The Bible as Comedy

Humour as Hope

Albert Radcliffe

The Bible as Comedy

Humour as Hope

Albert Radcliffe

Published by Pendlebury Press Limited
20 May Road
Swinton
Manchester
M27 5FR

www.pendleburypress.com

December 2017

ISBN: 978-0-9935945-7-1

Cover design by www.candescentpress.co.uk
Bible image copyright Kalina Vova/Bigstock.com

First Published by Albert Radcliffe for Kindle 2015

For My Wife, Daughters and Grandsons

And in Memory of

The Reverend Jack [John] Smith C.A.,

a prince among preachers

whose sermons alerted me to

Jesus' sense of humour

"Life is serious all the time, but living cannot be.

You may have all the solemnity you like in your neck-ties,

but in anything important (such as sex, death and religion)

you must have mirth or you will have madness."

G. K. Chesterton [1874-1936]

"For everything there is a season,

and a time for every matter under heaven…

a time to weep and a time to laugh…"

Ecclesiastes 3:1ff.

Table of Contents

THE OLD TESTAMENT or THE HEBREW SCRIPTURES

THE NEW TESTAMENT or THE CHRISTIAN SCRIPTURES

Preface

Why is there such a love of word games and verbal play throughout the Bible especially in some of its most serious parts? Why are these so seldom read in the same playful way in which they are written? As a holy book the Bible is a serious book, what then are we to make of this intrusion of human wit into the Word of God? These are some of the questions which *The Bible as Comedy* attempts to answer.

It was during Easter 1963, when I was a curate at Knotty Ash, Liverpool, that my Vicar alerted me to Christ's sense of humour. He was preaching about Jesus appearing to two of his disciples on the road to Emmaus, after his resurrection. [St Lk 24:13ff] They were discussing his crucifixion. Jesus feigned ignorance. They said they were astounded he hadn't heard of the "things" that had happened in Jerusalem. "What things?" Jesus quipped, still hurting from his wounds. It was the sort of wisecrack that appealed to a Liverpudlian. The first thing that Jesus did when he rose from the dead was crack a Jewish joke! Since then more instances of the Bible's comic dimension have been stored away, until, in retirement, the time seemed right to explore more seriously its role in our relationship with God as that relationship is set out in the Bible.

In putting these thoughts together, I'm grateful that I grew up in Liverpool, comedy's centre of gravity! I'm grateful, too, to my wife and daughters who have lived so patiently with the deficiencies of my own sense of humour. My appreciation must also include those comedians who were part of my wartime childhood: Rob Wilton, the first comedian I remember hearing, and Tommy Handley, who kept us laughing when invasion threatened and my mother thought that putting our sideboard into the street would stop Hitler's Panzers. Without comedy I'm certain we would have lost the war. It's as important as that. Its power is a spiritual power, though one that needs redeeming. I'm grateful too, to Ken Dodd, a fellow resident of Knotty Ash and a comic talisman for Merseyside and beyond. His sense of the ridiculous is a reminder of how theology's over-concentration on the serious has marginalised something as central to being human as humour. Without comedy Christian theology is a stunted growth. Ken Dodd's interest in the psychology of humour triggered my own. And then there was Les Dawson, whose love of word play was as teasing as the Bible's. It's not just that without comedy the world would be emotionally and culturally a poorer place; it's that, without it, it would also be spiritually dead.

When the Luftwaffe bombed my Primary School, I was

transferred to another where I came under the influence of Miss Dobells, a formidable teacher who turned the books of Genesis and Exodus into gripping story form. Would Pharaoh let the Children of Israel go? Would Hitler triumph? Were we doomed to be imprisoned in the circumstances of our lives? Of comedy as "being funny", Miss Dobells hadn't much that I can remember; but of divine comedy as our defence against wickedness, she had no doubt that we were all under-girded by hope.

I'm grateful too, in my exploration of biblical humour and Christian theology's lack of it, to my Jewish friends in the Council of Christians and Jews [CCJ] and to the various synagogue *shiurim* or study groups I've attended. A Jewish study group, with its probing after insight rather than factual knowledge is, in style, very different from a church bible study. My debt to Jewish friends is enormous and any failure to appreciate the subtleties of the Jewish approach to the Bible rests entirely with me.

Church and synagogue are unfortunately similar in their failure to read Scripture publicly according to its sense and so communicate liturgically the Bible's love of comedy. The Hebrew Scriptures are full of word play and comic situations. In most synagogues I've attended, the lessons are read at such a speed that the wit and comedy are lost. And while Jewish sermons are full of humour, few synagogue members seem any more alert to the Bible as comedy than Christians who attend church.

As soon as the Bible's comedy is recognised, unavoidable questions arise: why is it so often overlooked? Why is it neglected in Christian sermons? What purpose does it serve? In what way is it connected with God's self-revelation? Why is biblical comedy so often low key and so dark? What's the effect on Christian theology of reading the Bible as if the humour wasn't there?

It's not as if there weren't books to challenge this view of scripture as a comic desert. Even secular bookshops stock such works as Douglas Adams', *The Prostitute in the Family Tree,* [1997], J. William Whedbee's *The Bible and the Comic Vision* [1998], while Elton Trueblood's *The Humor of Christ,* was published as long ago as 1964. Yet, because the role of biblical comedy is still only partly explored, there is, I hope, room for one more book on the subject!

During Lent 2008, long-suffering parishioners of the church where my wife and I worship, discussed the book's first drafts. "I want to change the way you understand the Bible," I said optimistically, "finding God concealed in such things as ambiguity, irony and riddles. I'd like to open your mind to *The Bible as Comedy,* though it's a comedy that makes us smile rather than laugh. It's an approach which will enable us, I hope, to see Jesus as a human being, quick-witted, a man often concealed behind his titles, Son of God, Son of Man, as well as by ideas we have of his human perfection". Those present were alerted to nuances in the text they might have missed. Together we explored the relation of comedy to human evil, as well as its role in the Passion of Jesus. Though the discussions were vigorous and often encouraging, it was clear I'd been a little over-optimistic in my belief that the humour would be obvious to everyone. Christians especially seem fixed in the view that the sacred and the comic sit poorly together. Nevertheless, I remain optimistic! *The Bible as Comedy* is a project that's been creeping up on me all my life.

The Christian Bible is a foundation document of western civilisation. Once, everyone knew its stories and could recognise allusions to them, however subtle. For example, when, in 1866, the liberal reformer, John Bright, said of a fellow Member of the House of Commons, Edward Horsman, "The right honourable gentleman ... has retired into what may be called his political Cave of Adullam," everyone picked up the reference to King David's bolt-hole for outlaws in the desert. [1 Sam. 22:1.] Today, not many would recognise the significance of that cave.[1]

For 2000 years the Bible provided a wide range of cultural, spiritual and other symbols for the Christian world. These were living images that shaped the western mind. Their influence lingers on; and, as we shall see, their power is at root a comic power, transcending tragedy.

In quoting the Bible, I've sometimes used the King James Version, sometimes the Revised Standard Version but mostly the Revised English Version. The choice, when not whimsical, has been determined by the translation that seemed best to bring out the comic elements in the text. I've also used the Miles Coverdale version of the Psalms[2]. Far from the Bible being poor in comedy or lacking in wit, it's so rich a quarry that even several volumes would fail to reveal its wealth. What follows is only a selection to whet the appetite.

No book has been as closely interrogated as the Bible. The

---

1 Though in 1972, Walter Moore, MBE., in providing accommodation for the homeless and vulnerable called his organisation, *Adullam Homes.*

2 This is the version most Anglicans will be familiar with as it's the version used in the 1662 Book of Common Prayer. In 1535 Miles Coverdale [c1488-1569] produced the first complete printed translation of the Bible into English.

questioning has never stopped. Without such cross examination its pages are silent. *The Bible as Comedy* attempts to throw light on such questions as: what purpose does biblical comedy serve? What is the relation between comedy and revelation? Answering such questions will lead us to explore subjects as diverse as interpreting the Torah[3], religious extremism, the hiddenness of God, as well as entering the humour of Jesus to discover the man too often hidden behind the Church's beliefs about him.

Lastly, I'd like to thank those who have read and commented on the draft manuscript, in particular the late John Milner and Canon Alma Servant. I'm especially grateful to Eric Roth for his expertise in preparing the text for epublication. As with the views expressed any faults and shortcomings remaining are entirely mine.

---

3 Most English translations of the Bible translate "Torah" as Law, but as Torah means far more than Law. Torah is the preferred rendering here.

SETTING THE SCENE

Because the soul of man is not by its own nature or observation furnished with sufficient materials to work upon, it is necessary for it to have continual resource to learning and books for fresh supplies.
Abraham Cowley [1618-1667] *Of Solitude.*

The Bible is a book of sparkling wordplay and unending argument, as writer takes issue with writer over the great themes of our existence: the reality and nature of God; what it means to be human and the impossibility of avoiding evil or behaving rightly.

In a world of ideological extremes where religion seems to be its own worst enemy and where intolerance all too easily undermines our humanity, to argue, as *The Bible as Comedy* will do, that the Bible is the very antithesis of this might seem a lost cause and a wasted effort. Yet our problems today remain those that troubled the writers of the Bible. As they wrestled with human nature and with the elusiveness of God, they identified the themes that define our moral and spiritual existence and came to verdicts which, until recently, underwrote western civilisation.

And although the Bible does not sanction extremes of behaviour, it is a book in which the human love of extremes is explored until contradicted by divine generosity. It witnesses to the truth that religion exists to make us more and not less human. Its wisdom, preserved in a collection of many writings by many authors over at least 1200 years is not given to us in lists of infallible, not-to-be-argued-with statements. It is given to us instead in a living dialogue of mind with mind upon problems which continue to trouble us long after the closing of the canon[4] of scripture. The present loss of the Bible, particularly in British education, is nothing short of a cultural catastrophe, impoverishing the moral and spiritual aspects of public debate.

Once, the Bible was the most read and thought-over of books. Until a generation ago, it was taught in schools across the western world, and now its neglect is evident in the baffled "don't

---

4 The Canon of Scripture is the technical term for the authoritative list of books of which it is composed.

knows" of TV quiz contestants. For the young it's an unknown book. The cultural loss, let alone the spiritual and religious loss, is incalculable and badly needs addressing. As a result, works of literature once accessible to the ordinary reader are now as closed as the Bible itself. Yet the Bible is more than heritage and a literary classic. It's an invitation to join in the key debates of human existence as well as a vital resource when we do.

The Bible's surprise, however, is that from Adam to Jesus it does all this with an unexpected humour. From beginning to end it is a profoundly comic work. Its view of history is a comic view and its varied texts are alive with puns, irony, sarcasm and other kinds of wit. In the Bible, comedy and revelation[5] go together. They are inextricably intertwined. It's a connection that's unexpected and calls for exploration and explanation. Its surprisingly playful approach to divine things, far from discouraging the exercise of thought and reason, invites it. The Bible as the Word of God is not so much a book of revealed pronouncements as a library of divinely provoked discussions on important questions and answers.

The English Bible

> *The English Bible, a book which, if everything else in our language should perish, would alone suffice to show the whole world of its beauty and power.*
>
> Lord Macaulay [1800-1859] writing in the Edinburgh Review, 1828.

The Bible referred to in our title is the Christian Bible, consisting of the Old Testament (translated from the Hebrew),[6] the Bible of

---

5 Revelation is what God has revealed to us about himself, as well as what theologians understand that to mean. For Christians, God has revealed himself supremely in the life and teaching of Jesus, as well as in the teaching of Holy Scripture in both the Hebrew and Christian writings. When it comes to the particulars of revelation then opinion is sharply divided on a whole range of matters.

6 Jews, understandably, can take offence at the expression, "Old Testament" which implies that their Bible has been replaced by the Christian. For this reason, in order to be sensitive to Jewish feelings, especially in Interfaith Dialogue, the phrase, "Hebrew Scriptures" is often used.

Judaism, known to Jews as the Tanakh[7], together with the New Testament[8]. To these are added the fourteen books of the Apocrypha[9] printed in Anglican Bibles between the Old and New Testaments. These are the books of which the Church of England's Thirty Nine Articles of Religion says, *the Church doth read [them] for instruction of manners; but yet doth not apply them to establish any doctrine.* Other reformed traditions exclude the apocrypha, though often acknowledging that for a satisfactory overview of the Bible, a knowledge of its books is helpful.

Different churches have different Bibles. While all Christians recognise the same New Testament, Roman Catholics and Eastern Orthodox Churches include the so-called "deutero-canonical" books of the Apocrypha within their Old Testament. This is with the variation that Orthodox Christians include 3 Maccabees and Psalm 151, which other Christians exclude, while to complicate things 2 Esdras[10] which is included in Roman Catholic and Anglican Bibles is excluded by the Orthodox Churches as it survived only in Latin manuscripts.

In part, these differences arose because of the Church's origins in the Jewish faith which was divided between Hebrew speakers and Greek speakers. The New Testament was written in Greek and not in Hebrew because very soon in the early church Greek speakers outnumbered those who knew Hebrew or Aramaic, the language of Jesus. As Egyptian Jews[11] had already translated their Hebrew Bible into Greek, the translation known as the Septuagint [LXX], it was inevitable that this translation, which included the Apocrypha, should, with the Greek New Testament, have become the Bible of the early Church.

For a short time Greek speaking Christians and Greek speaking Jews shared the same Old Testament, though it was an arrangement that could not last. Sometime before 100 AD, the rabbis,

---

7 The word is made up from the initial letters of *Torah* [the Law], *Neviim* [the Prophets] and *Ketuvim* [the Writings].

8 Christians believe that the prophecy of Jeremiah [31:31] about a new covenant [testament] was fulfilled in Jesus, this is why Christians call their scriptures "The New Testament,'

9 "Apocrypha" comes from a Greek word meaning "hidden".

10 2 Esdras is important in that its understanding of the "comic" idea and role of the Messiah is much more developed than that in the Old Testament and is an important link to the death and resurrection of Jesus as Messiah in the New; an idea unknown in Old.

11 The word Jew comes from the word "Judean', meaning "of the tribe of Judah.'

fighting for the survival of Judaism, rejected the Septuagint and accepted as canonical only those books for which they had the Hebrew text. The Church, however, continued to use the Septuagint until, in the 16th century, the Protestant reformers argued like the Rabbis that only the books of the Hebrew Old Testament were part of the authentic Bible. Anglicans, typically, compromised so that the bible used by the Church of England and its sister churches have the non-Hebraic books of the Septuagint sandwiched between the Old and New Testaments as useful background and devotional material.

The Distribution of Comedy Throughout the Bible

Sarah laughed.
Genesis 18:12.

Near where I live there is a restaurant called *The Laughing Buddha.* Few English Christians could even imagine a restaurant called *The Laughing Christ.* But, as we shall see, Jesus did have a very distinctive sense of humour, one he used to great effect in his preaching. It was so central to his ministry that, if we fail to grasp its purpose or its effect on his listeners, we cannot fully understand either the man or his message, or the events that led to his death. We must ask then, why, if that's the case, has his Jewish sense of humour and its purpose been so largely overlooked for so long.

There is comedy throughout the Bible: God laughs[12], as do Abraham, Sarah and the enemies of the psalmist, though alas few others, which might seem tenuous support for an undertaking called *The Bible as Comedy.* Nevertheless, though laughter might seem in short supply, of comedy there's plenty, too much in fact for one book like this. All we can do is to illustrate the argument with a selection of examples.

Now, while all humour can be reckoned as comedy, not all comedy is humorous and certainly not laugh-out-loud funny, though the comedy's there.

Comedy as humour comes in many kinds with the Bible being better at some than others; nor is its humour evenly distributed. One would search with difficulty for a sense of fun in Leviticus or the Epistle of Jude, whereas Genesis, Tobit in the apocrypha and the gospels have more than enough to raise a smile. Biblical humour and comedy is found chiefly in its stories, histories and prophecies, with the greatest concentration being found in Genesis and the teaching of Jesus.

12 See for example, Psalm 2:4.

Here, where, in spite of the tradition of his never having laughed, Jesus emerges as the Bible's supreme humorist, where comedy climaxes to deep purpose in his teaching about the Kingdom of God.

Humour, then, comes in many varieties: absurdity, buffoonery, caricature, clowning, double entendre, drollery, farce, foolery, fun, irony, jest, joke, mockery, parody, paronomasia or word-play, paradox, play, pun, quip, riddle, ridicule, sarcasm, satire, scorn, slapstick, taunt, tease, trick, visual joke, wisecrack and witticism; examples of each of which can readily be found in scripture.

The Importance of Biblical Genres

> *Art does not classify objects, it does not pronounce them real or imaginary, does not qualify them, does not define them; it feels and presents them and nothing more.*
>
> Benedetto Croce [1866-1952] *Esthetic.*

Though we are not all writers, we all love to be critics, and it's as critics that we classify literature even though the boundaries between our categories are often blurred, like those, for example, between prose and poetry. In modern Bible translations, poetry is helpfully printed in lines of differing length, even though Hebrew poetry is defined by other characteristics such as its love of parallelism. Biblical verse is surprisingly diverse and includes prophecy, prayer, proverbs, psalms and songs; each with their preferred kinds of humour.

Hebrew prose is even more varied than Hebrew poetry and includes stories and history, as well as prophecy, sermons, psalms, prayer, ritual, apocalyptic visions, legal texts, letters and collections of wisdom sayings, each with appropriate humour. In psalm 9, for example, we find a comic image which occurs again and again in scripture – that of the wicked falling into holes they've dug for other people and getting their come-uppance in what in modern colloquial English is called a "pratfall". Well-deserved misfortune is among the most widespread of comic situations and as often as not in the Bible it signifies the vindication of the righteous, one of scripture's great comic and therefore redemptive themes.

I was a boy of six during the 1941 Liverpool blitz, and in one week I was caned twice for being late for school. When I arrived late again it was to find that my school had been bombed in the night by the Luftwaffe! "Serves you right!" I thought, imagining our headmaster's distress and sensing comedy and justice in the dust and ruin before me. The psalmist would have understood: *His mischief will recoil upon him and violence fall upon his own head.* [7:15]

The Bible's humour reveals it as a very human work. This is important, because it means that unless we take note of its comedy we will find ourselves in difficulties. If we fail to read the Bible as a product of human culture, but proceed directly to the belief that it is the unqualified and unmediated "Word of God", we do it a disservice, reducing scripture to little more than a quarry for Christian doctrine.

The Bible as Comedy

> *All tragedies are finish'd by a death,*
> *All comedies are ended by a marriage.*
> Lord Byron [1788-1824]. *Don Juan.*

The Bible as Comedy is intended to be an eye-catching title without being misleading. The Bible is as much a revelation of human nature as it is of God's. *The Bible as Comedy* aims to keep a balance, noting that for Christians it is primarily Jesus, the incarnate Word, who is The Word of God. The Bible can only be called The Word of God with qualification.

And because "comedy" can be such a slippery noun, it's as well to say something at the outset about the way in which it's used here. Comedy is used firstly in its technical sense as the opposite of tragedy. This is the use that has come down to us from the Greeks, especially from Aristotle in his *Poetics,* where he divided literature on the human condition into Tragedy and Comedy.

In Greek amphitheatres, actors wore masks, two of which can still be found in the décor of many theatres: one bearing a smile, for comedy, and the other, a sad expression for tragedy.

This Greek understanding survives in the title of Dante's poem, the *Divina Commedia,* the Divine Comedy; in the division of Shakespeare's plays into tragedies and comedies as well as in Honoré de Balzac's series of novels, *La Comédia Humaine.* On this classification, Dickens was one of the most prolific writers of comedy in English, though for most readers only *Pickwick Papers* might count as a comic work. As our epigraph shows, for Lord Byron tragedies end in death and comedies in marriage, or in some other way of things turning out for the best so that *All's Well that Ends Well.* On this reckoning, the Bible is the ultimate work of comedy. While it contains many instances of tragedy, overall, ending as it does with the redemption of the whole created order, the day when *Paradise Lost* becomes *Paradise Regained* it is world literature's supreme comedy. In treating history as a cosmic comedy the Bible goes far beyond Aristotle. It declares that, under God, history has meaning and will one day be redeemed.

While the gospels contain a great deal of tragedy, especially in the suffering and crucifixion of Jesus, the dramatic intrusion of his resurrection instantly transforms his life into comedy – though that is not usually how it's understood by most Christians.

Today, history as comedy is a Jewish-Christian idea under attack in both its religious and secularised versions, its moral status being perhaps the most controversial aspect of contemporary political theology. John Gray in his 2008 book, *Black Mass, Apocalyptic Religion and the Death of Utopia,* has trenchant criticisms of the effect of the Bible's comic legacy on secular historical and political thinking. It is, he argues, "illusory" and leads to violence and disappointment as one utopian vision after another, religious or secular, fails. Gray proposes instead that we explore what he calls, "The Lost Tradition of Realism".

The comic dimensions of scripture appear on many levels. There is comedy in its delight in puns and other kinds of word-play. There is comedy as well in the often quite farcical twists in plot-line. Its characters too are often comical: Jacob the trickster is an obvious example; God as trickster is less obvious. For example, though it was against the express commandment of God for an Israelite to marry a Philistine, in the folk account of Judges 14 God is said to be "at work" in Samson's desire because "he was seeking an opportunity against the Philistines." As the story ends with Samson killing thirty Philistine men this is grim humour and black comedy. It's not always morally attractive theology.

Can there ever be a genuine Christian tragedy? Auden thought not; Chesterton thought there could be and that Shakespeare's *Macbeth* was the supreme example. The debate continues; meanwhile, behind the arguments for and against, wherever literary culture has a biblical basis, the Bible's comic vision of final redemption remains the background against which every human drama is acted out. *All shall be well, all manner of things shall be well,* wrote the English mystic, Mother Julian of Norwich [c1342 – c1417] as she summarised the faith of her Church and her age.

About the time Aristotle [384-322BC] was dividing the plays of the Greek stage into comedies and tragedies, Jews who survived the Babylonian exile were writing up the history of their people as a divine comedy, with tragedies like their exile in Babylon as little more than painful episodes in their long story.

What is being attempted in using comedy as a critical tool like this is a kind of standpoint analysis. Being a library of books from different genres, the Bible needs to be understood from a variety of points of view. In the last 250 years it has been approached from every conceivable angle. We have had feminist criticism, form criticism, historical criticism, literary criticism, redaction criticism, source criticism and tradition criticism, all controversial and each devised to open a window on to some aspect of its truth. *The Bible as Comedy* is written for the ordinary reader, for everyone with a comic sense and a sense of humour.

Today, biblical faith no longer underpins western society as it once did, with the result that not only does human existence have little meaning, other than what we can project on to it, but that, with the fading of the comic vision, tragedy predominates as never before, leaving humanity to fend for itself. Much of our existence is inescapably tragic. Yet can we remain recognisably human if our existence is no longer thought of as a divine comedy? That's among the most important questions facing us today, when recent history seems a catalogue of failed experiments: Communism, Fascism, the Enlightenment with its liberal belief in progress, and most recently Market Capitalism, each a blind stumbling towards tragedy even as they presented themselves as secular salvation and comedy.

Comedy is also used in its other sense of "humorous" or "funny". It's what makes us smile or laugh, grin or chuckle. Yet, even in this sense, it depends on whether we see life as being essentially comic or tragic. In the absence of some meaning underwriting existence, life can appear to be no more than a cosmic joke, so that all jokes cracked within that joke are, at best, ironic; or at worst, a kind of gallows humour. Is there humour in the Bible? The common view would be that there's not; that the Bible is too serious to raise a smile, let alone make the reader laugh. This is a book that begs to differ.

Further Thoughts on Comedy and Tragedy

> *Farce is the essential theatre. Farce refined becomes high comedy; farce brutalised becomes tragedy.*
>
> Sir Edward Gordon Craig [1872-1966] *Index to the Story of My Days*

Not everyone who reads the Bible recognises it as a comic work whose tragic moments are cast within an overall comic framework. Comedy and tragedy may not be the only categories through which we can view scripture; yet for all that they polarise the way we see things, they remain essential if we are to make sense of life and literature. Without one illuminating the other or throwing it into contrast, the Bible, like life, becomes a closed and dull book.

Though comedy comes in many kinds we can note the following varieties: comedy as *Farce,* in which the plot is improbable and the situations far-fetched: Jacob and Esau; *Romantic Comedy,* in which lovers kept apart finally come together: Tobias and Sarah; and *Satirical comedy,* stories that make fun of human vice and folly: Samson and Delilah.

Tragedy is just as varied. In Hegelian tragedy, spiritual and other forces are in unending conflict, as when righteousness is opposed by evil. Elijah battling the prophets of Baal comes to mind. Tragedy may also result from character defects in otherwise great men: King Saul is a case in point. Tragedy is also often the result of pride or hubris over-reaching itself and receiving its deserts in nemesis. This was the fate of those who built the tower of Babel.

In tragedy, situations and individuals are lost: Judas. In comedy they are redeemed: St Peter.

In tragedy we despair: The Lost Sheep. In comedy we celebrate: the sheep is found again.

In tragedy, we are alone: Elijah. In comedy we belong: Esther.

In tragedy, things get worse: King Zedekiah. In comedy they improve: Job.

In tragedy, we die: Jephtha's daughter. In comedy we live: The widow of Nain's son.

Tragedy lies on the road to hell: Dives. Comedy, that to heaven: Lazarus.

In tragedy, hope dies: Judas. In comedy hope is realised: Jonah in the belly of the great fish.

Comedy as Avoiding the Nihil[13]

One can't be a part time nihilist.
Albert Camus [1913-1960]

One of the functions of comedy is to act as a spiritual defence against the experience of life as overwhelmingly futile and meaningless. The fear of nothingness, that is the nihil, is a theme that will emerge again and again in these studies, for example, in discussions of the book Ecclesiastes and in Jesus's cry on the cross, *My God, my God, why have you forsaken me?* [Mk 15:34].

The loss of the sense of transcendence that afflicts modern life: the belief that morality has no objective basis, or that it is impossible for human beings "to know" anything about anything; the widespread feeling of being lost in the world or of not having a clear sense of who we are or that in the end nothing makes any worthwhile difference– while these experiences can be ascribed to emotional troubles like depression, they can also be described as spiritual conditions which result from our culture's lack of a sense of the existence of God. The word which focuses this feeling of loss is *nihil,* an experience against which the Bible was a defence for over 2,000 years. Today, the nihil is an ocean of doubt on which believers must sink or learn to swim.

Absurdity, Nihil's Soul-mate

Over and above the absurdity of life there hovers the absurdity of death.
R.N.Coe.

Things that are absurd unsettle us at the same time as they can amuse us. Life's like that, and the Bible reflects the experience. The spiritual and the psychological are close neighbours. It was in exploring their relationship that I came across Bruce Hood's fascinating book, *The Self Illusion, Why there is no "You" inside your*

13 Nihil, Latin for "nothing", occurs in such words as "nihilism" and "annihilation". As an English noun it has, for many, come to be the defining word of our post-modernist age. Its use in this section heading can also be found in the title of Stephen Hand's book, *Apocalyptic Nights: Catholic Hope in the Nihil."* There is also an American rock band called Nihil.

head. Here was a book by one illusion, the author, written for another, the reader. We illusions are taking over the world!

That sense of the Absurd visited me again when following another interest, *Astrobiology,* the possibility of life on distant planets and moons elsewhere in the universe. So far none has been found but in spite of the non-existence of their subject there are now chairs and professors of astrobiology across the western world. Illusory selves studying non-existence subjects! Absurd? "Remind you of theology?" atheist friends might say.

The Bible can be absurd because reality can be absurd. But Jesus beat me to it. As a curate, learning the preacher's trade, I once heard a very earnest sermon on the parable of The Lost Sheep. [Lk 15:4]: Jesus said, *If one of you has a hundred sheep and loses one of them, does he not leave the ninety-nine in the wilderness and go after the one that is missing until he finds it? And when he does, he lifts it joyfully on his shoulders and goes home to call his friends and neighbours together. "Rejoice with me", he cries. "I have found my lost sheep".*

The preacher took the story seriously and, without questioning it, described in detail the plight of the poor creature as it climbed the rocky hillside, going "higher and higher, higher and higher," until it seemed more like a mountain goat than a sheep. We were reminded of when, as children, we too had been lost, as we identified ourselves first with the bewildered animal and then with the compassion of the shepherd.

It was at this point that, for me, the spell was broken; for what sort of shepherd would leave his flock to fend for itself to go after one lost sheep? By the time the shepherd returned, the abandoned sheep could well have been attacked by wild animals. I could imagine the crowd interrupting Jesus: "Oh, no he wouldn't!" they'd shout, like an audience at a pantomime. And so that he wouldn't look foolish himself, Jesus would have let his hearers know by the tone of his voice that he knew that they knew that no shepherd would be as daft as to abandon his sheep in that way.

The parable was comedy. It was an absurd story reflecting the desirable absurdity of the Kingdom of God. The Bible is a God-inspired book, but not a God-dictated book. His word of love for us is tucked way among very human words, many of them comic. The role of that comedy becomes clearer as it's probed, hopefully without killing it, for nothing dies as quickly as a joke explained. As we shall see later, the whole point of the Kingdom of God in Jesus' teaching is that it's the ultimate absurdity. Humour is absolutely central to the Kingdom of God. Salvation is both a comic concept and reality.

Paradox, Absurdity and Nihil's Friend

A paradox which comforts while it mocks,
Shall life succeed in that it seems to fail.
Robert Browning [1812-89]. *Rabbi Ben Ezra.*

The world is only logical and rational up to a point and the absurdity of much of life drives home that point. Paradox is a truth based on a contradiction! At first sight a paradox looks nonsense, but on closer examination its opposites make for a higher sort of sense. For example, in his first letter to the Corinthians [15:35ff], St Paul is trying to explain the apparently absurd Jewish and Christian belief in the Resurrection of the Dead, so he comes up with a paradox: *How are the dead raised? In what kind of body? What stupid questions! The seed you sow does not come to life unless it has first died; and what you sow is not the body that shall be, but a bare grain, of wheat perhaps..."* The spiritual truth, that we must die in order to live, is a comic, paradoxical truth.

And philosophers are no more comfortable around a contradiction in words than are mathematicians with paradoxes in numbers and symbols. For example, at the turn of the 19th century, the great German philosopher and mathematician Gottlieb Frege [1849-1925] was writing his master-work in which he hoped to show that in mathematics one thing could prove another to make all maths one incontestable, contradiction-free whole. And he thought he'd achieved his ambition, until that was, the English mathematician Bertrand Russell [1872-1970] came up with a devastating mathematical paradox, which for non-mathematicians he helpfully put into story form, now forever known as Russell's Barber Paradox.

It goes like this. *There is a town with a barber who shaves only the men who do not shave themselves. Who shaves the barber?* He cannot shave himself, because he only shaves those who do not shave themselves; and no one else can shave him because then he'd be one of those who do not shave themselves and so must be shaved by the barber! Put into mathematical language that contradiction sabotaged poor Frege's life-work just as his book was going to press.

This means that not only is life full of absurdities but that those absurdities sometimes reveal themselves as contradictions and paradoxes. That's just how things are, and if the Bible is to be true to life, then it has to reflect this and the most appropriate way it can do so is through comedy and humour. It's how God has made the world.

Paradox, like absurdity, has the power to win an acknowledging smile from us. Humour in the Bible always serves some serious theological and spiritual purpose.

The Importance of Stories

> *L-d! said my mother, "what is all this story about?'*
> Laurence Stern [1713-1768] *Tristram Shandy.*

Stories are the way the Bible prefers to do its theology. The result is to make the Bible look like a book devised by God to frustrate abstract theological speculation!

In the 1960s, when I first became involved in inter-faith dialogue, Jews I knew would say, with some pride, "We Jews don't do theology!" If I asked a rabbi a question he would answer with a story or a joke, if not another question. It was comedy of the kind I wished we had more of in church, where if you asked a priest the same sort of question you'd get a crash-course in philosophical theology! I love theology, but philosophy is only one way of doing it, and a very limited question-closing way at that. Biblical storytelling is another, and rabbinical story-telling, its offspring, is yet another, and I love that as well. With stories, questions are kept open and the possibility of dialogue preserved. More than anything else, the Bible is a book in which discussion promotes discussion.

If theologians are philosophers, rabbis are more like sages. However, in the last few years, I've noticed that Jews refer increase-ingly to "Jewish theology". Should this worry them?

The Bible as Comedy

THE OLD TESTAMENT OR THE HEBREW SCRIPTURES

1

THROWING DOWN THE GAUNTLET

It is not necessary to win in order not to lose
William the Silent [1533-1584]

When they were marched off to Babylon, the Jews lost their armed struggle against the world's greatest empire, but they had not lost their war against idolatry. That went on, even in the first verse of the first chapter of the history they wrote afterwards, the book we know as *Genesis*.

All around them great temples proclaimed the political, spiritual and intellectual invincibility of polytheism and, against that, what could a handful of captive monotheists do? Their answer was to write a book whose first three words were a play on words: *Bereshith bara Elohim.* "In the beginning God." The Bible begins with a joke.

"Why has a verb in the singular, *bara,* got its subject, *Elohim,* in the plural," I asked my first Hebrew teacher. "It's the Plural of Majesty," he said. "Elohim is plural, but here it doesn't mean "gods", it means "God". When Queen Victoria said, "We are not amused," that "We" was the Plural of Majesty"'. At the time I was happy with the explanation. I'm not now.

For the comparison with Genesis to work the Queen would have had to have said, "We (plural) am (singular) not amused". So what were these exiles up to playing havoc with Hebrew grammar? In making "gods" mean "God" and making a pagan plural word a Hebrew singular they were cocking a snook at their own idolatry as well as that of their conquerors[14]. They had turned the meaning of a word upside down. *Elohim,* that once meant "gods", now meant God. With that comic opening of Genesis the Jews had begun their spiritual come-back from apostasy and idolatry. As we will see, it also set a comic tone for much of the Bible.

---

[14] And it causes confusion too! In Genesis 3:5, the King James' Version translates "Elohim" as "gods" but most modern versions translate it as "God."

Other Beginnings

Bibles laid open, millions of surprises
George Herbert [1593-1633.]

When at six years old, I asked where my baby brother came from, my mother explained that he'd sprouted from a seed planted by my father in God's garden, though where that garden was or how my father planted the seed, she failed to tell me. It was only when puberty struck that her explanation made any sense, as did psalm 19 which we were singing in church one day in Miles Coverdale's translation. At verse four, I did a double-take. It seemed that at dawn, the sun rose like a *bridegroom coming forth from his chamber*. This was humour, and to a schoolboy mind vulgar humour at that! Was this really Holy Scripture? In stumbling upon one of the more erotic verses in the Bible, I had achieved what literary critics call a "close reading" of the text. Why had no one pointed out this incredible image before? Neither the Bible nor the sun rising would ever be the same again. True, it didn't make me laugh, but it certainly made me smile. As George Herbert said, the Bible is a book of surprises, and I was surprised.

About that time I also discovered "close listening," as verse after verse crept around my adolescent agnosticism. Sheltering from the rain one day, I wandered into Liverpool's Walker Art Gallery and, dripping wet, was brought to a halt before Solomon J. Solomon's [1860-1927] dramatic painting of Samson being betrayed by Delilah. The voluptuous Delilah had my complete attention! In Hebrew, even her name was a joke, as it can mean, "The One Who Weakened", and Delilah the prostitute had certainly weakened the mighty Samson. The painting caught my imagination, so much so that when the account was read in church I listened with heightened hearing. Samson had set the Philistines a riddle, and they had solved it by asking Delilah for the answer. When he discovered the betrayal, Samson was furious and said, vulgarly, *"If you had not ploughed with my heifer, you would not have solved my riddle."* [Judges 14:18] Was this a double entendre? No wonder the Vicar failed to mention biblical humour in confirmation class! For extra pocket money, I had started work Saturday mornings on a nearby farm and knew from older farmhands what "ploughing" meant when used like that. It might not have been the Bible as stand-up comedy, but it was humour that had me grinning.

At Holy Communion, Anglicans and Roman Catholics stand when the Gospel is read. It's to encourage attentiveness, though I know from experience that few can say afterwards what lessons read in church were about, especially those of St Paul! Two thousand years of tradition have conditioned the Christian ear not to expect comedy. If anything is heard at all it will be "sound doctrine." George Herbert may have expected surprises, but few have followed him in that respect. However during one Evensong I noticed that when a passage from Joel was read: *Blow the trumpet in Zion, appoint a solemn fast, proclaim a day of abstinence. Gather the people together, appoint a solemn assembly, gather the children, even babes at the breast; bid the bridegroom leave his wedding chamber and the bride her bower,* at the mention of the newly-weds interrupting their honeymoon to go to a meeting, one of our churchwardens grinned. Whether this would have amused listeners in ancient Judah is another matter, but that an occasion should be reckoned so important as to make the newly married postpone the consummation of their joy can surely make us smile. Scripture really is full of often quite earthy comic surprises.

One reason we smile so little at the Bible has to do with our expectation of total seriousness as its comedy is smothered by an all embracing solemnity of mind. And Christian theology doesn't help as preachers declare how the Bible is the Word of God, a serious book for serious people. Seldom is it suggested that a grin might be appropriate. God, we are told, is revealed through its inspired pages and it should be read by sincere believers with believing hearts; which is true enough, for the Bible is full of deep, spiritual thoughts and truths. It prompted our political freedoms and our social and moral ideals – but that's not the whole story. The Bible is also full of some very unlofty and darkly comic material. At theological college, I prayed that it would never be my turn to read how Ehud, one of the Judges of Israel, assassinated Eglon, king of Moab [Judges 3:15ff]. I knew I'd never be able to read the passage with a straight face: *When the people of Israel cried to the Lord, the Lord raised up for them a deliverer, Ehud, the son of Gera, the Benjaminite*[15]*; a left*

---

15 There is folk humour too in the name Benjamin, the son of Jacob, after whom the tribe was named. In Hebrew, "ben" means "son of" and "yamin" means "right," as opposed to "left," so that "benyamin', means something like "son of the right hand" or a "right-handed man". The twist lies in the fact that the tribe contained an unusually high proportion of left-handers, Ehud being one of them. The Book of Judges [20:16] records how, when the tribe mustered in support of the city of Gibeah, there were *seven hundred picked men who were left-handed, every one could sling a stone at a hair and not miss.* Eglon, being a right-handed man and ignorant of the joke was not expecting treachery from Ehud's left.

handed man. The people of Israel sent tribute by him to Eglon the king of Moab. And Ehud made for himself a sword with two edges, a cubit[16] *in length; and he girded it on his right thigh under his clothes. And he presented the tribute to Eglon. Now Eglon was a very fat man. And when Ehud had finished presenting the tribute, he sent away the people that carried the tribute. But he himself turned back at the sculptured stones near Gilgal and said, "I have a secret message for you, O king." And he commanded, "Silence." And all his attendants went out from his presence. And Ehud came to him, as he was sitting alone in his cool roof chamber. And Ehud said, "I have a message from God for you." And he arose from his seat. And Ehud reached with his left hand, took the sword from his right thigh, and thrust it into his belly; and the hilt also went in after the blade, and the fat closed over the blade, for he did not draw the sword out of his belly; and the dirt came out.*

The comic element is undeniable. It's there in the irony of, *I have a message from God for you,* as well as in the superfluous detail of, *the hilt also went in after the blade and the fat closed over it.* The phrase, *and the dirt came out* is pure comic excess. Fortunately, a fellow student, a professional actor, read the passage, and I was spared corpsing at the lectern!

It was passages like this that convinced me that as well as being in some way, "The Word of God", the Bible was also very much, "The Word of Man". As St Paul put it in Second Corinthians, *We have this treasure in earthen vessels* [4:7]. And though the apostle is describing his own human frailties it is an image that can just as well fit scripture as the Word of God. The Bible is the place where our search for God meets God's approach to us. It's a very human work, full of comedy even in its accounts of murder, betrayal and cruelty, and the Church has done itself no favours by playing down the humour. If it's bad theology to emphasise Christ's divinity at the expense of his humanity, then it's also bad theology to insist on the Bible as the Word of God while under-emphasising its place in humankind's literary traditions.

At my theological college, weekday mornings began with an exposition of one of the books of the Bible. Lecturers took it in turns and did a good job relating a passage, firstly to the time it was written and then to the contemporary world; yet not once do I recall anyone exploring the Bible's comic vision or the humour through which its visions were expressed.

This one-sided way of reading scripture was reinforced in the

---

16 A cubit was a measurement equivalent to about 18 inches or 45 centimetres. It would have been a short sword used in close combat.

1980s when it became the custom in the Church of England for the reader to say after a lesson, *This is the Word of the Lord,* to which the congregation replied, *Thanks be to God*. Not surprisingly, many found that there were times when it was difficult to announce that the passage read was in some way the unqualified Word of God, and so they reverted to the older, *Here ends our lesson.* It's something I've done myself.

Because biblical accounts of our relationship with God often include episodes of unashamed wickedness, readings sometimes raise more questions than they answer. For this and for other reasons, choosing lessons for public reading is often something of a problem. There are two ways in which a resolution has been attempted. The first is *Lectio Continua*[17], that is reading biblical books through from beginning to end[18]. The other is to match the passage read to a particular festival, fast or season of the Church's year. At theological college, I had, with *Lectio Continua,* the benefit of listening to long uninterrupted stretches of the Bible, passages not normally heard by those who only attended their parish church on Sundays. The result was a close acquaintance with the text and the discovery of its comic dimensions.

In rather less embarrassing taste than the story of Ehud and Eglon, but equally problematical, was this fine, poetical passage in *The Song of Deborah and Barak* [Judges 5:24ff.]. This ancient song, one of the oldest fragments of Hebrew poetry in the Bible, celebrates a victory by the Israelites over Sisera, leader of a powerful confederation of Canaanite city states. Sisera seeks refuge in the tent of Jael, a woman from a tribe he thinks is friendly. She deceives him by acknowledging his rank, even in defeat, and offering him milk in "a lordly dish." As Sisera bends to drink it, with a well practiced hand Jael reaches for a tent peg and drives it into his skull.

He asked for water: she gave him milk
She offered him curds in a bowl fit for a chieftain.

---

[17] The advantage here is that readings are appropriate to the season; the disadvantage is that some passages of the Bible are just never heard in church, and as private Bible reading becomes a thing of the past and Bible study groups engage the interest of a small part only of most congregations, the loss of familiarity with the Bible grows year on year.

[18] The great Fathers of the Church, St Augustine [354-430] and St John Chrysostom [c347 – 407] often used this method, and it was revived at the Reformation by the Reformers Huldrych Zwingli [1484-1531] and John Calvin [1509-1564].

She reached out her hand for the tent peg,
her right hand for the workman's hammer.
With the hammer she struck Sisera, crushing his head;
with a shattering blow she pierced his temple.
At her feet he sank, he fell, he lay prone,
at her feet he sank down and fell.
Where he sank down, there he fell, done to death.

The parallelism of those last three lines is a fine example of a classic Hebrew verse form, while the comedy mounts even higher in the ironic parallelisms of the succeeding lines:

The mother of Sisera peered through the lattice,
through the window she peered and cried,
"Why is his chariot so long in coming?
Why is the clatter of his chariot so long delayed?"
The wisest of her ladies answered her,
yes, she found her own answer:
"They must be finding spoil, taking their shares,
a damsel for each man, two damsels,
booty of dyed stuffs for Sisera,
booty of dyed stuffs,
dyed stuff and brocade, two lengths of brocade
to grace the visitor's neck."

These musings by "the wisest of her ladies" are genteel when compared with its comic equivalent among the courtiers of Eglon who, *finding the doors fastened, said, He must be relieving himself [*5:24]. Both passages were obviously written for smiles and laughs among fellow Israelites whenever the national epic was sung by their bards. The comedy of the writing was part of the storyteller's art. Details are spun out for comic effect in what is an all too human piece of writing. The song of Deborah and Barak ends with this thought:

So perish all your enemies, Lord;
But let those who love you be like the rising sun in strength.

There's nothing here about loving one's enemies [Lk 6:27]. It's not easy to say after such a bloodthirsty lesson in which captive women will be exploited as slaves and are the moral equivalents of fashionable clothing, "This is the Word of the Lord," even though the editor ends with an observation that comes as a welcome relief: *The land was at peace for forty years.*

People ask if this gloating and gore really is the Word of the Lord. "It's to show", clergy might reply, that *all things work together for the good of those who love the Lord*, [Rom. 8:28]. Or, "It's a revelation of divine providence, of God bringing his good out of our evil." But in that case why wrap it up in such an unashamed delight in comic gruesomeness?

A possible answer is that if the Word of God came to us not through culture-bound folk stories but through abstract utterances straight from heaven, the result would be a different and less persuasive kind of book. Instead, both the Hebrew and Christian scriptures are an all too human and comic account from below, of a truth and reality dimly perceived as coming in some way from above.

The Importance of the Reader

As writers become more numerous,
it is natural for readers to become more indolent.
Oliver Goldsmith [1728-1774] *The Bee.*

Biblical humour is a reminder of the importance of the reader, without whom every text is incomplete. The comedy not only keeps the hearer awake but triggers a response that hinders the indolence that Goldsmith feared. This is why Christians talk about wrestling with the Bible and why, in the Talmud[19], that treasure-house of

19 In Hebrew, *Talmud* means "teaching". and refers to the large collection of ancient writings that took shape around the Oral Law, the unwritten teachings that related to the revelation at Sinai. When the Oral Law was eventually written down, discussed and interpreted it gave rise to a body of writings known as the Mishnah. The Mishnah in turn resulted in an even larger body of recorded study known as the Gemara which means "completion" or "teaching". Together, the Mishnah and the Gemara make up the Talmud, of which there are two versions, the products of the two rabbinic schools of Babylon and Palestine. The Babylonian Talmud, with 36 tractates, is almost four times as large as the Palestinian with 39. Modern Judaism is the religion of the Torah as it is interpreted by the Talmud.

rabbinic[20] wisdom, the rabbis quizzed the text for answers to question after question. It's why Anglicans especially believe that without reason, tradition and imagination the Bible is a closed book. Meaning and applications cannot be read directly off the page. The presence of comedy prompts a response beyond that. Once we smile or repress a grin, we acknowledge that the text teases us, inviting us to enter more deeply and less certainly into the matter at hand. Comedy subverts, which is why those who crave certainty in spiritual things often miss the humour in their Bible.

But the Bible is not only the work of individual writers. It is also the product of believing and worshipping communities. Appropriately, therefore, it is best read among worshipping and questioning believers. In this way, the reader enters into dialogue with groups and traditions present and past. Nor does the Bible have only one voice, but many, just as there are many voices in the church answering those voices. In this extended conversation few things communicate as readily as humour.

From Genesis to Revelation, the books of the Bible are in dialogue with one another. When the canon of scripture was closed, the dialogue continued, and it continues in both Church and Synagogue today. Whatever revelation the Bible contains it is revealed only as its readers enter into that dialogue, which from beginning to end is a dialogue based on questioning. Throughout the Bible, text questions text and text answers text. The conversation never ends. The canon of scripture is closed but the questioning and the dialogue go on.

A Close Reading of the Text

You see, but you do not observe.
Sir Arthur Conan Doyle [1859-1930].

---

20 *Rabbi* is Hebrew for "my master" and was used to address those knowledgeable and wise in the Torah, or Jewish Law, as it was interpreted in the Talmud, where it was written, *Moses received the Torah from Sinai and handed it down to Joshua, and Joshua to the elders, the elders to the prophets, and the prophets handed it to the Men of the Great Assembly.* [Avot 1:1] The transference of authority to teach was by "the laying on of hands," so that every rabbi was a link in an unbroken chain of tradition. The chain was broken in the 4th century and could not be re-established, but the idea is perpetuated in many branches of the Christian Church in ordination of clergy through the laying on of hands by the bishop.

Poor Dr Watson, missing what was obvious to Sherlock Holmes! However, readers of *A Scandal in Bohemia* are not, I suspect, as quick to pass judgement as was the great detective. Seeing what's in front of us is seldom easy. My own favourite story of someone seeing what everyone else missed concerns the great French chemist Louis Pasteur [1822-95]. In 1849, Pasteur was working on a problem involving tartaric acid. Thousands of chemists before him had peered down their microscopes, but only Pasteur noticed that the crystals he was looking at came in two kinds: left handed and right handed. The technical term for this is *chiral*, that is, like gloves or human hands, crystals of tartaric acid are mirror images of one another. Why had no one noticed before? They had seen, but they had not observed. The Bible is like that.

2

WHAT IS HUMOUR? A THEOLOGICAL DIGRESSION

For the love of laughter, hinder not the humour of his design
William Shakespeare [1564-1616]
All's Well that Ends Well.

The Bible as Comedy offers only a partial view of the Hebrew and Christian scriptures, but what approach is not partial? It's true that comedy is a neglected perspective on biblical truth, but how significant is that neglect? An answer lies in the pages ahead, especially in their understanding of Jesus who, without the humour at the heart of both his ministry and his relationship with his disciples, would emerge from the gospels a very two dimensional figure indeed.

New Testament scholars have never made much of the presence of humour in the gospels, even if they've long acknowledged that it's there. The serious purposes it serves remain largely unexplored. The Bible that results from this neglect is all too often an intellectual's Bible, a Bible for those whose first love is the love of ideas. The presence of comedy rescues us from the mistake of supposing that it is only a book for theologians.

In psalm 37, God is credited with a rather questionable sense of humour: *The Lord will laugh at the wicked, for he sees that their day of judgement is coming* [37:13]. As God is elsewhere described as "merciful" and "slow to anger" it's obvious that the Bible is not straightforwardly self-interpreting. Questions have to be asked. The writer's and the reader's time, place and psychologies have to be taken into account. God laughing at the wicked is a morally disturbing image for us today though it clearly wasn't for whoever wrote the psalm. The Bible is not only a book that comforts; it also opens up the problem of the nature of humour itself.

Philosophers have written at length on every aspect of human existence but only briefly on humour! Many have begun their analysis well enough, only to run into difficulties. Humour dates quickly; one person's joke is another's embarrassment, and the subject does not yield easily to classification. *If a playwright is funny, the English look for a serious message, and if he is serious they look for the joke,* said Sacha Guitry [1886-1957], the French dramatist. What follows attempts to summarize some philosophical conclusions, so far.

Four Theories of Humour

> *We tried to count all the different theories of humour we came across, but gave up somewhere north of 100.*
>
> Jimmy Carr and Lucy Greaves. *The Naked Jape*.

According to Carr and Greaves there are four explanations of humour: the theories of Superiority, Incongruity, Ambivalence and Release, while the Concise Routledge Encyclopaedia of Philosophy reduces them to three by omitting Ambivalence.

1. The Theory of Superiority holds that the main purpose of humour is to boost our own standing by ridiculing that of others. It goes back at least to Aristotle [384-322 BC], who thought humour was "educated insolence". This was also Thomas Hobbes' and Henri Bergson's explanation and it accounts for a great deal, especially those jokes we describe as "put-downs", for example, Dorothy Parker's response when told that President Coolidge had died, "Why, I never even knew he was alive!" It was this kind of joke that Jesus turned upside down when [Lk 17:16] of the ten men he healed of leprosy only the Samaritan came back to thank him. *Were not all ten made clean? Was no one found returning to give thanks to God except this foreigner*? The despised foreigner! It's the non-Jew who is superior in this pointed twist on the expected.

Humour as an assertion of superiority is found in all societies; and it is also present in the Old Testament's love of satire. At the end of the book of Job, for example, it is God who is the satirist and a satirist who pulls no punches. *The Lord said to Job, Shall a fault finder contend with the Almighty… then Job answered the Lord, Behold I am of no account, what shall I answer?* [40:1&3].

After putting him down, the Lord berates Job from the whirlwind and poor Job doesn't stand a chance as God mocks him for his ignorance, and though we might think that what God says is too serious to be amusing, all mockery is a form of comedy and this is mocking superiority straight from heaven. *Can you,* God asks, *draw out Leviathan with a fish hook?* [41:1] And Job is beaten down as God asks one unanswerable question after another: *Who is this who darkens counsel,* God asks [38:1]. *In all your life have you ever called up the dawn* [38:12]; *Have you visited the storehouses of the snow or seen the arsenal where hail is stored?* [38:22] God browbeats Job like this for three chapters of magnificent poetic put-down until Job capitulates saying, *therefore, I despise myself, and repent in dust and ashes.* Surely, there's a little irony in Job's reply?

The Bible reflects all of human life and so much of that life is about conflict and controversy. There's not a verse in the Bible which has not got some controversy or other for its background; and the most effective humour in dealing with controversy is satire, the most superior kind of comedy. God taunts Job, and, in the world of the Bible, taunting was the weapon of choice in many of the conflicts it records.

When Elijah[21] battles on Mount Carmel with the prophets of Baal[22], he taunts them with a merciless satire on why the Canaanite fertility god, Baal, isn't answering their prayers: *Cry aloud, for he is a god; either he is musing, or has gone aside, or he is on a journey, or perhaps he is asleep and must be woken up.* [I Kings 18:27]. *Gone aside* is a euphemism as in a man might "go aside" to look for a convenient bush when he needed to empty his bladder! To apply the image to a god satirically like this was blasphemous comedy, and Elijah played it for all it was worth, maybe even pretending to snore when he added, *perhaps he's asleep.*

To mock is to scoff and scoffers are everywhere in the Bible. The psalmists are much troubled by them and psalm 79 responds with that unfunniest of responses, a curse. *Return sevenfold into the bosom of our neighbours the taunts with which they have taunted thee, O Lord* [79:12]. This is dark comedy indeed. No wonder Isaiah[23] looks forward to the day *when the scoffers cease* [29:20].

Wherever there's polemic, humour is seldom far away, even in such an innocent looking text as this from the creation account in Genesis: *And God made two great lights, the greater light to rule the day, and the lesser light to rule the night; he made the stars also* [1:16]. This sounds non-controversial until we realise that when it was

---

21 Elijah prophesied in the northern kingdom of Israel during the 9th c. BCE.

22 *Baal* in the Phoenician and Canaanite languages meant "Lord," and referred to the son of El, the high god. Unfortunately the names El and Baal also occur in Hebrew with rather different meanings which can complicate the picture. In popular Israelite religion, Baal, a fertility god, was more in demand than "the Lord" the God of Abraham, Isaac and Jacob. He was worshipped with his consort, Anath. Their worship involved sacred sexual activity and occasionally human sacrifice. Israelite attitudes varied from worshipping Baal instead of the Lord to worshipping the Lord through the ritual of Baal. From time to time, Baal worship had the support of powerful royal patrons, as in our example.

23 Isaiah's prophetic ministry took place around the middle of the 8th century BCE in the southern kingdom of Judah and lasted for at least 44 years.

written, the Jews were a tiny exiled group in Babylon, where the sun was the powerful god Shamash, while the moon, the father of Shamash, was the god Sin. Both gods had great wealth and enormous temples dedicated to their worship, and yet here were obscure and insecure, Jews boasting, "our God (whose own temple had been destroyed by the Babylonians) created your gods". The implied mockery there is the humour of superiority!

Shockingly, a desperate psalmist even taunts God: [Psalm 10:1], *Why stand far off, Lord, why hide away in times of trouble?* The taunt is made sharper in verse 12, with the suggestion that God is sleeping, *Arise, Lord, set your hand to the task; do not forget the afflicted.*

What sort of faith feels it can mock and taunt God like this?

2. Humour as Incongruity: If British philosophers like Thomas Hobbes]1588-1679] inclined towards superiority theory, German philosophers like Immanuel Kant [1724-1804] and Arthur Schopenhauer [1788-1862] favoured comedy as incongruity. Kant said that laughter resulted from "an affectation arising from a sudden transformation of strained expectation into nothing", while Schopenhauer thought it derived from "the incongruity[24] between a concept and the real object to which it was designed to relate".

We find something akin to this shift from an expected outcome to one that's unexpected, in the wisdom literature[25] of the Old Testament. For example, in the Book of Proverbs, there lies behind the text the comic image of two women soliciting young men as they leave the Torah academy. Women, of course, were not allowed to attend! One of the women proclaiming her charms was Lady Wisdom [1:20], the most desirable of women, while the other

---

[24] See *New Scientist* article *The Comedy Circuit* for 30 January 2010 where the title's pun refers to brain imaging in experiments designed to discover why some jokes which involve resolving incongruities are only funny to some people. One area of the brain involved in finding something funny is the limbic system which is associated with dopamine release and reward processing. Nonsense humour, it seems, is processed by the pre-frontal cortex; social humour by the fronto-insular cortex and the anterior cingulated cortex; nonsense humour by the hippocampus; and visual puns by the extrastriate cortex.

[25] Just as Israel's prophets prophesied, so the pursuit of wisdom was the life work of her Sages or Wise Men. The sages were responsible for writing books like Job, Proverbs and Ecclesiastes, books known collectively as Wisdom Literature.

was either a local “gang moll”, [1:10] or [2:16] a common prostitute. A wise student would follow Lady Wisdom. If he was foolish then he had ignored the advice of his parents [1:8].

Comic incongruity also lies behind the imagery of Amos in his prophecy concerning the terrible and surprise-filled *Day of the Lord* which the ignorant had supposed was a day to look forward to*: Woe to you who desire the Day of the Lord…. It is darkness, and not light; as if a man fled from a lion and a bear met him; or went into a house and leaned his hand against the wall and a serpent bit him.* [5:18]

Jesus was also fond of comedy as incongruity: *Would any of you offer his son a stone when he asks for bread?* he asked the crowd [Mt 7:9]. His listeners would have understood that this was exactly what he believed the Torah extremists were doing. It was not what God did. To drive the point home, he resorts to irony. *If you, bad as you are, know how to give good things to your children, how much more will your heavenly Father give good things to those who ask him?* [7:11]

3. Comedy as Ambivalence: When Jesus played his fellow Galileans for laughs by reminding them of what those in Jerusalem thought of them, he took a risk with his, *if you, bad as you are.* This is humour as *ambivalence;* that is comedy that depends on some ambiguity between opposing feelings of what is acceptable and what is not.

One of a psychoanalyst’s jobs is to peel away the layers of conscious thought to reveal the conflicts within. This is something which, according to theoreticians of humour like William Hazlitt [1778-1830][26], humour does well because it depends on it. The Sermon on the Mount is packed with knock-about ambivalence. Matthew places the sermon tellingly at the start of Jesus’ ministry when the crowd was not certain what to expect. They knew all about the hard-line religion of the authorities from Jerusalem, who’d come to Galilee to promote their kind of Torah observance, but they did not know what line their new, home-grown teacher would take. As we shall discover, unless we recognise the Sermon on the Mount as the comedy of ambivalence, it makes little sense. We don’t need to be psychologists to know that in our hearts we are all deeply ambivalent about things like peace and poverty.

4 Humour as Psychological Release was the favourite theory of Sigmund Freud [1856-1939] who saw depression and anxiety as the result of the social need to deny unacceptable thoughts and

---

26 See his essay on Wit and Humour.

feelings. In 19th century society these would be largely sexual in nature, while in biblical times they were more likely to be religious. In the Sermon on the Mount, Jesus preaches to a crowd who knew that Galileans like themselves could never be observant enough for the religious authorities in Jerusalem. Religious tensions were high in such a "big-brother" atmosphere, and so with a series of comic images Jesus sets about releasing the pressure: *When you give alms, do not announce it with a flourish of trumpets, as the hypocrites do in synagogues and in the streets to win the praise of others.* [Mt 6:2] This sort of mockery not only deflated religious pretension, it also made the religiously inferior feel superior to those who lorded it over them.

With comedy as release, humour becomes subversive, as Freud demonstrated when he was a prisoner of the Gestapo who, before they allowed him to leave Vienna, demanded a written statement testifying that he had not been mistreated. Freud obliged, and then added that he would recommend the Gestapo to anyone!

Just as nothing kills a joke as quickly as an explanation, so all explanations of humour fail to satisfy. Where comedy is concerned, we can appreciate Kant's assertion as a philosopher that things in themselves are unknowable, that, whatever reality might be, it's ultimately inaccessible. Everything is veiled. We cannot reach the foundations of humour because somehow they are also the foundations of our existence. Reason, like its siblings mathematics and logic, has limits. Quantum physics is not the only area in which we come up against uncertainty. To be a creature is to be limited, and limited in ways that make all exploration partial. *Truly,* says Isaiah, *thou art a God who hidest thyself.* [Is. 45:15] Just as God is hidden from us, so we will always be hidden from ourselves. Nature is only ever partly known. The more we know, the more there is to be known. This is the ultimate in comedy. Existence experienced as a joke is the joke the Bible explores. God is veiled and reality is veiled even when disclosed to creatures like us, who are veiled from themselves. When God answers Job out of the whirlwind [38:1] and berates him with that bullying list of questions, he is doing no more to Job than modern science does to the best minds among us. There is always a limit to human knowledge. Its frontiers may move, but there is always a perceived limit. God, like creation, is a tricky and comic reality. Unlike men and women, who are forever projecting their egos onto everyone and everything, God conceals the divine equivalent in his elusiveness.

As an aside, we can note that though the Jews of today have a well-deserved reputation for humour, historians seem only to date this from the 18th century and the impact of the Enlightenment on

European Jewry. *The Bible as Comedy* testifies otherwise.

Jewish Wit: Chutzpah

> *Oscar Wilde*[27]*: "I wish I'd said that."*
> *Whistler*[28]*: "You will, Oscar, you will.'*

Wit is an intellectual, clever kind of humour, often used to turn a difficult situation to advantage. Wits are quick thinkers, able with an amusing and unexpected phrase to escape difficult situations.

Chutzpah is a peculiarly Jewish kind of self-confident wit. It is impertinence redeemed by humour, the gall that can "get away with murder", and the Bible is full of it. Explaining chutzpah, a Jew today might give the classic answer of the young man who, having murdered his parents, pleaded he was an orphan!

Another example would be Joshua's prayer in Joshua 7:2, during the Israelite invasion of the Promised Land, when after defeat by the men of Ai and fearing annihilation at the hands of the Canaanites, he taunts God with sheer and mocking impertinence, *What will you do then for the honour of your great name?* Chutzpah as a humorous response to the divine presence is a biblical motif that will arise again in this study.

More thoughts on Humour as Ambivalence and Psychological Release

> *My way of joking is to tell the truth. It's the funniest joke in the world.*
>
> George Bernard Shaw [1856-1950]

Following their exile to Babylon in 597 BC, which will be explored more fully in the next chapter, it's impossible to say how ordinary Jews would have felt about the description of their past as the failure of polytheism, and their exile as the punishment and moral consequence of disobeying the Law of Moses. Not everyone would have agreed with the reformers here; many would have assimilated to the paganism of Babylon as the northern tribes seem to have done to that of Assyria. What interests us is the reaction of those who repented and promised future obedience to the Torah and who

27 1854-1900, writer, poet and famous wit.

28 J A M Whistler [1834-1900] was a painter and wit.

accepted the Lord as the one true God.

Monotheism frequently tends outwardly to social strictness and inwardly to stern self-control. When it operates like this, there can be little defence against it but humour. Not surprisingly, comedy as a defence against divine intrusion can be found throughout the Bible. A good example is in I Samuel 16, where Samuel is commanded by God to find a successor to King Saul from the family of Jesse. As he considers the eldest son, Eliab, t*he Lord said to Samuel, "Do not look on his appearance or on the height of his stature, because I have rejected him; for the Lord does not see as mortals see; they look on the outward appearance, but the Lord looks on the heart."* These are lofty and worthy sentiments but a few verses further on as Samuel considers the eighth and last son, who was *ruddy, and had beautiful eyes and was handsome,* the Lord said, "*Rise and anoint him".* As so often in the Bible, the humour is just the right side of transgressive. In Christian mythology, Satan rebelled against God; in the book of Jonah the prophet runs away instead and succumbs to depression; but, in describing the choosing of David's successor, the writer avoids both rebellion and depression and prefers to distance us from God with humour.

Comedy, Cruelty and Revelation[29]

> *He* [Macaulay] *has occasional flashes of silence that make his conversation perfectly delightful.*
>
> Sydney Smith [1771-1845].

The problem with so much humour is its cruelty. Jokes are too often at someone's expense. The taunt-songs of the Hebrew Scriptures are like curses served with comic relish, as in this taunt sung over the

---

29 Jews and Christians believe what they believe about God on the basis of what they believe God has revealed about himself. On this view, revelation is a gift of God. After that, however, the discussion becomes complicated. To what extent is revelation reducible to statements and propositions about God? What part does the Bible play in that? Do such beliefs change over time? Is there a hierarchy of revealed truths? In what way can such truths be described as infallible? What part do faith, reason, tradition and scripture play in exploring the content of revelation? Although these and other questions are important, this book is primarily interested in the connection between revelation and the Bible's comic vision of history and of God's role within it.

king of Babylon: *maggots are the mattress beneath you, and worms your coverlet.* [Isa 14:11]

Jesus once advised his hearers [Mt 6:7], *do not go babbling on in your prayers like the heathen, who imagine that the more they say, the more they will be heard.* In our more politically correct times, such comic caricatures are less acceptable. It is considered wrong to mock "difference", a sensitivity unknown in more robust biblical times when comedy could, by modern standards, be hostile and unfeeling. This was especially the case with the Taunt Songs of the prophets: *Come down and sit in the dust, O virgin daughter of Babylon; sit on the ground without a throne, O daughter of the Chaldeans! For you shall no more be called tender and delicate. Take the millstone and grind meal, put off your veil, strip off your robe, uncover your legs, pass through the rivers. Your nakedness shall be uncovered and your shame*[30], that is "your genitals", *shall be seen.* [Is. 47:1ff] This sort of vulgarity would probably be self-censored today. All taunting is a kind of satire and as such is comedy, cruel comedy, and there's a good deal of it in the Bible. Even God himself is taunted by the devout! *Rouse yourself, Lord; why do you sleep? Awake!* [Ps44:23] Taunting God could become part of the prayer of the righteous when they felt abandoned: *Has God forgotten to be gracious... Has his right hand grown weak?* [Ps 77:10].

So much of comedy involves cruelty, even a delight in cruelty, that this, together with obscenity, bad-taste and political incorrectness in a book believed to be in some way God's self-revelation, calls for explanation.

Until recently all known cultures were religious, though not to the same extent or in the same way. In Judaism and Christianity the relationship between God and humankind is paramount. The Bible is the story of that relationship, with God revealing himself in the blood-drenched cruelties we call history. God comes to us and we come to God in the mess that human beings make of things. As comedy and humour are essential sanity-preserving responses to that mess, revelation without them is unthinkable. A Bible without comedy would make us more suspicious of its spiritual worth than a Bible that posed no intellectual or moral difficulties.

And one further thought. The Bible is a collection of books that bear the scars of history. Its text is not always certain[31] and, where it is, its meaning is not always clear. The result is a library of books

---

30 Our word "pudenda" is from a Latin verb, *pudere*, meaning to be ashamed.

31 Modern translations will indicate with footnotes important variations in the ancient Hebrew and Greek text.

formed on the human side of revelation through natural processes. On the divine side, God's self revelation can only be given through those same processes. And just as, since Darwin, theologians have argued that natural selection was God's instrument of design in the created order, so we can say that in so far as the Bible can be thought of as "the word of God", God's self-revelation throughout its various books must also operate in a natural sort of way through the people and events that brought those books into being.

3

THE EXILE: THE BIBLE'S FIRST DEFINING MOMENT

If you want to make God laugh, tell him your plans for the future.
Woody Allen [1935-]

All that we call history is hindsight, and with the benefit of that hindsight we can say that the most decisive moment in the making of the Bible was the exile, in 597 BCE, of the Jews to Babylon where they were taken by the all-conquering king Nebuchadnezzar. It was the worst disaster of biblical times and with Judah's institutions destroyed and its leaders deported, it almost brought the history of the Jews to an end. Yet, seventy years later, under Cyrus II [d.529 BC], the vanquisher of the Babylonians and the enlightened and humanitarian founder of the Persian Empire[32] [538-333 BCE], many Jews returned to Judah as a nation intact and a people transformed. Those three generations of exiles saw the beginnings of a religious reformation whose effects have lasted to the present day. What happened is clear, how it happened is largely a matter for conjecture.

As the North Koreans learned in their conflict with the United Nations [1950 – 1953], once the leaders among prisoners of war are separated from their comrades, the remaining prisoners become easier to manage. This was a rediscovery of the policy of the Assyrians[33] who, in 722 BC, overthrew the northern kingdom of Israel

---

32 The Bible could well be described as a handbook on how a small nation survived the threat of six empires: the Egyptian [c1300 BCE]; the Assyrian [911-612BCE]; the Babylonian[612-539BCE]; the Persian[550-330BCE]; the Greek [336-49 BCE] and the Roman [49BCE – 135 CE]. Under King Solomon, Israel even had a small, local empire of its own [c971-931BCE]

33 Mesopotamia, the land between the rivers Tigris and Euphrates [present day Iraq] was the site of a number of ancient empires, Sumer and Elam being the first. The longest lived and most powerful was the Assyrian with its capital firstly at Asshur and then at Nineveh. Although the Assyrian Empire expanded and declined a number of times, it lasted from its origins under king Sargon of Akkad c. 2370 BC to the fall of Nineveh in 612BC, when it was succeeded by the Babylonian.

and exiled its leaders. It was a practice repeated by the Babylonians[34] when they annexed the southern kingdom over a century later.

The fate of the northern tribes is lost to history[35], although the people we know as the Samaritans[36] are in some way related to them. On the other hand, the fate of Judah, the southern kingdom, is one of the great survival stories of humankind. For reasons only partly understood, the Judeans were different. With their leaders taken from them, those left behind gave little trouble, while those in exile pondered their situation and came to far reaching conclusions and decisions. They did not disappear from history but organised themselves in such a way that they were able to transform their religion, return to Jerusalem, and become the Jewish people we know today.

The Neglected Covenant: Guaranteeing History as Comedy

> *The art of leadership...consists in consolidating the attention of the people against a single adversary and taking care that nothing will split up that attention.*
>
> Adolf Hitler [1889-1945] *Mein Kampf.*

With grim irony, this leadership principle used by Hitler to prepare the German mind for his assault on Europe's Jews, was used by the Jewish leaders in Babylon to preserve their nation.

The Judeans went into exile as polytheists and as demoralised prisoners of war; they returned with a religious dedication leavened by comedy. They had lost their temple, but in Babylon developed new, experimental institutions, which in time became the synagogue with its study of Torah. These today are the

---

34 In 627BC, the powerful city of Babylon successfully rebelled against its Assyrian overlords and with its capture of Nineveh in 612BC, became the capital of the short-lived Babylonian Empire [612-539BC]

35 It's almost certain that losing their distinctive identity they were assimilated into the ordinary Assyrian population becoming in two or three generations indistinguishable from their pagan neighbours.

36 The name derives from the city of Samaria which was the capital of the Northern Kingdom of Israel when, after the death of king Solomon [c960BC], the Israelites divided into the northern kingdom of Israel, consisting of ten tribes, and Judah, consisting of the two tribes of Judah and Benjamin.

heart of Jewish communities everywhere.

All this came about through their understanding of the exile as God's punishment for the sins of their ancestors, especially the sin of idolatry. Never again must Jews anger God in this way; and so the people renounced their idolatry and committed themselves to monotheism. They remembered the words of the prophet Amos to the leaders of the northern kingdom over a hundred years before: *Hate evil, and love good; establish justice in the courts; it may be that the Lord, the God of Hosts, will show favour to the survivors of Joseph.* [Amos 5:15].

History, which is tragedy under man, becomes comedy under God. This was the lesson Jewish leaders believed they had learned in Babylon. It was put into the mouth of the heroine, Judith, in her seduction of the Assyrian general, Holophernes: *no punishment ever befalls our race nor does the sword subdue them, except when they sin against their God.* [Judith 11:10]. It was an adaptation of the words of Jeremiah: *Israel, if you will come back to me, says the Lord, if you will banish the loathsome idols from my sight, and go astray no more, if you swear, "by the life of the Lord," in truth, justice and uprightness, then the nations will pray to be blessed like you.* [Jer. 4:1ff]

This renewed Covenant was to shape the future of Judah for the next six hundred years. Providing Jews kept the Torah, the law given to Moses on Mount Sinai, God would guarantee the survival of his people. This doctrine and policy turned the prophecies of Amos, Isaiah and Jeremiah into promises and summarised the lessons Judah's leaders believed they had learned in Babylon. They were determined that the covenant made by God with his people would never be broken again. Jews had power to preserve history as comedy as well as the power to turn it into tragedy.

The process by which Jews became a 'Torah observant' and 'Torah righteous' people has left little trace in the records[37]. An exile that began as a national tragedy had somehow ended on a comic note of hope for the future and a renewed faith in God. The Judeans had been warned by Isaiah: *my people shall go into captivity because they lack all knowledge of me* [5:13], but they had ignored his oracle. When it was almost too late, in Babylon they remembered. It was remembering the covenant that underwrote the Bible's vision of

---

37 By becoming Torah observant the Judeans became a distinctive people, the Jews. They were marked out by such Torah determined customs as circumcision, Sabbath observance and strict Kosher food laws. without these, the tribe of Judah would have been assimilated and lost to history as surely as the northern tribes of Samaria.

history as comedy. The Torah gave Jews their catastrophe-coping identity; one that survives today. But if anyone doubts the difficulty the reformers had in overcoming the idol worship of their people, they should read Jeremiah chapter 44 where we are left in no doubt of the love of ordinary people for the "Queen of Heaven.'

Idolatry: The Religion of the Jews before the Exile

There is a sad law which states that all religions tend towards idolatry.

Philip Toynbee [1916-81]. *Part of a Journey.*

No book of the Hebrew Bible as we now have it dates from before the Babylonian Exile. All were edited or written by Judeans resolved to be faithful to the Law of Moses. This explains the very negative stance of the Old Testament towards pre-exilic Israelite religion; for although the tribes were ostensibly monotheists in a covenant relation with the God of Israel, in practice they were polytheists. This is borne out in the failure of archaeologists to discover any evidence before the Exile of any significant difference between the Israelites and their Canaanite neighbours.

The biblical writer thought to be responsible for the books of Deuteronomy, Samuel and Kings, and known to scholars as the Deuteronomist, divided the rulers of Israel and Judah into good kings and bad. Good kings promoted the worship of Yahweh or Jehovah (almost always translated as "the Lord'); while bad kings not only did nothing to hinder idolatry but actively encouraged it by their own worship of the Canaanite fertility gods. The day-to-day religion of both kingdoms was polytheist. The God of Abraham, Isaac and Jacob who led the Israelites out of Egypt was the God of gods in name only. The lesser gods, the Baals or Baalim, were local deities resorted to for most day to day purposes. Before the exile, the belief that the Lord was the only God and not simply the nation's chief god was held by only a minority of Israelites. But all that changed radically during the Exile as monotheism began to displace polytheism.

Pre-Exilic prophets like Elijah [c860 BC], Isaiah [c740 BC], and Jeremiah [c 625 BC], and reforming kings like Josiah [640-609 BC] had appealed repeatedly to the people to abandon their worship of the Baalim, but without success. In an early sermon, delivered in memorable poetry, Jeremiah had berated his fellow Judeans for their apostasy: *Be appalled, O heavens, at this, be shocked, be utterly desolate, says the Lord, for my people have committed two evils: they have forsaken me, the fountain of living waters, and hewed out cisterns for themselves, broken cisterns that can hold no water.* [2:12]. In a land where families depended on water stored in rock-hewn cisterns a crack in the water-proof plaster lining was a domestic disaster. Jeremiah's was a dry wit and a telling image.

Isaiah too had made good use of sarcasm: *How can you say, I am not defiled, I have not gone after the Baals? Look at your way in the valley; know what you have done – a restive young camel interlacing her tracks, a wild ass used to the wilderness, in her heat, sniffing at the wind! Who can restrain her lust? None who seek her need weary themselves; in her month they will find her.* [2:23] The Baal worshippers at their devotions reminded Isaiah of a camel on heat!

This rejection of God by his people was traced by the reformers to as far back as the foundation of the nation in its flight from Egypt. In spite of the ten plagues and the miraculous crossing of the Red Sea, no sooner had the Israelites reached the desert than they hankered after other gods. *And when the people saw that Moses delayed to come down the mountain, the people gathered themselves together and said to Aaron: Up, make us a god who shall go before us,* [Ex. 32] which is how Aaron came to make the Golden Calf, which for later Jews would mark forever the idolatrous low point of their history. Yet, even in recording this most shameful act, the writer could not resist a little humour: *Aaron said, Let not the anger of my Lord burn hot; you know the people, that they are set on evil. For they said to me, Make us gods, who shall go before us; as for this Moses, the man who brought us up out of the land of Egypt, we do not know what has become of him. And I said to them, Let any who have gold take it off, so they gave it to me, and I threw it into the fire, and there came out this calf.* [33:22]. The phrases, "*As for this Moses*" and "*there came out this calf,*" are flashes of humour tinged with chutzpah.

The Deuteronomic Reformation: The Men of the Great Synagogue

> *By the waters of Babylon we sat down and wept when we remembered thee, O Zion.*
> Psalm 137:1.

The resolution by Judah's leaders in exile, that to avoid future disaster, their people would observe the Law of Moses and worship only the one true God, was the decision that saved the nation. It made the Jews a distinctive people whose impact on history would be out of all proportion to their numbers or political power. The tribes of Judah, Benjamin and Levi did not vanish as the northern tribes had done. As Isaiah had prophesied, *Zion will be redeemed by justice and her returning people by righteousness* [1:27].

According to the later rabbis of the Mishnah[38], who saw themselves as successors to the reformers, the credit for this far reaching reformation belonged to a mysterious group known as the *Anshei Knesset HaGedolah,* "The Men of the Great Synagogue." This was an assembly, perhaps mythical, of 72 (some say 85, others 120) scribes or scholars, sages and the last of the prophets, including Haggai, Zechariah and Malachi, who, it is claimed, passed on their knowledge of the Torah to succeeding generations. Later rabbis regarded those who laboured in this way for the salvation of the Jews and the preservation of their scriptures, as belonging to one or two generation only. Most historians, however, reckon it took several hundred years. As well as editing the Torah and initiating the practice of reading it on Sabbaths and festivals, the Men of the Great Synagogue are also credited with adding to the canon of Scripture the books of Ezekiel, Daniel, Esther and the twelve Minor Prophets. They are remembered too as liturgists, with many of today's synagogue prayers being traced to them. They were also said to have passed on the Oral Law, their interpretation of the Torah, which in its final development became first the Mishnah and finally the Talmud, the many-volumed interpretation of Jewish Law which is the basis of modern Judaism.

The American literary critic, Harold Bloom, would also include among those credited with producing the Hebrew Bible an unknown woman, the editor of the hypothetical document known as J[39]. But whoever it was who gave Christians and Jews their comic view of history, that under God all would end well, theirs proved to be a view

---

38 In Hebrew, "Mishnah" means "teaching," and refers to the final version of the Oral Law as it was written down, discussed, interpreted and codified by the Pharisees and their descendants the rabbis. The process began traditionally with Ezra the Scribe during the Exile and continued through generations of scholars, the Sopherim, the Zugot, the Tannaim until the final, authorised version was produced by Rabbi Judah Ha-Nasi, c 220 BCE.

39 Scholars who have attempted to trace the literary sources behind the first five books of the Bible, identified four, which they designated: J, P, E, and D and of these J, so called because its name for God was Jehovah, was the oldest. In *The Book of J,* Grove Press, New York, Bloom argued that the author of J was very probably a woman of the royal house at king Solomon's court.

which even when thoroughly secularised retained its basic optimistic form. In many ways, this has been the most lasting achievement of those ancient reformers. It means that even when western agnostics, atheists and secular humanists believe they have rejected belief in God, they nevertheless hold on to the comic patterns of human existence underwritten by Him in scripture.

Missing from the rabbinic list of Great Synagogue members were the priests, except for Ezra[40] and Ezekiel[41]. Also missing were the Sages, or Wisdom writers. After the *Wisdom of Solomon*, a book included in the Christian Apocrypha, the Wisdom tradition of Israel was absorbed into the rabbinic tradition as the rabbis began to call themselves sages.

These groups of priests, sages, prophets and early rabbinic scholars were responsible for preserving the Five Books of Moses: Genesis, Exodus, Leviticus, Numbers and Deuteronomy, the Torah, which are the heart of synagogue worship today.

Though scholars have worked hard to reconstruct the process by which the Old Testament came into being, details of how these various writings came to be written and preserved are now lost. Taken together, however, the Hebrew Scriptures form a remarkable comic vision of God's dealings with his people: how if they obey his laws, they would be blessed; but, if they disobeyed, they would be abandoned and the comedy of national blessedness transformed into tragedy.

History as a Jewish Theological Device

> *Life can only be understood backwards, but it must be lived forwards.*
>
> Søren Kieirkegaard [1813-1855]

The gods worshipped by Israel and Judah before the exile were nature gods; but as idolatry became a thing of the past and was

---

40 Ezra is remembered as one of the great reformers and heroes of Judaism during the exile in Babylon. According to Ezra 7:14, in 458 BCE, he led some 1,800 exiles home to Jerusalem with authority to impose the Torah upon the surviving community.

41 Ezekiel was a prophet and priest of the southern kingdom of Judah and prophesied for some 22 years in the years before and after the capture of Jerusalem by the Babylonians in 597 BCE.

replaced by the worship of YHWH[42], the one true God, the only God, his activity was sought not only in nature but in history. God the creator was also Lord of History. Without this radical shift in theology's centre of gravity, the Bible's comic vision could not have developed.

During and after the exile, dedicated scribes collected and edited all the surviving history and tradition they could find, both written and oral. Genealogies, old stories and songs, legend and history, legal texts and liturgical. All were written-up by them to promote a national programme of true worship in Torah righteousness, both in individuals and among the people as a whole. They did this by setting the commandments given to them by God within the great story of their history. At every opportunity, that narrative contained reminders of their apostasy and of God's covenant promise of blessing: *You must not bow down to them* [carved images] *in worship; for I, the Lord your God, am a jealous God, punishing the children for the sins of the parents to the third and fourth generation of those who reject me.* [Exod. 20:5] *Honour your father and your mother, so that you may enjoy long life in the land which the Lord your God is giving you.* [Exod. 20:12]

In exile, with barely three tribes surviving out of twelve, the Jews might easily have written up their story as a tragedy but, thanks to the vision of the prophets they wrote it up as comedy on a national, then a cosmic scale. Only if our western sense of history disintegrates into a disconnected, post-modernist succession of meaningless episodes will the work of the Men of the Great Synagogue be undone. Judah's neighbours, the Egyptians, the Assyrians and the Babylonians wrote chronicles. Apart from the Jews, only the Greeks attempted to interpret history as more than lists of dates and events.

In pondering their exile, the Jews gave the west their conviction that history has meaning and purpose which develops through time. It was a comic vision created to educate people in the Covenant they had ignored for so long but which guaranteed their existence. Without monotheism, this connection between the worship of God and the need for moral and well-ordered living would have been impossible. In polytheism, the behaviour of the gods mirrored human behaviour at its worst. It was the Jews who linked worship intrinsically to the pursuit of holiness and moral virtue.

---

42 The name of God, the Tetragrammaton. In Hebrew script the vowels are omitted so that its correct pronunciation is unknown, Yahweh being thought the most likely. Devout Jews usually say or write, Adonai, The LORD.

History as comedy is only possible under monotheism. Today's secular versions quickly collapse into history as tragedy. Under history as comedy, every kind of humour flourishes but when the comedy ends, all that survive are sarcasm, cynicism and other kinds of gallows humour. When monotheism ceases to nourish a comic and humanist view of life, history self-destructs.

The Great History of Israel

> *The modern consciousness of history is a consciousness of crisis, and all modern philosophy of history is in the last analysis a philosophy of crisis.*
>
> Jurgen Moltmann [b. 1926], *Theology of Hope*.

The difference between Moltmann's treatment of crisis as the central fact of history and that of the Hebrew Scriptures, is that the latter deal with the matter with playful humour, casting the tragic story of Israel and Judah's calamities within an over-riding comic and humorous framework. This extraordinary fact calls for explanation.

Taken together the books of the Old Testament form a grand historical narrative, a *Great History of Israel.* The Hebrew canon is the work of writers from many schools of ancient Israel, written and compiled over many years. Priests, prophets, sages, poets, storytellers, all contributed to telling how, after the creation of the world, things went badly wrong. The cause was idolatry. It was humankind's primal sin: the worshipping of anything but God. The prophets prophesied in vain until the kingdom was divided and its people exiled. Only the Judeans, the Jews, concluded that if they were to survive they must ensure that their worship was pure and their lives righteous.

In order to wean the exiles from idolatry, surrounded as they were by so many pagan temples, all of them politically powerful and architecturally appealing, Judah's founding fathers were mocked mercilessly for their idolatry, with comedy and humour as the weapons of choice. This is how Judah's historians came to write the story of their people as a satire. The great history of Israel mocked its founding fathers, as Jews were invited to chuckle at their ancestors in story after story. The message from the reformers was clear: "You are not to be like those whose wickedness brought us to this." To wean the people from idolatry was no easy matter. The message of the reformers was that if they went back to idolatry they would fail as a nation, becoming jokes and fools like their ancestors. In this way, the history of Israel also became a grand, comic confession of the nation's guilt.

The Great History in Outline

Laughter means to rejoice at another's expense, but with a good conscience.

Friedrich Nietzsche [1844-1900], *The Will to Power.*

Biblical comedy gets off to a good start as the history of Judah is traced back to the very creation of the universe! God said, "Let there be light," and the story gets underway.

What a piece of work is man, thought Shakespeare's Hamlet, *how noble in reason, how infinite in faculties, in form and moving how express and admirable, in action how like an angel, in apprehension how like a god*. This was Renaissance hyperbole handing on the torch of human excellence to the Enlightenment. But it was not the view of the author of Genesis, as what followed the six days of creation was a long and tragic descent into darkness. With Adam and Eve, the first couple, the world formed from physical chaos descended rapidly into the moral and spiritual kind, and what began as comedy ended in tragedy.

With the jealousy of Cain, murder entered the world; with the boasting of Lamech, it became untrammelled vengeance and with Lamech's son, Noah, God thought to begin all over again by destroying his creation with a great deluge. Salvation and comedy returned when he changed his mind. Noah is spared but only for chaos to return with the building of the Tower of Babel. This is history as insight into the human condition.

Then Abram the Patriarch, soon to be Abraham, the founding father of Israel, enters the story. He is an ambiguous combination of faith and cowardice, a nomad who receives God's promise of a homeland, a deeply flawed national hero, as are Isaac and Jacob the trickster, who in turn inherit the promise. This is no idealised version of history but a "warts and all" realist account of human nature far from Hamlet's thoughts on the subject.

With Jacob the trickster and Joseph the interpreter of dreams, progenitors of the tribes that would make up Israel, there is a further descent into darkness, this time into servitude in Egypt, from where, after 400 years, they are rescued by the stuttering Moses. After Moses, his successor Joshua leads the tribes across the Jordan and into the Promised Land where they are cared for by a succession of warrior Judges, the most famous of whom are Gideon, Samson and

Deborah.

These Judges are followed in turn by Samuel the prophet who anoints as king the unsatisfactory Saul. David, the adulterer and man of blood, follows Saul, the unworthy king, and in turn David is followed by Solomon, collector of wives, concubines and proverbs, and worshipper of foreign gods. Under his over-confident son, Rehoboam, there is civil war and the nation divides. Into this political chaos God sends prophets like Elijah, Elisha, Isaiah, Jeremiah, Amos and Hosea to remind an idolatrous people of the Covenant they are neglecting and the crimes that follow in the wake of their apostasy. Disaster strikes, and, marched a thousand miles across the desert to exile in Mesopotamia, neither Judah nor Israel could say that they had not been warned. But in exile, there's a spiritual and moral analysis of Judah's political history and the nation is reborn in repentance and obedience to the law. This is history as self-examination. It begins in tragedy, is written up with humour and turns life into a prayer for human existence as comedy.

Policing National Prayer

> *True prayer is a struggle with God, and man emerges victorious when God is the victor.*
>
> Søren Kierkegaarde [1813-55.]

Just as after the Glorious Revolution and the accession of William III, British historians wrote up their history as a grand progress towards democracy and the Whig Settlement, so after the Exile, the Jews wrote up their history as the long delayed crisis in idolatry followed by the re-establishment of the nation in the righteousness of a divinely-given law. It was the world's first and most successful comic history and it was based on the well tried educational devices of the carrot and the stick. The carrot was the opportunity to laugh at the folly of the nation's heroes. It was a gentle invitation to renounce idolatry; but persuading the people to become righteous according to Torah was another matter altogether, and for this, a stick was necessary.

Getting tough with inadequately repentant idolaters

> *Idolatry comes from the fact that while thirsting for absolute good, we do not possess the power of supernatural attention.*
>
> Simone Weil [1909-1943] *Gravity and Grace.*

The Book of Nehemiah describes how Ezra the Scribe read the Torah to the returned exiles: *On the first day of the eleventh month, Ezra the priest brought the law before the whole assembly, both men and women, and all who were capable of understanding what they heard. From early morning till noon he read aloud from it, facing the square in front of the Water Gate.* [8:1-3]

This single-minded commitment to the Torah is described even more dramatically in the book of Ezra: *On the twentieth day of the ninth month, all the men of Judah and Benjamin had assembled in Jerusalem, where they sat in the open space before the house of God, full of apprehension and shivering in the heavy rain. [10:9] The ninth month, Kislev, was the time of the winter rains. The crowd was cold and wet as they heard what the law asked of them. Ezra the priest stood up and addressed them: "You have broken faith in marrying foreign women," he said, "and have added to Israel's guilt. Now make confession to the Lord the God of your fathers, do his will, cut yourselves off from the peoples of the land and from your foreign wives"* [10:10ff].

To the liberal mind of today Ezra's demand were excessive, yet the people were reportedly enthusiastic. *The whole company assented loudly, "We shall do as you say."* The names of over one hundred leading citizens are recorded as obediently putting away their foreign wives and children in what is one of the most morally difficult and heart-rending passages in the Bible. With national survival at stake, Ezra had carried out a policy of unbloody ethnic cleansing. The transformation of the nation had begun. Jews must become people of the Torah, keeping even the least of its prescriptions. The Torah was Israel's road into the future, providing, that was, that Israel observed its demands. A comic perception of national history was being enforced through social pain and personal tragedy. In doing so, the returning exiles had discovered ideology, giving individuals no choice but to fit into a prescribed understanding of history. Whenever religion or politics become ideology, comedy becomes tragedy.

It's not known what became of those expelled as ideological refugees, but it's possible that they joined Torah-observant survivors of the old northern kingdom to become the people we know today as the Samaritans, named after the rival temple at Samaria. While the Judeans resolved to be not only Torah-observant, but also racially pure, with a policy of Judea for the Judeans, the Samaritans appear to have accepted everyone who observed their version of the Torah. As the Torah scrolls in both communities are almost identical, we can assume that its text had been agreed before the survivors of the two kingdoms developed into rival religions.

This radical and at times cruel nation-building transformation of Judaism is outlined in a speech of Judith, the eponymous heroine of the Apocryphal book. In the following passage, she is attempting to persuade the elders of Bethulia to agree to her plan to raise the siege of their city: *At the present day there is not one of our tribes or clans, districts or towns that worships man-made gods, or has done so within living memory. This did take place in days gone by, and that was why our forefathers were abandoned to slaughter and to pillage, and great was their downfall at the hand of the enemy. We, however, acknowledge no god but the Lord, and so have confidence that he will not spurn us or any of our nation.* [8:18ff] She expressed perfectly the policies of the Men of the Great Synagogue.

The hard-line policies of Ezra and Nehemiah are also found in the dark story of Numbers 25, in which Israelite men engaged sexually with the Moabite women who had invited them to the sacrifices offered to their gods. [Num. 25:1] This aroused the anger of the Lord, who said to Moses, *Take all the leaders of the people and hurl them down to their death before the Lord in the full light of day, that the fury of my anger may turn away from Israel. Each of you put to death those of his tribe who have joined in the worship of the Baal of Peor* [25:4]. Here, the offence is not that of marrying foreign women, for even Moses had a foreign wife, Zipporah, daughter of Jethro, a Midianite, but foreign women who led their families in the worship of foreign gods. *One of the Israelites brought a Midianite woman into his family in open defiance of Moses… when Phineas*[43] *son of Eleazar, son of Aaron the priest, saw him he got up from the assembly and took a spear, and went into the nuptial tent after the Israelite and the woman, where he transfixed the two of them, … pinning them together.* [25:7]. Here, in one of the Bible's grimmest, ironic images, a spear pins together the offending couple in the very act of their making love.

It was no easy task to persuade the people to give up idolatry, yet their leaders eventually succeeded through their skilful use of stories. It was through biblical stories that I first learned my faith and it was through these same stories that the children of Israel learned theirs.

---

43 In Roman times Phineas became the archetypal Zealot.

The Human Need for Stories

The most incomprehensible thing about the universe is that it is comprehensible.
Albert Einstein [1879-1955]

In order to survive, human beings need to make sense of an otherwise chaotic and meaningless world and we do this by interpretation and explanation, compressing large amounts of information into easily accessible, memorable and abbreviated interpretations of reality. It is a complicated process but the end result is always a narrative or story, some kind of symbolic drama. History is not only hindsight, it is hindsight as story and the Bible is a whole library of such stories.

In spite of the abstract mathematics and equations involved, even modern science reduces and compresses reality to the minimum number of dynamic symbols needed for a convincing account of the physical world. In the end, science too is communicated through narrative, though its stories are of a different kind to those involved in an historical account of life. Yet even stories as symbolic equations have their limitations and the abstractions used in science are only partly successful attempts to escape these.

Without narratives, human beings could never make sense of the world. Their form might vary from the plays of Shakespeare to Einstein's $E=mc^2$ but in the quest to make sense of events in space and time there's no escape from narrative. Biblical writers quickly mastered the art of telling a good story to a redemptive purpose.

Story, Comedy and Revelation

I'll tell that story on the golden floor.
A. E. Housman [1859-1936]

We are so accustomed in Church to receiving our faith through stories that we take them for granted. without asking how they communicate to us the being and nature of God. It was through stories that Jews did much of their theology. In the Bible, we find a whole mix of means and methods, from legal forms in Leviticus and proverbs in wisdom literature to comedy and stories in the Torah. In the churches we have preferred to do our theology humour and comedy free, gaining precision of thought but losing humanity, and thereby something of our sense of God and of the divine, in the process.

I think of these consequences whenever someone tells me they are a Bible-believing Christian belonging to a Bible-believing church. Whenever people say, "the Bible is very clear on this," I wonder if we are reading the same Bible. We are certainly not reading it in the same way. "Bible-believing Christians" can easily reduce the Bible to a book of propositions, as they seek the clarity and authority which the Bible's comedy and its stories cannot provide. Clarity and authority can easily become oppressive, while revelation and truth as story and comedy usually avoid these temptations.

Persuasion by Storyteller

It is an ancient story, yet it is ever new.
Heinrich Heine [1797-1856]

The stories that functioned as the carrots of encouragement we will come to shortly; stories as sticks, as threats of terror, were fewer but important, as paradoxically they helped sustain the overall comic vision of the Torah. In addition to those we have considered already we might note the following.

Abiram and his brother Dathan were among those *who challenged the authority of Moses* [Num. 16:1] and refused to obey orders. By law, the penalty for this was death but in the event it was God not Moses who carried out the punishment. *Hardly had Moses spoken when the ground beneath them split apart; the earth opened its mouth and swallowed them.* [16:31] It was another terrifying folk memory that served to strengthen the Torah obedience of the reluctant.

The horrific story of Phineas [Num. 25] referred to earlier, served a dual purpose, for when he speared Zimri and Cozbi in the very act of their love-making, 24,000 Israelites had already died in the plague which God was believed to have brought upon Israel for its sin of apostasy. The message was clear: serious sins have serious consequences. Keep the people holy.

Terror as an agent of comedy is a fearful concept, but for the more extreme reformers it seemed a necessary part of Torah. After the shameful idolatry of the Golden Calf, it was important that such sins should not go unpunished. Moses said, *Who is on the Lord's side? Come here to me; and the Levites all rallied to him. He said to them, The Lord God of Israel has said, Arm yourselves, each of you with his sword. Go through the camp from gate to gate and back again, each of you kill brother, friend, neighbour. The Levites obeyed, and about three thousand of the people died that day.* [Exod. 32:26ff]

Among the stories used as sticks to encourage the reluctantly righteous were Noah's Flood, [Gen. 6ff]; and the Destruction of Sodom and Gomorrah, [Gen. 19] which illustrated the reformer's belief that serious sins are inevitably followed by divine retribution and that history as comedy and redemption cannot be divorced from the tragedies of immorality and punishment.

The Limitation of Stories: Confabulation and the Narrative Fallacy

> *The narrative fallacy addresses our limited ability to look at sequences of facts without weaving an explanation into them.*
> Nassim Taleb [b. 1960]. *The Black Swan.*

Evolutionary psychologists explain the human love of narrative as a survival instinct: we either make sense of the world through stories or we perish. To explain is to find the story that makes the most convincing sense of things. It's a spontaneous "heuristic," that is a well-tried short-cut to reality. Rational thinking comes later as explanatory stories are critiqued and evaluated.

It was natural, therefore, that in exile the Jews would attempt to make sense of their predicament. Without stories it is impossible for men and women to operate as human beings. Given a series of unconnected events, those whose minds have ceased to function normally will go on telling stories, often of the wildest kind, simply in order to make sense of what has happened to them. Psychologists call this process confabulation. It is a reminder that, as with all things human, stories have their limitations. Stories are interpretations and simplifications and therefore run the risk of over-interpretation and over-simplification, varieties of confabulation that Nassim Taleb calls "the Narrative Fallacy".

It is for these reasons that within the Bible its stories are continually challenged by other stories. Long before theologians began analysing and criticising the Bible, the Bible criticised itself, frequently through comedy and humour. As we will see in the book of Job's questioning of Psalm 37, and in the challenge of the book of Ruth to Ezra's dismissal of foreign wives, confabulation and the narrative fallacy did not go unchallenged for long in the Bible.

The evolutionary biologists Stephen Jay Gould and Richard Lewontin suggested that we create religious stories to explain the otherwise random nature of world events. This is a possibility, of course, and the same argument can be made with respect to the truth-claims of scientific theories. In science and religion, beliefs seldom go for long without challenge. It's for this reason that in both fields of inquiry, theories and doctrines are constantly evolving and adapting as those holding them struggle for a better fit with reality.

Challenging the Narrative: Torah and the Death Penalty

A Sanhedrin which executed a person once in seven years was called destructive.
The Talmud.

When all law is God's law, crime is a sin and law enforcement the religious duty of the community. In Judah, failure to do so risked breaking the covenant with God. For each crime, the Torah prescribed an appropriate punishment, reserving the death penalty for the most serious infringements only. The list of capital crimes included blasphemy, idolatry, false prophecy, divination, sorcery, murder, working on the Sabbath, adultery, incest, homosexuality, bestiality, kidnapping, treason and the wilful disobeying of parents. This made Judah's comic vision of life one that, paradoxically, was undergirded by the threat and sanction of capital punishment. Death could be by stoning, the most common method, but also by burning, strangulation, or beheading.

It is a list which reflects the standpoint of the strictest among the Torah righteous. However, in practice, these punishments were often applied with great leniency and, by later rabbinic times, very reluctantly indeed as every effort was made to avoid capital punishment, even when prescribed. Rabbi Tarphon [c70-135 CE] and Rabbi Akiba [c50-c135], two of the greatest rabbis, said, *If we were members of the Sanhedrin, never would a person be put to death*; but Rabbi Simeon ben Gamaliel answered, *In that case they would multiply shedders of blood in Israel.*

The fear of the Lord is the beginning of wisdom, wrote the sages, [Prov. 15:27]. Fear as motivation might well be thought indispensable here as elsewhere in life, though it's soon discovered to be a poor policeman.

The tension between righteousness as legal strictness and righteousness as generosity of spirit, runs through both testaments, reaching its point of greatest divergence in the ministry of Jesus. Finally, as the dispute became religiously disruptive, the early Church separated from Judaism and each went its own way.

Judaism as the Pursuit of Torah Righteousness

I shall lead a wise and blameless life; when will you come to me?
My conduct among my household will be blameless,
I shall not set before my eyes any shameful thing.
Psalm 101:2.

We will return later to the role of the story teller in persuading the Jewish people to follow the reformers; but first we need to look more closely at righteousness as the nation's central concern and its essential connection with comedy.

The psalmist's resolve, quoted in our epigraph, summarised the determination of the returning exiles. It may seem odd to link such a single-minded and puritan sounding movement with the idea of *The Bible as Comedy*, yet once the nation's leaders were certain they had the means to prevent further disasters, then history for the Jews could, with God's blessing, only be a history of *shalom,* peace. With its happy ending guaranteed, Jewish history became comedy in the first sense, thereby creating room for comedy in the second. For this to happen, three things were necessary: a definitive copy of the Divine Law; its exposition by scholars devoted to its study; and an educational and liturgical programme to encourage Torah righteousness among all Jews.

When St Matthew describes Jesus step-father, Joseph, as a "just" man [1:19], we are to understand that Joseph was a Torah faithful Jew, a man resolved that nothing in his life should bring disaster on his people. Abolishing idolatry had been only the first step in this purification of the nation. No detail in ritual or moral living was too small a matter for the devout. Jews were now defined by their quest for righteousness and beyond righteousness, holiness. On Sinai, God had said to Moses, *You will be to me a kingdom of priests, my holy nation.* [Ex. 19:6]. Righteousness is a moral concept, holiness a spiritual. Holiness is the righteousness that becomes transparent to God through a life of prayer.

This belief that no disaster would befall the Jewish people if only they kept the Torah was one that saw them safely through successive military occupations by the Babylonians, Persians, Egyptian Ptolemies and the Seleucid Greeks. It survived the destruction of the temple by the Romans in 70 CE, and, two generations later, the loss of the land itself after the failure of the Second War against Rome under the would-be messiah, Bar Kochba. The devout explained Israel's misfortunes as the result of some failure to observe the Torah until, that was, the horrors of the Holocaust, the Nazis' systematic destruction of 6 million European Jews, many of them devoutly Torah observant. What, Jews asked, could we have done to deserve such suffering? And though some still clung to the old explanatory formula, for most Jews, the belief that obedience to the religious law protected the nation from disaster was shaken. Judith's assertion: *no punishment ever befalls our race nor does the sword subdue them, except when they sin against their God,* could not go unchallenged after the death of a million children in Auschwitz and other death camps.

But, until the horrors of the Shoah, the belief that God would reward Torah righteousness served the devout well. The Bible took its comic shape around it, though dissenting voices were never silenced. Righteousness is a pivotal word in both testaments, once it is allowed that love, justice and holiness are part of its moral, social and spiritual structure. Of all the events that make up Israel's history, the decision to stake the nation's future on obedience to the Mosaic Law was the most far reaching.

If the nation's pre-exilic ruling elite had been idolatrous, the post-exilic was decidedly puritan. Nothing was allowed to stand in the way of religious renewal. King Josiah had failed in his reforms, but the returning exiles would not fail in theirs. Fortunately, however, the Jewish love of debate proved stronger than their tendency to ideology, though it was often a close run thing. A further counterweight to this drift to extremism was that the fear of angering God by failing to observe his Law was often accompanied by joy in observing it. To this day, when the Torah scroll is carried through many congregations, it is accompanied by dancing, bringing to mind psalm 119, *In your statutes I find continual delight* [v16].

Eventually, the Rabbis identified 613 scriptural commandments as comprising Torah Righteousness. To make their demands bearable these were to be experienced not as a crippling burden but as prayer: *How I love your law* [Ps. 119:97], even though the same writer also says: *The dread of you makes my flesh creep; I stand in awe of your decrees.* [Ps. 119:120] If Christian mysticism is centred on the love of Christ, Jewish mysticism is focussed on love of the Torah.

This commitment to Torah observance as a way of maintaining control over history is what cultural historians call historicism, the belief that knowing how history works is the first step towards managing it. Some Jewish sects, the Essenes, Apocalypticists and Zealots often came close to historicist and ideological thinking but in Judaism there were always moderating voices against the tendency. The Book of Ruth, for example, can be read as a reaction against such extremists – but of Ruth, more later.

Before the Exile, idolatry was the major problem faced by the Jews; afterwards, it was the quest for righteousness. Even the temple became subordinate to its personal and social pursuit. Here too, a long-lasting pattern was laid down, one that was to determine the nature of European civilisation, even the emergence of democracy and socialism as the means through which social righteousness might be promoted.

History as the Failed Pursuit of Righteousness

Righteousness exalteth a nation.
Proverbs 14:34.

If human beings are to live together successfully, then agreed rules of conduct are necessary. In ancient Greece, as in ancient Egypt and throughout the Middle East, ethical living was linked to *philo-sophia,* philosophy, the love of wisdom. The book of Proverbs in the Old Testament testifies to this essential connection, as do departments of "Ethics" and "Moral Philosophy" in western universities today.

After the Exile and the re-establishment of life around the covenant made at Sinai, virtuous living as taught by the sages became defined as the pursuit of righteousness according to the Torah. Western society is heir to these wisdom and rabbinic traditions, the first predominantly, though not entirely, secular; and the second entirely religious. History as managed change is the attempt by nations to write their story as a pursuit of ethical goals; only recently has the motivation for this swung from one driven by religion towards one argued for in secular terms.

The pursuit of righteousness is a comic pursuit. It has left a remarkable legacy and an often tragic story. It was a pursuit that guided English Puritans in their shaping of parliamentary democracy. It contributed to the abolition of slavery, promoted civilised entrepreneurial capitalism as well as launching our contemporary concern with universal rights. Modern atheists in their conviction that religion is universally pernicious betray a great ignorance of their own origins.

But, if the quest for righteousness has produced great benefits, it has also produced great evils, including the crusades and the religious conflicts of 17th century Europe, those wars of rival righteousnesses which arise from the temptation to self-aggrandisement to which the pursuit of all virtues, especially righteousness, are prone.

Righteousness as a Temptation

Resist at the beginning; the remedy may come too late.
Ovid [43BC-17AD]

No man that is not tempted, shall obtain the kingdom of heaven, said Jesus in an agraphon[44], a favourite non-biblical saying of the early Church father Tertullian.

Temptations are spiritual tests and every situation in life is subject to them. Schoolchildren know how teachers are prone to sarcasm and junior doctors how senior consultants like to play God; while those who pursue righteousness are inclined to self-righteousness – even the psalmist, as in: *the Lord repaid me as my righteousness deserved; because my conduct was spotless he rewarded me.* [18:20]; It was this attitude of religious self-congratulation that Jesus would preach against.

A more serious temptation, however, was that of intolerance towards the less observant. Wherever there was an emphasis on the Torah the rigorists were anxious lest the recovered covenant was broken again and further catastrophe unleashed. This was a development that resulted in a growing religious exclusivity, devout Jews holding aloof from those thought insufficiently observant. *The Passover was eaten by the Israelites and all who had returned from exile and by all who had held themselves aloof from the peoples of the land and their uncleanness.* [Ezra 6:21]

Ezekiel takes up Jeremiah and challenges the Deuteronomists

No morality can be founded on authority, even if the authority were divine.
A. J. Ayer [1910-1989] *Essay on Humanism.*

---

44 An *agraphon* is a saying of Jesus found outside the four gospels. There is a famous agraphon in the Acts of the Apostles: *It is more blessed to give than to receive.* [20:25]. There are many more scattered throughout the Church Fathers; for example, the agraphon quoted above is found in the early writer, Tertullian [c160-220AD], who also recorded:*No man that is not tempted, shall inherit the kingdom of God.* [De Baptismo 20:2]. One of the most commonly quoted is: *Be ye wise bankers.* Scholars are not agreed as to either their value or their authenticity, though they should undoubtedly be more widely known. A useful introductory book on the subject is Robert Dunkerley, *Beyond the Gospels,* Penguin Books, 1957.

The explanation of the Deuteronomists, and Men of the Great Synagogue, was that the Exile was God's punishment for the idolatry of earlier generations, an understanding that dominates much of the Bible. But this simplistic view did not go unchallenged. It was questioned by writers who took issue over what kind and degree of righteousness would assuage the wrath of God; and most radically it was challenged by the Prophet Ezekiel who found difficulty with the very notion that the exile could be thought of as the punishment of God for the nation's idolatrous history.

This tension between the teaching of the Deuteronomist and the prophecy of Ezekiel is found later in the teaching of Jesus.

Writing from Jerusalem, Ezekiel took issue with the whole idea of someone, and by implication, the nation, being punished for the sins of others, including the dead. *What do you all mean by repeating this proverb in the land of Israel: Parents have eaten sour grapes and their children's teeth are set on edge. As I live, says the Lord God, this proverb will never again be used by you in Israel. Every living soul belongs to me; parent and child alike are mine. It is the person who sins that will die.* [18:1] Ezekiel is here expanding a prophecy on the same proverb found in the prophet Jeremiah [31:29] who was perhaps making general a legal particular in Deuteronomy, *parents are not to be put to death for their children* [24:16].

Ezekiel's next challenge was even more radical. He reversed the traditional understanding that salvation followed repentance: the sinner sinned, God punished, the sinner repented, God restored. For Ezekiel the order was different: God was gracious, the sinner sinned, God forgave and restored, and then the sinner repented.

Ezekiel's prophecies are theologically complex. The exiles were in need of pastoral care; the divine name had suffered calumny in the Exile [36:20] and needed to be vindicated. God achieves this by ending the Exile *for the sake of my holy name* [36:22]. But this left the problem of how a faithless people could observe the Torah in future. Jeremiah had solved the problem with his prophecy that God would write the Torah on hearts directed by his spirit. Ezekiel takes the metaphor further and prophesies that God will give his people new hearts. In a magnificent passage he wrote: *I shall take you from among the nations and gather you from every land, and bring you to your homeland. I shall sprinkle clean water upon you, and you will be purified from everything that defiles you; and I shall purify you from the taint of your idols. I shall give you a new heart and put a new spirit within you; I shall remove the heart of stone from your body and give you a heart of flesh. I shall put my spirit within you and make you conform to my statutes; you will observe my laws faithfully.* [36:24ff].

Only then is there the possibility of true repentance! *I assure you that it is not for your sake that I am acting, says the Lord God, so feel the shame and disgrace of your ways, people of Israel.* [v32] This is doing theology by prophecy as the relationship between repentance and forgiveness is reversed. This reversing of expected order occurs even more completely in the ministry of Jesus where its comedy describes the essence of the kingdom of God.

The heady mix of righteousness, punishment, blessing, Torah observance, forgiveness and repentance remains a source of conflict to this day. It set up rival schools of understanding that can be traced in the Christian Scriptures and beyond. The fundamental tension between ethical liberals and hardliners, religious extremists and humanists is there in the ministry of Jesus and in modern synagogue and church life. History as comedy is often a chaotic battlefield upon which the Name of God is more dishonoured than ever it was in Ezekiel's day.

The Jews as the People of the Book

> *A book that furnishes no quotations is, "me judice", no book – it is a plaything.*
>
> T. L. Peacock [1785-1866]

During their exile, the Jews became the people of a book. Wherever they settled they would be defined as the people of the Torah. It was everywhere the same book and they would be the same people wherever they were. The Torah formed them spiritually and nationally. It would achieve all that their oral and partial histories could never have achieved, and it would give them a unity of belief, outlook and practice, especially when, after the exile, they became a dispersed people. In a diaspora[45] which stretched from Babylon to Egypt, they might adapt local customs and speak the local language[46], but as long as they observed Torah, they were recognisably the same people. And their book was a comedy. It

---

45 Diaspora comes from a Greek word meaning "dispersion." By the time of Jesus, the Jews had become the most dispersed of the many peoples absorbed into the Roman Empire, with at least five times as many Jews living outside Judea as lived within it.

46 The rabbis understood Nehemiah 8:8, "*So they read in the book of the law of God distinctly, and gave the sense, and caused them to understand the reading,*" meaning that though the Torah was written in Hebrew the Jews themselves spoke Aramaic, a related language.

sounds straightforward, but the difficulty is that the comedy of the Bible was a dynamic one.

4

HISTORY AS REDEMPTION, THAT IS AS COMEDY

All history...is an inarticulate Bible.
Thomas Carlyle [1795 - 1881]

The role of storytellers in the rebirth of Judah was central. We have looked already at their use of stories to warn of divine or community punishment for anyone who disobeyed the law of God. However, as law enforcement officers everywhere discover, fear and terror are not always good educators. Telling the young to remember Lot's wife who was turned into a pillar of salt because she disobeyed the angel and looked back [Gen 19:26] probably met with only limited success among the nation's teenagers.

As a young priest, I was advised, "Don't tell people that they should pray. You'll only fill them with guilt when they don't. Instead, make prayer so attractive that they'll want to pray". It was the same for the returned exiles who used stories to promote a desire for Torah righteousness.

Scattered throughout the Hebrew Scriptures are books which read like folk-tales, in which the hero or heroine is a Torah observant Jew. They were written in a popular style to bring righteousness and its blessings to as wide a public as possible, while avoiding the extremism of Ezra and Nehemiah. They presented the reformers' policies in a way that appealed to ordinary Jews, and in doing so they gave us the books of Ruth, Jonah, Esther, Daniel and Job, in the Hebrew Bible; Tobit, Judith, Susanna, Bel and the Dragon in the Apocrypha, together with the lives of the patriarchs that make up much of the book of Genesis.

Scholars have had difficulty in finding a name for this particular genre. With their happy, comic endings and often gory plot lines they can seem little more than folk-tales. They can also sit lightly to the history they claim to embody. They are known variously as romances, novella or "didactic stories". While they contain obvious elements of fantasy and imaginative fiction, their purpose was the serious one of sustaining the Jewish people in times of persecution and the temptation to apostasy. They were reckoned by those who drew up the Hebrew canon as books inspired by God and worthy of a place in scripture.

Daniel and the Priests of Bel

> *Things and actions are what they are, and the consequences of them will be what they will be; why then should we desire to be deceived?*
>
> Bishop Joseph Butler [1692-1752]

Many stories were told about the Jewish sage, Daniel, and two of these, *Susannah* and *Bel and the Dragon*[47], were originally attached to the Greek version of the Book of Daniel. For non Roman Catholics they are now found in the Apocrypha. Both are early detective stories designed to discredit polytheism.

Bel and the Dragon is a two part comedy written to promote loyalty to the living God of Judah, whose rival in exile was Bel-Marduk, the patron god of Babylon. Bel's claim to be a "living god" was demonstrated, it was said, by his daily consumption of flour, sheep and wine! As a Torah observant Jew, Daniel refused to worship Bel's image and explained his refusal to King Cyrus: *Do not be deceived, O king; for this is but clay inside and brass outside, and it never ate or drank anything."* [1:7] In protest, seventy priests of Bel asked Cyrus to set out food as usual, then seal the temple with everyone locked outside. However, before the king left, Daniel scattered ashes over the floor so that when the priests and their families emerged in the night by a secret door, they left their footprints behind as proof of their deception. *Then the king was enraged, and he seized the priests and their wives and children; and they showed him the secret doors through which they were accustomed to enter and devour what was on the table. Therefore the king put them to death and gave Bel over to Daniel, who destroyed it and its temple.* [1:21] The comedy lies in Daniel's ingenuity and the priests getting what they deserved.

In the second story, the king, acknowledging that Daniel would only worship "*The Living God*" seeks to catch him out with a joke of his own involving a word play on the word "living". He asks Daniel to worship a "live" serpent or dragon, depending on the translation. It is possible that the serpent represented the dragon in the Babylonian creation myth which itself represented the primal chaos in the creation stories of the time. *Daniel said, I will worship the Lord my God, for he is the living God. But, if you, O king, will give me*

---

47 *Bel* being a variant of Baal.

permission, I will slay the dragon without sword or club [1:25]. The king gave permission and Daniel proceeded to feed the dragon with indigestible cakes made from pitch, fat and hair. *The dragon ate them and burst open. And Daniel said, "See what you have been worshipping".* [1:27]

Understandably, the Babylonians were not pleased at losing their god through trickery and they threatened to kill the king unless he handed Daniel over to them. They then *threw Daniel into the lions' den and he was there for six days. There were seven lions in the den, and every day they had been given two human bodies and two sheep; but they were not given to them now so that they might devour Daniel.* [1:31].

How would Daniel escape the lions? Here, we must think ourselves into the crowd hanging on the storyteller's every word as Daniel is rescued miraculously by the prophet Habakkuk who had been told by an angel to take the dinner he had prepared, to Daniel, in the lions' den. *Habakkuk said, Sir, I have never seen Babylon and I know nothing about the den.* [1:35] With that, the angel grabbed him by his hair and transported him to Babylon right over the den. *Then Habakkuk shouted, Daniel! Daniel! Take the dinner which God has sent you.* [1:37] *On the seventh day, the king came to mourn for Daniel. When he came to the den he looked in, and there sat Daniel. And the king shouted with a loud voice, Thou art great, O Lord God of Daniel, and there is no other beside thee.* [1:40]. The last six words, repeated again and again in Isaiah 45, became the creed of the returned exiles.

Strange as these stories are to modern ears, the message behind their comedy is clear: those who worship the one, true God and keep the Torah will never be abandoned.

The answer to the question, "why is there so much comedy in the Bible?" is now partly answered. It is because its stories were a part of popular culture and popular culture, then as now, was saturated with comedy. "You have to laugh," was a phrase I heard constantly as a child in 1940s England, threatened with invasion. It would have been little different in 6th century BCE Babylon.

Popular culture is a comic culture. It is because so much of the Bible originated in popular culture that it contains so much comedy. Nor do biblical theologians escape lightly, their theology being revealed by the Bible's comedy as a high brow study of often low-brow material! Before the exile, Jewish popular culture was pagan and polytheist. During and after the Exile, popular culture was transformed and enlisted in the service of the God of Abraham, Isaac and Jacob.

The Book of Ruth

Perhaps the self-same song that found a path
Through the sad heart of Ruth, when, sick for home
She stood in tears amid the alien corn
John Keats [1795-1821], *Ode to a Nightingale*.

The book of Ruth is read in synagogues at *Shavuos*, the Festival of Weeks, known to Christians as Pentecost. It is a romance, full of folk-tale material and is sometimes published in Britain as a straight-forward love story in popular magazines for older women. It could well date from the time in which it is set: the period of the Judges [c. 1100 BCE], though it was probably adapted sometime after the return from exile to counteract the decrees of Ezra and Nehemiah against marrying foreign wives. As it begins with starvation and death and ends happily with marriage it qualifies as a comedy!

The story opens with a famine and with a couple from Bethlehem, Elimelech and Naomi, together with their sons, migrating to Moab in search of food. Elimelech dies. The sons marry foreign wives, Orpah and Ruth, only to die themselves shortly afterwards. With no men to look after them, the women must starve or return to their families. Orpah opts to return to Moab, but Ruth converts to Judaism and goes with Naomi to Bethlehem. What happened next turns on the provision in the Torah of what is known as Levirate Marriage by which a man could marry a deceased relative's wife to provide for her. A child resulting from the marriage was deemed to belong to the dead man. Prompted by her mother-in-law, and after a few twists in the plot, Ruth marries Boaz, a wealthy relative of her husband, so that the son born to them was reckoned as Elimelech's.

The point of this winning comedy becomes obvious in its last verse: *"Naomi has a son; we shall call him Obed." Obed became the father of Jesse, David's father.* [4:17] In other words, king David, who played a key role in the history of Israel, was the great-grandson of a foreign woman, a Moabitess, a one-time worshipper of the god Chemosh. This is even more remarkable as those responsible for the text of Deuteronomy had preserved the decree that: *No Ammonite or Moabite, even to the tenth generation, may become a member of the assembly of the Lord.* [23:3].

This story, which contradicts the main thrust of post-exilic Torah theology, is yet another illustration that those responsible for the canon of scripture did not oblige the Bible to speak with one voice. Scripture is not always self-consistent, and mutually contradicting texts can be found throughout the Bible. Ruth is a further illustration that the best defence against intolerance is often humour, especially that of the "so there!" kind. There's a further example of this in the story of the Moabite king, Balak, who employed a gentile, Balaam, a professional curser, to curse the Israelites on their journey to the Promised Land. After investing much time and wealth attempting to persuade Balaam, Balak is disappointed and the episode ends with a gentile being the first to bless Israel. [Num 24.] As a comic twist within this comic story there is also the once well-known episode of Balaam being saved from death by a conversation with his donkey! [Num. 22:22ff]

The Book of Ruth as Sexual Comedy

I'm going to introduce sex into Romeo and Juliet.
Robert Helpman 1909-1986]

Sex is a universal fascination and source of temptation, a vital theme in the comedy of popular culture, even that of the Bible. In the Authorised Version, Boaz tells Ruth, *have I not charged the young men not to touch thee?* [2:9] The Revised Standard Version is less coy: *Have I not charged the young men not to molest you?* In Patriarchal societies a woman without the protection of a male relative is vulnerable and at risk in this way. Women captured in war were among the most likely to be sexually exploited by being reckoned as booty. In the Song of Deborah and Barak [Judges 5:24ff], the mother of Sisera muses, *a damsel for each man, two damsels.*

In the book of Ruth, sexual tension is heightened when Ruth is advised by Naomi, *It is well, my daughter that you go out with his maidens, lest in another field you be molested.* [2:22] Seeing Boaz behave so caringly towards Ruth, Naomi comes up with a plan to snare him into marriage. Ruth is to wash, put on perfume and her best clothes. Dressed like a bride she is to find out where Boaz sleeps and lie down near him. At this point, the Hebrew is sexually intriguing, for Boaz sleeps in the privacy of the threshing floor which, as the prophet Hosea makes clear [9:1], was a favourite haunt of prostitutes. Ruth's plan is that Naomi should next "uncover his feet" which elsewhere in the Bible are a euphemism for genitals. With so much erotic tension none too subtly conveyed, it's a tantalising story. But Ruth's boldness goes beyond her mother-in-law's advice and when Boaz wakes up she proposes marriage by saying, *Spread the skirt* [wings] *of your cloak over me.* The "wings" of Boaz's skirt echo playfully his reference to the protective "wings" of the Lord in 2:12.

The episode is knowingly told and erotically charged. The book was a popular comedy conveying the reality of God's providence in Ruth's deliverance from poverty and insecurity, while also challenging the extreme Torah righteousness of Ezra. While the story originated in popular culture, the ends it served were higher.

Esther, the Comedy of a Jewish Girl Who Became Queen and Saved her People

> *Because women can do nothing except love, they've given it a ridiculous importance.*
>
> W. Somerset Maugham [1874-1965] *The Moon and Sixpence.*

It is at first puzzling that in the patriarchal society of the Bible there should be such an emphasis on women as saviours of their people. The editors were careful to include in the story of the Jews not only the matriarchs Sarah, Rebecca and Rachel but also Miriam, Deborah and even Rahab the harlot. A possible explanation is that the post-exilic commitment to holiness had created a new dignity for women, giving them a greatly expanded role within the family, a role which included teaching the Torah to their children. However, it's also likely that women were given these heroic roles for their popular comic effect, as examples of the humour of incongruity, as no man would normally expect to be upstaged by a woman. However, with God, the Lord of history, even that was possible! Men got the better of by a mere woman, now that was comical!

Unlike in the book of Ruth, God is not mentioned at all in Esther, though there is a clear trust throughout in his providence working through events. Nor is there much interest in Jewish life or institutions. For these reasons, the book barely made it into the Bible and, as no fragments have been found among the Dead Sea Scrolls, it was clearly not a work thought important by many Torah observant Jews.

The book of Esther is set during the Babylonian exile, probably in the reign of Ahasuerus of Persia, [Xerxes I, 485-465 BCE]. Comic effects are present from the outset in the description of the banquet thrown by the king. An exaggerated love of detail is used in folk tales the world over. It's not a device much used in tragedy.

The story begins when the beautiful Queen Vashti holds a feast only to have it interrupted by the king commanding her to appear before his drunken courtiers, where she knows she'll be ogled. Vashti refused, the king was humiliated and the story's details with its lists of wise men and eunuchs flow as extravagantly as the wine.

Following her spirited display of independence, Vashti is dismissed as queen and dispatches are sent to all the king's provinces, *to every province in its own script and to every people in their own language, in order that each man, whatever language he spoke, should be master in his own house.* [1:22] We can hear already the murmuring approval of the storyteller's hearers in what was probably an all male audience: *Let there be sought out for your majesty beautiful young virgins; let your majesty appoint commissioners in every province of your kingdom to assemble all these beautiful young virgins and bring them to the women's quarters in the capital Susa…the girl who is most acceptable to the king shall become queen in place of Vashti* [2:3ff].

The beautiful orphan Esther now enters the story. She is the adopted cousin of Mordechai, a Jew exiled by Nebuchadnezzar, and she is among the virgins selected for the king's pleasure. However, before she is introduced to the luxurious life of a royal concubine, Mordecai advises her not to disclose *her race or family* [2:10].

When it was Esther's turn to sleep with the king she proved a great success, the king loving her more than any of his other women. *He treated her with greater favour and kindness than all the rest of the virgins, and placed a royal diadem on her head, making her queen instead of Vashti.* [2:17]. Meanwhile, Mordecai was keeping a close watch on palace politics and discovered that two of the eunuchs were plotting against the king. Mordecai told Esther, and Esther told the king, with the result that the plotters were hanged [2:23].

Then, just as everything is going well, the story takes a sinister turn when the king promotes a courtier, Haman, *above all his fellow officers* [3:1]. Unfortunately Haman was an Agagite, a descendent of Agag, the Amalekite[48] enemy of King Saul. It was Agag who had been *hewed in pieces* by the prophet Samuel *before the Lord at Gilgal* [I Sam. 15:33]. This detail would not have been lost on the hearers. Irony and coincidence are now compounded because Mordecai, the Benjaminite, is none other than the *son of Jair, son of Shimei, son of Kish,* [2:5] and is therefore of the family of king Saul!

---

48 *Amalek* was a nomadic tribe that lived in the Sinai desert between Egypt and Canaan. They had attacked the Israelites at Rephidim and became an enemy whose extermination was ordered by God [Dt 25:19]. Saul's failure to obey this dreadful command [1 Sam. 15] led to his losing the throne of Israel. They were finally destroyed in the 8th c BCE by King Hezekiah [I Chron 4:43].

Haman and Mordecai had no choice but to become enemies.

In court ritual, Haman was entitled to receive a bow, and everyone obliged except Mordecai who explained that as a Jew he was unable to observe the custom. Mordecai was within his rights but Haman was furious and *having learnt who Mordecai's people were, scorned to lay hands on him alone; he looked for a way to exterminate not only Mordecai but all the Jews throughout the whole kingdom.* [3:6]

What follows is the first recorded instance of what, in the 19th century, would be called anti-Semitism: Haman said to king Ahasuerus: *Dispersed in scattered groups among the peoples throughout the provinces of your realm, there is a certain people whose laws are different from those of every other people. They do not observe the king's laws, and it does not benefit your majesty to tolerate them* [3:8].

Haman was continuing a centuries old vendetta against the Jews. The book of Deuteronomy tells how the conflict between Jews and Amalekites was a fight to the death: *Bear in mind what the Amalekites did to you on your journey from Egypt, how they fell on you on the road when you were faint and weary and cut off those from the rear, ... they showed no fear of God. When the Lord your God gives you peace from your enemies ... you must without fail blot out all memory of Amalek from under heaven.* [Dt 25:17ff]. Ahasuerus had no idea of this threat of genocide in his empire.

Haman continued to poison the king's mind against the Jews: *If it please your majesty, let an order be drawn up for their destruction. [3:9]. The order was accordingly issued by the king to destroy, slay, and exterminate all Jews, young and old, women and children, in one day, the thirteenth day of the twelfth month, the month of Adar* [3:13].

When Mordecai learns of the plot he gets word of it to Queen Esther but, as she had not been sent for by the king, there seemed little she could do unless she intruded on the royal presence unannounced, for which she could be sentenced to death. But Esther had no choice and so the entire Jewish community in Susa, the capital, fasted and held its breath.

On the third day, Esther presented herself at court. Fortunately, Esther pleased the king and he asked what she wanted. Esther, crafty as well as beautiful, invited both the king and Haman to a banquet. With splendid irony, Haman boasts about this to his wife and friends, adding *Yet all this gives me no satisfaction so long as I see that Jew Mordecai in attendance at the king's court. His wife Zeresh and all his friends said to him, "Have a gallows set up, seventy five feet high and in the morning propose to the king that*

Mordecai be hanged upon it. Then you can go with the king to the banquet and enjoy yourself." This advice seemed good to Haman and he set up the gallows. [5:14].

That night the king, unable to sleep, was reading the state papers and learned of the plot thwarted by Mordecai. Enquiring further, he discovered that Mordecai had gone unrewarded and, as Haman was conveniently at court, asked him: *What should be done for the man whom the king wishes to honour?* [6:6] Thinking the king was referring to him, Haman suggested the most lavish reward he could think of, only to find later, in a monumental occasion of role reversal and comic comeuppance, that he had to confer on Mordecai all the honours he'd hoped for himself!

When Mordecai tells his wife and friends what has happened, their response is equally unwelcome: *If you have begun to fall before Mordecai, and he is a Jew, you cannot get the better of him; your downfall before him is certain* [6:13]. Mordecai now dreaded going to the banquet, so that when the king asked Esther what favour she wished him to grant her, she asked for her life and that of her people. Ahasuerus demanded to know who had ordered the genocide. *This wicked Haman* [7:6] she answered and in an ironic and comic reversal of fortunes, Haman is hung on the very gallows he had prepared for Mordecai.

Instructions for the massacre were then cancelled and the king granted permission to the Jews *in each and every city to assemble in self defence, and to destroy, slay and exterminate every man, woman and child, of any people or province which might attack them and treat their goods as spoil.* [8:11] The death toll was 75,000, *but they took no plunder* [9:15]. Today, this vengeful ending is raced through at its annual Purim synagogue reading.

The book ends happily with the deliverance of the Jews and its celebration in the festival of *Purim* or *Lots*, so named because it was by lot that Haman had set the day for history's first pogrom. Purim's comic dimension is reflected to this day in its party atmosphere, when levity and even inebriation is allowed. Whenever the name of Haman is mentioned in synagogue today a tremendous din is made with the help of rattles called "gregers". There can be no doubting the books comic status.

Jonah: Clown, Fool and Prophet

> *Shipmates, this book, containing only four chapters – four yarns – is one of the smallest strands in the mighty cable of the Scriptures.*
>
> Herman Melville [1819-91] *Moby Dick*, Fr Mapple's

Sermon.

The central figures of the Old Testament are not kings, priests or sages but prophets. Moses, Elijah, Isaiah, Jeremiah, Amos and Hosea are its heroes of faith, striding across its pages as spiritual giants, the servants and judgement-givers of God. The exception is the comic figure of Jonah, the prophet who fled from God and from his vocation to preach judgement at the heart of the Assyrian empire. Jonah could not believe that God cared for non-Israelites and became depressed at the success of his own preaching, even sulking when God forgave the wicked city of Nineveh.

Although the book can be read as a satire, a polemic against Torah exclusivism, at school our scripture teacher insisted that it was to be understood literally. Our entire class protested in vain that the story was clearly an allegory, that even killer whales couldn't swallow a man whole, let alone spew him up again alive and well after he'd swum for three days in its gastric juices!

Jonah is prophecy as folk-story, with the storyteller enjoying his own tale. *The word of the Lord came to Jonah son of Amittai: Go to the great city of Nineveh; go and denounce it, for I am confronted by its wickedness."* [1:1]. Jonah's response is to run away to sea, only to find that God is as much present there as on land. As with the book of Ruth, the joke was on those who supposed that God was only interested in his chosen people.

When a storm threatened the ship, its sailors cast lots to discover whose actions had brought such wrath upon them. Jonah is identified as the culprit, he is thrown overboard and the storm dies down. Already a failed prophet in this tongue-in-cheek story, Jonah cuts a clownish and pathetic figure as he stumbles from one predicament to another - for *The Lord ordained that a great fish should swallow Jonah, and he remained in its belly for three days and three nights.* [1:17]

While in the fish's belly, Jonah prayed. [2:1]. His psalm not only expresses the devotion of a devout man, but with verse 8, *those who cling to false gods may abandon their loyalty, but I with hymns of praise shall offer sacrifice to thee*, it manages the sort of irony, satire and ambiguity found in the book of Genesis. Yet, who are these who renege on false gods? Is it Jews in exile or pagan Assyrians about to be preached to by Jonah? Few preachers are able to resist the old joke: "Why did Jonah sing a psalm in the belly of the great fish? Answer: "Because everybody sings in Wales.'

To the comic incongruity of a prophet who runs from God, is thrown into the sea, swallowed by a fish and spewed out onto dry land, the storyteller adds the irony of Jonah's being lost in Nineveh, *a city of 120,000 people* [4:11]; *a vast city, three days journey across.* [3:3]. Undismayed ,Jonah proclaims the city's doom: *In forty days Nineveh will be overthrown.* Every doubter in those times of oversupplied prophecy believed that prophets could be ignored as a matter of course, and yet, *the people of Nineveh took to heart this warning from God; they declared a public fas,t and high and low alike put on sackcloth.* Then, a tall story becomes even taller: *When the news reached the king of Nineveh, he rose from his throne, laid aside his robes of state, covered himself with sackcloth and sat in ashes.* In short, pagan foreigners will do what the people of God are reluctant to do. Next, the Assyrian king gives voice to the theology of the Jewish reformers: *Let all pray with fervour to God, and let them abandon their wicked ways and the injustice they practice. It may be that God will relent and turn from his fierce anger; and so we shall not perish.* [3:8]

And God does relent. *When God saw what they did and how they gave up their wicked ways, he relented and did not inflict on them the punishment he had threatened.* [3:10] Most preachers would have been delighted at such a result, but here the narrator provides a further comic twist: *this greatly displeased Jonah.*[4:1] The prophet did not want these foreigners to repent – but God did! Jonah is now revealed as no better than the most extreme and intolerant among the reformers. He tells God: *It was to forestall this that I tried to escape to Tarshish*[49]*. I knew that you are a gracious and compassionate God.* [4:2] What sort of prophet is this? His every reaction is the opposite of what all other prophets have led us to expect!

The temptation of the over-righteous is to resent the moral achievements of those they think unrighteous! The psalms are full of examples of this crippling spiritual condition. Jonah's resentment is so much stronger than his loyalty to God that his sulking ends with his wishing himself dead. *Now take away my life, Lord; I should be better dead than alive.* [4:3] But God won't have it but challenges Jonah's self-righteousness: *Are you right to be angry?* [4:4] he asks. But Jonah is so annoyed that the Assyrians have repented that he defies God, sits under a makeshift shelter to see if the city will be destroyed. But God can play a good joke and *ordained that a climbing gourd should grow up above Jonah's head to throw its shade over him and relieve him of his discomfort.* Here the storyteller probably paused for effect: *and Jonah was very glad of it.* [4:6]

---

49 Possibly a Phoenician port and colony in what is now Spain.

Yet God's sense of humour in dealing with his stubborn and self-destructive prophet is not exhausted: *At dawn the next day God ordained that a worm should attack the gourd, and it withered.* [4:7] In short, God's providence can operate through a giant fish or a hungry worm.

Next, the narrator tightens the screw further on the hapless prophet: *and when the sun came up, God ordained that a scorching wind should blow from the east.* [4:8] Without the gourd to protect him, the sun beat down on Jonah's head *till he grew faint, and prayed for death.* [4:8] Only then is Jonah's refusal to love non-Jews finally overcome. God asked, *Are you right to be angry over the gourd? Yes, Jonah replied, mortally angry.* Then God clinches his argument: *you are sorry about the gourd, though you did not have the trouble of growing it, a plant which came up one night and died the next* [4:10]. Jonah had lost the argument. There is nowhere for him to run and the comic trap closes as he gets his comeuppance and God puts down his unsatisfactory prophet with, *then should I not be sorry about the great city of Nineveh, with its hundred and twenty thousand people who cannot tell their right hand from their left,* [4:11] that is, they are without moral law and therefore to be pitied, not condemned. The compassionate understanding of God here is very different from that in the story of the destruction of Sodom and Gomorrah, though nearer to that found in the account of Noah and the flood. Such conflicting accounts were allowed to remain unreconciled side by side in the national epic. Neither the writers of these stories, nor those who put the final canon of scripture together, made any attempt to get their differing theologies to agree. That mistake was left for later theologians in their efforts to tidy up the Bible as they pursued the illusory goal of spiritual and intellectual consistency.

Jonah is a tale brilliantly told by an unknown writer who wanted to put a stop to the foreigner-hating extremism of Torah fundamentalists. Jonah is Judah; the exile is the fish's belly, his story the hoped-for history of the Jews. With the book of Jonah, national literature echoes the dispute between the major schools of Torah interpretation: the hard-liners and the liberal-humanists.

This tale of a petulant prophet is the one biblical book that ends with a joke, that of incongruity: *and also much cattle?* [4:11] In 3:8, covered with sackcloth, the cattle too had repented! Jonah is a serious, polemical book but difficult to read with a straight face.

Some Thoughts on Scripture as Revelation

When a member of my family complains that he or she has bitten his tongue, bruised her finger, and so on, instead of the expected sympathy I put the question, "Why did you do that?

Sigmund Freud [1856-1939] *The Psychopathology of Everyday Life.*

In 2009, in an interview with the *Church Times*, a spokesman for an organisation which believed that the Bible was being ignored in an important debate said, "If you can't trust one bit, how can you trust the rest?" Does the Bible support or subvert this view? The presence of so much comedy and the satirical and playful uses to which it is put only serve to undermine the belief that the Bible's message is primarily one of authoritative pronouncement or that it speaks with only one voice. Stories like those of Ruth and Jonah will not allow such a literal, "the Bible says" interpretation; while for Christians the radical teaching ministry of Jesus makes it a lost position. The Bible is a record of continuous, ongoing argument, debate and theological development. Text is in dialogue with text and the reader is invited to enter into a dialogue that remains open to this day. The Bible is not a book of self-consistent theological pronouncements like the Westminster Confession of 1656[50] and cannot be read as if it was.

Instead, we are obliged to ask why books from popular culture like Ruth, Esther and Jonah are there at all. All comedy is subversive of authority. Jonah, the prophet with an attitude problem, does not speak to us with "authority." He is there to make us question and re-think those parts of the Bible that speaks with the sort of authority that refuses to be contradicted! Jonah and Ruth were mocking and contradicting other voices in the Bible convinced that they had Torah on their side.

The books of the Bible are the product of intense questioning and argument over what were life and death issues. Many responded with autocratic seriousness, while others contradicted their assertions with erotic flippancy and tongue in cheek superciliousness. In a Holy Book, this is extraordinary. It overturns counter-intuitively ideas of what a Holy Book should be like.

At the Lambeth Conference of 2008 the Anglican Church was riven by the debate over gay Christians. Ezra would have felt at home

50 This was a confession of faith in the Calvinist tradition drawn up at Westminster and was adopted by the Church of Scotland as an expression of its beliefs.

with those concerned for the moral purity of the Church and who wished to distance themselves from homosexuals who claimed they had a priestly vocation. The Bible was quoted as authoritative for this position. What was missing in the debate was the Bible's lightness of touch. If we take the Scriptures seriously, then we have to take its use of comedy seriously especially when debates become acrimonious. In all the hard-hitting debates in which Jesus was caught up, he made good use of satirical comedy. *Life is of course absurd, and it is ludicrous to take it seriously. Only the comic is serious,* wrote Ionesco, a view the Bible often supports!

If the Bible is in some way God's self-disclosure in the writings of those who seek to honour and obey him, then humour and comedy are important vehicles for that revelation. Biblical theology is as impossible without humour as it is without prayer. The Bible forbids us to take either ourselves or our theology too seriously. That's the way to cruelty and inhumanity as well as folly. Why is the Book of Jonah part of Holy Scripture? Because the Bible as a whole belongs to Jewish and Christian humanist literature. God in his power is on the side of our weakness because without the Bible"s sense of the ridiculous, holy texts all too easily become oppressive texts. Jonah is a low-brow refusal by low-brow believers to be brow-beaten by their high-brow betters. The Bible as the Word of God is very much God's self-revelation though through the words of men and women in all their literary and spiritual diversity.

Tobit and the Vindication of Torah Righteousness

Be in general virtuous and you will be happy.
Benjamin Franklin [1706-1790] *On Early Marriage.*

Tobit is the story of a devout exile of the northern kingdom of Israel who, after much misfortune, realised how God's providence guides the righteous towards blessing and a good death. It contains some of the Bible's greatest comic passages.

I, Tobit, have made truth and righteousness my lifelong guide. I did many acts of charity to my kinsmen, those of my nation who had gone with me into captivity at Nineveh [1:3]. *After the deportation to Assyria in which I was taken captive … everyone in my family and nation ate gentile food, but I myself scrupulously avoided doing so* [1:10]. Together with circumcision, it was the observance of the

Kosher[51] food laws which enabled exiled Jews to hold on to their religious identity. Tobit's was just the sort of religious loyalty the author wished to encourage.

Tobit's honest life wins the approval of king Shalmaneser who makes him buyer for royal supplies. It's a job that makes Tobit rich and, for safe keeping, he deposits his savings with Gabael, a relative. In the hope of encouraging fellow Israelites to follow his example, Tobit lists his good deeds: *I would share my food with the hungry and provide clothing for those who had none, and if I saw the dead body of anyone of my people thrown outside the wall of Nineveh, I gave it burial.* [1:16]. As the opening of Psalm 79 make clear, unburied bodies rendered cities unclean. When the virtuous Tobit buried the bodies of Sennacherib's victims at the siege of Jerusalem, his good deed got him into trouble with the king, *all that I possessed was seized and confiscated for the royal treasury and I was left with nothing but Anna my wife and my son Tobias.* [1:20]

However, things began to look up again and through the influence of his nephew, Ahikar, Tobit is restored to royal favour. But then, just as he is about to invite a poor man to the family's Pentecost meal, another body is found for him to bury and things go wrong again as a passing sparrow empties its bowels into his eye and blinds him. As a result of these coincidences in a further comic twist his wife Anna has to work to support him. Tobit's misfortunes multiply further when Anna's grateful employer rewards her with the gift of a kid goat. Tobit assumes wrongly that she has stolen it and a family misunderstanding results. Taunted by his wife and neighbours, Tobit prays for death. Coincidently, as he does so, a relative, Sarah, in far off Ecbatana, is also beset with taunts and misfortune. *Sarah had been given in marriage to seven husbands and, before the marriage could be duly consummated, each one of them had been killed by the evil demon Asmodaeus.* [3:8]. Sarah too prays for death; but God hears Tobit's prayers and sends the angel Raphael just as Tobit remembers to tell Tobias about the money deposited with Gabael. He also gives him some fatherly advice on living a righteous life.

As he's preparing for his journey Tobias meets a man looking for work. The man is Raphael, an angel, in the guise of a distant relative and together they set off to recover Tobit's money. On the way, as Tobias cools his feet in a river, he is attacked by a fish. *The angel said to him, "Seize the fish and hold it fast."* [6:3] Tobias drags the fish ashore. *The angel said, "Split open the fish and take out its*

51 Kosher is the Yiddish form of the Hebrew word *kosher* meaning "proper". It is used of things that are ritually fit for use and sanctioned by Jewish Law, the Torah.

gall, heart, and liver; keep them by you, but throw the guts away; the gall, heart and liver can be used as remedies [6:4]. Tobias duly salts them and takes them with him.

Smelling no doubt strongly of fish, Tobias arrives at the house of Raguel, father of the unmarriageable Sarah. As Sarah's next of kin, Tobias has the right to marry her. When Raphael offers to arrange this, Tobias remembers Sarah's seven husbands: *the very night they went into the bridal chamber to her they died.* [6:13]. Told by a master storyteller, comedy as dark as this would have had listeners eager to learn what happened next.

The marriage is arranged. Raguel calls his wife and says, "*My dear, get the other bedroom ready....* This has to be a contender for "the funniest verse" in the Bible! *Edna went and prepared the room and brought Sarah into it. She wept over her, and then drying her tears said, Take heart dear daughter; the Lord of heaven give you gladness instead of sorrow* [7:18].

The scene is now set for one of the Bible's finest pieces of comic writing. Will Tobias survive his wedding night? Will Sarah prove to be a femme fatale for the eighth time? *When they had finished eating and drinking and were ready for bed, the young man was escorted to the bedroom. Tobias recalled what Raphael had told him; he removed the fish's liver and heart from the bag in which he had them, and put them on the burning incense.* [8:1ff]. One can imagine the reaction of the seven times disappointed bride as the stench of fish overpowers her perfume; for *the smell from the fish kept the demon away, and he made off into Upper Egypt* [8:8].

With the marriage still not consummated, the plot's development is interrupted by prayer in a daring combination of erotic writing and genuine devotion, as Tobias says, *So now I take this my beloved to wife, not out of lust but in true marriage. Grant that she and I may find mercy and grow old together. They both said, "Amen, Amen", and then slept through the night.* Nowhere else does the Bible follow a couple to their marriage bed like this, stretching comedy and prayer to the breaking points of privacy, decency and good taste, yet it works and is a marvellously effective piece of comic writing.

Next morning, the comedy gets better still as Raguel rises and summons his servants, and they go out and dig a grave, for he thinks, *Tobias may be dead, and then we shall have to face scorn and taunts. When they had finished digging the grave, Raguel called his wife: Send one of the servant-girls, he said, to go in and see whether he is alive* [8:9ff].

All is now set for a happy ending and more good advice as Tobias returns home with a wife, the money, an angel and the carefully preserved fish-gall which, spread on his father's eyes, does for his blindness what the fish's heart and liver did for the demon.

Eventually, Tobias died, greatly respected, 117 years old, with his righteousness, his faith and prayers based on it vindicated by God. *Tobias lived long enough to hear of the destruction of Nineveh by King Ahasuerus of Media* [14:15]: A dark ending that is pure comedy.

Judith and the Changed Status of Women after the Exile

> *I'm not denyin' the women are foolish: God Almighty made 'em to match the men.*
>
> George Eliot [1819-1880]. *Adam Bede*.

Whenever changes are made to religious belief or practice there are social and psychological consequences. Often these are far reaching, as was the case during the Exile when Jews began to abandon polytheism and Jewish life became increasingly focussed on loyalty to God and stricter Torah observance in morals and the rituals of everyday life. For these changes to be possible, a more structured personal and family life was essential.

With these changes in place Jews became even more distinct from their neighbours with the differences being most obvious in marriage and the observance of kosher food laws. Individual identity and family and social cohesion were strengthened. Perhaps the most far-reaching changes, however, were in the role and status of women, for without their co-operation, the reforms of the men would have had little success. Outside the home, life was patriarchal, but within the family, Torah observance gave women a far more important role than ever they'd had before. A good Jewish family required a good Jewish mother to run a good Jewish kitchen and manage a good Jewish household. For women, this meant an enhanced social status[52]. As a result, women became stronger and more independently minded. Nowhere is this better seen than in the book of Judith.

One of the storyteller's tasks was to encourage Jews under stress to persevere in the Torah and draw strength from the example of heroic figures of the past. This is one reason the Bible is so full of stories of improbable comic triumphs over adversity. As might be expected, most of these stories were of men like Moses, Joshua, Gideon, Samson and Elijah. However, there are also stories of heroic

---

52 Proverbs 31:10ff makes good sense when read against the Torah's enhancing of the role of women.

women who were equally instrumental in preserving the nation: Deborah, Jael, Esther and Judith, not forgetting the unnamed woman in the comic episode at the tower of Thebez, who *threw a millstone down on Abimelech's head and fractured his skull. He called quickly to his armour-bearer and said, Draw your sword and dispatch me, or it will be said of me, a woman killed him.* [Judges 9:53] What a shameful death that would have been! Nevertheless all Israel knew that it took a woman to save the nation from the upstart Abimelech[53]. Similarly, it took a woman to save the Jews from the all-conquering army of the Assyrian general Holophernes. Never mind that the story is a difficult fit historically. Its comedy lies in its being a great tale of feminine wiles in the service of God. Only in a patriarchy could deliverance through a woman be thought humorous as well as comic.

The first eight chapters of Judith describe the punitive expedition launched by Nebuchadnezzar against those who defied him. This expedition was followed by another under Holophernes, his commander-in-chief: f*ear and dread of him assailed the inhabitants of the coast of Tyre and Sidon and the people of Sur and Okina, and of Jemaan; terror seized the population of Azotus and Ascalon.* [2:28] As the Israelites were determined to resist, *the entire population of Judah and Jerusalem fasted before the temple of the Lord Almighty.* [4:13]. Planning strategically, they closed *the passes through the hill-country, fortifying all the heights, and putting obstructions in the plain.*[5:1] Holophernes responded with intelligence gathering: *Tell me, you Canaanites, what people is this that lives in the hill-country? What are their cities? How large is their army?* Achior, the Ammonite commander, repeated to Holophernes the belief of the returned exiles that providing they observed the Torah, they would always defeat their enemies. Enraged, Holophernes besieged Bethuliah, the city of Judith, a rich, beautiful and devout widow. It was a description guaranteed to rouse the interest of the men in the audience.

When the city's water supply ran short, the magistrates agreed to surrender after five days, providing a relief force had not arrived by that time. Judith was appalled. *Who are you,* she asked, *to put God to the test at a time like this, and usurp his role in human affairs?* [8:12]. The frightened citizens asked Judith to pray for rain, while Judith had something more radical in mind, though what she would not say. *I shall go out with my maid and, before the day on which you have promised to surrender the town to our enemies, the*

---

53 Abimelech [c12th c BCE] was the illegitimate son of Gideon, a Judge who delivered Israel from the Midianites. Abimelech murdered all his 70 brothers except Jotham, and ruled over Shechem for 3 years until overthrown.

Lord will deliver Israel by my hand [8:33].

Slowly, the storyteller revealed how Judith the widow became Judith the heroic seductress. *She removed the sackcloth she was wearing and laid aside her widow's dress. After bathing she anointed herself with rich perfume. She arranged her hair elaborately, tied it with a ribbon, and arrayed herself in the gayest clothes, those she used to wear when her husband Manasses was still alive. She put sandals on her feet and adorned herself with anklets, bracelets and rings, and all her ornaments, and made herself very attractive, to catch the eye of any man who saw her.* [10:3ff]

This is a wonderfully titillating piece of comic writing. The returned exiles were in danger, but in scripture comedy in the face of impending tragedy often indicates that God is about to save his people. Humour in no way detracts from piety or marginalises God; rather the presence of genuine prayer in many of these stories, often taking up an entire chapter, only increases the serious purpose of the comedy: Jonah prays in the belly of the great fish; Tobias prays before he and Sarah consummate their love and Daniel blesses God when Nebuchadnezzar's dream is revealed to him. And now, Judith prays [Ch 9] committing her plan to God before setting out for the Assyrian camp. Lest anyone suppose that the story's entertainment value is what is important, Judith's prayer says otherwise: *May your whole nation, every tribe, be made aware that you are God, God of all power and might, and that you and you alone are Israel's shield.* [9:14]

Judith's plan is to make Holophernes believe she is willing to betray her people. With beauty to bait the hook, who could resist such a "honey trap." What follows is another fine piece of storytelling. Judith is eventually alone with Holophernes, who was *beside himself with desire for her. He trembled with passion and was filled with an ardent longing to possess her; indeed ever since he first set eyes on her he had been seeking an opportunity to seduce her.*[12:16] This is as near to a bodice-ripping narrative as the Bible gets; and as Judith teases Holophernes, so the storyteller teases the reader as it is revealed that Holophernes *drank a great deal of wine, more than he had ever drunk on any single day in his whole life.* [12:20] The humour here is that found in the porter scene in Shakespeare's Macbeth, where alcohol *provokes desire and takes away the performance.* [Act II, Scene III]

Judith is now alone with the sleeping Holophernes, all parts of her plan in place. As a devout Jew she prays for success, and goes *to the bed-rail beside Holophernes head, reached down his sword, and drawing close to the bed she gripped him by the hair. "Now give me strength, O Lord, God of Israel," she said, and struck at his neck twice with all her might and cut off his head.* [13:6]. It is an execution whose drama has inspired many painters, among them Caravaggio, Artemisia Gentileschi, Christofano Allori, Cranac the Elder, Giorgioni, Mantegna, Michelangelo and, more recently, Gustav Klimt.

Judith was able to make her escape because, cleverly, she had led the guards to think that she was leaving Holophernes' tent to say her prayers. As she left, she concealed his head in mosquito netting so that next day it could lead the Jewish counter-attack. Without their leader the Assyrians panicked and the Jews triumphed, Judith having been careful to explain, *The Lord has struck him down by a woman's hand! And I swear by the Lord who has brought me safely along the way I have travelled, that, although my face lured him to his destruction, he committed no sin with me, and my honour is unblemished* [13:15].

Judith's purity is unsullied, her fame assured, the booty immense and Judah freed from invasion. The book, which is a propaganda publication on behalf of those pressing for a Torah righteous nation, concludes with a classic comic happy ending, *No one dared to threaten the Israelites again in Judith's lifetime, or indeed for a long time after her death.* [16:25].

The comedy in Judith, like so much biblical comedy, is dark. It is about the wicked getting what they deserve. It is about justice being delivered by sagacity. In Victorian cartoons in Punch magazine the reader was often invited to laugh at the discomfiture of the self-important. In the Bible, that sort of comedy is reserved for the well-deserved fate of the wicked who have inflicted on them the humiliation they intended for others. Often what brings about this comic loss of face is not Torah but Wisdom, and Wisdom comes from God.

5

LOVE AS COMEDY: AND SEX GAMES AT THE PALACE

Do not rouse or awaken love until it is ready.
The Song of Songs [2:7].

The *Song of Songs*, also called *The Song of Solomon* and *Canticles,* is among the unlikeliest books to find in the Hebrew Scriptures, containing neither mention of God nor the Torah. How did it get there?

It was written to be sung as *The Best of Songs* and celebrates the search for love and its consummation by King Solomon and the most beautiful woman in his harem. The presence of a chorus makes of the couple's desire for one another a very public, ritualised game of love. Theirs is love as amorous play, set to music and dance and played out before guests. This is love as comedy and erotic pleasure which today's media might headline as "Sex games at the Palace".

Because Hebrew is short on punctuation and other aids to understanding, it is not always clear who is saying what or what is going on behind the poetry. What is obvious, however, is that this is love chiefly from the point of view of one of Solomon's wives or concubines. The woman has three speeches, the man, one. The woman teases and warns, *I adjure you, O daughters of Jerusalem, by the gazelles or the hinds of the field, that you stir not up or awaken love until it please,* [2:7] while the man *like a gazelle or young stag* [2:8] must peep through a window!

Courtship as a game like this is love as erotic comedy. In 7:1-9, as the man praises his lover's body, he works his way upwards until he reaches the spot between her thighs and belly. Playing for laughs, he sings euphemistically of *the round goblet* of her "navel"!

The poetry of The Song of Songs is wonderfully lyrical even in translation: *My beloved spake, and said unto me, Rise up my love, my fair one and come away. For lo, the winter is past, the rain is over and gone; The flowers appear on the earth, the time of the singing of birds is come, and the voice of the turtle is heard in our land, The fig tree putteth forth her green figs ... Arise my love, my fair one, and come away.* [2:10]. This is comedy as celebration and delight, becoming by turns, as love does, a game of hide and seek, then a lovers' tiff with pining and lost love, followed by even more subversive comic forms, including role and gender reversal. At the beginning and the end of the songs, it is the woman who, reversing the conventions of a patriarchal society, is the dominant figure, inviting her lover to kiss her, *O that you would kiss me with the kisses of your mouth* [1:2]; until finally [8:14], sending her lover away to a far off *mountain of spices*.

This courtly celebration of sexual desire and fulfilment is a strange book to find in the Bible, for on the surface there is nothing religious about it. However, the beauty of its poetry and the appeal of romantic love would have guaranteed it a place in the affections of the public. Sophisticated readers began interpreting its erotic poetry as an allegory of the love between Israel and God. It was this, especially with the support of Rabbi Akiva and the Hillel school, that secured its place in scripture and led to its being read in the synagogue and at home at Passover.

Hidden Meanings for a Hidden God

Canst thou by searching find out God?
[Job 11:7]

The prophet Isaiah described the God of Israel, the chief player on the stage of history, as a God who hid himself [Is. 45:15]. God is elusive. In being a library of many books with many voices, the Bible as comedy mirrors this: that God remains hidden even as he discloses his presence.

It was believed that with the prophet Malachi prophecy came to an end in Israel, so that all the Jews had left of God's self-revelation was the Torah. By about 400 BCE, Judaism had become a religion in which God was in danger of being reduced to a memory and his voice to a collection of well-told stories and laws[54]. Something more was needed therefore to keep prayer and the meaning of sacrifice alive, and one solution was to accept as further revelation the emerging interpretations of the Torah by the Rabbis in what would later become the Mishnah and Talmud.

But what if God was hiding in scripture and the key to finding him was to read scripture as allegory? This is what happened with the Song of Songs. A book about sexual love became scripture the moment that human love was seen as an allegory of divine love. Its

---

54 In post-biblical rabbinic times, when it was believed that prophecy had ended, the rabbis spoke of the *Bat Kol,* literally, "daughter of a voice", that is an "echo". It was said that the Bat Kol was heard by individuals and groups at time of great importance only.

admission into the canon was guaranteed. *Wear me as a seal over your heart, as a seal upon your arm; for love is as strong as death, passion as cruel as the grave; it blazes up like a blazing fire, fiercer than any flame. Many waters cannot quench love, no flood can sweep it away,* [8:6ff]. While the Rabbis were not enthusiastic about the mystical approach to scripture, they made an exception for allegory.

Until the end of the Middle Ages, allegory was also the preferred method of interpretation in the Church. St Paul had drawn parallels between human love and Christ's love for the Church and the Song of Songs lent itself to this approach. In Russia, for example, the verse, *I sleep but my heart waketh,* [5:2], became associated with the Jesus prayer, which, when repeated again and again transferred itself from the mind to the heart, to continue being prayed even as the penitent slept.

Among Roman Catholics, the Song was understood as expressing the love of the Church for the Virgin Mary, so that the words: *My sister, my bride, is a garden close locked, locked, a fountain sealed,* [4:12], were transferred to the perpetual virginity of the Virgin Mary so that in Christian art she is often portrayed as a locked garden and a sealed fountain.

Homo Ludens

At the end of the game you'll see who's the winner.
A proverb collected by George Herbert.

It would seem the most comic twist of all that revelation should depend on our human love of playing games. Yet play can be as serious and as important as that. If the Bible makes one thing clear it is that from Abraham's bargaining prayer on behalf of Sodom to the sport of love in the Song of Songs, games and truth often go together. It is there in God as a trickster playing life and death games with Jonah and in his providence at play in the trickery of Jacob, not to mention his bet with Satan in the book of Job.

And games come in many kinds. Some games are played for fun, some for physical exercise; while others are played for some life and death purpose. When God brought the plagues upon Egypt and when the soldiers placed the crown of thorns on Jesus' head, these were cruel and comic games designed to humiliate.

When Jewish scholars played games with scripture, they were taking our love of play to where it had never been before. If God was hiding from his people like lovers hiding from one another in the

Song of Songs, then allegorical understanding might find him in what was written, just as prophecy had revealed him in history and wisdom his presence in nature, life and thought.

The Search for the Reality Behind Appearances

> *To the true Christian poet, the whole world and all the incidents of life tend to be sacraments – signs of God, signs of his love working in the world.*
>
> Thomas Merton [1915-1968].

In many ways, searching for God in scripture was a version of the old search for the reality underlying the physical nature of the world, a quest which modern science inherited from ancient philosophies and medieval theology. One can make a good case for tracing the origins of experimental science to the need of monotheism to explore the hiddenness of God. It's not so long a stride from the hidden God to the roots of physical reality hidden in nature.

For the Rabbis, the problem was most acute with those texts thought trivial or unworthy. *Woe to the man who asserts that the Torah intends only to tell of commonplace things and secular narratives.... When angels wish to descend to earth they have to put on earthly clothing; how much more is this true of the Torah.... The stories of the Torah are merely its outer garments.* [Zohar 3:53[55]]. Allegory was a way of discovering the divine presence even where it seemed absent. The problem, however, was that there was no way of telling which interpretations were reasonable and which were fantasy. For the Butler's dream in Genesis 40, three interpretations were offered for the branches of the tree: they could be the Temple, the King or the High Priest; yet who could say which? To be playable, games must have rules and at first allegory was a game without a rule book. Attempts were made to provide one, yet, in the end, it was all a matter of which allegories were the most convincing. At first, the Song of Songs made most sense if the lovers were God and Israel. This was later replaced with woman as the soul and her lover as God. In the medieval Church, the same process could be seen as the Church and Christ gave way to the soul and God.

---

55 The 14th century Book of Zohar [*zohar* in Hebrew means "splendour"], is a book in the Jewish mystical tradition of Kabbala.

Gematria: More Games Played With the Bible

They say there is divinity in numbers, either in nativity, chance or death.

William Shakespeare [1564-1616], *The Merry Wives of Windsor*

Those Jews who pursued righteousness discovered that, for all their faithfulness to the Torah, they did not always experience the presence of God. Was He hiding as Isaiah thought, or departed as others suggested? For the devout, God was hidden, with allegory as one way of reaching behind his seeming absence and Gematria another.

In Hebrew, numbers are indicated by letters; each letter having a numerical value. This meant that words and phrases could be read as sums and numbers and their equivalents found elsewhere in a sacred game known as *Gematria.* For example, in Genesis 42:2, when Jacob says to his sons *Go down to Egypt,* the Hebrew for "go down" is *redu,* which has a numerical value of 210, the number of years of the Israelite captivity there.

One justification for gematria was found in Psalm 137:17. *How precious also are thy thoughts to me, O God, how great is the sum of them. If I should count them they are more in number than the sand.* Once numerical correspondences had been identified there was no end to them or their usefulness in interpreting difficult texts. Gen.28:12, for example, tells of Jacob's dream in which a ladder, the Hebrew word is *sullam,* stretches from earth to heaven. As the numerical value of *sullam* is 130, the same numerical value as Sinai, medieval exegetes argued that the Torah revealed on Sinai is man's ladder to heaven.

Gematria was a serious game and just as the rabbis devised rules for interpreting Torah, so they drew up rules for gematria. If God was playing hide and seek among the words of scripture, gematria was a way to discover his whereabouts. The Bible as comedy was being explored by interpretation as play.

Gematria and the Rise of Modern Science

This whole visible world is a book written by the finger of God.

Hugh of St Victor. [1096-1146]

The metaphor of nature as a book alongside the book of scripture existed long before Hugh of St Victor and continued long after him.

For Galileo, nature was "a book written in the language of mathematics" an idea echoed by Sir James Jeans [1877-1946] when he wrote, "the Great Architect of the Universe now begins to appear as a pure mathematician".

The idea that God was the reality hidden behind the world and that through the Bible he was revealed even when hidden, survived in modified form when nature too came to be understood as a book of revelation. For scientists like Galileo and Newton, nature was a book that needed to be decoded if underlying realities like gravity were to be discerned. During the late renaissance, European scholars were well acquainted with the use of numbers and letters in gematria and it was a small step to assuming that what worked for scripture would also produce results when applied to nature through mathematics.

The modern idea that science and religion are inevitably opposed to one another would have seemed nonsense to early physicists. Galileo argued in one of his letters that because the books of scripture and nature were by the same author they could not be in conflict while as his papers show, Newton, for his part, spent more time reading his Bible through mystical techniques like those of gematria, than he did reading nature through mathematics!

A strong case can be made then for arguing that deciphering the Bible through gematria as a theological and spiritual game was a template upon which the decoding of nature through mathematics was developed. Yet, when nature is deciphered scientifically the reality uncovered is not God, as had been hoped, but further, well concealed, deeper levels of reality. God is still hidden, only now he is hidden behind the quarks, leptons and bosons of the Standard Model of the atom. He remains for believers the reality hidden behind nature's concealed realities. However serious this kind of play[56] might

56 It will be clear by now that the biblical text is often a playful text and that this is reflected in the way in which Jews often study their Bible. At one shiur I attended, we were studying *Bereshith* [In the beginning], the first *Sedrah,* or weekly Sabbath morning Torah reading. At verse 9 in Genesis 1, the rabbi stopped at the word *yikavoo,* "be gathered together." Attention was drawn to the three consonants, *ykv* which form the backbone of the verb "to gather". We were asked to think of other words formed around those same letters and the group came up with *mikvah*, the ritual bath for purification, and *tikvah* the word for hope. It was an insight into how the rabbinic mind played over the surface of a playful text as Aquinas said the Wisdom of God played throughout the world. *Because of the leisure that goes with contemplation, the Divine Wisdom (Continued...) (56*

be, it is still play and as such never far from comedy.

The search for the reality that underlies appearances goes on. In modern physics, the search focuses on The Theory of Everything, which it is hoped might take us to the deepest level of reality of all. If it is discovered, wrote Stephen Hawkins in his *A Brief Nature of Time,* "we would know the mind of God." Isaac Newton could not have put it better.

Are there limits to what can be known?

Not how the world is, is the mystical, but that it is.
Ludwig Wittgenstein [1889-1951].

Or more pressing still: "What *it is*!" If, in scripture, it is God who is elusive, in the modern world we must add to that hiddenness of God, the hiddenness of reality itself. What is it of which we are part? What lies behind the world of matter and energy? What is it at root?

Ever since the German philosopher Immanuel Kant [1724-1804] argued that we can never know "things in themselves," western men and women, Christian or otherwise, have stood at least one remove from what they think of as reality. It is in this sense that there are limits to human knowledge. All our knowledge, whether of God, the world or ourselves is a constructed and indirect knowledge, even knowledge which seems to be direct and immediate. Take away the means through which we believe we know and we know nothing. And the means by which we believe we know is always symbolic. This is as true in science, philosophy and poetry as it is in theology. Ultimately we know what we know only through symbols, through letters and numbers. Science and religion are at bottom two complementary symbol systems. Whatever reality is, it is a teasing, taunting and therefore a comic reality. Like the theories of phlogiston and the ether, gematria was a dead end in science, yet, like the other mystical sciences of alchemy and astrology, it acted as midwife at the birth of our mathematical physics and technology of today.

---

continued) itself, Holy Scripture says, "is always at play, playing through the whole world." St Thomas Aquinas [c1225-74]. Commentary on Proverbs 8:30ff.

6

THE BIBLE AND THE SEARCH FOR WISDOM

The only infallible criterion of wisdom to vulgar judgements – success.
Edmund Burke [1729-97]

The Bible's wisdom literature includes, besides Proverbs, the books of Job, Ecclesiastes, the Song of Songs, a number of Psalms [1, 37, 49, 73, 112, 127, 128, 133, 139], and, in the Apocrypha, The Wisdom of Solomon and Ecclesiasticus.

It was the sages of Israel who wrote its books of wisdom. Their interest was not primarily in prophecy or law, but in passing on to the next generation advice on living wisely. Priests, prophets and sages were, together with soldiers, merchants, landowners and Judah's political leaders, at the heart of the nation. As the king's policy advisers, the sages were part of the civil service and as such often came into conflict with the prophets who frequently had other ideas, particularly on foreign policy. These three groups, priests, prophets and sages wrote the books which form the Bible. While the priests and prophets were concerned with faithfulness to the Torah, the Sages, with their international sympathies[57], took a more humanist approach. Was Torah the key to the good life, or was it Wisdom? Often prophets and sages disagreed over this, until by the time of the rabbis Torah was seen as the ultimate wisdom and rabbis became the sages of their day.

Six centuries after the Fall of Jerusalem, the rabbis began compiling the Talmud, that enormous commentary on the Torah, which reconciled Law and Wisdom. But that reconciliation lay in the future. During the time that Judah was part of the Persian Empire [538-333BC] and throughout the period of Greek influence, the sages struggled to come to terms with the new emphasis on righteousness as total faithfulness to Torah

---

57 All the great courts of the Middle East, from Mesopotamia to Egypt, had their schools of resident sages. It is clear from the documents that survive that whereas they might disagree profoundly in their religious beliefs, in their writings about wisdom there was far greater agreement.

Ecclesiastes: Looking into the Abyss

A donkey with a load of holy books is still a donkey
Arab Proverb

Has the Bible a single message or many? If the answer is many then the next question has to be: can these be reconciled and if they cannot, where does that leave us?

We have noted already that the book of Ruth takes issue with the severity of Ezra's interpretation of Torah righteousness and to Ruth we must add the troubling voice of Ecclesiastes.

Ecclesiastes is a perplexing work that appears to subvert the rest of scripture, asserting the futility of human existence, the inscrutability of God and the pointlessness of living unless it is to enjoy life. It is the nearest the Bible gets to a nihilistic vision of human existence and as such is a denial of the comic vision that shapes the rest of scripture. The author of Ecclesiastes, known as *Koheleth*, the Hebrew for Preacher, is a thinker who dared to look deeply into human existence and find little meaning there. Not surprisingly, not everyone wants to gaze into that abyss with him.

No one knows who Koheleth was, or why the rabbis admitted such a dark work into the canon of scripture. The book's few positive statements hardly balance its negative pronouncements. Most scholars date it to about 300 BCE, the period when Persian influence was giving way to Greek. This was a troubling time when Jews were making every effort to fashion national life around the Torah. Ecclesiastes ran counter to that. It was the also the outlook of a scholar without disciples.

Futility, utter futility, Koheleth begins. [1:2] *All things are wearisome.* [1:8] To brighten his life he tries everything, even gardening! He achieves greatness and wealth. He pursues wisdom, though interestingly not Torah righteousness. *The good and the sinner fare alike,* he says [9:2]. His only word for the righteous is a throw-away comic line, a scholar's joke. It is so terse as to be easily missed. *Do not be over righteous,* he advises. [7:16]. We can imagine how that was received by those defending the Torah against Greek cultural imperialism. *Be not righteous overmuch,* was a favourite sermon text of 17th century Anglican Latitudinarians in the years following the Puritan stranglehold on English life.

Ecclesiastes was a lone voice. The single-minded pursuit of righteousness all too easily results in morally unattractive lives. It was why, after the Restoration of Charles II in 1662, the English could not wait to re-open theatres, bring back Christmas and throw off the

Puritan yoke.

Then, with a scholar's sense of humour, Koheleth advises us, *and do not be over-wise!* [7:17] The author of Ecclesiastes is a writer standing on the edge of the chasm of meaninglessness and futility, with his sense of humour intact. There are many examples of black humour in the Bible but this has to be among the blackest and most brave. Ironically, the righteous had the last word. In its final version, the book was brought into line with orthodox opinion: *This is the end of the matter: you have heard it all. Fear God and obey his commandments; this sums up the duty of mankind.* [12:13]. The final editor attempted to kill the comedy!

Koheleth and the Nihil

There's probably no God, Now stop worrying and enjoy your life.
London Atheist Bus Slogan, 2009

Contemporary music culture sometimes refers to what Koheleth experienced as the *Nihil,* a Latin word meaning Nothing.[58] It is possible, of course, that all he was suffering from was boredom! However, it's more likely that what he felt went deeper than that and is an early recorded encounter with life as meaninglessness.

Nihil is a word that resonates with many people's experience of modern life. It is the name of an Irish Black Metal Band, while the German Industrial Rock Band, KMFDM, issued an album of that name. Nihil is, therefore, a good word to describe life that's lived without the comic underpinning of biblical religion.

The Importance of Folly

Anacharsis would say...At Athens wise men did propose and fools dispose.
Francis Bacon [1561-1626].

The sinner only becomes a comic figure if he's also a fool. My teacher, Miss Dobells, who taught wisdom to nine year old Bootle lads, believed that boys were universally inclined to silliness. This was serious enough in her eyes had it not been made worse by her conviction that silly boys grew up to be foolish men. Esau, she thought, would have been at home in our class! Her lesson on

58 It's from *nihil* that we derive our words "nihilism" and "annihilate.'

Jacob's foolish son was masterly and it was my introduction to folly as comedy.

In Junior School, we arrived at Esau's foolishness after tracing the fortunes of the promises God had made to Abraham: how he would bless him: *All the peoples on earth will wish to be blessed as you are blessed* [Gen. 12:3]; how he would make of him a great people, *Look up at the sky, and count the stars, if you can. So many will your descendants be.* [15:5]. She told us how the covenant with Abraham had been passed on, not to Ishmael, but to Isaac and how, after Isaac, it should have gone to Esau, but didn't, because Esau was foolish while his twin brother, Jacob, was crafty. It was gripping stuff and sibling rivalry was a subject which many of us reckoned we knew more about than our teacher! The first twin to emerge from the womb *was reddish and covered with hairs like a cloak, and they named him Esau. Immediately afterwards his brother was born with his hand grasping Esau's heel, and he was given the name Jacob.* [25:25] In Hebrew, there are puns on the boys' names and the colour red. *As the boys grew up, Esau became a skilful hunter, an outdoor man, while Jacob lived quietly among the tents.* When she came to the words, *Isaac favoured Esau because he kept him supplied with game, but Rebecca favoured Jacob.* Our teacher subtly broached the whole business of family politics: "Were Isaac and Rebecca wise parents?" she asked. Taking our cue from her tone of voice, we replied, "No, Miss," each of us reflecting on our own position in our parents' affections and noting that Miss Dobells had no favourites. Then she came to the heart of the story: *One day, Jacob was preparing broth when Esau came in from the country, exhausted. He said to Jacob, "I am exhausted: give me a helping of that red broth." This is why he was called Edom*[59]*. Jacob retorted, "Not till you sell me your birthright as the first born." Esau replied, "Here I am at death's door; what use is a birthright to me?" Jacob said, "First give me your oath!" So he gave him his oath and sold his birthright to Jacob. Then Jacob gave Esau some bread and some lentil broth, and he ate and drank and went his way. Esau showed by this how little he valued his birthright.* [1:29ff]

In telling the story our teacher used the phrase, *a mess of pottage,* from a chapter heading in the Genevan Bible of 1560. Fools, it seemed, always sold themselves short like Esau, giving away too much for too little. Esau was a foolish man who had, no doubt, once been a silly boy.

Esau was my introduction to the important but neglected biblical

---

59 In Hebrew, Edom means "red country," referring to the red rocks of the region, and so continues the play on the word red.

notions of folly and wisdom, which, together with sin and righteousness were central to Jewish identity after the Exile. *Let me hear the words of God the Lord: he proclaims peace to his people and loyal servants; let them not go back to their foolish ways.* [Psalm 85:8]

It's easy to forget the role of the Wisdom writers in the formation of the Bible and the salvation of Judah. If the priests and prophets had reckoned it was the "sin" of transgressing the Torah that had brought the Jews to the edge of destruction, the Sages were in no doubt that it was "folly." In the comic imagery of the book of Proverbs, Wisdom and Folly are two women of the street calling to the young men as they came out of school. *Wisdom cries aloud in the open air, and raises her voice in public places. She calls at the top of the bustling streets; at the approaches to the city gates she says, "How long will you simple fools be content with your simplicity."* [1:20].

The sages who helped shape post-exilic Judah were part of an international network. It was easy for a priest like Ezra to insist that Jews separate themselves from everyone else but no sage could have suggested such a thing. It would have been foolish. The sages, with their international viewpoint, would have been among those promoting stories like Ruth and Jonah whose purpose was to thwart separatists and extremists. For example, the *Thirty Wise Sayings* of Proverbs. 22:17 ff. is, in the opinion of some, adapted from the Egyptian Wisdom of Amenemope.

The sages were determined that their fellow Jews should avoid folly. Life as comedy, that is life with a happy ending, was best guaranteed by living wisely. The way to tragedy was to live foolishly. Proverbs was therefore as much an intended guide to successful living as the Torah. Unfortunately, while sin is easy to define, folly is not; and whereas we know pretty well in advance what might be sin, foolishness is evident chiefly when events refuse to conform to the anticipations of the wise – which perhaps explains why the Bible's wisdom writings are on the margins of the canon rather than at its centre.

For centuries, wisdom was one of Israel's chief intellectual pursuits, just as it was in ancient Greece; and though what wisdom was exactly was everywhere assumed and nowhere defined, it clearly had to do with leading a virtuous and meaningful life by making sound judgements in complicated situations. Though our word philosophy means "love of wisdom," ironically, modern philosophy, even moral philosophy, has little interest in the subject. To the sages of Israel this would have been folly.

Western intellectuals are the social commentators of our time, ready to mock folly, especially political folly, but seldom able to identify the wisdom that might avoid it. *My son, safeguard sound judgement and discretion, do not let them out of your sight… then you will go on your way without a care, and your foot will not stumble.* [3:21]

When Belief and Experience Clash: Psalm 73 and the Book of Job

No wise man wants a soft life.
King Alfred [849-901]

The decision of the returning exiles to stake their future on strict Torah observance produced an immediate problem. Those who observed the Law were promised that God would bless them. They would be like *a tree planted beside water channels; it yields its fruit in season and its foliage never fades. So too, he prospers in all he does.* [Psalm 1:3]. Yet, that promise of divine blessing and protection was not the whole story, for as the writer of Ecclesiastes pointed out: *In my futile existence I have seen it all, from the righteous perishing in their righteousness to the wicked growing old in wickedness.* [7:15]. This was not supposed to happen. Righteousness was meant to ensure that life as tragedy became life as comedy. Koheleth's answer was to accept that that is how things were and settle for those pleasures that came his way as gifts from God. Yet not all wisdom writers could accept such a disconnection between righteousness and blessedness.

Psalm 73 begins by asserting the faith of the returning exiles, *Assuredly God is good to the upright, to those who are pure in heart* [v1]. The psalmist's faith is tested, however, *because boasters roused my envy when I saw how the wicked prosper. No painful suffering for them* [v3]. The problem for the psalmist arose when the wicked escaped suffering and the righteous didn't! Social psychologists refer to this clash between belief and experience as Cognitive Dissonance. Providing the dissonance is not too great, it can be tolerated, but should it become insupportable it has to be resolved. This can be achieved in several ways. When it is resolved by rejecting beliefs that cannot be reconciled with experience, "loss of faith" results. Koheleth was the one biblical writer for whom the dissonance was so great as to lead to a loss of faith. He was able to hold on to what remained of God as the guarantor of life as comedy only by the most slender of threads.

The author of Psalm 73 also suffered acute dissonance: *Indeed it was all for nothing that I kept my heart pure and washed my hands from guilt.* [v13]. But his dissonance is resolved by his re-interpreting his beliefs so that they harmonise with his life. *I set my mind to understand this but I found it too hard for me, until I went into God's sanctuary, where I saw clearly what their destiny would be. Indeed you place them on slippery ground and drive them headlong into utter ruin. In a moment they are destroyed, disaster making an end to them.* [v19]. That is, the prosperity of the wicked is short lived. Their comeuppance is only delayed. *Those who are far from you will perish; you will destroy all who are unfaithful to you. [v27].* The English philosopher, A.N. Whitehead [1861-1947], had a similar idea when he wrote that *the instability of evil is the moral order of the world.* However, for another of Israel's sages the resolution of dissonance was not so easy.

The Book of Job

> *No man I think will ever be of much use to his generation who does not apply himself mainly to the questions which are occupying those who belong to it.*
>
> Frederick Denison Maurice [1795-1872]

The book of Job is not primarily about the problems of innocent suffering or radical evil, though that is sometimes claimed; it is a book about the undeserved suffering of the righteous. The suffering of the unrighteous was not a problem for Jews. It was what they deserved; but, that the righteous should suffer went against the beliefs of the dominant Deuteronomist party, for whom the "righteous man" *prospers in all he does.* [Psalm 1:3]. Job was what we would call today, the disconfirmation of their reading of history.

Job was a righteous man – and with that note of reassurance for the devout reader, the book gets off to a good start! Yet, already there's an intriguing complication. Job was a native of Uz, making him an Edomite, not a Jew. As the Edomites were the enemies of the Jews and had helped the Babylonians sack Jerusalem, this teasing comic start would have perplexed those who had hoped for fewer complications in dealing with religious dissonance.

Job is narrative theology as dramatic verse but with a comic prose introduction and epilogue. It belongs with comedies like Jonah, Esther, Tobit and Daniel, except that where they affirm the orthodox belief that God guards the righteous, Job, like Ecclesiastes, confronts us with the fact that this is not always the case.

Job is both righteous and immensely wealthy, a sign of his blessedness until, within a few chapters, he loses everything. And that was not supposed to happen. The comedy is signalled in the first chapter, where Job's sufferings are traced to a wager between God and the chief prosecutor in the Court of heaven, Satan. To the pious the idea was outrageous. It was how pagans saw their gods behaving.

And not only is Job not a Jew but two of the three friends who comfort him are not Jews either. Eliphaz, his oldest friend, is also from Edom, a land famous for its wisdom. As the prophecies of Obadiah are devoted to predicting the doom of Edom, the irony begins to mount. Eliphaz talks a lot but is no help as he disappointingly repeats the Deuteronomic argument that Job is being punished for some wrongdoing because misfortunes like his do not happen to the righteous. [5:17]. Eliphaz even accused him of being a fool who turned his back on wisdom by banishing the fear of God from his mind and by doing so *cutting off all communication with him* [15:4].

Job is visited next by Bildad the Shuhite, another non-Jew, whose name was once known to every child in England as the answer to the joke question, "What's the name of the shortest man in the Bible? Bildad assures Job that *God will not spurn the blameless man.* [8:20].

Job's third visitor is Zophah the Naamathite, possibly a Jew from the lowland area of the Shephelah, the lowland plain between Judah and Philistia; but he's no help either, telling Job that *God exacts from you less than your sin deserves* [11:6]. Job is so certain of his innocence that he blasphemously challenges God himself, *Let the Almighty state his case against me.* [31:34].

After 31 chapters his friends *gave up answering Job, for he continued to think himself righteous.* Hearing Job challenge God, a younger man, Elihu the Buzite, also a non-Jew, comes angrily onto the scene: *Do you reckon this to be a sound plea, to reckon that you are in the right against God?* [35:2] and Job endures another long speech, which ends wittily and ambiguously with the words, *the Almighty we cannot find; his power is beyond our ken, yet in his great righteousness he does not pervert justice.* [37:23]. Elihu also argues that Job's punishment is a righteous punishment but Job, in a deliberate and mischievous misunderstanding, takes him to mean that God will finally vindicate him, *I know that my vindicator lives and that he will rise last to speak in court. I shall discern my witness standing at my side.* [19:25].

Up to this point, Job has been defiant in defending his integrity, even against his wife whose support was lacking from the outset, *When the Adversary left the Lord's presence, he afflicted Job with running sores from the soles of his feet to the crown of his head, and Job took a piece of broken pot to scratch himself as he sat among the ashes. His wife said to him, Why do you still hold fast to your integrity? Curse God and die! He answered, You talk as any impious woman might talk. If we accept good from God, shall we not accept evil? Throughout all this, Job did not utter one single word.* [2:7ff]. Job refuses to accept that his misfortunes are the just reward for his sins. He refuses too to resolve the dissonance between faith and experience either by abandoning his faith or re-interpreting it. Instead, he lives heroically with the tension unresolved.

Job has been as righteous as Daniel or Tobit, yet to everyone except himself he has been punished for his sins. Job sticks to his conviction that righteousness is not a defence against misfortune, nor misfortune proof of unrighteousness, whatever the righteous say. Then, when God does speak he as good as ignores Job's problem, doing no more than reminding Job of his creaturely finiteness and, by asking questions Job cannot answer, he defines the limits of the Wisdom tradition.

Although these last chapters are intended to be the key to the book, it is not clear what they actually say in their labyrinth of ironies and ambiguities. For example, the Lord said to Job, *Is it for a man who disputes with the Almighty to be stubborn? Should he who argues with God answer back?* [40:2] That can mean either that if Job answers back, he is only compounding his impertinence; or it can be read as a challenge to answer if he can, just as Abraham answered God and argued with him over the fate of Sodom. Job's response is to rest his case, [40:4] which could mean that now God is on trial and guilty, while he, Job, is innocent; for when God speaks again, it is to challenge Job a second time, *Would you dare deny that I am just, or put me in the wrong to prove yourself right? Have you an arm like God's arm; can you thunder with a voice like his?* [40:9].

Finally, on one interpretation, Job capitulates. *I yield, repenting in dust and ashes.* [42:6]. And yet he has nothing to repent of, apart, that is, of speaking *of things which I have not understood, things too wonderful for me to know.* [42:3]. Other, more defiant interpretations are possible.

God does not come out of his encounter with Job well. After all, Job is only asking the question posed by other devout Jews, Why do the righteous suffer? Has God won the argument, has he won his wager with Satan? In a nice comic twist, the book is not even interested in the question! And if God does win, it is not by fair means. Job is not out-argued, his question and defiance are valid and he speaks for more than himself. God pulls rank and beats Job down. With the resources of the wisdom movement exhausted and, worn out by his misfortunes, Job capitulates, only to end up with more blessings than he began. *The Lord restored Job's fortunes, and gave him twice the possessions he had before.* [42:10] His tragedy has becomes a grand comedy!

Neither Job nor Koheleth support the orthodox view that the righteous prosper while sinners are punished. They are realists. Life is not like that. Both beliefs are biblical and the tension between them is unresolved.

Job is a forerunner of the story, first told to me by a Holocaust survivor, in which a group of Jews in a death camp put God on trial for allowing such an undeserved tragedy to happen. They find God guilty, and then go back to their prayers. The Holocaust is the ultimate challenge to Torah righteousness as the guarantee of Jewish survival.

On any reckoning the book of Job is a masterpiece of world literature. All the resources of the wisdom movement went into its writing, yet at the end, the question of why the righteous suffer remained unanswered.

To balance the comic opening there is a comic, non-sequitor ending in which God rebukes Eliphaz and his friends, *because unlike my servant Job, you have not spoken as you ought about me.* [42:7]. So what was wrong with what they said? We are not told. Does God approve then of Job's impious stance? Yet, all ends well, and Job being a righteous man intercedes for his friends.

Why did the book's unknown author write this most important of Jewish theological problems as a tongue-in-cheek wager between God and Satan and a comic debate involving non-Jews? As literature, the book is a triumph: a theological play written by a philosopher. As a theological answer to a pressing question it is an intriguing failure. But, like most good theology, it sharpens and intensifies a question, opening it up rather than closing it down.

Today, Job's troubles are usually put this way: "Why do bad things happen to good people?" The writer of psalm 37 [v25] did not believe that they could. *I have been young, and now am old: and yet saw I never the righteous forsaken, nor his seed begging bread.* It's as if the book of Job was written against just such a standpoint.

Deus Absconditus, the Hidden God: More Contradiction

There is enough light for those who only desire to see, and enough obscurity for those who have a contrary disposition.

Blaise Pascal [1623-62.]

In the end, God reveals himself but does not tell Job anything he didn't know already: God remaining hidden even as he reveals himself. We have been here before. *Verily, thou art a God that hidest thyself,* says the prophet [Isaiah 45:15] known as "Second" or "Deutero" Isaiah[60]. Sooner rather than later we must all come up against God's hiddenness. To Martin Luther [1483-1546] God was Deus Absconditus, the Hidden God. It was inevitable that Job would not be answered in the way he wished – nor we ourselves for that matter.

---

60 Most scholars are of the view that the Prophet Isaiah did not write all 66 chapters of the book that bears his name, but only the first 39. These were written in Jerusalem. Chapters 40 - 55 are attributed to a later prophet, usually known as Second Isaiah, writing in Babylon sometime about 540 BC, towards the end of the exile. Chapters 56-66 are believed to reflect the life of the returned exiles written by several authors known collectively as "Third Isaiah" or "Trito-Isaiah."

7

THE BIBLE'S SECOND DEFINING MOMENT: WAR AGAINST THE GREEKS

Whatever it is, I fear the Greeks even when they bring gifts.
Publius V Maro Virgil [70-19BCE]

From the fall of Babylon in 539 BCE, to the defeat in 332 BCE, of Darius, the last king of Persia, by Alexander the Great, the returned exiles were under the tolerant and paternalistic rule of the Persians. The temple was rebuilt and Torah holiness promoted. In spite of the resistance of those like the authors of Ruth, Jonah and Job, who were open in their attitudes to non-Jews, Judah's self-imposed separation from foreigners intensified. God had punished his people, it was argued, because they had tolerated the worship of other gods. That must not happen again. Non-Jews who offered to help with the rebuilding of the temple were rebuffed by the Jewish leaders Zerubbabel and Joshua [Ezra 4:1-5].

In spite of opposition, this policy of isolating a Torah obedient people from the nations around Israel proved successful. The Jews were more united than before with a clear sense of their own identity. They were becoming a self-disciplined nation built on a Torah centred family life. It is true there was some persecution from neighbours that Judah despised, a fact acknowledged in the books of Ezra and Nehemiah, and there were occasional rebellions recorded by the later Jewish historian Josephus[61] [37- c105CE]; yet, for 200 years, no major disasters befell the Jewish people. They were a God-fearing and God-protected people.

With the Torah safely in the hands of the priests and an emerging rabbinate, there was no longer a need for prophets to warn against entanglement with foreign powers and their gods, or having continually to remind rulers to care for the poor, the orphan and the

61 Flavius Josephus was the Roman name of Joseph Ben Matthias, a Jewish historian and soldier who commanded the northern rebel Jewish forces in Galilee during the great revolt of 66CE. Realising that the Romans would win, he gained favour by surrendering and spent the remainder of his life in Rome, where he wrote his *History of the Jewish War* and the *Antiquities of the Jews,* both important source material for historians.

widow. After the prophet Malachi [c500-c450 BCE], prophecy more or less died out and was replaced by the apocalyptic movement, about which more shortly. Anything a prophet might say was covered by the ordinary provisions of the Torah, though Malachi found occasion to condemn priests who sometimes flouted it. He also supported the hard-line on foreign wives. *May the Lord banish from the dwellings of Jacob any who do this.* [2:12]

But, as prophecy came to an end, so did humour. While there is word play and wit throughout the gloom of Jeremiah there is none in Malachi unless the claim that the gentiles honour God's name while his own people don't, is, like the ending of the book of Jonah, an example of sarcasm as the humour of incongruity. With Malachi, prophetic history as redemptive comedy was being superseded by apocalyptic history, in which national continuity was underwritten by Torah faithfulness - yet only, that was, until history itself came to an end, when *burning like a furnace; all the arrogant and all evildoers will be stubble, and that day when it comes will set them ablaze, leaving them neither root nor branch, says the Lord of Hosts.* [4:1]. With Malachi, history's comic ending has been become the destruction of the wicked and the triumph of the righteousness. This is comedy without humour, a comedy losing its humanity. Meanwhile, the religion of Judah was about to undergo a further transformation.

The Greeks ignore the Jewish Wish to be Left Alone

> *I am not aware that any community has a right to force another to be civilised.*
>
> John Stuart Mill [1806-1873]

Alexander the Great died in 323 BC after destroying the Persian Empire. His generals inherited his conquests. Judah came under the rule of Ptolemy, Egypt's new Pharaoh, and remained under the Ptolemies for a century of comparative peace and stability. Little is known of this period, though Greek speaking Egyptian Jews produced a Greek version of the Torah which became the core of the translation we know as the Septuagint. Then, in 198 BCE, at Panium, the Caesarea Philippi of the gospels, where Peter confessed Jesus as Messiah, Antiochus III, the Great [223-187BCE], the Seleucid ruler of Syria, defeated the Egyptians and annexed Judah.

According to the Jewish historian Josephus, the Jews welcomed Antiochus with great joy and for a time were not disappointed. The rights they enjoyed under the Persians were confirmed: generous tax concessions aided the recovery of a war-torn economy and even the wood for temple sacrifices was tax free. Then, the situation changed.

The Greek way of life was a confident one. It transformed the societies it conquered in a process known as Hellenisation. Cities were reorganised and democratised along the lines of the Greek city state, with games, theatres and other institutions unknown in Judah. Intellectual life was vigorous and like most things Greek proved attractive to many non-Greeks including Jews. Greek became the language of trade and education and, in time, the language of the New Testament. Many Jews adopted Greek customs and ideas, especially in Egypt but, in Jerusalem too, younger Jews began to live like Greeks, some even reversing their circumcision in order to take part in the games where athletes competed naked.

As always, when different cultures meet, the question for Jews was whether they should assimilate or remain a people apart. The nation was divided on the matter. Things came to a head when Antiochus IV Epiphanes, the Seleucid ruler of Syria, succeeded to its throne. Syria was the largest of the states into which Alexander's empire had fragmented. To his humour-loving Jewish subjects, his title *Epiphanes*, meaning "god manifest" became *Epimanes*, or "madman".

Antiochus had inherited a Syria bankrupted and humiliated in its recent defeat by Rome. To strengthen his kingdom, Antiochus began a policy of enforced Hellenisation, by which he attempted to impose Greek culture on the Jews. To finance his programme, he helped himself to the treasuries of Syria's wealthy temples. In addition, to foster the worship of the Greek gods he identified them with local deities and issued coins on which he appeared as Zeus, the king of the gods - all of which threatened Jewish identity as a Torah abiding nation.

Even so, many Jews were happy to oblige Antiochus, including the High Priest, Jason, who had gathered around himself a group of gymnasium-loving younger priests. To the righteous, the nation was again slipping into idolatry in a crisis as serious as that produced by the Exile.

Matters came to a head when Jerusalem was attacked, its temple incorporated into the Greek enclave within the Jewish city, and the God of Israel redefined officially as the local manifestation of Zeus, king of the gods on Olympus. Many Jews resisted these developments and their defiance drove a desperate Antiochus to abolish their privileges and outlaw Judaism. Temple sacrifices were replaced by those offered to Zeus, Sabbath observance ceased, copies of the Torah were destroyed, circumcision was forbidden and Jews compelled to eat pork. Non-compliance meant death. Jewish existence was once more under threat. Many younger Jews, believing their faith was outmoded, went along with Antiochus. The repressive reaction of the Greeks was severe and successful; until, that was, a priest called Mattathias refused to offer a pagan sacrifice. When another priest was prepared to oblige, Mattathias killed him along with the official on duty. As he fled to the hills with his sons, John, Simon, Judas, Eleazar and Jonathan, Mattathias called on all Torah observant Jews to trust in God and join him in rebellion. These rebels were called the *Hasidim*, the Pious Ones; and when Mattathias died, leadership passed to his third son, Judas, nicknamed Maccabeus, "The Hammer."

The Maccabean Revolt, named after him, began in 167BCE, but against the might of the Greek war machine, it seemed, at first, doomed to failure and yet it ended three years later with the Seleucids defeated and the temple rededicated to the Lord, an event celebrated to this day in the Jewish Festival of Hanukkah.

Sabbath Observance: When tragedy contradicts comedy

Human kind cannot bear very much reality.
T.S.Eliot [1888-1965], *Burnt Norton*.

With Genesis, the Bible opens on an undeniably tragic account of life and closes in Revelation with an equally confident comic vision. No biblical writing is without conflict between the two. Yet the Maccabean rebels were so convinced of God's support in their struggle for the Torah that when, on the Sabbath, a group of them were attacked they refused to defend themselves on the grounds that because fighting was work they would have broken the Sabbath. Experience and faith were again in conflict. It was another instance of cognitive dissonance and was resolved by the rebels deciding realistically that if they were attacked again on the Sabbath they would defend themselves. [1 Macc. 3:29ff]. Experience had modified the Bible's comic vision. Spiritual truth is never a static truth. Belief is always subject to modification by reality. Any theory of revelation must take account of that.

Judaism had again been brought to the edge of extinction. Yet, miraculously, the phalanx, the all-victorious killing machine perfected by Alexander, had been humbled in battle by the guerrilla tactics of the Maccabees in what today would be described as Asymmetrical Warfare. Understandably, the Jews attributed victory to the policies which had secured their survival during the previous four centuries, namely loyalty to the Lord of Hosts and the pursuit of personal and national righteousness through strict observance of the Torah. And just as the Babylonian exile had produced a flowering of comic religious literature, so too did the threat of national extinction under the Seleucids. It was at this time that the book of Daniel was written.

Daniel – the End of History and the coming of Apocalyptic

The world's history is the world's judgement.
Friedrich von Schiller [1759-1805]

At first, the book of Daniel seems to be just another short story written to encourage Jews to hold fast to the Torah, this time in the face of the Greek onslaught. Set in the days of King Nebuchadnezzar, the folklore element is strong as is the emphasis on trusting God to champion the faithful.

Daniel is a young, handsome and educated Jew who, with three friends, is chosen to serve at court. Unfortunately, as a civil servant he is required to eat the non-kosher food provided. To avoid breaking Jewish law, he and his friends ask to be allowed a vegetarian diet for a trial period: *At the end of the ten days they looked healthier and better nourished than any of the young men who had lived on the food from the king.* [1:15]. To the first hearers of this comic account the moral was clear: you may not be as handsome as Daniel but you can be as Torah observant and, if you are, you will be as blessed. *To these four young men God gave knowledge, understanding of books, and learning of every kind, and Daniel had a gift for interpreting visions and dreams of every kind.* [1:17] As happens in popular tales the king is impressed with his young courtiers and finds them *ten times superior to all the magicians and exorcists in his whole kingdom.* [1:20].

Daniel then goes on to pass further tests. Unlike his Chaldean rivals, he knows, without being told, what dreams the king dreamt and is able to interpret them. In this, Daniel resembles Joseph at Pharaoh's court, only here Nebuchadnezzar's dream and Daniel's interpretation mark the beginning of a radical comic development within Judaism. *As you watched,* he tells the king, *there appeared to your majesty a great image. Huge and dazzling, it stood before you, fearsome to behold. The head of the image was of fine gold, its chest and arms of silver, its belly and thighs of bronze, its legs of iron, its feet part iron and part clay.* [2:31]

People everywhere are fascinated by dreams and the first

listeners would have followed every word keenly: *as a stone hewn from a mountain by no human hand struck the image on its feet of iron and clay and shattered them.* [2:34]. As Daniel interprets it is clear that something is happening here to the popular story form itself. Daniel tells the king: *you yourself are that head of gold. After you there will arise another kingdom, inferior to yours, then a third kingdom of bronze, which will have sovereignty over the whole world. There will be a fourth kingdom, strong as iron, just as iron shatters and breaks all things, it will shatter and break all the others.* [2:38-40]

It is as if a lid was being lifted from off history. The scribes, in writing up their people's story had given them an overview of their history which went back to Abraham and beyond to Adam, the first man. And whereas with the prophets it was particular events which held religious significance, now, with Daniel, something new was emerging. The history of Jews as the Chosen People was becoming a story within the much larger sweep of world history. Yet, whereas the prophets made no attempt to conceal their message, these new interpreters, acknowledging the intrinsic hiddenness of God, wrapped their account in obscure and dreamlike imagery.

Scholars call this visionary overview of history *apocalyptic,* from a Greek word meaning "revelation" or "uncovering." The older view, preached by men like Jeremiah, was that God was in charge of world events and rewarded Torah faithfulness. Now, as prophecy gave way to apocalyptic with its claim to understand both the minutiae of historical events and the grand comic narrative of which they formed part, so the short story began to include symbol-laden visions across vast stretches of time and space. Prophets had been replaced by visionaries and, as the new genre developed, secrets were revealed of the cosmic struggle between good and evil. These were conveyed to the seer in obscure symbols which needed to be explained by angels. Apocalyptic was a heady mix, embodying ideas more potent than the simple comic stories of Ruth, Jonah, Tobit and Esther; though, like them, the aim of the new genre was to assure Jews that history was on the side of the Torah faithful. With apocalyptic, history as comedy had gone global, even cosmic.

Apocalyptic is thought to have originated in Zoroastrianism, the pre-Islamic religion of Persia, its beginnings in Judaism being traceable to the prophet known as Second Isaiah who wrote in the time of Persian rule.

During their exile in Babylon, the Jews had been on their guard against pagan religions like those of Marduk and Nebo, but Zoroastrianism was different. It was unlike any religion they had come across before. It was so like Judaism that it was difficult to ignore. Zoroastrians were monotheists worshipping one God, Ahura Mazda, the "Supreme Wisdom", a God of light. Zoroastrians also had sacred scriptures, the Avesta. Their founder, Zarathustra, Zoroaster to the Greeks, had, like the prophets, also preached against polytheism. In addition, it was a compelling explanatory system in which, although Ahura Mazda was supreme and would eventually prevail, he was opposed by forces of darkness and chaos. History was understood as a cosmic conflict in which individual Zoroastrians struggled to lead a moral life. The Jews had never met a faith so like their own. It is noticeable that while Second Isaiah makes fun of Bel and Nebo, *Bel has crouched down, Nebo stooped low; their images, once carried in your processions, have been loaded on to beasts and cattle* [46:1], Zoroastrianism alone is spared the wit of biblical comedy.

The encounter between Jews and Zoroastrians has had scholars debating ever since the extent to which Zoroastrian ideas influenced the Jews and their scriptures. For example, the phrase "*God of Heaven*" is only used in the Bible in Persian contexts, prompting the question: Was it a term for Ahura Mazda borrowed by the Jews? The two faiths had so much in common that it is difficult to see how even with the rigorous policy of the separatists, the Jews could avoid all influence. When Second Isaiah wrote: *I am the Lord; and there is no other, I form light and create darkness; I make weal and create woe, I am the Lord who does all these things,* [45:7] he was dangerously close to making God the creator of evil as well as good. The understanding that God was involved in the conflict between light and darkness, good and evil was probably a development stimulated by contact with Zoroastrians. Scholarly debate continues.

Apocalyptic was a theology of the symbolic imagination and incredibly rich and powerful in its imagery. It was a creative way of dealing with the dissonance triggered by the impact of Greek upon traditional Hebrew culture. In time, apocalyptic would become, in its more extreme developments, a dangerous ideology leading to the disastrous war with Rome [66-70CE], a disaster far worse than any it was launched to avoid; while, when secularised two millennia later, in the atheistic visions of the Communists and Nazis, it brought unprecedented sufferings on the world.

Philosophers like John Gray have traced the philosophy of the American Neo-cons, and their desire to project liberal democracy across the world, to a secularised version of apocalyptic which retains the ideal of a perfect world order while abandoning the religious idea of divine providence. Unlike biblical prophecy, secularised apocalyptic is very much alive in western political theory, just as it was once alive in Communism and Nazi racism. In secular apocalyptic, theology has died while the comedy lives on in such perverted non-comic realities as torture and state terrorism.

But in the book of Daniel, apocalyptic was still a comic vision of history promising a benign end to tumultuous events. It was a theology devised to encourage those who, in spite of their special status under God, felt history was passing them by.

Afraid, perhaps, that he might overtax the patience of his readers, the storyteller abandons apocalyptic imagery for the further adventures of Daniel and his friends in the fiery furnace [3:1ff], where once again God rescues the faithful. In the next chapter [4:1], king Nebuchadnezzar imagines himself as an animal, a psychological illness known as *Insignia Zoanthropia.* Yet even this is within the providence of God. On recovering his sanity, the comedy continues as Nebuchadnezzar worships the God of the Jews.

Then, the pace of the drama quickens as Nebuchadnezzar's son, Belshazzar, throws a feast in which an unknown hand writes on the wall a prophecy of the end of the kingdom, while *That very night Belshazzar king of the Chaldaeans was slain and Darius the Mede took the kingdom* [5:30]. The apocalyptic theme of history as divine judgement had become part of the story.

Compared with the twisting plot lines, characterisation and humour in Tobit or Judith, the adventures of Daniel make a less satisfying story, disjointed and without conclusion, other than the cursory note, *Prosperity attended Daniel during the reigns of Darius and Cyrus the Persian.* [6:28]

The last part of the book is dominated by visions and their meaning, becoming a very different genre to the short stories that dominated Jewish theology before the onslaught of Greek imperialism. With the humour gone, apocalyptic was left as comedy without wit.

The audience for the short story would have been a popular one. For the new apocalyptic there would have been a smaller readership but one with more sophisticated literary tastes. Apocalyptic was a coded form of communication, written for a religious elite which prided itself on being privy to the secrets of history. Before apocalyptic, history was seen as a comic-tragic flow of events secure in the hands of a living God who sometimes intervened on behalf of his people, but with the coming of apocalyptic, it became a predestined process biased in favour of the righteous.

When, in 1991, Francis Fukuyama declared that western liberal democracy had triumphed on the world political stage and therefore marked the culmination of history, he was secularising comic ideas traceable to the book of Daniel.

The Resurrection of the Dead and the Age to Come

> *We therefore commit his body to the deep, to be turned into corruption, looking for the resurrection of the body (when the sea shall give up her dead).*
>
> Forms of Prayer to be Used at Sea, the Book of Common Prayer.

Jews, Christians and Muslims believe in the apocalyptic doctrine of the resurrection of the dead, a belief found first in the book of Daniel: *At that time there will appear Michael the great captain; who stands guarding your fellow countrymen; and there will be a period of anguish such as has never been known ever since they became a nation till that moment. But at that time your people will be delivered, everyone whose name is entered in the book; many of those who sleep in the dust of the earth will awake, some to everlasting life and some to the reproach of eternal abhorrence.* [12:1ff]

Belief in the resurrection of the body appeared during the Maccabean revolt. Without it, Jesus' appearances after his death would have seemed even more perplexing than they were. The doctrine was one of several developments in prophecy which resulted from the clash of Hebrew and Greek cultures in the second century before Christ. With it came the idea that history was divided into "the present age" and "the age to come", the latter being always on the point of arriving until it would eventually be inaugurated by the Messiah whose advent would bring with it the Day of Judgement. Because these beliefs promised a happy ending to world history, their function was a comic one, even though they were short on humour and word-play – though there is a nice example of chutzpah, or brazen impertinence, in Daniel 9:18, where Daniel is pleading for his people: *It is not because of any righteous deed of ours, but because of your great mercy that we lay our supplications before you. Lord, hear; Lord, forgive; Lord, listen and act; God for your own sake do not delay, because your city and your people bear your name.* This comic muddle of a prayer begins by admitting that the righteous have no claim on salvation, and then appeals to God's self-interest, *because your city and your people bear your name.*

Where had the humour gone in apocalyptic? It had vanished as folk-stories were subverted by the apocalyptic love of symbolic code. The story form lingered but theology was turning into ideology, and theology without a folk element quickly becomes ideology without humour.

Jewish Sectarianism and the Pursuit of Torah Righteousness

Doubts amongst Divines, and difference of texts,
From when arise diversity of sects
And hateful heresies.
Edmund Spencer [c1552-1599].

The Old Testament took its final shape in the years following the capture of Jerusalem by the Romans in 70CE. These were years that witnessed the outcome of the struggle for the future of the Jewish people.

Sooner or later, all religions divide into groups separated by differing beliefs and practices and Judaism was no exception. In the period after the Maccabees there were some 20 different sects whose rivalries formed the background to the life of Jesus as well as determining the contents of the Hebrew Scriptures.

The struggle to keep Jews faithful to the Torah was an unending one, especially among Diasporan communities scattered across the Parthian and Roman Empires. There was always the tendency to assimilate to non-Jewish neighbours, though the Hasidim, the "devout ones", constantly encouraged Torah-slackers to return to their observance. Not a great deal is known about the Hasidim though most were probably laymen. Psalm 119, with its love of the Law, is theirs, and their influence can also be seen in Psalms 31, 34, 52, 73, 101 and elsewhere. It was from these Torah faithful Hasidim that the Maccabees would later draw their supporters and the sect we know as the Pharisees would emerge.

Like denominations everywhere, the Pharisees divided into moderates and hard-liners. Their Hebrew name, *Prushim,* meant "Separated Ones." They were a radical group marked out by their serious commitment to Torah and their dynamic and progressive way of doing theology through constant debate. Rabbinic Judaism today sees itself as the direct descendent of these early Pharisees whose Rabbis were responsible for the canon of the Jewish Bible and, thereby, of the Old Testament canon adopted by the 16th century Protestant Reformers.

The politically powerful Sadducees were the most conservative and traditional of these sects, their name deriving either from *Tsadik*, meaning "righteous," or from *Zadok,* the High Priest under David and Solomon, from whom they claimed descent. They were a priestly group, associated with the temple and, before the rise of the Pharisees were officially responsible for interpreting the Torah.

Being conservative in theology, they did not believe in the resurrection of the dead, angels, or the oral law; nor did they accept holy books other than the Torah. Had the Sadducees triumphed in this struggle between the sects, the Jewish scriptures would have consisted only of the five scrolls of Genesis, Exodus, Leviticus, Numbers and Deuteronomy.

It is possible that the *Hasidim* were the authors of comedies such as Tobit, as it is unlikely that hard-line sects like the Essenes could have written anything so humorous, though a copy has been found at Qumran. Because the Essenes were stricter than the Sadducees and considered the Jerusalem High Priestly families to be upstarts, they kept very much to themselves, an isolation which made them even more "The Separated Ones", than the Pharisees.

The Essenes were greatly attracted to apocalyptic with copies of such non-biblical works as "The War Scroll" and "The Messianic Apocalypse" in their library. In the unlikely event of their having triumphed in the struggle between the sects, the Hebrew canon would have had fewer tales like Judith and more apocalyptic books like Daniel and The Apocalypse of Zephaniah.

The Zealots, who for Josephus made up the Fourth Party of Judaism, came quite late to the sectarian scene. They first appeared shortly after 6CE, in Jesus' boyhood, when the Romans incorporated Judaea into their empire as part of the province of Syria. The Zealots agreed in most things with the Pharisees, except that where the Pharisees tolerated the Romans in exchange for religious freedom, the Zealots were committed to their armed overthrow. "They have," said Josephus, "an inviolable attachment to liberty, and say that God is to be their only Ruler and Lord." Theirs was a righteousness backed by violence, an early form of terrorism. This increasing fragmentation of the Jewish people into party groupings was one of the more disastrous outcomes of the successful rallying of the nation against the Seleucid threat.

8

THE BIBLE'S THIRD DEFINING MOMENT: WAR AGAINST ROME

O you hard hearts, you cruel men of Rome.
William Shakespeare [1564-1616]. *Julius Caesar.*

If the Jews hoped that the Roman yoke would prove as light as the Persian, they were disappointed. Taxation was more exploitative, appointments to the High Priesthood more cynically contrived, while Judaism itself was viewed with a contempt worthy of the Seleucids. In addition, the Romans favoured Gentiles and Romanised Jews over traditionalists.

Matters came to a head in 39CE, when the emperor Caligula [37-41CE] ordered his statue to be set up in the temple. The Jews objected, the emperor ordered the temple to be destroyed but died before his wishes could be carried out. To the righteous, God had again delivered his people, though the Zealots had noted the precariousness of their freedoms under Roman rule.

For a generation after that Judea was relatively peaceful, until, in 66CE, the garrison at Caesarea allowed birds to be sacrificed in front of a synagogue. In retaliation, prayers for the Emperor were stopped in Jerusalem. When Florus, the procurator, responded by confiscating the temple silver, its escort was massacred on their return journey to Caesarea, even though they had been promised safe conduct. As Judea was vital to Roman defences against the powerful neighbouring Parthian empire, a punitive expedition was launched from Syria and when the Zealots destroyed it, it seemed to many Jews that God had yet again vindicated the righteous.

However, the situation was now critical, and fearing rebellion elsewhere, the Romans sent in two of their best legions. It was a long and tough campaign, taking over a year even to subdue Galilee. The Sadducean leadership in Jerusalem, realising revolt was hopeless, did nothing to help the Zealots; while the future historian of the war, Josephus, initially the rebel commander in Galilee, defected to the Romans. More than 100,000 Galileans died. When the survivors of the revolt reached Jerusalem, they massacred and replaced the moderate leadership and were able to hold out for four years until, in 70CE the city finally fell and the temple was destroyed by Titus.

The rebellion, fuelled by apocalyptic theology and belief in the military efficacy of Torah righteousness was disastrous. It ended with the survival of but two of Judaism's many sects: the Pharisees and the Christians. The black comedy of militarised righteousness was over and a new chapter begun in the tragic history of the Jews. Of the three great catastrophes of biblical times, the Babylonian Exile, the Wars of the Maccabees and the National Uprising against Rome, the last was the most bloody and far-reaching, its consequences shaping the history of the west down to this day.

The reason the war did not bring Jewish history to an end was the resilience of the Pharisees who, in their pursuit of Torah righteousness, had resisted the intoxication of apocalyptic theology. In their struggle with the Christian, or Messianist Jews, for the future of Judaism, the Pharisees defined the canon of Scripture and began the codification of their Torah based theology in a humane and moderate way. The result was the Mishnah and Rabbinic Judaism. Those Jews who followed Jesus, though they were apocalypticists, were also moderates and pacifists, and many of them, like James, Jesus' brother, the first bishop of the church in Jerusalem, were also Pharisees. In view of the tragic sundering of Judaism into two rival religions where previously there had been only two sects, it is important to ask how this happened.

A number of factors were involved; none was decisive but together they resulted in a fateful parting of the ways. The first was the influx of large numbers of gentile converts into the churches. Many had previously attached themselves to synagogues as God-fearers. As God-fearers, gentile men did not need to be circumcised or observe the ritual rules of the Torah. They needed only to keep the moral or Noachic commandments, as set out in Acts 15. However, whereas God-fearing gentiles had previously identified themselves as Jews in some way, the moment the term "Christian" was coined, gentile followers of Jesus began to see themselves as having a distinct non-Jewish religious identity. This tendency was amplified with the rebellion against Rome, when Jews became subject to automatic gentile suspicion. It was then natural for Christian Jews to identify themselves as gentiles and distance themselves as much as possible from "their co-religionists".

Other factors involved in this tragic redefinition of opposing sects as rival faiths were the Christian claims that Jesus was the incarnate Word of God and that through him God had extended his promised salvation to the gentiles. It's possible that such very Jewish ideas as these would have found suitable Jewish expression anyway; but, as the Christian church began to look more to Hellenistic ways of doing its theology the divide widened with the result that the Romans came to see Jews and Christians as different religions. These finally became established as separate communities throughout the empire. As the rivalry between Gentile Christians and Rabbinic Judaism grew, so each defined itself increasingly in opposition to the other.

But what of those Christians who still lived as Jews? Their position was undermined in a number of ways, not least because after the war with Rome, their bishops were replaced by gentile Christians. Even the *Desposyni*, the blood relatives of Jesus, lost their status and their inherited leadership roles.

On the Jewish side of the divide, the Sadducees, Essenes, Zealots and other Torah loving groups had been swept away and the very survival of the Jewish people put at stake. In response the rabbis opted for a non-militaristic love of the Torah backed by scripture that minimised the role of apocalyptic. Even though Torah observant followers of Jesus had previously been accepted as Jews, they were now distanced. Jews would be gentile friendly but Torah separate. The outcome for Jewish Christians was that they were rejected both by the growing gentile church as well as by fellow Jews rallying around the Pharisees. Exactly when these Jewish Christians disappeared no one can say, though it is possible that small Aramaic speaking communities survived until the Arab-Muslim invasions of the seventh century.

Sometime after the war against Rome, Jews and Christians went their separate ways as the peoples of two covenants. For Christians, the Bible became a divided book, its two testaments providing the comic framework for rival identities.

Many tragedies later, our two faiths are still opposed, though since the Holocaust under the Nazis [1941-45], they are more tolerant and peaceable in their differences. Three quarters of the Christian Bible is a shared book. Exploring what that means is where the Bible's comic overview sheds light on the growing secular fear that history might turn out after all to be meaningless and therefore tragic.

9

STARTAS YOU MEAN TO GO ON

Nothing so difficult as a beginning,
In poesy, unless perhaps the end
George Gordon, Lord Byron [1788-1824]

The Hebrew Bible was created by the descendants of the Judean exiles who returned from Babylon. These Torah-obedient Jews rescued and edited the sacred documents and traditions of Judah and Israel, adding new works so that everything was shaped by a single-minded faithfulness to God and obedience to his commandments. These Hebrew Scriptures defined Judah as God's covenant people and their history as a comic vision for the world.

To understand the Old Testament as comedy is to take an overview beginning with Genesis and ending with the Wars of the Maccabees. It's a long story, full of tragedy and human wickedness held within, and contained by, the cosmic comedy of God's redemptive purpose.

The Torah, a Comic Masterpiece

A Man's life of any worth is a continual allegory, and very few eyes can see the Mystery of his life – a life like the scriptures, figurative –which such people can no more make out than they can the Hebrew Bible

John Keats [1795-1821]. *Letters.*

As we saw in chapter 1, the Bible's comic love of word play begins with the opening words of Genesis, *In the beginning God created,* and though it's lost in translation, the fate of so much light-heartedness in scripture, it continues *And the earth was without form and void.* In Hebrew, the last three words are famously, *tohu v'bohu,* which is as neat a word-play summary as any tabloid editor could devise.

Children use the same comic device when they say *easy peasy.* Politicians used it during the Cold War with their *"tremblin' in the Kremlin".* It may come as a surprise that something similar is found in a sacred text. It is the pleasure of language playfully used; a way of making a weighty point without theological abstractions intruding. The subject could hardly be more serious: God and creation in the first sentence; then, in the second, a cheeky reminder that the spirit of man hovers creatively over the text like the spirit of God over the waters.

Creation out of Nothing?

Nothing comes from nothing.
Parmenides [c.520-450 BC]

In saying this, Parmenides of Elea set logical limits to what was conceivable. It's a thought that hovers over modern cosmology in scientific attempts to explain the beginning of the universe without bringing God into the equations. The writer of Genesis removed those limits by doing just that, by bringing God into the account.

The biblical account of creation is a comic account, combining something of the humour of superiority and of incongruity. In exile, the Jews would have heard the great Babylonian epic the *Enuma Elish,* in which the god Marduk kills the sea monster, Tiamat, and, in the presence of other gods from the body's halves, creates heaven and earth. In Genesis, God is alone. No struggle is involved. His word alone is necessary[62]. In his creating *ex nihilo,* that is from nothing, the Babylonian gods are mocked. With the humour of superiority, the exiles have the last laugh; while the incongruity of an inconsequential people belittling the world's mightiest empire only drives the point home. Yet to achieve this meant opening a door that is not easily closed, that of nothingness. The fear of a return to chaos is bad enough; the dread of a return to nothingness is far worse.

In the psalms [74:13-14], and in Isaiah [51:9], there is evidence that the Jews had also accepted the belief that God and not Marduk created the world by slaying a primal monster; while in the stories of Noah and the misfortunes of Job, the fear of a return to chaos is very real. History as a divine comedy holds that chaos at bay; but life as nothingness, the nihil, threatens to undercut even that.[63] The thought that something could come from nothing was inconceivable to Parmenides and the Greeks. To non-monotheists it was a nonsensical concept.

---

62 In a world in which magic was a fact of life, this was important, as no magician could perform magic using only words.

63 For a long time in the western world, mathematicians seem to have avoided the use of zero because of the dread that the concept of non-existence evoked. The square root of minus one, also a "non-existent" number, produced a similar existential reaction.

Creation as Comedy

The end is where we start from.

T.S.Eliot. *Little Gidding.*

Five times during the six days of creation Genesis declares that God saw that what he had created was good [1:10]. In this repeated saying, the Bible stakes out the whole of creation as a comic arena. The Jewish commentator Rashi [1040-1105] said that the reason why the vault of heaven, created on the second day, was not declared good was that it was not completed until the third day: only then could the verdict be announced. By describing creation as good, which is the necessary end of all comedy, creation is, by definition, pure comedy. It is good at its beginning rather than where we'd expect, at the end. In the Bible, the end is where we start. When in Eden, things go wrong in the tragedy of "the Fall", as it is known in Christian theology, though not in Jewish; what has happened is nothing less than a fall from Divine Comedy.

Depending on one's point of view, the statement that God rested on the seventh day is either a mundane piece of information or a rather splendid joke. The strongest argument for the latter is that the practice that distinguished the Jews from all other ancient peoples was their refraining from all kinds of work on the seventh day, the Sabbath. This was because, they claimed, when the Holy One, Blessed be He, had finished his work of creation, he rested. Jews should do the same. This is the humour of incongruity, comparing the Sabbath rest of an ordinary person to God's creating the entire cosmos!

And, the very idea of God resting was itself a comic one. Whenever God failed to intervene in the world the temptation was the taunt that he was resting! He could only rest when creation was complete!

The Garden of Eden: Tragedy out of Comedy

Where the apple reddens
Never pry –
Lest we lose our Edens
Eve and I

Robert Browning [1812-1889]

This Hebrew love of word play continues with a pun in chapter 2, where God creates "man" [*Adam* v7] from the ground [*adamah*]; and continued with another in the account of the creation of Eve, Adam's "helper", from one of his ribs. [2:21ff]

It is as if human beings are compulsive comics by nature; that the need to entertain is present even in our dealings with God and in our writing upon sacred subjects. This word-play also coincides with the Bible's first use of situational irony. This occurs between the creation of the man and God's providing him with a help-meet. *The Lord God made trees grow up from the ground, every kind of tree pleasing to the eye and good for food; and in the middle of the garden he set the tree of life and the tree of the knowledge of good and evil.* [2:9]

Like a gun conspicuous on the table in some murder story, the reader knows that the tension created by this juxtaposition of comedy and the threat of tragedy is central to the plot. Sooner or later the gun will be fired and that apple tree scrumped.

We are not left waiting long. The man is placed in a garden, and almost as an aside is told: *You may eat of any tree in the garden, except from the tree of the knowledge of good and evil, the day you eat from that, you are surely doomed to die*. It's against this background of the forbidden tree that the lonely Adam is given a wife. Only years of solemn reading in church and at home have dulled the expectation that something is going to go wrong. The irony is Shakespearean in its service of tragedy.

Just as there cannot be trees whose fruit gives the knowledge of good and evil, so serpents, however good at hunting, cannot talk. The story is an allegory, a metaphor, the embodiment in folk-humour of how humanity has a god-like nature within its grasp and allows it to slip through its fingers. It is not an abstract analysis of our human predicament. The truth is in the imagery. Revelatory insight is wrapped-up in a story.

There follows a piece of tragi-comic dialogue whose masking wit reveals the deep things of our human condition. The serpent, *more cunning than any beast of the field* [3:1], opens the conversation with a little Socratic irony, pretending not to know what instructions the Lord had given to the couple. The serpent teases Eve in the same way as the story- teller teases the reader. The teasing promises pleasure as it delivers disaster. In other words, comedy can serve evil as easily as it can serve God. We forget that to our peril!

> **The serpent**: *Is it true that God has forbidden you to eat from any tree in the garden?*

The woman: *We may eat the fruit of any tree in the garden, except for the tree in the middle of the garden. God has forbidden us to eat the fruit of that tree or even touch it; if we do, we shall die.*
The serpent: *Of course you will not die, for God knows that as soon as you eat it, your eyes will be opened and you will be like God himself, knowing both good and evil.*

The inevitable happens, the gun is fired! *She took some and ate it; she also gave some to her husband, and he ate it.* Even here, as the episode reaches its climax, the writer cannot resist punning on the words *cunning* and *naked*. Because of the way Hebrew words are formed around basic root letters, puns are not as difficult to create as they are in English. *Then the eyes of them both were opened, and they knew that they were naked; so they stitched fig-leaves together and made themselves loincloths.*

In the Christian understanding of this passage, something so catastrophic has occurred in the relationship between the human race and God that the man and his wife are expelled from the garden – and here too, the writer cannot resist a little comedy:

The Lord God: *Where are you?*
The Man: *I heard the sound of you in the garden and I was afraid because I was naked, so I hid.*
The Lord God: *Who told you that you were naked? Have you eaten from the tree which I forbade you to eat from?*
The Man : *It was the woman you gave to be with me who gave me the fruit from the tree, and I ate it.*
The Lord God: [To the woman] *What have you done?*
The Woman: *It was the serpent who deceived me into eating it.* [Gen. 3:9ff]

The comedy lies in "the blame game" played out as the Man blames the Woman and the Woman blames the serpent.

Because humour can be so mischievous we need to ask: "What exactly is going on here?" In St Augustine's view, all human woe could be traced to this primal disobedience of Adam and Eve: sin, war, political oppression, economic and other forms of exploitation, all have their roots in this sundering of fellowship with God. The doctrine of the Fall and its perpetuation in Original Sin are a powerful Christian summary of the passage. Its weakness is that it ignores the playfulness of the original, and reduces the tragic-comic to unqualified tragedy.

While, as a Christian, I value Augustine's reading of the story as a Fall from primal innocence, I also find the rabbinic interpretation of events, as a mix of blessings and curses, also valid, for all was not lost in Eden. The tragedy was not total, as the presence of folk humour illustrates: death enters the world though so too does knowledge and wisdom. There is evil but alongside that evil there is good, and therefore the possibility of a comic account of human woe. In spite of all the tragedies we unleash upon ourselves, the human condition is still an extraordinarily rich and ambiguous one, replete with creative as well as destructive possibilities. By confronting disaster with humour, it was as if the writer was saying to Augustine, "You're right," and to the rabbis, "You're right as well', and ironically that retort is also an old Jewish joke!

How much greater *Paradise Lost* might have been if only Milton had been more alert to the presence of humour in Genesis. Satan would not so easily upstage God and the plot line would not be judged quite so mechanical and starved of human interest.

Things Continue To Go Wrong [Genesis 4:1ff]

O, my offence is rank, it smells to heaven;
It hath the primal eldest curse upon't
A brother's murder.

William Shakespeare [1564-1616]. *Hamlet.*

After the expulsion from Eden, the stories continue with further word play. *And the man knew Eve his wife; and she conceived and bore Cain, and said, "I have gotten a man with the help of the Lord".* In Hebrew, the verb *kanah*, means "to get," the "k" and "n" echoing the same consonants in Cain. It's as if the author, identified by scholars as "J', could not resist lightening her account with humorous and humanising touches. In contrast, scholars have traced the preceding chapter to a more serious Priestly writer, "P', in whose narrative God says, *Let us make man in our image, after our likeness* [1:26]. Man is therefore the noblest of creatures, an icon of the divine. But when J fills out P's account, mischievously he, or she, has Man created from red clay. We might be images of the divine but we are also animated dust - a comic thought which brings the reader down to earth again!

Adam's first-born, Cain, does not remain an only child for long, however. He soon has a brother, Abel. Cain, being older, works the land, now cursed by God, with his father; while Abel is given the lighter task of shepherding the family sheep. No reasons are given for what happens next, only that when the brothers offer to God tokens of their work, Cain's sacrifice is rejected while Abel's is accepted. As a result of this "slight", Cain, feeling spurned, murdered his brother, and comedy has again become tragedy. When the Lord asks, "*Where is your brother, Abel?"* fratricide is followed by the first recorded lie: Cain says defiantly, "*I do not know,"* and resorts to chutzpah: *Am I my brother's keeper?*

In these fragments of high comedy and low humour, Genesis is painting an impressionistic portrait of the human condition. Something went wrong in Eden and murder was among the consequences.

Lamech: Boasting and the Dark Side of Comedy

> *I apologise for boasting, but once you know my qualities, I can drop back into a quite brilliant humility,*
>
> Christopher Fry [1907-2005]

Until recently, the truth of the 14th century English proverb, *A boaster and a liar are all one,* helped discourage boasting in most parts of British society. Old attitudes die hard and most people still regard excessive boasting as intrinsically comical. In Shakespeare's *Henry V*, Sir John Falstaff and Pistol, two braggart professional soldiers, are portrayed as clowns, the humour lying in their compulsive exaggeration. Cervantes spun out the same effect endlessly in *Don Quixote.* The author of Genesis limited herself to just two verses.

Cain's descendant, his great, great, great grandson Lamech, boasted to his wives, Adah and Zillah:

> *I kill a man for wounding me,*
> *a young man for a blow.*
> *If sevenfold vengeance was to be*
> *exacted for Cain,*
> *for Lamech it would be*
> *seventy-sevenfold*
>
> [Genesis 4:23-4].

Lamech was the brother of Tubal-Cain, the man credited with creating metal weapons. Here Lamech boasts of his ability to use them without compassion or moral restraint. This is comic exaggeration of the grimmest kind, reminding us how humour and evil all too often go together. There is a story that the Soviet dictator, Joseph Stalin, found the execution of Grigory Zinoviev [1883-1936], as described by three drunken sycophants, so funny that, helpless with laughter, he had to signal for the joke to stop. And that "seventy seven fold" was taken up by Jesus in his famous reply to Peter. [Mt 18;22]

Another Ancient Fragment, Genesis 6:1-4

Gather up the fragments that remain.
Jesus of Nazareth [c7BC-c33AD]. [St John 6:12].

It soon becomes obvious in modern translations that not only is the Bible not one book but many, but also that these books are not written-through. They are, with few exceptions, compiled from fragments put together in such a way as to make overall sense of their bits and pieces. One such section is the strange story in Genesis 6:1-4.

In this fragment of ancient mythology, it is said that no sooner had human beings given birth to daughters than the sons of the gods saw how beautiful they were and took for themselves the women they wanted. But the Lord said, "*My spirit will not remain in a human being for ever; because he is mortal flesh, he will live only for 120 years.* Once again God seemed afraid that human beings might become "*like one of us". What if he now reaches out and takes fruit from the tree of life also, and eats it and lives for ever.* [3:22]. Not even after sexual assault by a race of immortals would human beings be allowed the immortality they craved.

It's far from clear who the sons of the gods or of the daughters of men were. The former could be pagan gods, angels, the sons of Seth or ordinary men; while the latter were possibly ordinary women or the descendants of Cain. Nor is anything said about punishing *the sons of the gods* for rape. The fragment has one function: to explain why the human life-span is divinely capped. All this happened, the writer is saying, in mythological times, when there were giants and heroes on earth. *In those days as well as later, when the sons of the gods had intercourse with the daughters of mortals and children were born to them, the Nephilim were on the earth, they were the heroes of old, people of renown.* [6:4].

The comedy here lies in the recurrent theme that sin produces mayhem as the world is reduced to tragic pantomime. As the story plays no further part in scripture or in Jewish or Christian theology, we need to ask why it's there. It's possible that when they were written these were important mythological themes. That time has long passed and as even the most conservative readers usually ignore the story its redundancy ought to temper any absolute biblicist claim to truth. Comedy is a biblical reality principle. Stories can't always be reduced to theological propositions.

Even so, in today's technological world, as our human lifespan grows ever longer and our ability to redesign ourselves increases exponentially it's a story that seems to be ever more telling in its analysis of human hubris.

The Dissatisfied Creature: Man as tragedy

And the worst friend and enemy is but Death.
Rupert Brooke [1887-1915]

Deep down, we human beings are creatures who feel cheated and as a consequence rebel against our creatureliness. *He has put eternity into man's mind,* wrote Ecclesiastes [3:11] explaining the origins of our human indignation at being deprived of immortality. Death is a perpetual reminder of what as creatures we are not. This primal deprivation is also alluded to in the words of God to Adam, *you may eat of any tree in the garden, except from the tree of the knowledge of good and evil; the day you eat from that you are surely doomed to die.* [2:16] A little later, this withholding of immortality is underlined: *the man has become like one of us, knowing good and evil; what if he now reaches out and takes fruit from the tree of life also, and eats it and lives for ever.* [3:22]. Three chapters later, the source of mankind's resentment against God is re-asserted, *the Lord said, My spirit will not remain in a human being for ever, because he is mortal flesh.* [6:3].

These ancient writers knew that death and human limitation were experienced as affronts to our dignity and that our obsession with immortality never fades. It is there in the Epic of Gilgamesh[64] with its echoes of the story of Noah. Gilgamesh's quest was a search for immortality. It is a story the exiles would have known. They will have known too how, in the building of the pyramids and other royal tombs, the whole economy of Egypt was devoted to securing immortality for the Pharaohs. In today's secular world, celebrity and

---

64 This is an epic poem preserved on 12 clay tablets which was discovered in the library of Ashurbanipal, a 7th c BC king of Assyria. It probably originated in a much old Sumerian work. Much of the poem has to do with the hero Gilgamesh's quest for immortality.

the search for undying fame are its poor substitutes.
To long for eternity while being condemned to mortality is among the Bible's insights into our human predicament. It is the tragedy underlying our existence, to which the Bible as comedy is a response.

The human resentment of death and the profound sense of loss at being denied immortality may also explain why so much biblical comedy borders on chutzpah. Just as comedy is in continual tension with tragedy so chutzpah can be understood as the believer's reluctance to submit either to the human condition or what convention takes as being the will of God. Our rebellion is also against the perceived unjust limitations imposed by our creatureliness.

Noah and the Return to Chaos

And Noah, he often said to his wife when he sat down to dine,
I don't care where the water goes if it doesn't get into the wine.
G. K. Chesterton [1874-1936]

If the story of Cain and Abel is about the social breakdown that followed their parent's expulsion from Eden, and the boasting of Lamech witnesses to the world's growing moral degradation, then the story of Noah's flood [Gen. 6-9] reveals the full extent of the disaster that resulted when Adam and Eve broke the law of God. *When the Lord saw how great was the wickedness of human beings on earth, and how their every thought and inclination were always wicked, he bitterly regretted that he had made mankind on earth.*

Noah *was a righteous man, the one blameless man of his time,* [6:9]. He was the son of Lamech, the boaster who was only able to father him in his one hundred and eighty second year! The one thing this braggart needed to boast about, a son, was denied to him for over a century and half! Lamech was a humiliated boaster when all around him his peers were fathering sons by the dozen. Finally, when a son, Noah, is born to him, the boy turned out to be a non-violent paragon of virtue, an ironical reproach to his father, an irony which began a rich run of punning humour explored by Whedbee, Bloom and others writers. Whedbee points out that since the medieval Wakefield Mystery Plays, "dramatists have found the biblical flood story an ever-flowing fountain of comic characters, motifs, and scenes".[65]

Before the rise of the geological sciences in the 19th century

65 See page 49 in J.Wlliam Whedbee's, *The Bible and the Comic Vision.* Fortress Press 2002.

and dating techniques based on nuclear decay in the 20th, Christians accepted the Flood as a memory of an actual historical event. This confusion of categories – the insistence by some on reading all biblical stories as if they were factual history when their playfulness makes it clear that they are something else, has come in the 21st century to confuse the public use of scripture.

Even though few Christians today take the story of Noah literally, but understand it as myth or allegory, its spiritual and moral meanings are clear: in the Genesis story, the human race is adrift from God and wickedness and social breakdown of every kind are a universal experience. A good, well-ordered world created from physical chaos has been reduced to moral and spiritual disorder, so much so that God is said to have had second thoughts about having created the human race in the first place. There is, however, one exception: Noah, even though God is angry enough with everyone else to cover the earth with a mountain-height flood "*to a depth of fifteen cubits*".

To escape, God commands Noah construct a gigantic ship, the Ark, in which his family and the world's animals will find refuge. Then it rained for forty days, so that *every living thing that moved on earth perished.* [7:21]. The story, however, ends as comedy with Noah and his family rescued and worshipping God, and God promising, *Never again shall I put the earth under a curse because of mankind, however evil their inclination may be from their youth upwards, nor shall I ever again kill all living creatures as I have just done.* [8:21]. God makes a covenant with Noah never to wreak destruction upon the earth again, and he seals the covenant with the sign of the rainbow.

Unfortunately it proved to be a fresh start that made little difference; things still went wrong. Said to be the first tiller of the soil and with God's curse upon the ground removed, Noah becomes the first man to grow vines, discovers how to make wine, and gets drunk. The nakedness which shamed Adam and Eve in Eden is repeated as Noah, naked in his tent, falls into a drunken sleep. [9:20ff]. It is difficult for us in the west, saturated with images of nudity, to appreciate what a powerful symbol of degradation Noah's nakedness was. When Ham tells his brothers Shem and Japheth of their father's shame, in order to cover him decently with a cloak, they have to walk backwards, averting their eyes. To modern, western eyes, their embarrassment offers a scene little short of slapstick comedy in its tragedy.

The tragic humour here is that the divine work of destruction and new beginnings is undone. It is a "what was the point of" kind of story. This is the humour of futility that runs to full flood in the book of

Ecclesiastes. And it gets worse, for when Noah wakes up and discovers what had happened, he takes out his self-disgust not on Ham who saw him in his drunken shame, or on Shem and Japheth who rescued him from it, but on his unsuspecting grandson, Canaan![66] *Cursed be Canaan! Most servile of slaves shall he be to his brothers.* [9:25]. This marks the entry of injustice into the world. Its inappropriateness and disconnection with what went before is a farce that lacks even a breath of humour. Comedy and tragedy have become confused. The fruit of the Tree of the Knowledge of Good and Evil has proved to be sour. It meant too, that when the Israelites invaded Canaan, what was a blessing for them became a curse for the Canaanites, a curse traced to Noah cursing his grandson! It is a curse that echoes in the land of Canaan to this day.

Genesis follows this tragedy of human corruption through to the time when supposedly all the world spoke a single language. As people journeyed in the east, they came upon a plain in the land of Shinar and settled there. They, said to one another, "*Come let us make bricks and bake them hard".* Then they said, "*Let us build ourselves a city and a tower with its top in the heavens and make a name for ourselves, or we shall be dispersed over the face of the earth."* [Gen. 11:1ff]

The black comedy of our origins has now reached the story of the Tower of Babel, where the descendants of the flood's survivors repeat Adam and Eve's trespass on the sovereignty of God. *The Lord came down to see the city and tower which they had built, and he said, "Here they are, one people with a single language, and now they have started to do this; from now on nothing they have a mind to do will be beyond their reach. Come let us go down there and confuse their language, so that they will not understand what they say to one another." So the Lord dispersed them from there all over the earth, and they left off building the city. That is why it is called Babel, because there the Lord made a babble of the language of the whole earth.* [Genesis 11v5ff.]

Again, the writer cannot resist a little word-play, this time on "Babel" and "babble", though the real comedy lies not in the punning but in our picturing the confusion which results from the sudden inability to communicate. We can imagine the storyteller filling out the detail with funny voices and nonsense language. Good storytellers

---

66 As Canaan was the presumed father of the Canaanites, the enemies of the Hebrews on their entry to the promised land, and the chief cause of their lapse into idolatry, this prospective and prophetic curse on Canaan seems to us rather contrived. The story clearly serves more than one purpose.

will illustrate comic scenes with comic antics. Sadly, whenever oral tradition is written up, the humour is diluted – and then it is lost a second time whenever the story is used to support some theological abstraction.

Biblical theologians are interpreters of Bible stories, though where, for the storyteller, it is the story's effect on the hearers that matters; for theologian it is the doctrine the story illustrates that's important. This means that the comic tale of the Tower of Babel is shrunk onto some abbreviation of its theoretical meaning, for example, "After the hubris of ambition, comes the nemesis of pride". Philosophers call this, "Reductionism", because it reduces the substance of something in such a way that part of its essence is lost. In the case of the Bible, it is comedy and what it represents that disappears.

From now on nothing they have a mind to do will be beyond their reach. Today, as advances in artificial intelligence and technology reshape the world this is arguably the most prescient verse in the whole Bible! As human beings strive to be godlike, God seems almost afraid of the challenge, though the truth is that we, the over-reachers, are the ones who are anxious. We are afraid of ourselves and project our fear, in our waywardness on to God.

Disappearing Humour: Bible Stories and Narrative Theology

> *A man is always a teller of tales, he lives surrounded by his stories and the stories of others, he sees everything that happens to him through them.*
>
> Jean-Paul Sartre [1905-80]

Ever since the Church Fathers explored the mystery of the Godhead in the language of substance and persons, the Church's theology has been wedded to the philosophy of its time. This has meant that theologians have read the Bible's stories in a reductionist kind of way, until all that is left is a formula which is declared to be the narrative's underlying truth. This was largely how theologians used the Bible until scholars like Karl Barth [1886-1968] and H. Richard Niebuhr [1894-1962] realised that the revelation of God in scripture is given largely in narrative and story form. It was the beginning of what is now known as Narrative Theology, the attempt to mirror in theology the role of narrative in the Bible. Alas, the project proved impossible as theologians again set about their task by substituting abstract academic theorising for narrative. Inevitably, theological thinking turned stories into ideas and the study of biblical narrative into "Narratology", and in which, not surprisingly, comedy vanished once more.

10

MEANING IN HISTORY-
PROMISE AND COVENANT

History was forged for Israel in the living situation itself, in the dramatic conflict of will between themselves and God.

Ronald Gregor Smith [1913-1968], *The New Man*

When the Jews in exile invented history by turning chronologies into stories and edited the memories of their nation they shaped them around their relationship with the living Lord of history. They were a people who believed that they were constituted around the promises of God and in a covenant relationship with him.

Those who compiled the biblical history of the Jews wrote it up as comedy, whose epic narrative was as much about God as it was about his people. As the only God, their God was a God for the world and not for Jews only. The comedy of which they were part was inclusive with one God for one world. The details might be as minor as the boasting of Lamech but their scope was a universality traced back through many flawed human beings to Abram, the Father of the Nation and to Adam and Eve as the world's parents.

Abram and Abraham [67]

Consider Abraham your father and Sarah who gave you birth: when I called him he was but one, I blessed him and made him many.

Isaiah 51:2

The first part of Israel's national epic can be summarised as "A Comedy of Errors," beginning with events in the Garden of Eden and ending with the confusion of The Tower of Babel. Its comic hope of

67 Although many modern scholars think that Abram and Abraham are dialect variants of the same name, in the book of Genesis [17:1ff] the change of name is linked by God to Abram's new covenant status. *This is my covenant with you, you are to be the father of many nations. Your name will no longer be Abram, but Abraham, for I will make you the father of many nations.*

everything turning out well in the end was preserved through the covenant promise of God to all mankind made through Noah. [Gen. 9:15]

The next episode in the Genesis history of the world begins with the call of Abram, a nomad whose wanderings scholars date to about 1700 BCE. At this time, the middle-east was made up of a vast network of city states which, through the levying of tribute and systems of allegiance, were organised into empires whose names and borders were forever shifting. Only Egypt had any real political permanence. Throughout these territories, nomads wandered freely, entering into temporary relations with local communities, sometimes settling down and displacing former occupants as Israel would later do in Canaan, though more often moving on in search of fresh pasture. Abram enters the Bible as just such a nomad.

The Lord said to Abram, *Leave your own country, your kin and your father's house, and go to a country that I will show you. I shall make you into a great nation; I shall bless you and make your name so great that it will be used in blessings.*]12:1] For the writer of Genesis this call of Abram forms the first part of God's plan to restore harmony to his creation.

At 75, Abram, with Sarai his wife and his nephew Lot, set out for Canaan. Unfortunately, their arrival coincided with a famine and they were compelled to go to Egypt where, thanks to the fertile waters of the Nile, food was seldom in short supply.

The Comedy of Errors Continues in Egypt

O what a tangled web we weave
When first we practice to deceive.

Sir Walter Scott [1771-1832]. *Marmion.*

The stories may change, but the Bible's underlying spiritual thrust remains constant. Any thoughts that the nation's Father, Abram, was a worthy recipient of God's promise of future greatness are promptly undermined. *As he was about to enter Egypt, Abram said to his wife Sarai, "I am well aware that you are a beautiful woman, and I know that when the Egyptians see you and think, 'She is his wife,' they will let you live but they will kill me. Tell them you are my sister, so that all will go well with me because of you and my life will be spared on your account."* [Gen. 12:11ff].

Much of the comedy in this second part of Genesis depends on the bearers of God's promise telling lies or resorting to deception. In passing his wife off as his sister, Abram, the deeply flawed patriarch, is not only a coward but risks condemning Sarai to the life of a concubine in Pharaoh's harem. Worse still, in doing so he endangered the very promise on which the future of the Jews as God's chosen people depended. Things grew worse when Pharaoh's courtiers see Sarai *taken into Pharaoh's household.* [12:14] As the wealthy Abram now grows even richer, it prompts the realisation that his cowardice had made him a pimp.

Meanwhile, the Lord inflicted plagues on Pharaoh and his household on account of Abram's wife, Sarai. [12:17]. Tragic events are now turning into farce.

When Pharaoh discovers what has happened he asks Abram, *Why have you treated me like this? Why did you say she was your sister, so that I took her as a wife?* [12:18]. Like Job, Pharaoh had been punished by God even though innocent. It is an interesting twist to the plot. The guilt was Abram's, his behaviour appalling, yet with inexplicable humanity, *Pharaoh gave his men orders, and they sent Abram on his way with his wife and all that belonged to him.* [12:20]

Considered morally, this is a very confused story, yet throughout divine providence remains at work. The plot becomes even more convoluted when later, Abram, now Abraham, tries the same trick on King Abimelech of Gerar. Only then do we learn that Sarai, now Sarah, is in fact Abraham's half-sister, as they have the same father, though different mothers, a domestic arrangement later condemned in the Law of Moses [Lev. 18:11]. Once again, Abraham had profited through deceit.

Afterwards, in Genesis 26, Abraham's son Isaac attempts the same ruse, only this time God intervenes and spares the kingdom of Gerar by warning its king that he is about to commit a terrible sin. The bizarre plot lines in these stories are pure comedy; the outcomes, real or potential, are tragic. The account of how the promise to Abram survives and is passed on is a comic tale of how providence triumphs over the farcical weakness and wickedness of the human race.

The Inheritance of the Promise to Abraham as Comedy

> *Lord forgive all the little tricks I play on you, and I'll forgive the great big ones you played on me.*
>
> Robert Frost [1875-1963], attributed.

The promises to Abraham are handed down the family like a piece of property, subject not only to accident and misfortune but to the most disgraceful kinds of family politics. Isaac's son Jacob, whose twelve sons were the founding fathers of the tribes of Israel, is portrayed as a scoundrel, a man who cheats both his brother and his dying father. It is not an edifying tale. [Gen. 27].

Jacob, the arch-deceiver, is guided by his equally reprehensible mother when he tricks Esau out of his father's last blessing. Rebecca cooks Isaac's favourite meal for Jacob to take to him. Isaac is blind, and Jacob uses the skin of a young goat to make his hands and neck seem as hairy as his brother Esau's. Rebecca's plan works; Isaac is deceived and Jacob receives the blessing meant for his brother. Not surprisingly, when his father died, Jacob went into hiding to escape Esau's revenge.

The comedy in these episodes centres on the irony that the most valuable possession of the Jews in exile, the promises made to Abraham, are treated so casually by those responsible for passing them on. It is not so much, how can Ishmael forgive Sarah, or Esau, Jacob; as how can God forgive any of them for their insult to his name? In these stories, one finds the best and the worst in the spiritual life of humankind. The knowledge of God and communion with him have become the playthings of all that's wrong with human beings. The bearers of the covenant treat it with contempt. The comedy is "Bible black" and breathtaking in its treatment of all that happened before the Exile. There is little respect by the writers here for their forebears. Babylon really was a watershed in the history of the Jews as so much of what went before is as good as laughed off.

Whenever a people write up their history, they usually attempt to make their story the envy of the nations around them, emphasising the heroism and wisdom of their founding fathers. The Jews did the opposite, even when on the edge of extinction. Why did they make of their national story such a prolonged and shaming comedy? The more one ponders this strangest of holy books the more one is astounded at its originality and apparent perversity. Why didn't their seriousness in observing the Torah carry over into writing their history? Perhaps the writers realised that only the comic genre can bear the burden of hope and lasting redemption.

As Isaac lies dying, the comedy continues with Esau plotting to kill Jacob. Realising that time is short, the manipulative and histrionic Rebecca tells her dying husband, *I am weary to death of Hittite women! If Jacob marries a Hittite woman like those who live here, my life will not be worth living.* [27:46]. Knowing that like Esau he is no match for Rebecca, and being something of a trickster himself, Isaac sends Jacob to find a wife from among his wife's brother's family in far off Mesopotamia. After being confirmed in the Blessings and Promises he had won from Esau by deception, Jacob sets off and reaches the home of his uncle, Laban. There he meets his cousin Rachel, who is *beautiful in both face and figure,* and promptly falls in love with her. [29:9] A deal is struck by which, in return for Rachel, Jacob will work for Laban for seven years. However, when the seven years are up, Jacob the trickster is out-tricked by his trickster uncle! *It is against the custom of our country,* said Laban, *to marry off the younger sister before the elder.* [29:26]. It i 's a cruel joke, whose memory is perhaps perpetuated in church weddings today where brides are obliged to lift their veils before the couple make their vows. Instead of spending his wedding night with Rachel, Jacob spent it instead with her much less attractive sister, Leah, whose comically ambiguous name meant either "wild cow" or "gazelle."

Poor Jacob was only able to marry Rachel after agreeing to work for his father-in-law for a further seven years! The trickery, however, does not end there, for it is then the Lord's turn to out-trick the trickster. When God sees that *Leah was unloved, he granted her a child, but Rachel remained childless. Leah conceived and gave birth to a son; and she called him Reuben.* [29:32] Reuben means, "*Look, a son!"* his name expressing Leah's scorn for her infertile sister. *The Lord has seen my humiliation, but now my husband will love me.* The triumphant Leah produces still more sons, Simeon, Levi and Judah, whose names, by drawing attention to God's favouritism, further humiliated Rachel. Simeon meant "hearing," the message to Rachel being, "God has heard me and not you!" The name of the second son, Levi, meant "attachment," *now that I have born him three sons my husband will surely be attached to me.* [29:34]. Judah, which meant "Praise", was given by Leah to remind Rachel of the sons for whom her fertile sister had thanked God. The comic vindictiveness in this choice of names illustrates the dictum of the 19th c. French political thinker, Charles Peguy, that, "*Everything begins in mystique and ends in politique".*

By this time, Rachel was desperate: *Give me sons or I shall die,* she says to Jacob. [30:2] Following Sarah's example, Rachel gives Jacob permission to sleep with her slave-girl, Bilhah, *and she conceived and bore Jacob a son,* the baby counting as her own. *Then Rachel said, God has given judgement for me.* The boy was named Dan, which in this family game of children's names meant "judgement." When Bilhah conceived again and produced another son, Rachel said, "*I have devised a fine trick against my sister, and it has succeeded;*" so she named him Naphtali, which meant "trickery." This is history as self-parody as Jacob the trickster now had a son called "trickery" the result of Rachel tricking her sister.

The family saga underwent a further twist when Leah too became barren, and offered Jacob her slave-girl, Zilpah. When Zilpah bore a son, Leah said, "*Good fortune has come", and she named him*

Gad, which meant "Good Fortune." And, when Zilpah gave her yet another son, he was named "Asher", meaning "happy" or "blessing", for *Leah said, Happiness has come, for women will call me happy."* [30:13]

But this droll tale of dynastic competition doesn't end there, for when Reuben comes across some mandrakes, a root thought to be a powerful aphrodisiac, he gives them to his mother, Leah. As one of the Hebrew words for love is *dod,* and that for mandrakes is *dudaim,* the word-play continues. Desperate for ever more children, the competitive women enter into an agreement which sheds a great deal of light on the family arrangements of the Father of the Nation's domestic life. *Rachel said, In exchange for your son's mandrakes let Jacob sleep with you tonight. In the evening, when Jacob came in from the country Leah went out to meet him, "You are to sleep with me tonight, she told him. I have hired you with my son's mandrakes."* [30:15]

In a family of schemers and manipulators Leah proves as capable a manipulator as her mother-in-law. *Jacob slept with her that night, and God heard Leah's prayer.* Is there also an attempt to manipulate God here? *Leah conceived and bore a fifth son.* She called him "Issachar", which means "Reward", saying, *God has rewarded me because I gave my slave-girl to my husband.* [30:16]. The farce continues with the birth of Zebulon [Prince], and Joseph, whose name means "May he add," that is, "May God add another son to me".

After working for Laban for almost twenty years, Jacob now has two wives, a large family and flocks of his own. It was time, he reckoned, to settle with Laban, return home and take his chance with Esau. But Laban is reluctant to let him go. As Jacob has made him rich, Laban can afford to be generous with his severance settlement, especially as all that Jacob asked for were the black lambs and brindled and spotted goats. Yet though the request seemed modest, Laban suspected a trick and fearful of losing his grandchildren, removed from his flocks all that Jacob asked for, then departed, putting three days journey between Jacob and himself.

Rather than leave with nothing, Jacob out-smarted his double-crossing father-in-law one last time by breeding selectively from the remaining flocks, the black, striped and spotted animals that had been agreed. [30:35ff] Quite how he did this is not clear. The text has usually been interpreted as reflecting ancient folk beliefs that a foetus can be affected by what the mother sees, in this case wooden rods from which the bark had been peeled. As genetically the explanation is impossible, it is thought that they must have had some other more practical sexual function, which Kaltner, McKenzie and

Kilpatrick explore in a chapter in their book headed, [68]"Did Jacob use Sex Toys?"

As Jacob grew ever richer, Laban's sons became jealous and when Jacob noticed that *Laban was not so well disposed to him as he had once been,* [31:2] he hurriedly left for Canaan. To complicate things, Rachel took with her her father's household gods. In view of the monotheism of the post-Exilic community, it might have been expected that reference to Rachel's idolatry would have been edited out as she was, after all, one of the matriarchs of Judah but this was an honest history. Narrative tension mounts further when Laban asked Jacob, *why did you steal my gods?* [31:30] and Jacob's replies, *Whoever is found in possession of your gods shall die for it.* When Laban enters his daughter's tent he finds her sitting on the camel-bag in which she has hidden them. She escapes detection with cunning worthy of her husband, *Do not take it amiss, father, that I cannot rise in your presence; the common lot of woman is upon me.*

Jacob's story does not end there but enough has been said to show how it is told within an overarching comic framework. It is a gripping tale of a compulsive trickster. It answered a nation's questions about its origins by explaining how God's promises to Abraham had been passed on so that even in exile and during the uncertain years of their return, God was still faithful. However, it also raises as many questions as it answers. Why did God choose and reveal himself to such patently unrighteous people? And why, too, is God portrayed as a character in a comedy as flawed and as unattractive as that of the Patriarchs, Abraham and Jacob?

The Story of Joseph

> *The first law of storytelling…'Every man is bound to leave a story better than he found it.'*
>
> Mrs Humphrey Ward [1851-1920]

Of Jacob's twelve sons, Joseph was his father's favourite and with him the epic tale of the patriarchs reaches its climax. The complications arising from parental favouritism are a recurring theme in the Bible, and the sibling rivalry between Jacob and Esau is now magnified as Joseph, the child of Jacob's old age, repeatedly taunts his brothers with accounts of dreams in which he constantly emerges as top brother. In one dream, he told them, *We were out in the field binding sheaves, when all at once my sheaf rose and stood upright,*

[68] *The Uncensored Bible*, Harper Collins, 2008.

and your sheaves gathered around and bowed in homage before my sheaf. [37:7] This is the humour of superiority in which the baby of the family is clearly getting above himself. The brothers did not need to be experts in Freudian dream analysis to work out what was going on. The dream had something of the humour of incongruity as well.

Foolishly, Jacob had made Joseph a distinctive coat, the Hebrew being translated either as "a coat of many colours" or "a long robe with sleeves." This combination of parental favouritism and a younger brother's inflated sense of his own importance led his brothers to plot his murder, but at the last moment they failed to go through with their plan and Joseph was sold into slavery instead. To conceal their crime the brothers tell their father that he had been killed by wild animals, producing as evidence his coat soaked in goat's blood. The storytelling here rivals in its love of word-play and other comic devices those stories found elsewhere in the Bible and Apocrypha. The tale of how Joseph the slave delivers Egypt from famine, rises to become the second most powerful man in the land and saves his family from starvation, is so rich a comedy that all that can be attempted here is to pick out one or two examples.

Behind the humour of these stories, the twists of their plots, their flawed characters and unrighteous behaviour and the jokey word play of the narrative, the underlying aim is the serious one of showing how, through the providential care of his people, God brings good out of human folly and wickedness.

On arriving in Egypt, Joseph was bought as a slave by Potiphar, captain of Pharaoh's guard and *prospered because the Lord was with him.* [Gen. 39:2] Because Joseph proved trustworthy, Potiphar placed him in charge of his household. Potiphar's wife, however, infatuated with her young Hebrew slave, attempted to seduce him. Joseph resisted, *How can I do such a wicked thing? It is a sin against God.* Until, *one day when he came into the house to see to his duties, and none of the household servants was there indoors, she caught him by his loincloth, saying, "Come, make love to me," but he left the loincloth in her hand and ran from the house.* Joseph is then accused of attempted rape and thrown into jail.

In the Bible's comic view of history evils that befall the righteous can, through God's providence, be turned to blessing. Joseph's life is no exception. Just as he rose to the chief position in Potiphar's household, so in prison he is placed in charge of the other prisoners, including both Pharaoh's baker and cupbearer, each deeply troubled by their dreams. Like Daniel, Joseph is able to interpret them, and, as he predicted, the baker is hanged and the cupbearer released.

After two years had gone by, it is Pharaoh's turn to have

disturbing dreams, two nightmares in one night. And just as the wise men of Babylon were not able to interpret Nebuchadnezzar's dream, so the official interpreters of dreams at Pharaoh's court are also unable to help. It is then that the cupbearer remembers Joseph and tells Pharaoh of his skill in dream interpretation. Joseph is summoned. Pharaoh describes his dreams and is told that they predict seven years of abundant harvest, followed by seven of famine. Asked for advice, Joseph recommends building grain stores and is put in charge of the construction programme. When events prove Joseph right, the story's comic structure is clearly visible. And there is word play too. In [40:13] Joseph tells the cupbearer that *within three days Pharaoh will raise your head and restore you to your post.* Thinking that he will also receive good news, the disgraced baker also tells Joseph his dream, only to be told that *within three days, Pharaoh will raise your head...and hang you from a tree.* [40:19] The humour, with the repeated phrase, *will raise your head,* is decidedly dark, but it is a good tale well told.

The Plot Deepens

Behind a frowning providence
He hides a smiling face.
William Cowper [1731-1800]

In Genesis the comedy never stops. By the time the famine arrives, Joseph has become the virtual ruler of Egypt. The grain stores are full, and among the hungry of other lands who travel to Egypt for food are his brothers, ten of them, only little Benjamin having been left behind to keep his ageing father company.

Joseph is busy overseeing the sale of Egypt's grain surplus when he recognises his brothers, though they fail to recognise him. The stage is now set for one of the best comic games in scripture, in which Joseph plays with his brothers' anxieties until, in a comedy of surprises, he reveals who he is and persuades them to bring his father to Egypt.

Joseph begins by accusing his brothers of spying. They deny it: *There were twelve of us, my Lord, all brothers; sons of one man back in Canaan, the youngest is still with our father, and one is lost.* [42:13]. In that euphemism, "*one is lost*", they stand self-condemned. It is a moment of profound psychological effect and power. The reader knows what is going on and Joseph knows, and the story hovers between tragedy and comedy as Joseph takes his revenge by making his brothers run to and fro between Egypt and Canaan, contriving each time some means of obliging them to return.

After accusing them of being spies, Joseph further racks up the tension by calling them thieves. Next, he confuses them by hiding their purchase money in a grain sack and imprisoning Simeon, his half brother, making him a hostage guaranteeing their return with Benjamin, his full-brother. It is a cruel game, yet a just one as it is only what they deserve.

When the brothers return full of anxiety and bringing Benjamin with them, Joseph unleashes his idea of humour as surprise and ambiguity. They are unable to read his intentions as he welcomes them back not with imprisonment but with a party to celebrate! *The steward conducted them into Joseph's house, and gave them water to bathe their feet, and provided feed for their donkeys.* [43:24] Full of apprehension they are met with kindness. If there is one passage in the Hebrew Scriptures which illustrates the grace of God reflected in human behaviour, it is this. Yet it is also deeply ambiguous, because Joseph is playing games with his brothers' feelings. Is there here, as in the wager between God and Satan in the book of Job, the subversive thought that history itself might after all be but a game played by God as Joseph played with his brothers? It can sometimes feel like that!

When he finally speaks to Benjamin, Joseph has reached emotional breaking point. Seeing his brother, he asks in feigned innocence, *Is this your youngest brother, of who you told me?* And to Benjamin he said, "*may God be gracious to you my son!*" As the psychological tension becomes unbearable Joseph breaks down, and overcome by his feelings for his brother, and almost in tears, went into the inner room and wept. [43:30]

He weeps, yet his game goes on a little longer, until finally he can keep it up no more, by which time his brothers are completely confused. *Joseph was no longer able to control his feelings in front of all his attendants and called, "Let everyone leave my presence!" There was nobody present when Joseph made himself known to his brothers, but he wept so loudly that the Egyptians heard him, and news of it got to Pharaoh's household. "Joseph said to his brothers, "I am Joseph, is my father still alive?".* [45:1-3]

The story illustrates perfectly Freud's theory of humour as psychological release. It's also comedy as a theory of history when he tells his brothers, *God sent me on ahead of you to ensure that you will have descendants on earth, and to preserve for you a host of survivors. It is clear that it is not you who sent me here, but God.* [45:7].

Which was how, in his old age, Jacob came to live in Egypt. Yet, there is one last comic twist to the story as Jacob dies and his body is taken for burial in Abraham's tomb at Machpelah. The brothers, still fearing vengeance, begin to doubt Joseph's sincerity and their fears return. In an attempt to guarantee their safety they send him a cleverly worded message: *In his last words to us before he died, your father gave us this message: "Say this to Joseph: I ask you to forgive your brothers' crime and wickedness; I know they did you harm."* [50:17]

Are they lying as they plead for their lives? *We beg you: forgive our crime, for we are servants of your father's God.* The ambiguity is very much a part of the comedy. It's akin to Potiphar's wife's invitation for him to make love to her - a test of his integrity. *Joseph replied, Do not be afraid. Am I in the place of God? You meant to do me harm; but God meant to bring good out of it by preserving the lives of many people, as we see today.* [50:20]. Joseph's last words embody the faith of the exiled reformers in Babylon. It is a grand comic tale, in which the Hebrew ancestors of the Jews have arrived in Egypt where they will be as much in exile as those who later sang their laments by the waters of Babylon.

11

EXODUS: RIGHTEOUSNESS AND THE ROAD FROM TRAGEDY TO COMEDY

I took the road less travelled by.

Robert Frost [1874-1963].

In compiling Exodus from old tribal sources, the exiles put together a comic tale of exile and deliverance and combined it with a theophany of the One True God at the giving of the Torah on Sinai, the source of the righteousness that guaranteed Jewish survival.

From the outset, there is wordplay. When the infant Moses is rescued from the bulrushes and Pharaoh's daughter adopts him as her son, *she names him Moses,* [Heb. Moshe] *for she said, I drew him out* [Heb. Mashah] *of the water.* [Ex. 2:10.] There is humour too in the way in which Pharaoh's attempts to oppress the Hebrews are continually frustrated, while God's plans for his people always come to fruition. Moses is abandoned for the crocodiles to eat, but is brought up under Pharaoh's nose!

It took Ten Plagues to persuade Pharaoh to let the Israelites go: the Nile turned to blood; frogs overwhelmed the land; then gnats, followed by flies; then came animal disease; after which boils, then hailstorms; eighthly, locusts devoured the harvest, then darkness covered Egypt until finally and most cruelly, the firstborn of man and beast died. Only then does Pharaoh let the Israelites go. Between the hail and the locusts God says: *I have made Pharaoh and his courtiers obdurate, so that I may show these signs among them, and so that you may tell your children and grandchildren the story: how I toyed with the Egyptians.* [10:2]. This is history as tragedy, and tragedy as comedy.

There is comedy throughout the entire Exodus account. For example: *The Lord said… If Pharaoh demands some portent from you, then … Take your staff and throw it down in front of Pharaoh, and it will turn into a serpent. When Moses and Aaron came to Pharaoh, they did as the Lord had told them; Aaron threw down his staff … and it turned into a serpent. At this Pharaoh summoned the wise men and the sorcerers, and the Egyptian magicians did the same thing by their spells, every man threw his staff down, and each staff turned into a serpent. But Aaron's staff swallowed up theirs.* [7:8ff]. The humour lies in the turning of the tables as the Egyptian magicians are upstaged by the faith of Moses and Aaron. It's a pattern of deliverance repeated as an intransigent Pharaoh is forced into submission by plague after plague. [7:14 – 12:32].

And there's further deliverance at the crossing of the Red Sea [14:5-29] where, at the moment the Egyptians trap the Hebrews against the impassable waters of the Red Sea,: *Moses stretched out his hand; and the Lord drove the sea back by a strong east wind all night, and made the sea dry land, and the waters were divided. And the people of Israel went into the midst of the sea on dry ground, the waters being a wall to them on their right hand and on their left.* [14:21]. And just as the Egyptians are about to catch up with them, Moses again stretches out his hand, the waters return and the Egyptians are drowned. Although it may be difficult for us today to see such tragedy as comedy, nevertheless, because all ends well for the Israelites it is how, without their using the word, the story would have been understood by those exiled in Babylon.

As the escaping Israelites began their journey to the Promised Land, again and again their situation looked desperate and each time disaster was averted by the intervention of God. Exodus could well be called The Book of Narrow Escapes. During the last of the plagues, the death of the first born, the Hebrew slaves were able to fend off the destroying angel by painting the blood of the Passover lamb on the door posts and lintels of their houses. [12:1-30].

Then in the wilderness, when the Israelites ran short of water at Marah, God rescued them once more by showing how to make its bitter water drinkable [15:22ff]. Later, when their food ran out, he sent a flock of quails [16:12]. This was followed by manna, the bread from heaven. Scrape after scrape is accompanied by rescue after rescue, each a much needed reassurance for the exiles in Babylon that the God who brought their ancestors out of Egypt would not forsake them.

Humour along the Way: The Burning Bush [Exodus 3:2]

The fire which lights us at a distance will burn us when near.
H. G. Bohn, A Handbook of Proverbs, 1855.

When tending the sheep of his father-in-law Jethro, priest of Midian, Moses led the flock along the west side of the wilderness and came to Horeb, the mountain of God. There an angel of the Lord appeared to him as a fire blazing out from a bush. Although the bush was on fire, it was not being burnt up. [Ex 3:2]

This is the humour of incongruity triggered by seeing the impossible: a bush that burns yet is not burnt! It is why in the Bible miracles are revelation by comedy and why in secular life a good conjurer can prove so entertaining.

In Gen. 15:17, the flaming torch seen by Abram symbolises the divine presence. The burning bush seen by Moses is clearly such a divine fire.[69]

The Comic Climax of the Book of Exodus: The Giving of the Law

Where laws end, tyranny begins.

William Pitt the Elder [1708-1778]

In the Exile's reform of Judah's religion, the future of the Jews depended upon their accepting their vocation as the Chosen People and their faithful observance of Torah. That vocation was set out in the first five books of the Bible. The climax of the book of Exodus comes when Moses meets with the One True God, the God of Abraham, Isaac and Jacob, the Hidden God of Isaiah, at Mount Sinai and receives the tablets of the Law bearing the Ten Commandments. These, together with 603 other commandments, defined the righteousness demanded by God. The whole programme for righteousness is there [20-23] and is the basis of the comic vision of Judaism down to today.

69 To the medieval Christian mind the burning bush seen by Moses was a symbol of love as charity. Erotic, or sexual, love was the love that burned and consumed. Charity was the divine love that burned and was not consumed.

12

TWO WAYS OF INTERPRETATION

It is my judgement that church interpretation [especially where historical criticism is concerned] has tended to trim and domesticate the text.

Walter Breuggemann. [b. 1933-]

Both Christians and Jews hold the stories of Genesis and Exodus to be central to their faith, yet read them in very different ways. For Christians, the Fall of Adam and Eve in Eden and the disasters that followed were the result of the couple's free choice in disobeying God. Theirs was a fall from innocence into a universal condition of sin from which the human race still awaits deliverance. On this interpretation there is a direct line which runs from The Fall of Adam to the world's salvation on that other tree, the Cross of Christ.

As often happened, the church in the east developed the doctrine differently from the church in the west. While in the west, with theologians like St Augustine, the Fall was the mother of all catastrophes, a perpetual wound in human nature, the Greek Fathers of the east tended to minimise its consequences, stressing human responsibility in resisting its effects. If the west emphasised bondage to sin, the east held that, though fallen, human beings remained essentially free.

In the western church, the human condition since the Fall is one of inherited enslavement to sin and a guilt compounded with helplessness. Christians in the East, on the other hand, were less forensic and content to emphasise the spiritual consequences of being born into a stricken world.

As we have seen, this way of doing theology reduced the Church's understanding of the Bible to philosophical abstractions. It is a very Greek way of treating a Hebrew text. The result has been that the stories on which theories of the human condition are based have been largely lost to view, surviving in the liturgy chiefly as evidence for the doctrines that replaced them. Whenever Christians read their Bible they are tempted to see it as a collection of proof texts for particular doctrines. This is *eisegesis*, reading meanings into a text rather than out of it.

One result of reading the Bible doctrinally is that its comedy shrivels. When it comes to humour, philosophers are not good at philosophising and Christian theologians long ago decided that they were God's philosophers. To this day, philosophers have no satisfactory theory of comedy. It is one reason why, while there is humour in the Bible, there is little in church doctrine, a fact that should keep theologians awake at night.

Fortunately, the Church still has its liturgical reading of the Bible as a defence against humourless theology. The worry here, however, is that as lessons read in church grow ever shorter in order to match supposed modern attention spans, congregations are deprived of whole stretches of scripture. In the Church of England, three lessons are appointed to be read at the Eucharist, but, to keep services short, the Old Testament lesson is often dropped. When Bible stories are lost, their comedy is lost as well.

To see more clearly the difference in approach between Jews and Christians, we need only look at what the rabbis made of Adam and Eve. Where Christians see evidence of a Fall from Primal Innocence and the Grace of God, the rabbis took a more oblique and playful approach. They noticed that in the Hebrew of Genesis 2, where, in verse 7, man is "formed" from the dust of the ground, the Hebrew word is וייצר [vayyitzer] and has two "yods," [the letter י], but in verse 19, where animals are created, the same verb has only one yod, ויצר [vayitzer]. The rabbis asked, "Why the difference?" Their explanation illustrates the difference between the rabbinic way of interpreting a text and the Christian.

The rabbis explained that there were two yods in describing human creation but only one for that of animals, because, while man has two yetzers, a *yetzer tov*, a good inclination, and a *yetzer ra,* an evil inclination, animals have only one yetzer, for unlike human beings they lack a moral sense and experience no moral conflict. This was a view of human nature far removed from the Christian Doctrine of Original Sin. The rabbis also believed that, when disciplined, the evil inclination could serve God. To love God with all the heart, [Deut. 6:5], meant loving him with both the evil and the good yetzers.

Finding meaning in the text by treating its letters playfully until they suggested some insight was a comic approach to the Bible that became a significant part of the rabbinic method. Like the Maccabees, the rabbis turned their back on Greek ways of thinking and developed instead the traditions of interpretation they had inherited from the Pharisees.

Once at a shiur I attended, the rabbi asked: "Why, in Genesis 6:9 is Noah described as "righteous and blameless," and in 7:1 only as "righteous'? No one came anywhere close to the answer of the sages which was that when God addressed Moses to his face [7:1] he received only one word of praise: he was "righteous;" but, when God spoke in his absence, he was both "righteous" and "blameless".

They deduced from this that we should give only part of the praise due to someone when they were present, but give them full praise in their absence. That sounded good advice, but when I explained it to a former teacher, she took issue with the rabbis. This was because many of the children she had taught had been deprived of praise from childhood so that further deprivation would do them no good at all. The discussion goes on! The rabbinic sages would have been delighted. The Bible exists to provoke spiritually informed debate about the great issues of life.

Midrash

> *Midrash: the discovery of meanings other than literal in the Bible.*
> The Encyclopedia of the Jewish Religion.

Jewish and Christian Bibles contain but a small selection of the total output of sacred texts in their communities. By the time the rabbis closed the canon of the Hebrew Scriptures, and the church decided the limits of the New Testament, dozens of books had been excluded from each. Together they reveal the vitality and diversity of the two faiths. The range of this non-canonical literature was enormous and it's important in helping set the Bible in its historical context. These excluded books also throw light on how Jews and Christians did their theology.

For Christians there were rival gospels, epistles and apocalypses. For Jews, there were apocalypses, wisdom writings, hymns and psalms, prayers, rule books and hagiographies. Much of these Jewish materials are commentary on, and interpretation of, biblical texts. They come in a number of varieties, for example, writings known as *pesher*[70] interpreted prophetic books as codes that required deciphering. Of this great body of Jewish interpretation and expansion of scripture, the category that most fascinates Christian scholars, and throws most light on our interest in The Bible as Comedy, is *Midrash.*

When Christian theologians began exploring their faith with the help of Greek philosophy, the rabbis had already developed their own distinctive way of interpreting scripture through *Midrash*, a Hebrew word meaning "exposition". The earliest Midrashim were concerned with Jewish law and are the legal rulings known as *halakhah*. But alongside these there grew up a non-legal kind of Midrash, imaginative, non-systematic and folksy, moral and spiritual,

70 Hebrew for "deciphering".

sometimes poetic and often amusing. These *haggadic Midrashim* form about a third of the Talmud and, apart from rational, Torah based jurisprudence, can be said to be the chief way Jews have done their theology. Unlike Christian theology, the Midrashim take up the easily overlooked comic aspects of the Hebrew Scriptures.

In the Midrashim of the 4th century Rabbi Tanhuma bar Abba, we find this tongue in cheek observation, "Four things make a man age prematurely: fear, anger, children, and a bad-tempered wife", while a Midrash on Proverbs advises, "Give the wise a wink, the fool a fist". In the Genesis Rabbah we are advised, "Even if all of a slander is not believed, half of it will be." A great deal of Midrash is theology as insight as well as theology as comedy. A Midrash on the Psalms observed that, "the prosperity that the wicked enjoy here is a measure of the rewards that the righteous will receive in the hereafter." And when it comes to the study of history, the Midrash Tanhumma has this: "Many pens are broken and seas of ink consumed, to describe things that never happened".

Midrash is the human face of theology, as in this Mekilta midrash on Exodus: "To welcome a fellow man is to welcome the Shekhinah", the Shekhinah[71] being the Divine Presence. Midrash seldom strayed far from a biblical sense of comedy: "The stone fell on the pitcher? Woe to the Pitcher. The pitcher fell on the stone? Woe to the pitcher." [Esther Rabbah].

Midrash is also theology as wisdom which theology as philosophy has forgotten even though the word "philosophy" means "love of wisdom." "Don't try to identify the Tree of Knowledge," advised the Genesis Rabbah, "you may cast suspicion on someone who is innocent."

Unlike philosophical theology, Midrash is non-rational. It darts from thought to thought finding subtle and surprising connections between the unconnected. It was this, it has been suggested, that prompted Freud to create "word association" as a psycho-analytical tool: "Life is a passing shadow," says Scripture. The shadow of a tower or of a tree? No: the shadow of a bird – for when a bird flies away, there is neither shadow nor bird". [Genesis Rabbah].

If Christians have heard of Midrash at all, it is probably the following example that they have in mind, and deservedly as it packs whole volumes of moral theology. After the Israelites crossed the Red Sea, it's said that God rebuked the angels for joining in the song of

---

71 In Hebrew, Shekhinah means "indwelling". It derives from verses like Exodus 25:8 which have to do with God dwelling with his people. It is used by later Rabbis in the Talmud as a way of avoiding direct mention of the name of God.

victory sung by Moses and Miriam [Exodus 15]. God said, "My children are drowning and would you rejoice?" The rabbis clearly found the Bible too triumphalist at this point and humanised it with compassion and wit. It's a glorious way to do theology!

There were even midrashim to argue that midrash might need defending when it came to discerning theological truth: "Let not a simple parable seem trivial in your eyes, for through it you acquire an insight into the complex law." [Song of Songs Rabbah]. It is clear from this example that with his love of parables, Jesus was very much a Jew in the Midrashic tradition.

New Testament scholars have become increasingly interested in the relation of Midrash to the gospels, Midrashim usually being a reflection on a particular text. In his 1996 book, "*Liberating the Gospels, Reading the Gospel through Jewish Eyes*, John Shelby Spong [1931-], the retired American Episcopalian bishop of Newark, argued that the gospel accounts of the nativity and resurrection of Jesus were Midrashim on his life and teaching. In my view, this is an argument too far, in that Spong over-extends the non-rational category of Midrash to argue for a rationalist reduction of the gospels to non-historical documents. One effect of this is to leave the comic elements in the gospels without any historic means of support.

Midrash and Christian Theology

> *What has Athens to do with Jerusalem or the Academy with the Church?*
>
> Tertullian [c 160-c 225] *De Prescriptione.*

Just when, how and why Church and Synagogue separated into rival religions remain questions for scholarly debate. What is certain is that after the fall of Jerusalem they came to define themselves over against each other, a process familiar to sociologists. As they developed, both faiths needed to make sense of their changing identities.

In the Church, individuals and groups attempted this by writing gospels and epistles as well as a variety of other works, some of which remain important in exploring the origins of mainstream Christianity – works like the Letters of St Ignatius and the Shepherd of Hermas. Others, less mainstream, for example the gospels of Judas and Thomas, represented theology done on the margins of orthodoxy. Alongside this way of doing theology, there developed another which, leaving behind its Jewish roots, preferred to do its thinking in Greek philosophy. Tertullian [c160-c225], the Father of

Latin theology, was opposed to this way of doing theology, even though his own style of argument was from the world of classical paganism. "What', he asked, "has Athens to do with Jerusalem, or the Academy with the Church?" Nevertheless, the emerging Christian creeds, though derived from the Jewish world of the New Testament were phrased in the language of Athens and the Academy.

A number of things followed from this: the first was that humour and comedy disappeared from Christian theology. This dehumanised it, for when we lose hold on life's comic aspects we forfeit some of our humanity. Because in the synagogue theology was done in the popular, biblical style of storytelling it remained nearer the people; while in the Church theology became increasingly the preserve of an educated clergy, separated from the people, most of whom could recite the creeds but not explain them, a situation that to a large extent remains to this day!

Christian theology is nowadays largely confined to the universities and is unintelligible to most churchgoers. To what extent this path will be followed in the Synagogue, now that many Jews talk of "doing theology", remains to be seen. But for the present, humour and the comic sense of life remain more at home in a synagogue than a church.

Storytelling and the Inevitability of Biblical Humour

> *Adequately set forth, the history of the princess Taik and of the virtuous youth occupies all the energies of an agile storyteller for seven weeks.*
>
> Ernest Bramah [E.B.Smith] 1868-1942.

During my teens, Ernest Bramah's Chinese storyteller, Kai Lung, was among my favourite fictional characters. His humour was understated and his stories improbable; yet they fixed in my mind the realisation that, to be successful, stories require some element of comedy and wit, while the storyteller needs to be a bit of an actor. Storytellers are entertainers who must engage their listeners. This is true for the Bible as its stories were part of an oral tradition long before they were written down.

"Form Criticism" is the academic study of biblical passages which are believed to have been originally passed on orally. Those who wrote them down as part of the larger narrative are known as "redactors". The study of their methods is called "Redaction Criticism." Much has been written on Form and Redaction Criticism but little of it seems to have been aware of the comedy and humour in the biblical text. Nor has there been any really serious attempt to understand the function of biblical humour.

Another of Ernest Bramah's characters, Kin Yen, the Picture Maker, says of one story, "the whole narrative is permeated with the odour of joss-sticks and honourable high-mindedness". He could have had in mind those Bible commentators who write for fellow academics while missing what would have delighted the story's first audience.

Questioning the Bible

Questions are never indiscreet. Answers sometimes are.
Oscar Wilde [1854-1900]

Of any book that has as much claimed on its behalf as the Bible, a key question is always: "Can you build a civilisation on it?" As history is littered with failed books that once looked promising in this regard, it''s an important question.

In spite of growing secularisation, western culture is still very much a civilisation built on the Bible. No one can understand the west, either its social and political history, or its cultural and intellectual frameworks, without a working knowledge of the Bible. The loss of the Bible in our educational system has resulted in widespread cultural impoverishment as well as a spiritual vacuum at the heart of secularised lives. It was hoped by 19th century secularists that great literature, great music, and great painting would fill the gap. Instead we have Consumerism and Celebrity Culture!

Others hoped that *Das Kapital* would serve as an alternative source of values; but, in the end, that too failed. Perhaps the trouble lay in its version of history as comedy but with a lack of humour as well as its inability to change the hearts of its readers as well as their minds. Where there is no comedy, there is no humanity, and without it these all books which have some design on people's souls are doomed to fail. Books which cannot be chuckled at cannot easily be questioned: Chairman Mao's *On the Elimination of Contradiction Among the People,* or Hitler's *Mein Kampf,* are books that ended up devouring lives. Whenever, the Bible has been reduced to that kind of soul-devouring literature the consequences have been disastrous. One way to hold the door open on the Bible's humanity is to see it as both a Divine and a Human Comedy.

Not only is the Bible the most read book in history, it is also the most questioned. It even questions itself. We could say that its humour is its first level of criticism. The Bible becomes spiritually dangerous when its readers feel that it is so holy as to be above criticism.

When John Bunyan [1628-88] and William Cowper [1731-1800] read their Bible, they found there John Calvin's doctrine of Double Predestination which served only to exacerbate their proneness to depression. This was the belief that God, in his inscrutable wisdom, predestined some to salvation and others to damnation. If ever there were doctrines that needed humanising by biblical humour it was these doctrines of election and predestination. Without humour, Bible reading would be insupportable. As beings buckling under the combined weight of our creaturely nature and our Maker's majesty, we would be crushed. What saves us is our knowledge of his love for us and the sense of humour without which we could not survive as his creatures.

The Bible and Meditation

The Art of Meditation constituted one of the great developments in European Culture.

Louis Martz [1919-2007] *The Poetry of Meditation.*

Humour and comedy are often the result of meditation. Thanks to Louis Martz', *The Poetry of Meditation*, I came to appreciate what a difference the Christian art of meditation made to western cultural life in the 15th to 17th centuries, and even beyond into the 19th. Meditation was not only powerful prayerfully but it also greatly sharpened Christian perception. At its heart was the Bible, as readers who followed the exercises of writers like St Ignatius Loyola [c1491-1556], used feeling and understanding to enter imaginatively into its text. I found it of immense help myself, not only in prayer but also in writing poetry. It even changed the way I walked the dog, noticing things I would otherwise have missed; and it changed most of all the way I read my Bible and listened to lessons as they were read in church.

It became very clear too, that Jesus meditated. And like poets before and after him, he also meditated on nature. With that realisation came an example of George Herbert's promised surprise, an example sprung by Christ himself, one about which commentators can be coy and polite society resort to euphemism.

In Matthew 15:17, it's clear that Jesus meditated on what happens in the "loo" if you are English middle-class, "toilet" if you're working class or the "bathroom" if you're an American.

When the Pharisees tackled Jesus about his disciples eating with unwashed hands, he changed the subject and said to the crowd gathered to overhear a good dispute: *Listen and understand! No one is defiled by what goes into his mouth, only what comes out of it.* Later, in an earthy image, he explained to Peter, *do you not see that whatever goes in by the mouth passes into the stomach and so is discharged into the drain?*

The point Jesus was making was that it was not what went into a man's mouth that defiled him but what came out of it from the heart. His meditation was preserved because in the early church, gentile Christians no longer had to watch what they ate, only what they said.

Christ's meditation has a certain ironic component because of the way in which he makes physical uncleanness teach moral cleanliness. Again, it is not enough to make us laugh, but it is enough to make us smile, providing of course we are not coy, in which case it will make us squirm.

Comedy as an Oblique and One-Sided Approach to the Bible

> *The world is a comedy to those who think, a tragedy to those who feel.*
>
> Horace Walpole [1717-1797]

While approaching the Bible through comedy like this gives a somewhat biased view, it's also a profitable one. Because biblical authors always had God before their minds, it can also only ever be one that is tragic in part. Overall, prophesying as it does eventual fulfilment and justice for the world, the Bible is inevitably a comedy. We must take the Bible as we find it and not how we think it should be. Arguments of what Victorians called "antecedent probability" are the temptation here. These are the arguments that say, "if it is this then it's probably that", when it does not necessarily follow. Once it is said that the Bible "is" the Word of God then, some will argue, it cannot contain error or mistakes. It must be always literally true.

To many it sounds a reasonable argument, especially when voiced with sincerity, that God will communicate to us only what is absolutely the case. All we need are a humble heart and a readiness to obey. Who are we, it is said, to stand in judgement over the revealed Word of God?

Yet, the Bible will not allow us to see things that way. Except for its legal decrees and prophecies, it does not purport to be collection of divine utterances, however much we think it should be. It's a book with a history, marked with the scars of history. Most of all, it has comedy and there are conclusions that comedy does not encourage us to assume. For all that the Bible is, in some way, The Word of God, it is also a very human book. Its comedy will not allow us to abandon that thought. Bibliolatry is one more idolatry.

13

WE CAN TAKE OUR FAITH TOO SERIOUSLY

Wit is abrupt, darting, scornful and tosses its analogies into your face; humour is slow and shy, insinuating its fun into your heart.

E. P. Whipple, Literature and Life.

One Easter long ago, I answered the phone to a caller who wished to complain about a cartoon in a local newspaper in which Jesus was shown entering a restaurant and booking a table for thirteen. "It's blasphemous," he said, and launched an attack on "these people," and demanded I complain to the editor.

'Humour's a funny thing," I said. "What was one of the first things Jesus did after his resurrection?" "You tell me," he snapped. "You're the expert!" So I told him: "he cracked a joke!" He grew angrier. "Is this what they teach you in college nowadays? No wonder people don't go to church!" and he slammed his phone down. The joke was that mentioned here in the Preface!

The Playfulness of Old Testament Hebrew

Because of the leisure that goes with contemplation, the Divine Wisdom itself, Holy Scripture says, "is always at play, playing through the whole world."

St Thomas Aquinas [c1225-74]. *Commentary on Proverbs* 8:30ff.

Most of the humour in the Bible comes under the heading of *paronomasia,* or word play, usually a kind of pun. A pun is a play on the double meaning of a word, making us either laugh or groan depending on the level of surprise. The more contrived the pun, the louder the groan!

Although today the pun invites only groans, few can resist them. My own favourite was an advertisement in a camping shop which, flattering its readers' knowledge of Shakespeare, read: *Now is the discount of our winter tents.* Almost as good is the joke about the disciple of the Maharishi who had a wisdom tooth extracted without anaesthetic because he wanted to "*transcend dental medication*". And, when in 2008, John Coward, co-pilot of a BA Boeing 777, skilfully crash-landed his stricken plane at Heathrow airport saving the lives of all on board, the *Sun* newspaper could not resist a little paronomasia and led with the headline, *COWARD IS A HERO.*

Perhaps the Victorians loved puns too much for present tastes, but who could resist Sir Charles Napier's one word telegram to London on his conquest of the Indian province of Sind, *Peccavi!* I have sinned! The Old Testament loved this sort of thing.

An Evening of Puns and Riddles

> *Man only plays when in the full meaning of the word he is man, and he is only completely man when he plays.*
>
> Friedrich Schiller [1759-1805].

A Christian Arab I knew once invited me to his home. I was made welcome as only Arab hospitality can welcome a guest. After a splendid meal, the entire family of thirty or more, of all ages, formed a circle for conversation, during which grandfather suggested we play a game. I expected charades but for a good hour or so we exchanged puns and riddles – and to my astonishment– it was played in English! To my shame, when it was my turn I could offer nothing better than the old English playground riddle, "What is it that goes ninety-nine, plonk! Ninety-nine plonk?" The answer, which they didn't seem to know, was a centipede with a wooden leg!

Their puns were often very clever. Were they used in local schools in teaching English, I wondered? When my turn came again, I was thrown back on my knowledge of the Bible and I asked them Samson's riddle, in Judges 14: "*Out of the eater came something to eat; out of the strong came something sweet.*" And, because they knew their Bibles, they knew the answer: "*What is sweeter than honey? What is stronger than the lion?"* [14:18]. One of the teenagers told how, after Samson had killed the lion at the vineyards of Timnath, he returned to find a swarm of bees had made their hive in its carcass. Braving the bees, Samson scraped out some of the honey to share with his parents. There were nods of approval all round the room. They even knew that Samson's lion and bees, with the words, *Out of the strong came forth sweetness,* were the trade mark on a tin of Tate and Lyle's Golden Syrup which, in the days of the Mandate, had been sold throughout the British Empire!

The love of words I found that evening and the fun to be had from them was biblical through and through. Perhaps it was the sort of evening Jesus had enjoyed. Judah and Galilee of his day, with a synagogue and school in most villages, meant that the Jews were the first people who could boast of universal education, with the Torah and the prophets for textbooks.

When Isaiah said [5:1], *I shall sing for my beloved my love song about his vineyard*, he was casting his prophecy as a riddle, explaining [v7] that the vineyard of the Lord of Hosts was Israel, Judah the plant he cherished. Riddles are comedy as games. Is life the riddle God plays with us and religion the game we play with God?

Struggling to Retain Humour in Translation

Translation is at best an echo
George Borrow. *The Bible in Spain*.

Immanuel L Casanowicz's, *Paronomasia in the Old Testament* lists more than 500 examples of wordplay in the Hebrew Scriptures; while Elbert Russell's *Paronomasia and Kindred Phenomena in the New Testament,* gives a further 200 examples, mostly from the gospels. Considering that parts of the Bible, like Leviticus and Revelation, have little use for verbal fun this means that entire sections of other books radiate with it.

Unfortunately, this kind of verbal jesting is easily lost in translation, though occasionally a good translation preserves something of the joke. For example, in the Genesis account [2:23] of the creation of woman from the rib of the first man, the Hebrew pun is mirrored in the English because of the way in which the word "man" forms part of the word "woman." The Hebrew pun works in the same way. *Adam said, this is now bone of my bones, and flesh of my flesh; she shall be called Woman [ishshâ], because she was taken out of Man [îsh].* Having to explain the pun like this all but kills the joke that survives the translation; but the pun is there and knowing that changes our attitude to the text.

Prophets and their love of punning

A pun is a pistol let off at the ear; not a feather to tickle the intellect.
Charles Lamb [1775-1834]. *Popular Fallacies*.

Even the weakest pun is an intellectual conceit delighting some and annoying others. My own discovery of the love of the prophets for puns happened when I was a student studying the prophet Amos [8:1]: *Thus the Lord God showed me: Behold a basket of summer fruit [qayits]. And he said, "Amos, what do you see?" And I said, "A basket of [qayits] summer fruit." Then the Lord said to me, the end [qets] has come upon my people Israel."* The word play here is on *qayits* and *qets.* The impending destruction, the *qets* of Israel, is suggested to the prophet's sense of humour by a basket of *qayits,* summer fruits. So that the reader won't miss the working of the prophet's mind, the RSV provides helpful footnotes.

When the nation is threatened with defeat and captivity, Amos wraps the news in a quip. There's more than questionable taste involved in this way of communicating a message – there's also something of our third theory of humour, ambiguity. There is ambiguity in a prophet trying to be funny-clever with impending disaster; and there is further ambiguity when we find the Word of God wrapped in the word of man as comedian.

It is possible that this is how the prophetic imagination sometimes worked. For example, early in his ministry, Jeremiah was contemplating an almond tree. As we'll discover with Jesus, prophets and poets are similar in their ability to concentrate their attention creatively on everyday things. On this occasion the prophet was focusing his attention on an almond tree [Jer. 1:11]. *The word of the Lord came to me, saying, "Jeremiah, what do you see?" And I said, I see [shaqed] a rod of almond. Then the Lord said to me, "You have seen well, for I am [shoqed] watching over my word to perform it."* Again, with its tiny superscript letters the Revised Standard Version of the Bible alerts the reader to the pun, as does the Oxford Revised English Study Bible. For this reason, I've always advised that godparents buy those being confirmed not only a Bible that contains the Apocrypha but a version with study notes.

The King James Version

> *Great and manifold were the blessings, most dread Sovereign, which Almighty God, the Father of all mercies, bestowed upon us the people of England, when first he sent your Majesty's Royal person to rule and reign over us.... But among all our joys, there was none that more filled our hearts than the blessed continuance of the preaching of God's sacred Word among us.*
>
> Preface to the Authorised Version of the Bible, 1611.

With the helpful footnotes of modern translations there is little excuse for the belief that the Bible is a book without humour, a prejudice we owe to the Authorised Version of 1611.

When King James I commissioned a new translation of the Bible he also solved a political problem. He did not want it to give his subjects politically unsettling ideas which Bibles with explanatory notes might do. He believed that translations with footnotes all had axes to grind.

The new Bible must be allowed to speak for itself. Any explanations that were needed would be given in sermons preached by clergy appointed by bishops who would be appointed by the king. James had his way and the translation that is called after him won universal acclaim for its accuracy and style. It failed, however, in one respect in that it gave the reader little idea of the wit and comic innuendo found in the original Hebrew and Greek. For example, when Hagar, the slave wife of Abraham, is sent into wilderness with her son Ishmael, the text of Genesis says that, *God heard the child crying;* the Hebrew, *God has heard*, is a pun on Ishmael's name, [21:17]. More humorously, in Deuteronomy 32:15, *Jeshurun,* which means "an upright man" is found as a variant of Jacob, Israel's first name; and Jacob, the trickster, as we are told, was anything but upright!

Reading the Lessons in Church and Synagogue

> *"That's the reason they're called lessons," the Gryphon remarked: "because they lessen from day to day."*
>
> Lewis Carroll [1832-1898], Alice in Wonderland.

It might be thought that when the Law and the Prophets are read in synagogue that worshippers would be more aware of the wordplay than are Christians hearing the same lessons read in church; but this seems not to be the case. In Orthodox synagogues I've attended, the pace of the readings is so rapid that Jewish congregations are no more alert to the sparkle of the text than are Christian. Interesting wordplay will need to be explained in the sermon. In some synagogues, worshippers will be given a copy of Dr J. H. Hertz's helpful *Chumash*, in which the Hebrew text is printed with the English Translation and a Commentary. Turning to my own copy, I see that in his note for Genesis 3:20 where Adam calls his wife Eve (her name in English), her name in Hebrew is *Havvah*, which means "life". The text itself tells us that this was because "she was the mother of all living," but Hertz corrects this in a note to read that she was "the mother of all humankind", paradoxically undermining the attempt in English to leave the pun on her name intact!

Fun with Serious Words in the Apocrypha

And the other Books [as Hierome saith] the Church doth read for example of life and instruction of manners but yet doth it not apply them to establish any doctrine.

Article 6 of the 39 Articles of the Church of England.

Because the books of the Apocrypha are mostly Greek translations, it is not surprising that word-play there is rarer than in the original Hebrew. Nevertheless, there are examples in the one chapter work, *Susannah,* which was added to the book of Daniel in order to emphasise Daniel's wisdom.

Often described as the world's "first detective story", Susannah is a virtuous young Jewish woman, falsely brought to trial and accused of adultery by two respectable elders whose advances she had rejected. Daniel defends her honour and questions the elders separately. He asks them under which tree the sin had been committed. As they each identify a different tree Susannah is acquitted and her accusers put to death as prescribed in the Torah, *you shall then do to him as he had meant to do to his brother.* [Deut. 19:18-21]. Their fate is both comedy and irony because what they had intended for her they had brought on themselves.

In the Greek of the Apocrypha, Daniel asks, *under which tree did you see them together?* In the Revised English Version the word play is preserved: the elder answered, *Under a clove tree* [*schinon*]. Daniel said, *Very good. This lie has cost you your life, for already God's angel has received your sentence from God, and he will cleave [schisei] you in two.* A footnote points to the wordplay on "clove" and "cleave".

Daniel's interrogation of the second elder also involves a play on words. "*Under what tree did you surprise them together?" The elder replied, "Under a yew tree." [prînon] Daniel tells him, This lie has cost you your life, for the angel of God is waiting, sword in hand, to hew [prisai] you down and destroy the pair of you."* Again, a footnote explains that "yew" and "hew" translate a play on words in the Greek. It's pure luck that the word play is brought out naturally in the English translation.

Revelation and the Human Delight in Wit

His foe was folly and his weapon wit.

An inscription to W.S.Gilbert, by Anthony Hope.

Puns are a kind of wit, the lowliest kind many think. Some argue that they are lower even than sarcasm. Yet they are universal. Not even *New Scientist* can resist their appeal! In an article on 24th November 2007, on *The Origin of Laughter* there is this: "*Father [reprovingly], "Do you know what happens to liars when they die?" Johnny: "Yes sir, they lie still.*"

In an age when joyless fundamentalism is proving such a spiritual and political temptation, this reminder that the Bible is rooted in the fun-loving side of human nature as well as in the serious, is timely and welcome. The fact that even in its most serious passages there is an attempt to raise a knowing smile says something about the nature of the sacred and the danger of taking it too seriously. To spot a pun in a sacred text is to have its writer intrude, taking attention away from some serious point, only for us to discover, moments later, that the point has been emphasised by the very distraction. With Amos and Jeremiah the revelation is often in the pun! The prophet is showing off with his word games, very human games but through which God is revealed. Humour humanises the Bible.

14

MOVING ON FROM THE PUN: IRONY, SATIRE AND BEYOND

L'ironie est le fond du caractère de la Providence.
[Irony is the very substance of Providence.]
Honoré de Balzac [1799-1850]
Eugénie Grandet.

The range of humour available to us today is vastly greater than in Jesus' time. Since the 1960s, *Postmodernism* has been the label given to those aspects of western culture that are believed to define it. Until recently it was impossible to escape the word, even though it was so catch-all a concept that it made more sense to talk of postmodernisms. Within those postmodernisms the subject, as a personal self, was deemed to have disappeared even though narcissism and self-knowingness were everywhere, and the boundaries between traditional categories so breached as to make talk of them meaningless. All world-views were declared redundant, including the Christian. Any "privileged" standpoint was swallowed up in the idea of knowledge as "play" and human existence was reduced to a kind of comedy in which the dominant category was "irony." Irony was everywhere life's primary expression. Nothing could be understood clearly because everything was perceived as ironic including the selfhood of the knower. The last quarter of the 20th century was a perfect opportunity, therefore, for a perplexed Christian to become familiar with the presence of irony in the Bible.

A dictionary definition will usually point to the comic difference between expectation and revelation: in what a word generally means and what in context it actually means. In Dramatic irony the difference is between what the characters on stage know and what the audience knows. In Socratic irony, the questioner pretends to ignorance in order to expose someone's misunderstanding.

In my first parish, whenever I showed visitors the grave of James Smithies, and explained how, at Waterloo, he had survived the greatest cavalry charge in British history only to be knocked down and killed in old age by a local horse, people would say, "That was ironic". Fate, we know, often is, but what of God?

Irony in the Hebrew Scriptures

As philosophers claim that no true philosophy is possible without doubt, so by the same token one may claim that no authentic human life is possible without irony.
Søren Kierkegaarde [1813-55]

The Bible's first irony [Gen. 3:1ff] is a clever one in which truth is put into the mouth of the serpent, the father of lies. When the serpent tempted Eve he was at his most subtle. How clever can irony get? As clever as the serpent in Eden.

Similar irony is attributed to God at the Tower of Babel [Gen. 11:1-9]. God says, *Behold they are one people, and they have all one language; and this is only the beginning of what they will do; and nothing they now propose will be impossible to them*. Whether the writers realised it or not, in this most prescient of insights into human knowledge, there is irony in God's irony, for there is irony in what God does not say; and which, being God, he does not need to spell out because he already knows it! *Nothing they now propose will be impossible to them*. Everything human beings have ever wanted to do: fly, create the ultimate weapon, create undreamed of wealth, devise ever more sophisticated machines, and not only to understand nature, including our own, but to adapt nature to our dreams and will – in brief, to play at being God – all this we have done and as a result we worry about where it's taking us. And it's all there ready to unfold in the story of the Tower of Babel, and foretold with terrifyingly accurate puns and irony. It's arguable that the teasing, irony and other comic elements in the first eleven chapters of Genesis shield us from full exposure to the spiritual terrors they mask.

Revelation and Irony

What gods will deliver us from all these ironies?
Friedrich Schlegel [1772-1829]

With puns it is usually easy for the reader to make a connection between the Bible's love of word games and revelation. With irony it's different. Irony does more than embellish a text. Even in a postmodern world which understands itself as all "surface", irony is a vehicle for communicating the human condition's problematical and inescapable depths. In the Bible, ironies function like images in parallel mirrors.

In the psalms, the comic image of the man who falls into a pit he has dug for someone else is an ironic thought that delights the godly again and again. *The nations have plunged into pits of their own making, their feet are entangled in the net they have hidden*. [Ps 9:15]. Like the financial wizards of 2007, made bankrupt by their own sorcery in 2008, there was something troublingly satisfying in this comic image – unworthy, tragic, but satisfying all the same!

Irony was also loved by the Bible's wisdom writers, the sages. These were Israel's intellectuals and proto-scientists. With their rational and considered approach to faith they were frequently in conflict with the prophets. They advised the king, and were responsible for educating the civil service and running the diplomatic corps. Predictably, they tended to be conservative in their calculating ways. The prophets were more radical and, claiming to speak under direct inspiration from God, often had more authority. If the prophets liked puns, then the sages favoured irony. The sages were also more likely to question current expressions of religious faith, which is why Ecclesiastes is one of the least read books of the Bible, among Jews as well as among Christians. On the ever shifting boundaries between faith and doubt, we find the writer of Job, arguably the most irony-ridden writing in scripture, using irony in Job's reply [12:1] to Zophar. Zophar had exhorted Job to repent, suggesting that his troubles were less than he deserved at the hands of a just God whose ways were deep and past finding out. Job said to his friends, *No doubt you are intelligent people, and when you die, wisdom will perish!* There is no doubting the sarcasm here. Sarcasm is irony in which apparent praise is really an insult. It is the kind of irony that would be recognised in every school playground and office in England. "Sarcasm I now see to be in general, the language of the Devil," said Thomas Carlyle in *Sartor Resartus*.

When the book of Job was written, the worlds of the wisdom writers and the prophets were in crisis. The social structures which supported them had been so shaken, that when Job says, *when you die, wisdom will die with you*, his words are so saturated with tragic irony as to go far beyond mere sarcasm. Doubts about the wisdom movement's future haunt his words. The author knows that if he cannot come up with an answer for the problem of why the righteous suffer in a world that rests in the hands of a righteous and all powerful God, then wisdom will perish with the death of his friends.

No literary device illuminates the darkness of human existence as well as irony. The book ends with God's reply to Job. As Job was sarcastic with his friends so now God is sarcastic with Job, who gets what he deserves. The biter is bit. *Brace yourself and stand up like a man; I shall put questions to you, and you must answer.*

Would you dare deny that I am just, or put me in the wrong to prove yourself right. Job is compelled to consider the great beasts, "Behemoth" and "Leviathan" whose existence wisdom cannot explain. Job submits but the only answer he receives is irony wrapped in irony. All the ironies of the book are wrapped in the easily overlooked irony of the prologue; for the whole tale is after all only a joke, a wager between God and the Satan[72], the Prosecutor whose job was to accuse human beings in the court of heaven.

Job as the Old Testament's Serious Joke

You have heard of the patience of Job.
The Epistle of James [5:11]

Because meaningless suffering is more than most humans can bear, the book of Job tackles the question of how an all powerful, all loving God can give meaning to existence in the sufferings of the righteous. If he is all loving, how can he stand by and do nothing? Could it be he's not all powerful? Again, if he's all powerful and does nothing to help, how can he be all-loving? This is the Problem of Theodicy, the problem of the righteousness of God.

By wrapping Job's sufferings in layers of irony then packaging his troubles as a divine comedy in which, at the end, everything turns out well, the book of Job leaves us wondering if this is not all the humour of incongruity. We, the reader, asked for bread and are given a stone! Job's afflictions are mischievously explored yet at the end we are no wiser. There is no answer to the darkest puzzle of a believer's existence. Irony has done all it can and, like the wisdom movement itself, plays itself out with little to show for the trouble it has taken.

Divine Trickery: The Darkest Comedy of all

Dare to be true: nothing can need a lie.
George Herbert [1593-1633]

If setting the problem of righteous suffering within the story of a

---

72 Originally, Satan was a legal officer in the High Court of Heaven. God was the Judge, the Satan was the Prosecutor. This was his role in the book of Job. Later, when apocalyptic began to displace prophecy, the role was demonised, and Satan became chief among the angels who had rebelled against God.

wager between God and Satan failed to reach the bedrock of truth, then the account of the Prophet Micaiah and King Ahab is one to make us dig yet another deep hole. [I Kings 22.]

Jehoshaphat of Judah, the king of "jumping" fame in that mildest of Victorian expletives, was asked by King Ahab of Israel for military help in his attempt to retake the city of Ramoth-gilead[73] from the Aramaeans. Jehoshaphat replied with typical middle-eastern extravagance, *What's mine is yours: myself, my people and my horses, but,* he said, *first let us seek counsel from the Lord.*

As the kings sat side by side on their thrones, the court prophets of Ahab were sent for, four hundred of them, and the comedy began. The prophets were unanimous, *Attack,* they said, *the Lord will deliver it into your majesty's hands.* Impressive though their unanimity was, Jehoshaphat was not convinced, thinking perhaps that such a grand display had been engineered by Ahab. *Is there no other prophet of the Lord here through whom we may seek guidance?* He asked. *There is one more,* the king of Israel replied, in one of the Bible's great comic passages: *there is one more through whom we may seek guidance of the Lord, but I hate the man, because he never prophesies good for me, never anything but evil. His name is Micaiah son of Imlah.*

What follows is cast in the language of ancient diplomacy. Jehoshaphat says, with mock horror, *My Lord King, let no such word pass your lips*. But it did and the king of Israel called one of his eunuchs and told him to fetch Micaiah with all speed.

When later the kings reconvene at the main gate of Samaria and watch the prophets put on another show, one of the prophets, Zedekiah son of Kenaanah, having made for himself a pair of iron horns to dramatise his prophecy, said to the kings, *This is the word of the Lord: with horns like these you will gore the Aramaeans and make an end to them;* at which point, the prophets all come in on Zedekiah's side, backing his message: *Attack Ramoth-gilead,* they chorus, *and win the day; the Lord will deliver it into your hands.* [22:12]

The messenger sent to fetch Micaiah reported that the prophets had unanimously given the king a favourable answer. *And mind you agree with them*, he added. *"As the Lord lives," said Micaiah, "I shall say only what the Lord tells me to say."*

When he came into the king's presence, the king asked, *Micaiah, shall I attack Ramoth-gilead, or shall I refrain?* It's here that whoever is reading the lesson must pack his voice with sarcasm if the

---

73 Ramoth-gilead, "The Heights of Gilead," was a strategic fortress east of the river Jordan.

story's comedy is to be preserved. *"Attack, and win the day," Micaiah replied, "the Lord will deliver it into your hands."* But the king knows his dissident prophet too well. *How often must I adjure you, said the king, to tell me nothing but the truth in the name of the Lord.* At that Micaiah turns on the poetry:[74]

I saw all Israel scattered on the mountains,
like sheep without a shepherd,
and I heard the Lord say,
They have no master;
let them go home in peace.

Those words, *I heard the Lord say, "They have no master;"* is a hint that Ahab will be killed if he goes into battle. But as politicians do, when given advice they do not like, he waves it away: *the king of Israel said to Jehoshaphat, "Did I not tell you that he never prophesies good for me, never anything but evil."* It is then that the prophecy of Micaiah becomes for today's Bible reader very problematical indeed.

Micaiah went on, *Listen now to the word of the Lord; I saw the Lord seated on his throne, with all the host of heaven in attendance on his right and on his left. The Lord said, "Who will entice Ahab to go up and attack Ramoth-gilead?" One said one thing and one another, until a spirit came forward and, standing before the Lord, said, "I shall entice him." "How?" said the Lord, "I shall go out," he answered and be a lying spirit in the mouths of all his prophets. "Entice him; you will succeed," said the Lord. "Go and do it'*[75]. Is Micaiah speaking the truth? Did he have such a vision? Or is he playing his opponents' game? It is an image of God as darkly comic as that found in the prologue of Job.

Micaiah says to Ahab, *You see then, how the Lord has put a lying spirit in the mouths of all these prophets of yours for he has*

---

[74] The prophets often delivered their oracles in poetry, as the page layout will show in the Revised Standard Version and other modern translations of the Bible.

[75] "It is distinctly taught that man should not imitate God in the following four things, which he alone can use as his instruments. They are, jealousy [Dt. 6:5], revenge, [Ps 94:1] exaltation [Exod. 15:21; Ps 93:1] and acting in devious ways." Schechter p 204. God may use these for comic outcomes, but when used by man and women it results in tragedy.

decreed disaster for you. And as Micaiah implied that Zedekiah was lying, *Zedekiah strikes him in the face. "How did the spirit of the Lord pass from me to speak to you?" he demanded. Micaiah says, "That you will find out when you run into an inner room to hide."*

The tension is broken when Ahab orders Micaiah to be arrested and committed to the custody of Amon, the Governor of Samaria and Joash, the king's son. "*Throw this fellow into prison," he said, and put him on a prison diet of bread and water until I come home in safety." Micaiah tells him: "If you do return in safety, the Lord has not spoken by me."*

With Micaiah safely locked up, Ahab and Jehoshaphat march against Ramoth-gilead. Yet they do not completely ignore the prophet's advice, because Ahab enters battle in disguise. He says to Jehoshaphat, *I shall disguise myself to go into battle, but you must wear your royal robes*

However, their enemy, the king of Aram, had a battle plan and *ordered the thirty two captains of his chariots not to engage all and sundry, but the king of Israel alone.*

For a while, Ahab must have thought his plan was working and that he was fooling both the enemy and God, for when the *captains saw Jehoshaphat, they thought he was the king of Israel and turned to attack him, but Jehoshaphat cried out, and when the captains saw that he was not the king of Israel, they broke off the attack on him.*

Then comes the denouement; the enemy might be fooled, but no one can fool God, for an Aramaean archer drew a bow "at a venture", and the king was hit where the breastplate joins the plates of the armour. The king said to his driver. "*Turn about and take me out of the line, I am wounded". When the day's fighting reached its height, the king was facing the Aramaeans, propped up in his chariot, with the blood from his wound pooling on the chariot floor, until at nightfall he died.* This is an incredible image, with the dead Ahab propped up like El Cid and leading his troops in battle.

The story ends with more unforgettable imagery. At sunset the herald went throughout the ranks crying, "*Every man to his city, every man to his country." Thus the king died. He was brought to Samaria and buried there. The chariot was swilled out at the pool of Samaria where the prostitutes washed themselves, and the dogs licked up the blood, in fulfilment of the word the Lord had spoken.*

The moral is that however they try, not even kings can escape the judgement of the Lord of history, who is the only God, and more powerful by far than all the gods of nature.

Much as I love this story and revel in its ironies and comedy I find it difficult to know how to understand Micaiah's explanation of God sending a lying spirit into Zedekiah and Ahab's court prophets, though there may be some more recent parallels.

In 1940, when Hitler halted his panzers before Dunkirk allowing the British Expeditionary Force to escape; and later, when, without needing to do so, he declared war on the United States, had God in his providence somehow slipped these follies into his mind so that he would lose the war. I have heard it argued that way. But then what about Vietnam or the invasion of Iraq?

Micaiah's story contains a difficult argument, even leaving out the suggestion that God manipulates history by lying to human beings. Or could God, perhaps, be meeting a human *ruse de guerre* with a divine? Our story might be comedy, but it is a difficult, thought provoking comedy in which history as "nihil" stares us in the face.

False Prophets and a Joke Told With a Straight Face

Beware of false prophets, which come to you in sheep's clothing.
Jesus of Nazareth. [St Matthew 7:15].

Prophecy was important in Israel, but easily undermined by prophets telling kings what they wanted to hear, or else failing to predict the future correctly. Attempts were therefore made to safeguard its integrity – none of which worked, not even when backed by the death penalty. *The prophet who presumes to speak a word in my name which I have not commanded him to speak, or who speaks in the name of other gods, that same prophet shall die.* [Deut. 18:20.] The passage continues with a test for false prophecy which we can only think was put forward tongue in cheek otherwise it is a truth so obvious that it is inconceivable that anyone could have put it forward with a straight face: *How may we know the word which the Lord has not spoken? – when a prophet speaks in the name of the Lord, if the word does not come to pass or come true, that is a word which the Lord has not spoken; the prophet has spoken presumptuously, you need not be afraid of him.* [18:21] It doesn't take a revelation from on high to tell us that, though it is generous in its assumption that the prophet only "thought" he was giving a word from the Lord. It is a test that works best as a knowing joke told with a straight face.

Was God Joking with Moses About His Name?

Here was the world's worst wound.
And here with pride
'Their names liveth for ever', the Gateway claims.
Was ever an immolation so belied
As these intolerable nameless names.

Siegried Sassoon [1886- 1967]

When Moses met God at the burning bush [Ex. 3:6], He revealed himself as *The God of Abraham, Isaac and Jacob* and commanded him to lead the Israelites out of Egypt. Because this was asking a great deal, Moses reckoned he needed further explanation. What if the Israelites asked for the name of the God who was sending him on this impossible mission, what should he say? As Egypt was a land with hundreds of gods, covering every aspect of life, it was not a foolish question. All that God said in reply was: *I AM that I am.* The Hebrew, for this is, *Ehyeh-Asher-Ehyeh,* which is not so much a name as a refusal to give a name. Then, God abbreviated his answer to *Ehyeh. Tell them that I AM* [Ehyeh] *has sent you to them.*

There are parallels here to the comedy in Genesis 32:23, a passage describing how Jacob wrestled with an angel at the ford of Jabbok. When asked for it by the angel, Jacob gives his name, but only for the angel to change it to *Israel,* which means, *God strove.* When Jacob in turn asks the angel for his name, the angel evades the question and gives him a blessing instead. Scholars have struggled to understand what this wrestling encounter with God might mean. At any first meeting the opening question is always for the other person's name. That formality opens up a relationship as well as the possibility of some claim being made on the other. In the ancient world, prayers, blessings and curses were thought not to work in the absence of the relevant name.

Jacob does his own bit of renaming by changing the name of the place to *Peniel, the Face of God,* as the angel could only have been the angel of the Divine Presence. What is important, however, is that when asked, the angel withholds his name. So we are not surprised when Moses encounters God on Sinai and the only name he is given is the teasing, *Ehyah,* "I AM," which is also, of course, the identity of Moses as well as of everyone who will ever hear the story. We are each of us an *I am who I am.* For Moses, no name would mean no relationship. So, what is God doing here by being so abstractly philosophical and clever? He is turning the request for his name into a word game in which the withholding of the name becomes the name. If the prophets can play at paronomasia, so can God.

One reason scholars believe that there are different traditions and writers behind the accounts of the Exodus is that in 6:2, God does tell Moses his name, though what that name was exactly we are not sure, because all that has come down to us are the four Hebrew letters of the tetragrammaton, YHWH, the vowels being omitted as is usual in Hebrew. After the return from exile only the High Priest was allowed to utter the Divine Name. To this day Jews still refer to God as haShem, the Name. Devout Jews coming across the tetragrammaton are forbidden to guess what the missing vowels might be; instead they are to pronounce the word as *Adonai,* "Lord.'

My first Hebrew teacher was a devout Jew who, when I added the vowels suggested by Christian scholars and read it first as the old fashioned *Jehovah,* followed quickly by the more modern, *Yahweh*, my teacher buried his head in his hands and groaned loudly. "You must never, never, say the divine name". he told me. "When you come across the sacred letters, you must always say, *Adonai.* If you are translating, say simply, 'the Lord.'" I have done so ever since.

So again, we are into word play which seems to crop up whenever we are faced with God's self-revelation. Whenever in the Bible human beings relate to God, there's comedy of some sort. Many go to their Bible for clarity and authoritative pronouncements. What they are given instead is often word play. Word games are never far away. The Bible is a book that plays with the reader.

Just why this kind of comedy should form an important part of the biblical narrative is a worthwhile question as is the question of why the humour in such passages should be so frequently dark. One possible answer has to do with class differences in ancient Judah. The sages with their sophisticated love of irony would have come from the upper social orders; the story tellers with their love of word games, from lower down the social scale. Those editing the final documents of Israel's history incorporated both traditions together with their different forms of comedy.

Satire: When Humour Becomes Offensive

> *I'll publish right or wrong:*
> *Fools are my theme, let satire be my song.*
>
> George Gordon, Lord Byron, [1788-1824.]

Satire uses wit, irony, burlesque and sarcasm to hold up crime, vice and folly to ridicule or scorn. Satire is the humour that makes enemies. Its use in the scriptures might, therefore, seem at first sight surprising, but that is the case only for those who expect the Bible to be an uplifting or comforting work.

My own discovery of biblical satire was as a teenager attending Matins at our parish church. In those days it was customary to sing to Anglican chant all the psalms appointed for that morning. It was when we came to Psalm 115, *Non nobis, Domine*, in Miles Coverdale translation, that I found myself grinning.

> *Their idols are silver and gold;* I sang*, even the work of men's hands.*
> *They have mouths and speak not; eyes have they, and see not.*
> *They have ears and hear not; noses have they and smell not. ...*
> *They that make them are like unto them; and so are all such as put their trust in them.* [vv 4-8.]

Satire as sarcasm is not designed to make friends though it may be so wrapped in comedy as to make the insult palatable; which was not the case with the prophet Amos [41:1], *Hear this, you cows of Bashan,* he says. Bashan was the most fertile part of the Northern Kingdom, a plain famous for its wheat and cattle. To the psalmist, the much sought-after bulls of Bashan were an image of the enemies of the godly [Ps. 22:12]; while for Amos, the area's well-nourished cows put him in mind of the rich, pleasure seeking women of Samaria, the cows *who oppress the poor, who crush the needy, who say to their husbands, "Bring that we may drink."'*

Whenever men and women satirize one another the comparison with animals seems to be universal. In western society men are likened to rats, pigs, dogs and tomcats; women to cows, vixens and shrews. Comparing public figures to animals is the stock in trade of political cartoonists everywhere, but should the Word of God contain language as vulgar and demeaning as this? Yet, if this is what particular individuals are like, why not? The Bible will reflect the worst of us as well as the best. The worst of these women oppress the poor and boss their husbands around! The best among them would have concern for the under-privileged and for love in family relationships. In this way, even the most childish things that men and women have to say about one another is brought into the story of God's dealings with his people.

Just how offensive can biblical satire be? The answer is as strong or vulgar as the language of the writer. Martin Luther, with his peasant background, breached in his table-talk most modern notions of decency, going well beyond the "cows of Bashan." Those who edited the Old Testament allowed most of the satire, however vulgar or aggressive, to remain unchanged; but, when it came to the joke that ended Solomon's Empire under his son Rehoboam, the limit had been reached. When the assembly of Israel say to Rehoboam, *Your father made our yoke heavy. Now, therefore lighten the hard service of your father and his heavy yolk upon us and we will serve you*, [I Kings 12:1 ff] Rehoboam takes time to reply, then rejects the delegation's plea and says elliptically, *My little finger is thicker than my father's loins.* In Hebrew, loins are more than thighs, and the Hebrew, "*little one*", didn't mean finger. Our scripture class of 14 yr old boys spotted the euphemism. As his father had seven hundred wives and three hundred concubines, Rehoboam's reply was a vulgarity well below the belt, and our coy translations, like the Hebrew, mark the limits of biblical decency. As the gospel says, *Let the reader understand*.

Other kinds of Old Testament Comic Writing

> *Comedies of manners swiftly become obsolete when there are no longer any manners.*
>
> Sir Noel Coward [1899-1973]

Puns, irony and satire are far from exhausting the kinds of comedy found in the Bible. "Situation comedy", was anticipated more than 25 centuries before it appeared on our television screens.

The story of David and Goliath [1 Sam. 17] is one of the Bible's great apparent reversals of outcome, in which a poorly armed boy kills a well-armed giant; though, as every soldier knows, poor Goliath didn't stand a chance. The encounter illustrated the military superiority of mobility and fire-power over fixed and well-armed defence, where you can get at the enemy but the enemy can't get at you. Though Goliath might have looked invincible he was at a decided disadvantage; for while David, skilled with the sling after long hours of practice guarding sheep, could deliver a deadly blow with a well-aimed stone, Goliath could get nowhere near David to deliver his killer-strike. Most generals in most situations will choose fire-power and mobility over static defence.

Then the story of how Samson, blinded by his Philistine captors [Judges 16], brings the temple of Dagon crashing down upon his pagan persecutors is another great comic reversal of outcomes. The God of Israel triumphs over one of the Baalim. Comedy is always a morale-boost for the weaker side.

In the story of the destruction of Sodom and Gomorrah [Gen.

18] we move from military conflict to diplomacy and negotiation. Abraham *drew near to the Lord* to ask, *Will you really sweep away innocent and wicked together*? Then, questioning, like Job, the judgement of the judge of all the earth, he began to intercede for the inhabitants of these wicked cities in a way that is reminiscent more of the market place than the practice of prayer.

In the spring of 1967, I led a pilgrimage to the Holy Places in the Old City of Jerusalem. Time had been allowed for an afternoon visit to the *suq*, or market. After buying presents for the family, I had one item on my personal shopping list - an inlaid chess board from Damascus. My budget was 5 dinars, £5 sterling. "How much is that fine chessboard," I asked the friendly stall-holder. "Two dinars," he told me. "I'll take it," I said, before he could change his mind, and I left feeling pleased with myself. Later, Arab friends groaned when I told them. "But you took all the pleasure out of shopping," they said, "both for you and for him. You should have admired the goods, enjoyed a cup of coffee and bargained him down to one dinar. That's how it works here."

And that's how it works in the story of Abraham pleading for the lives of the wicked men of Sodom, in which the issue is that of righteousness, the key concern for post-exilic reformers. Abraham puts pressure on God! *Shall not the judge of all the earth do right*? [Gen. 18:25]. The humanity here is as notable as the chutzpah. The humour lies in the incongruities. Abraham is "pushing his luck," seeing how far God was prepared to go, something few Christians would even dream of attempting in prayer. In doing so, he brings down the level of his prayer to the kind of bargaining that went on at the market stalls of Sodom. At issue was the survival of an entire community, a pagan community at that, and it is being decided like a haggle over a jar of olives!

As the Lord no longer answers when the haggling gets down to ten righteous men, there are clearly fewer than that in the city. In the next chapter, Sodom and the surrounding cities are destroyed and what began as comedy ends as tragedy.

As we have seen, Jews today describe Abraham's behaviour as *Chutzpah*, "sheer impudence, gall, bare-faced cheek." Chutzpah would have begun as a social device used by the weak against the strong, here it is being used by the faithful in prayer.

Continuing where Abraham left off

The critic is a haunter of unquiet graves.

M.J.C. Hodgart, *The Ballads*

Abraham's is a faith that argues with God. It does not rebel against God, like Satan and his angels in Milton's *Paradise Lost.* The comedy in the account of his interceding for Sodom demonstrates that though Abraham is no rebel, he is not easily overawed by God either. He maintained the right to question and to think for himself. This is why when modern atheists assert that religious faith is blind faith, they can be wide of the mark. For Jews and Christians the greatest faith is still a questioning and an arguing faith. When faith's capacity for criticism dies, intelligent faith dies with it. What is left honours neither God nor his creation.

So why, when the number of righteous had been haggled down to ten, did God abandon Abraham to his prayers. After all, Genesis claimed that God had saved the whole earth on account of the righteousness of Noah – why not save far fewer in Sodom? Was the city that wicked?

My own suspicion is that one of the functions of biblical comedy is to mark the limit of reason. Life and faith go on when our rational faculties have reached their limit.

The Persistence of the Connection between Sin and Punishment

> *Suffering is permanent, obscure and dark and shares the nature of infinity.*
>
> William Wordsworth [1770-1850]

The modern tragedy most akin to Noah's flood or the destruction of Sodom and Gomorrah is the Shoah, or Holocaust - the cold, rational, continent-wide, bureaucratised attempt by Hitler to exterminate European Jewry. Any attempt to explain this along the lines of the Deuteronomist, that it was God's punishment for some offence against him, seems absurd and offensive.

Even while it was happening Jews were asking what they could have done to deserve such a catastrophe and no convincing answer was or has been forthcoming. The same question was asked by the devout after the destruction of the Temple by the Romans, and among the answers suggested was that parents had not educated their children properly in the Jewish faith. Many were satisfied with this explanation, but it doesn't convince today. It is not that explanations are not forthcoming but that no one can think what sort of explanation would suffice.

And what of the Christian side of the debate, for the Shoah

took place among a people who, though in the grip of a delusional and destructive non-Christian philosophy, still for the most part identified itself as Christian? Not long after the war, a group of Protestant churches met to discuss the catastrophe that had descended on the Jews in their midst. Their conclusion was that it had happened because Jews had rejected and crucified Christ. This was absurd, offensive and rightly failed to convince. It was replaced by greater awareness of the problem, and the growing honesty in answering it, that came with the publication in 1965 of *Nostra Aetate* and the debates in the Second Vatican Council.

Elsewhere in the Christian world the temptation to link natural catastrophes with divine punishment, though still in evidence, seems to be weakening. When the extent of the HIV epidemic first burst upon a frightened public, a number of Christian leaders from biblical literalist backgrounds, declared that it was a well deserved reminder from God that society needed to get its moral act in order. Very quickly, however, this all too-easy connection was challenged and the moralising it involved disappeared from the media.

When as a curate I began hospital chaplaincy work, I'd occasionally meet a patient who had been told that to deserve their illness they must have done something very wrong. "What did I do to deserve this?" is a natural response, one which the Bible supports and denies. Of this, more later.

15

CLOWNING AND MORE SITUATION COMEDY

It is meat and drink to me to see a clown.

William Shakespeare [1564-1616], *As You Like It.*

It was a story [I Kings 3:16ff] that had me on the edge of my seat. I was 9, and Miss Dobells was a great story teller. Was Solomon really going to cut the baby in two? That would be pure tragedy, but I felt in my bones that this was grim, dark, threatening comedy. Perhaps he was only pretending! My mind was torn between the story's surrealism and the knowledge that Solomon was an absolute monarch who could do, if he wanted to, exactly what he threatened.

Many years later, parishioners told me of a case in a local magistrates' court. A lad in the parish had "put a girl in the family way" and had refused to pay child maintenance. The abandoned mother took the boy to court, but he had persuaded a number of his mates to swear on oath that they had each slept with her. "Very well," the magistrates said, "half a crown a week each." The story went around the town like a good joke and the clerk of the court behind the decision became a local hero. It remained a tragedy for the girl but comedy for everyone else.

Prophets as Clowns

I remain just one thing, and one thing only – and that is a clown. It places me on a far higher plane than any politician.

Charlie Chaplin [1889-1977]

False prophets were a problem in Israel. The problem lay in recognising them, especially when both true and false prophets dramatised their messages with what scholars call "prophetic symbolism," a kind of "acted parable". For example, to show that God would shortly bring disaster upon Jerusalem, the prophet Jeremiah bought an earthenware flask from a local potter then led a group of elders and senior priests *to the Valley of Ben Hinnon at the entry of the Potsherd Gate.* This was the gate that took its name from the shards, the pieces of broken pottery dumped there. Surrounded by broken pots, instructed by God and with all eyes upon him, Jeremiah raised the jar and smashed it, saying, *Thus says the Lord of Hosts, So will I break this people and this city, as one breaks a potter's vessel so that it can never be mended.* [Jer. 19:11]

Is this comedy? Perhaps not in the usual sense, but considering the way in which his words are dramatised, an element of comedy is present, just as it was with Nikita Khruschev [1894-1971] when, in the autumn of 1960, first, he banged his fist on the table at the United Nations and later his right shoe. As Khruschev's antics were clowning for effect, so too were Jeremiah's at the Potsherd gate.

Prophets often made their point in this way, though not every occasion qualified as clowning: Jeremiah's buying his uncle Hanamel's field, for instance, to show that he had faith in the future. [Jer. 32:7-9] On the other hand, Isaiah's wandering around naked for three years in a society where nudity was not an optional lifestyle, certainly bordered on the bizarre. [20:1-6] He did this to illustrate how the Assyrians would lead the Egyptians into captivity with their buttocks shamefully exposed. Isaiah was playing the clown, just as he was with his public declaration of celibacy to show that the future would be so bad that it would be wrong to bring children into the world.

The same kind of serious clowning can be found in the prophet Hosea's marrying a prostitute, as well as in Ezekiel's strange behaviour with his hair [5:1 ff], cutting it off and dividing it into three heaps, burning one part in the city centre, cutting up another as he walked the streets, and scattering the remainder to the wind, all to symbolise the coming degradation of Jerusalem. If this isn't clowning what is?

The Prophets and their children

Do you hear the children weeping, O my brothers?
Elizabeth Barrett Browning [1806-1861]

The prophets of ancient Israel never lost an opportunity to take their message to the people, often saddling their children with the most attention grabbing names they could think of. For its shock effect, Hosea's wife, Gomer, a woman of loose morals, was married by the prophet in order that her "harlotry" might illustrate Israel's own unfaithfulness to God. When, as a poor sermon illustration, she bore him a son, *the Lord said to Hosea, "Call him Jezreel, for in a little while I am going to punish the dynasty of Jehu for the blood shed in the valley of Jezreel".* [1:4] Nothing is said about what this choice of name did to the boy's emotional and spiritual development; though an even worse fate befell his sister. *The Lord said, call her Lo-ruhamah,* [1:6] which means *unloved.* The world is full of unloved children but it is doubtful if before Hosea any parent burdened a child with such a self-damning name. The poor girl was walking testimony to God's displeasure with his people. Nowadays, the prophet would be had up before the court for child abuse!

Yet this blighting of his children's lives did not stop there. As soon as Lo-ruhamah was weaned, Gomer *conceived and bore a son* [1:9] and, at the Lord's command, Hosea gave him the most terrible name of all, *Lo-ammi*, *Not my people*. These were dark names for dark times. The nation was in crisis, threatened with destruction and the names of the three children were perpetual reminders of this. It is as if today, someone was to name their children, *Rampant Capitalism*, *Unsustainable Development,* and *Global Warming.*

Not that all prophets were as uncompromisingly bleak in their choice of names as Hosea. When, in 735 BCE, the Judeans faced an overwhelming onslaught by the Assyrians, Isaiah went to meet Judah's king, Ahaz. To emphasise what he had to say, Isaiah took with him his son, *Shear-jashub,* whose name meant "A remnant will return." Ahaz understood that while Judah's fate would be bad enough, mercifully it would not be a lasting destruction! It would have a comic ending.

The name of Isaiah's next son was made public even before he was conceived: *Maher-Shalal-Hash-Baz,* [Isaiah 8:1&3], the longest name in the Bible. It meant, "Speeding for Spoil, Rushing for Plunder", those doing the speeding and plundering being the armies of Assyria.

The Comedy Doesn't Get Blacker Than This

> *He was, and is yet, most likely, the wearisomest, self-righteous Pharisee, that ever ransacked a Bible to rake the promises to himself and fling the curses on his neighbours.*
>
> Emily Brontë [1818-1848] *Wuthering Heights.*

The Bible is always read selectively, as much by quarrelsome scholars as devout laity; and, in a society in which, apart from a few immigrant communities, it is now extinct, cursing has become a lost art form.

In churches across England no choir ever sings psalm 58; and, wherever curses occur in other psalms, the brackets placed around them in 1928 indicate that they are unfit to pass Anglican lips. As for the Book of Common Prayer's "Commination Service", or Denouncing of God's Anger and Judgements against Sinners, written for use on Ash Wednesday, and which includes nine curses, I doubt if it has been used once in the last hundred years:

> **Minister**: *Cursed be he that removeth his neighbour's landmark.*
> **Answer**: *Amen.*
> **Minister**: *Cursed be he that maketh the blind to go out of his way.*
> **Answer**: *Amen.*

I realised my own blindness to the presence of cursing in scripture when I accompanied a group of American Baptists on a pilgrimage around Galilee. At the ruins of Capernaum, our guide, a devout and knowledgeable Christian Arab, said, "This is Kfar Nahum, the city of the prophet Nahum, which never flourished again after our Blessed Lord cursed it". A gasp went up from those around me. Our guide then referred us to the Woes in Matthew [11:23] and Luke [10:15], which most scholars understand as warnings or expressions of sorrow and translate as "alas," but which our guide insisted were curses. Back at the hotel, I explained how such curses would be understood in ancient Israel as a prophet pronouncing the judgement of God, and that seemed to make it all right!

Cursing is the flip-side of prayer as blessing. How could I have missed something so central and darkly anti-comical in scripture? I knew it was there, of course, but not how much a part of daily life it had been in biblical times. In psalm 52, for instance, in which the psalmist has tired of the wickedness of the powerful, he resorts to a curse: *So may God fling you to the ground, sweep you away, leave you ruined and homeless, uprooted from the land of the living.* [v5] There's little else the psalmist can do but curse and so he becomes quite poetical in his vented contempt.

But it is the next verse which reveals the darkest comedy: *The righteous will look on, awestruck, then laugh at his plight: "This is the man," they say, "who would not make God his refuge, but trusted in his great wealth and took refuge in his riches".* This resentment against the uncaring rich is echoed across the western world today, not least in the West, with the coming of the super-rich and the growing impoverishment of the middle-class. With the present crisis among the world's financial institutions, political commentators began to laugh as darkly as the psalmist. This self-congratulation of the righteous is a spiritual temptation to which we will return later.

Creative cursing may be a redundant art form in the post-Enlightenment west, but it is alive among the traditional societies in our midst, existing as an expression of an outrage that while avoiding vengeance seeks justice in black prayer and comedy.

In the Bible we are forbidden to curse God, our parents, or the deaf. The penalty for the first two is death.

In the New Testament, Jesus instructs his followers to *Bless those that curse you.* Early Christians lived in a world where professional cursers were employed by those with grievances to blight the lives of their enemies. Christians were not to engage their services.

The Bible is shot through with the imagery of cursing and the comic thought that a curse might recoil on those doing the cursing. Christians were to bless anyone who cursed them.

Though who was it, we might ask, who was doing the cursing in this puzzling and darkly comic text in St Paul's letter to the Galatians [3:13]? *Christ brought us freedom from the curse of the Torah by coming under the curse for our sake; for scripture says, "Cursed is everyone who is hanged on a gibbet.*" [Dt 21:3] That was the Revised English Bible, which like many modern translations softens the text for modern sensibilities. The King James Version is less nervous when it translates that Christ was made a curse for us. In Jewish Law an executed man was a curse upon the land and his body had to be taken down by nightfall, hence the haste to bury Jesus on that first Good Friday. But made a curse by whom? Some have suggested God himself! Would that be an irony too far?

16

MORE THOUGHTS ON ECCLESIASTES

The more the universe seems comprehensible, the more it seems pointless
Steven Weinberg [b. 1933], *The First Three Minutes.*

I once attended a Synagogue Study Group, and was made most welcome. They were discussing *Koheleth*, which Christians call *Ecclesiastes*, or *The Preacher*, famous for its phrase in the King James Version, *Vanity of Vanities, saith the Preacher; all is vanity* [1:2].

The discussions were vigorous and I was fascinated by how the rabbi probed the text with questions. All seemed to go well for three weeks, until the woman next to me had had enough and remonstrated with the rabbi: "This isn't a Jewish book at all." she said. "It's too negative. Judaism is joyful and positive. All the things we Jews value, it dismisses as futility. It should never have been included in the Bible".

The general feeling was that interesting though the book was, the woman was right. Apart from a few verses [3:17; 7:18; 12:9-14], probably added later to render the work more acceptable, Koheleth is at odds with the rest of the Hebrew Bible.

The message of Ecclesiastes is bleak: God and his ways are inscrutable. The same fate, death, comes to all, to people and to animals; to good people and to bad. There is no distinction. Life is futile, human effort pointless. Life is an absurd joke! Koheleth pushes the argument in Job to its limit. As a sage, he had pursued wisdom to its logical conclusion. The result was that in spite of all its promises, wisdom gave no sense of purpose to life. It was but a step away from atheism. What finally saved the book for believers[76] was its strong comic sense, in a passage that was perhaps added by an unknown hand, that in the end all would be well; God was hidden, not non-existent, that ultimately he could be trusted and that a sense of playful, prayerful good humour was the answer to the believer's

76 In addition, that is, to reading the book allegorically and mystically.

greatest fear: nihilism.[77]

Koheleth's bleak, initial conclusion was reached more than 2,000 years later, however, by the physicist Steven Weinberg in the epigraph that heads this section. Today the pursuit of reason has arrived at the same frontier of nihilism as the ancient pursuit of wisdom. We have only to note the pursuit of hedonism in the late 20th c. to realise that modern culture is pure Koheleth*: a man hath no better thing under the sun than eat and drink and to be merry* [8:15].

The Heroic Nature of Modern Atheism

An atheist is a man who has no invisible means of support.
Harry Emerson Fosdick [1878-1969] [attr.]

At the end of the 20th century, a number of western atheists grew increasingly militant, accusing religion of having caused most of history's wars, of being irrational and depending not on evidence and reason but on unthinking, blind faith. Religion was held up to scorn and compared unfavourably with rational, scientifically based secular humanism.

In a universe without meaning, in which the only transcendence is self-transcendence and where there is no God to underwrite human effort, men and women are thrown entirely upon their own resources. It is up to individuals to project meaning on to an uncaring cosmos. Yet atheism, too, is a spiritual condition, an heroic, non-religious, spiritual condition, one which should be evaluated sympathetically not mocked, as it has echoes in much of what can be found in the Bible.

In Job and Ecclesiastes especially, religion, like life, is presented as something of a joke. God is experienced as *Deus absconditus,* the Hidden God, *a God who hides himself,* said Isaiah [45:15] in a text that rings many bells in today's world. It's an experience spiritually akin to the absence of God. In that way, it is close to, yet different from, modern atheism.

77

Nihilism is the belief that accepted moral values and truths have neither meaning nor existence. While, historically, nihilism has been embraced by a number of radical political and intellectual movements, especially in pre-revolutionary Russia (the term was coined in 1861 by the Russian novelist and playwright Ivan Turgenev) the vast majority of people everywhere avoid it at all costs.

Is there atheism in the modern sense in the Bible, where God seems not just absent, but non-existent? There are two psalms [14:1 & 53:1, where this is a possibility, in which a devout Jew could well be contrasting his own faith with that of the "fool" who says in his heart that *there is no God.* The Hebrew word for fool is a variant on the "vanity", "emptiness" or "futility" found in Koheleth. Commentators argue that the phrase refers to a practical theism, that the fool in his impiety lives "as if" there was no God. That's a possibility but it might also be the negative conclusion to an Israelite line of thinking about the divine that was discussed in ancient Israel.

Before the Exile, the God of Israel was one god among many. In the prophets, it's made clear that these rival gods and goddesses are a joke, that only the LORD was God, other gods were illusory. If that was the case, what prevented those who, in experiencing his absence, concluded not that he was hiding but that he didn't exist? *The fool has said in his heart, there is no God,* may well point to something like atheism in ancient Israel.

Atheism as a Spiritual Condition

Suicide is the only logical reaction to the death of God.
Fyodor Dostoevsky [1821-1881], Kirilov, in *The Devils*.

In the West, in Europe especially, religious believers have only recently begun to take seriously the emergence of atheism as a widespread spiritual condition, for not only does the world appear to be meaningless for many, but religion too has lost its ability to give meaning to life. In his 1942 essay, *The Myth of Sisyphus*, Albert Camus wrote, *There is but one serious philosophical problem and that is suicide. Judging whether life is or is not worth living amounts to answering the fundamental question of philosophy.* The problem of meaning is as important as that.

In following the path traced in the Bible by humour, we have come to a very dark place indeed, in which each side, believers and unbelievers, berate and belittle each other when what is needed is dialogue. *The day is not distant,* wrote the Jesuit palaeontologist Teihard de Chardin [1881-1955], *when humanity will realise that it is forced to choose between suicide and adoration.*

Is this talk of suicide as a response to meaninglessness an over-reaction, or merely an inadequate analysis? Already the search for oblivion through drugs and alcohol is a preferred strategy among many of today's young. Is this a religious, social or spiritual problem, or all three?

Different strands of religious thought in ancient Israel also led to a range of conclusions. For most Jews the problem was how to achieve the righteousness that God commanded, for others the major issue was that of the undeserved suffering of the righteous, while a minority were concerned with the hiddenness of God and the apparent futility of human existence. In each of these quests for truth in Jewish religious life, wit and humour were central. The faith of Israel was expressed through comedy. Humour was never far from prayer. In the modern world, dialogue between Christians, Jews and Atheists and not polemic has to be the way forward.

17

MORE ON THE FUNCTION OF OLD TESTAMENT COMEDY

Nothing useful if not honest.
The motto of John Dee [1527-1608/9]
Warden of Manchester.

Humour comes in many kinds and most are found in the Bible. Irony, sarcasm, word-play and puns are all there, as well as dark humour, some very black indeed. They are there because, with the exception of the Torah, those who created the Bible had no idea how their writings would be valued, preserved, argued over and collected for use in worship as sacred scripture. They wrote as people of their time, writing from the double perspective of their own view of things, as well as from the experience of the community in which their lives had been shaped.

As the books of the Bible are human products about God and a nation''s experience of God, they can reflect the best and the worst of human nature. The characters they portray and the situations they describe are often immoral. Only occasionally are there role models showing the way to personal and social righteousness. In places the text is poorly preserved. Nor with the best scholarly help is it always clear what the writers originally meant. Yet, for all that, the Bible remains a collection of books centred on God and upon how the human race in general, and the people of Israel in particular, relate to him. They also show how, millennia later, readers who enter into its struggle to relate to God and live righteously can share in its wisdom and spiritual riches.

Humour and comedy are there because they are central to human existence. We could not live without them. They are spiritual necessities and as much part of religious life as secular.

Human beings live in continual need of transcending everyday life. Comedy makes this possible. Laughter and amusement express it. Even in the most terrible suffering, men and women will joke. It expresses defiance. It is a sign that the human spirit is stronger than death. For as long as we can joke, we can hope.

Because it is such an unequal, rather one-sided matter, humour is necessary in our relationship with God. How is it possible for men and women to hold on to their God-given independence and dignity in the over-awing presence of their Creator? How may mere creatures stand before God and feel neither insignificant nor discounted? God is great and human beings small and dependent.

What, though, if deep down we resented being creatures? If this was only true in our relationship with God, it would be bad enough, but seems to be the case too in to our relationship with other creatures. We behave towards them as if we were free even from the constraints that govern them, with the result that our abuse of the planet threatens all our survivals. We are creatures who insist on living as if we were gods; and this is as true for atheists as it is for believers.

In the story of the primal disaster in Eden, Adam and Eve attempt to solve the problem of their creatureliness by rebelling against God; rebellion being an heroic way of holding on, by aggressive self-assertion and spirited independence, to something we are afraid of losing. In the Bible, comedy seems to function as an alternative to rebelling both against God as well as our own creatureliness. Abraham does not approve of what God is proposing to do to Sodom. Like Job, he questions God's sense of justice. How can he make his point without, as a creature, sinning against his Creator? He uses chutzpah, comedy.

And in scripture, God is also presented as using dark humour. In the wilderness, when the Israelites, "fed-up" with eating manna, are on the point of rebellion and longing for the flesh pots of Egypt, God said to Moses, *say to the people: Sanctify yourselves in readiness for tomorrow; you will have meat to eat. You wailed in the Lord's hearing; you said, If only we had meat! In Egypt we lived well. The Lord will give you meat and you will eat it. Not for one day only, nor for two days, nor five, nor ten, but for a whole month you will eat it until it comes out at your nostrils.* [Num. 11:18ff].

Comedy as an Alternative Strategy

> *I wish our house had a bigger garden so that sister Beatrice might have a little more work to do.*
>
> St Teresa of Avila, Letter 331.

I first came across humour as an alternative to rebellion about the time I heard of Solomon's proposal to cut a baby in half. Miss Dobell had given us a lesson on the book of Proverbs. I suppose the class was not working hard enough because she advised us that next time we saw an ant's nest we should remember Prov. 6:6, *Go to the ant thou sluggard: consider her ways and be wise.* Miss also explained that the alternative to being cheeky was *a soft answer.* It was there in our Bible: *A soft answer turneth away wrath.* [15:1].

Later, having been brought up to be an honest lad, I raised my hand to admit that it was I who had cleverly repaired a torn hymn book using the side-strip from a war-effort savings stamp – a hymn book, the class was told, that had crossed the Atlantic at great risk to the sailors who transported them, all so that we could sing "O God our help in ages past". I attempted a *soft answer,* explaining that it was better that I tore a strip off the stamps than that Miss tore a strip off me! "Are you being funny with me, Radcliffe?" "But a soft answer turns away wrath, Miss," I said. Only it didn't! It fetched me "a clip behind the ear" instead.

Is that how humour sometimes functions in the Bible, as an alternative to rebellion as a way of relating to God? In psalm 44 [v23], where the psalmist has lost all sense of God's presence and is hoping that a soft thought will avoid his anger, teases God, or taunts him, if we can accept the stronger adjective. He says *Rouse yourself, Lord; why do you sleep?* He's reacting to the experience of God's absence in the way Elijah reacted to the prophets of Baal.

It's not easy being human. Life doesn't always make sense. Bad things happen to good people and there are days when the pain of being ourselves outweighs the joy of being alive. Nor are other people always helpful when God seems distant. Yet the human spirit is not easily crushed and comedy is the Bible's response of faith to life's seriousness as well as to the utter seriousness of God. There's enough humour in the Bible to show that we never need despair either of our humanity or of God.

Human Creativity and Divine Inspiration

I must create a system, or be enslaved by another Man's;
I will not reason and compare; my business is to create.
William Blake [1757-1827], *Jerusalem.*

How can the words of men also be the Word of God? How could the Eternal communicate himself to mere mortals? One answer is preserved in the book of Proverbs: *The Spirit of man is the candle of the Lord* [20:27]. God was the Hidden God who could reveal himself even in erotic love songs. As observational scientists the Wisdom writers had worked out that the morning dew falling on Jerusalem was connected in some way to the snow of Mount Hermon. [Ps 133:5] As human knowledge is only as good as its symbol systems, they could not at the time progress further. This is as true for theology and philosophy as it is for physics and mathematics. Their candle metaphor might translate today as: *the curiosity and understanding of the mind is the only light we have on the world or on God.* The Word of God can only come to us through human creativity and without humour that creativity would be a very dim candle indeed.

Humour and Spirituality

Spirituality has to do with becoming a person in the fullest sense.
John Macquarrie [1919 – 2007]

Spirituality is such a slippery word that it is necessary to attempt a definition. It means, by derivation, everything that relates to the human spirit which, because of its association with disembodied beings like ghosts or demons, is now intellectually a redundant, pre-modern concept. Nevertheless, it retains some value today as the category which concerns those aspects of human existence that transcends all that is purely physical, rational, moral or emotional.

In science, curiosity, which is linked to the desire to increase knowledge, can be described as a "spiritual" activity because it is not exhausted by rational and emotional descriptions of scientific research programmes. There is some transcendent or spiritual aspect to all human creativity. The traditional term for this ability of the mind to transcend what's physical, rational, moral or emotional is "spirit," and though it survives in metaphors such as "high spirits", it has now no academic place in modern thinking about human nature, though its derivative, "spiritual" has been pressed into service across a whole range of secular substitutes for religion.

The last western thinker to explore seriously the category of the human spirit was the Russian philosopher Nikolai Berdyaev [1874-1948]. After Berdyaev and the loss of the noun, we have had to make do with the all-purpose adjective, "spiritual," which relates not only to religious subjects such as prayer, and for which in church circles it is often a synonym, but also for everything which nourishes the non-physical, non-rational and non-emotional dimensions of human nature – so that music and literature, dancing and paintings are now understood as "spiritual activities." Even when human beings are no longer thought to possess a "spirit," they are still described as "spiritual." .

This broadening of the idea is something Christians should value, for not only can prayer and the Bible be understood as sustaining our inner-lives, but clearly comedy and humour can also function spiritually as well.

Before exploring the relationship between humour and

spirituality, we must note that "spiritual" is a morally neutral term. A "spiritual" person can be a saint, like St Francis; or decidedly wicked like Hitler, arguably the most spiritual man of the 20th century! If only there had been a saint whose holiness had matched Hitler's wickedness. Unless we can see Hitler's hold over his followers as being also a spiritual hold, we will not be able to understand him or ourselves.

As a library of books, the Bible reflects many different kinds of humour, not all of them acceptable to the modern reader; for example this piece of stereotypical characterisation of women. *I find more bitter than death the woman whose heart is a net to catch and whose hands are fetters. He who is pleasing to God may escape her, but the sinner she will entrap. "See," says the Speaker, this is what I have found reasoning things out one by one, after searching long without success: I have found one man in a thousand worthy to be called upright, but I have not found one woman among them all.* [Eccl. 7:26]

There's humour in the nets and fetters but it is a misogynist humour born from disappointment. As for what it does for the modern reader's spiritual well-being, the reader must decide for herself! As in life, so in the Bible, humour and comedy can in themselves be morally and spiritually neutral while the uses to which they are put need not be.

Re-visioning the Bible as Comedy

Not everyone can initiate a policy, but everyone can judge it.
Pericles. [495-429 BC].

In the Bible, God is the major player on the world stage. While most human relationships are in some way unequal, humanity's relationship with God is not even remotely equal. We are created in God's image, but he outclasses us in every way. Are we creative? So is God. The best we can do is Beethoven, Shakespeare and Michelangelo, whereas God created the entire Universe.

Is God powerful? So are we. We now have the ability to destroy the planet that gave us birth – yet what is that compared to the power to create a cosmos that has itself the power to create and sustain all that comes from its existence? Theologians have long known that it is easier to say what God is not, than what he is. Our relationship with him is unequal because of infinite differences in scale and it is doubly unequal because of the complication of sin, our ability not only to make mistakes but to get everything we do wrong in some spiritually corrupting sort of way.

Even atheists cannot escape being children of the universe, a situation which is as shot through with paradoxes as being creatures of the divine. *I don't believe in God, but I miss Him,* wrote Julian Barnes in *Nothing to be Frightened of.* Biblical writers might respond with, I *believe in God, but you have to laugh.* For Barnes, humour is a way of coping with death; in the Bible it can also be a desperate way of coping with God.

In the ancient world, the way to relate to God was as a subject relates to his king. It is a model that has served believers well. Even in republics like the USA, God is still thought of as an absolute monarch with our relationship to him being one based on submission. Unfortunately, submission implies obedience, which is where the problem begins, for this means that there is an unavoidable contradiction at the heart of our existence as creatures. If God created us in his own image then that means he created us to be in some way free. How then can we be free yet obedient at the same time? We cannot, and so we rebel. In Milton's *Paradise Lost,* a third of the angels rebelled. In the Garden of Eden, Adam and Eve rebelled and ever since men and women have been in rebellion not only against God but against their own nature as creatures.

This is, of course, an oversimplification, because in the Bible human creatureliness does not involve total submission and unquestioning obedience. We are creatures with free will and considerable freedoms of other kinds, although there are limits to those freedoms and being a creature means accepting those limits. This is what the forbidden tree in Eden represents. Unfortunately, being a creature is a limitation human beings cannot or will not accept. We lash out at the limitations on our lives, struggling to transcend our position in the universe as its creatures. It is what makes us who we are. It is the spiritual function of science to be forever attempting to rewrite the script of human existence even though it gets us into endless trouble, not least in threatening self-destruction as the pride of management imagines it is able to manage human nature.

Management theory has become the hubris of our age. It is believed that with the right personnel and management structures, optimum outcomes could be found for all situations – this in spite of the management disasters of Vietnam, Iraq and Afghanistan in the most managed and mismanaged wars in history. This is our spiritual predicament.

Just how current proposals to redesign human beings will work out, we have no idea. Even though what cannot be predicted cannot be managed, few doubts seem so far to have crept into the minds of the managerially minded. All of which is only humanity's penultimate problem. Our ultimate management problem is God himself. How are we to manage our relationship with God in a world half ruined by our failure to manage history, a failure which results from our failures to manage ourselves.

Our most pressing temptation is to imagine that we can manage God by managing without Him. Our God-given task, however, is to manage our relationship with him as best we can; and that's where comedy and humour come to the rescue!

Revelation, the Bible and Dialogue

The conversation of prayers about to be said.
Dylan Thomas [1914-1953]

The Bible is an open-ended book. The dialogue it began and embodies continues to this day with Jews and Christians still following their rival lines of dispute and enquiry. We need dialogue through humour to complement history as comedy.

An Honest Book: A Revisionist Faith with a Non-Revisionist History

Subtlety may deceive you, integrity never will.
Oliver Cromwell [1599-1658]

We have seen that the Bible is not a book that meets our assumptions of what a Holy Book should be. It is an untidy record of revelation through faith as trial and error. Polytheism doesn't deliver and so the Jewish nation adopted monotheism and the pursuit of a God-centred righteousness. This defined the faith of Judah as a risk-taking, pragmatic faith. The Bible is a partial record of how they worked out that faith as comedy with humour. The astounding thing is the extent to which they resisted the temptation of all historians to revise and re-write. *Russia is the only country where the past is unpredictable,* ran a Russian joke during the Soviet Era. The Men of the Great Synagogue and the Rabbis who drew up the canon of the Old Testament resisted idealising history by retelling it as how things should have gone. Abraham was a liar and moral coward, David an adulterer and man of blood. Even their experience of God was written up with all its moral and historical shortcomings. If God seemed to behave less well than he expected his people to behave, it was retained as part of the story. *No mortal may see me and live,* [Ex

33:20] God said to Moses at Sinai; but then Isaiah had a vision of God [6:1ff] and Ezekiel too. [1:4ff] and no attempt was made to render the accounts consistent. If history is finally comedy then its inconsistencies and suffering can be faced up to, but only as long as it is faced with a faith that incorporates humour.

Why Are There So Many Barely Religious Books in the Hebrew Scriptures?

> *We do not need to prove religion to men but to prove to them that they are religious.*
>
> George Tyrrell [1861-1909] attr.

God is not mentioned much in Proverbs or at all in Esther; while, unless it is read as an allegory, The Song of Songs is little more than a collection of erotic poems. As for Koheleth, by insisting on the inscrutability of God and the meaningless of human activity, other, that is, than by the pursuit of pleasure (for only with this does God enter human existence), Ecclesiastes establishes itself as the most religiously subversive book in the Bible. *To eat and drink and experience pleasure in return for his labours, this does not come from any good in a person: it comes from God. For without God, who can eat with enjoyment? He gives wisdom and knowledge and joy to whosoever is pleasing to him, while to the one who fails to please him is given the task of gathering and amassing wealth only to hand it over to someone who does not please God. This too is futility and a chasing of the wind.* [2:24]. God hardly comes into the picture, except as the means by which a wise man can turn life as tragedy into life as comedy.

It is a fact that even the most devout among the religious are not religious to the same degree, or even religious in the same way. Nevertheless, it is the temptation of the devout to wish that everyone was as religious as themselves. As an Anglican visitor to Pentecostal and other "sound" conservative, evangelical churches, I know that someone will probably ask me if I am "born again", or "saved', or "know the Lord" or am a "Bible believing Christian". Mischievously, like Jesus, I will answer the question with a question and ask what these phrases mean. Without using additional code words few can attempt an answer. Their desire is only that I would reveal myself as their kind of Christian. If the Bible can tolerate wide variations of religious expression, why can't those who value it above all other books? Why can't those who believe in the God of the Bible believe he has something important to say through the Bible's diversity? It's because human beings are so different that biblical comedy is possible. The Bible as comic and revelatory is a book of the broadest religious sympathies interpreted too often, alas, by the narrowest of unsympathetic minds.

A Comedy Without its Final Act

We dance around in a ring and suppose,
But the secret sits in the middle and knows.
Robert Frost [1874-1963].

The Hebrew Scriptures are a comedy of salvation without a clear or climactic ending. There are a few scattered hints that in the end all will be well one day with history, and that creation will finally be redeemed, but there's nothing definite. The promise of a Messiah, and the resurrection of the dead, these and other promises of fulfilment developed slowly and haphazardly in the centuries between what Christians call the Old and New Testaments. Without them, the New Testament makes little sense, for it's the Christian claim that in his life and ministry, death and resurrection, Jesus of Nazareth filled the gap between the two and brought the comedy of the Old to its final act in the New as all the humour and word play of the Hebrew Bible, the stories, the irony, the puns, paradoxes, satire and sarcasm, were used by Jesus in his preaching about the Kingdom of Heaven in order to bring the comic end of history into clear and practical focus.

The historical gap between the two Testaments was filled with a multitude of religious developments: the rabbis expanded the Law of Moses through the Oral Law and the writers of apocalyptic busied themselves with creative elaborations of the coded visions of Daniel and other figures, while in the background wisdom seemed to stagnate and there hovered for many the unfulfilled prophecy of the "Prophet like unto Moses," of Deuteronomy 18:15. For Christians the life and teachings of Jesus seemed a clear fulfilment of much that was explored in this period, which was itself an illustration of Søren Kieirkegaard's observation that *Life can only be understood backwards, but it must be lived forwards.*

.

.

THE NEW TESTAMENT

OR THE

CHRISTIAN SCRIPTURES

18

JEWISH HISTORY AS COMEDY CONTINUED IN JESUS OF NAZARETH

However certain our expectation
The moment foreseen may be unexpected
When it arrives.

T. S. Eliot [1888-1965]
Murder in the Cathedral.

Sometime about 26 AD, Jesus left his home village of Nazareth, among the hills of Galilee and began his ministry in the lakeside fishing town of Capernaum, about 25 miles away. It was a time when Judasim was a faith in transition. Jews were a people under Roman occupation; their great institutions like the Torah, the Temple, the Synagogue and Jewish family life were intact but questions and uncertainties about the understanding of Torah, the coming of the Messiah(s) and the Kingdom of God were topics of intense interest and discussions everywhere. The coming of Jesus, his impact on those debates and what followed from them would change radically not only the history of his own people but that of the wider world as well.

The question provoked by his ministry was, "Who is this man?" To some he was just one more wandering rabbi, a teacher of Torah, like those who came up from Jerusalem to persuade Galileans to adopt a particular style of orthodoxy; to others he was a throw back to ancient prophets like Elijah, while a few wondered if, perhaps, he was the Messiah who might even bring a restored kingdom to Israel.

The Messiah

He hath indeed better bettered expectation
than you must expect of me to tell you how.

William Shakespeare [1564-1616]
Much Ado About Nothing.

A generation later, about 50AD, the followers of Jesus began to be called Christ-ians, that is, Messianists, followers of Jesus as Messiah. "Christian" was a nick-name which like many nick-names changed an identity. To understand how this happened we need to know something of the growth of the Messianic expectation in Israel.

In the two hundred years before Jesus was born, apocalyptic theology had developed in a number of directions, each related in some way to the coming, at *the End-Time* of a redemptive and therefore comic figure, anointed of God, known as the Messiah. His task was to inaugurate the Kingdom of Heaven, that is, God's rule on earth. Different religious groups interpreted this in different ways. Not everyone believed he would be preceded by the return of Elijah. In the Psalms of Solomon, he is a king of the line of David, whose task was to purge Jerusalem of the godless, setting up instead a kingdom of the devout; while in the Testament of Levi, the Messiah was a Levitical priest. The ancient library known as the Dead Sea Scrolls knew of three Messiahs: an Eschatological Prophet like Moses, a Messiah of the royal house of David, and an anointed priest. To complicate matters, in addition to the Messiah, there was also the mysterious figure of the Son of Man; as well as in the background Second Isaiah's Suffering Servant.

There was, then, no single, settled expectation of the Messiah for Jesus to fulfil. Apocalyptic expectation was in flux. All that was agreed was that, through the Messiah, God would save his people and inaugurate the coming of his kingdom. The expected Messiah was therefore a comic role which Jesus was free to fulfil in his own creative way; and, as we shall see, he did this with a very distinctive sense of humour, one that embodied much of the humour in the Old Testament. That sense of humour is the best window we have on to Jesus the man.

The Magnificat

They loved the Rich, whom all the world abhors.

D. B. Wyndham Lewis [1891-1969], *Paean.*

The comedy began with his mother even before he was born. Mary was visiting her relative, Elizabeth, who was pregnant with the future John the Baptist. The moment Mary greeted Elizabeth, the child "leapt" in Elizabeth's womb. Mary's response was the hymn of thanksgiving known as the *Magnificat* [Lk 1:46ff], the key verses of which are a perfect expression of history as the comic reversal of misfortune and tragedy.

In the 1662 Anglican Book of Common Prayer, those verses read: *he hath scattered the proud in the imagination of their hearts. He hath put down the mighty from their seat: and hath exalted the humble and meek. He hath filled the hungry with good things: and the rich he hath sent empty away.* The words echo the *Song of Hannah*, the mother of the prophet and judge Samuel [1 Sam. 2:1-10]. In a secular world, Mary's song would be seen as political manifestos. Not surprisingly, because of its popularity among rebel groups in the 1980s, the Guatemalan government forbade its public reading.

Although such revolutionary sentiments are found among oppressed peoples everywhere they can come as a shock when Christians, who are used to singing the Magnificat devotionally, stop to think what the words actually mean. Expressed less poetically, they could have been written by Karl Marx or sung by the Paris mob on their way to the Bastille.

Those who find it difficult to read the song of Mary as divine comedy have only to consider the history of political cartoons to see how often the rich and powerful are shown being toppled from their comforts and privilege.

As it is unlikely that Mary composed the hymn herself, we have to ask where she got it from. One possibility is the Zealots, who were active at that time, especially in Galilee. A case can be made for Mary and Joseph, and Elizabeth and Zechariah belonging to a group of devout and moderate Zealots. The Magnificat, as well as the ministry of John the Baptist, might lend support to this view, as would Matthew's description of Joseph as "a righteous man," [1:19.] together with Mary's unhesitating acceptance of the will of God at the Annunciation [St Lk 1:37].

As family stories are important in shaping the lives of children, it is possible that Jesus' earliest thoughts of the kingdom of God as the world turned upside down were triggered by hearing the Magnificat's divine comedy repeated by his mother. It is possible too that St Luke's inclusion of the Magnificat so close to the beginning of the gospel was his way of drawing our attention to its importance in providing Jesus with a theme that would have such a central role in his teaching.

The Family of Jesus

All life is bad, but family life is worse.

Julian Mitchell. [1935 -]

The family home is our first school, especially where religion is concerned and we know that Jesus' parents were both religious. As devout Jews they each sought to lead a Torah righteous life, though events around Jesus' birth led Joseph to moderate his Torah strictness.

In the gospels there are clues that family life was not straightforward for Jesus and that where his own religious faith was concerned he followed a rather lonely path. For example, we are told that on one occasion, near the beginning of his ministry, his four brothers, James, Joses, Judas and Simon, went up to Jerusalem for the Feast of Tabernacles and wanted him to go with them [St Jn 7:2-5]. They said, *You should leave here and go to Judaea so that your disciples may see the great things you are doing. No one can hope for recognition if he works in obscurity. If you really can do such things as these, show yourself to the world.* Then John explains, *For even his brothers had no faith in him.*

While Roman Catholic and Eastern Orthodox Christians believe that Mary remained a virgin all her life so that the "brothers of Jesus" were in fact his step-brothers, Joseph's sons by a previous marriage, Protestants and most Anglicans believe that they were his natural brothers, sons of Mary by Joseph. Either way, it makes little difference to the fact that as the beliefs of Jesus were forming and developing in his home-life he did not always have the full support of his family.

As well as brothers, we also know that Jesus had sisters [Mk 6:3], though we are not told how many or their names. Perhaps they were present when St Mark [3:21] records that his family, hearing of the crowds he was attracting, *set out to take charge of him. He is out of his mind,* they said.

The gospel picture of Jesus' family is then a mixed one. His "stepfather" Joseph is described as a "righteous man" [Mt 1:19], almost Ezra-like in his adherence to Torah righteousness. When he discovers that his bride-to-be is pregnant, *being a just man, and not willing to make her a publick example, he was minded to put her away privily.* It took the appearance of an angel in a dream to rescue Jesus from the Torah righteousness of Joseph. In view of Jesus later avoidance of even the appearance of "over-righteousness" we might wonder if this also dates from his hearing as a boy those stories of his birth passed on to us by St Luke.

But, if Jesus' family appeared embarrassed by his ministry, his response to them can best be described as one of chutzpah. As it would have broken the fifth commandment to have severed relations with them, Jesus cleverly and publicly avoided sinning in this way by seeing his predicament as affirming a religious and ethical principle. Few things could be more humiliating for a prophet's family than for them to attempt publicly to persuade him to abandon his ministry, especially when that family was well-known for seeking God's kingdom and adhering to the Torah. On this occasion however, "a soft answer turned away wrath". [Prov. 15:1] Jesus said to the man who brought a message that his mother and brothers were standing outside, "*Who is my mother? Who are my brothers?" And pointing to his disciples, he said, "Here are my mother and my brothers. Whoever does the will of my heavenly Father is my brother and sister and mother."* [Mt 12:46.]

When his family sought to distance themselves from him, Jesus, as he so often did, took refuge in witty ambiguity. Was he cutting his ties with them, or was he simply enlarging the family of which he was head to include everyone covered by that teasing last clause? They probably thought him too clever by half to put them in their place like that! He had not excluded them, but included them instead in the kingdom's wider vision of the family.

Jesus' Scandal-Ridden Family Tree

Good families are generally worse than any others.
Anthony Hope [1863-1933].

Jesus was born into irony. The evidence is in his family tree which is traced back to King David and Abraham by St Matthew and to Adam by St Luke. Lists of family names are quite common in the Bible, but most readers skip them if they can. It's only if they increase family status or provide small-talk that we linger over even our own! Jesus' lineage is fascinating on both accounts.

From a comic point of view, it is Matthew's which is the most interesting[78], containing as it does two prostitutes, a royal adulterer, an idolater who sacrificed his son to a pagan god, and a fratricide who killed all six of his brothers to secure the throne! What makes this so grimly comical is the incongruousness of it all, because this is the Messiah's family tree!

St Matthew's intention was to show that Jesus was a good Jew and a member of the royal house of David in spite of being a Galilean of uncertain parentage. Along the way he drops names that

---

78 St Matthew even included a little gematria in his genealogy, in the form of number-play upon the name David. He presents Jesus' ancestors in three groups of fourteen names, fourteen being the number value of the name David. In Hebrew, the vowels are omitted, which leaves the three consonants DVD. As D [Daleth] is the fourth Hebrew letter and V [Vav] is the sixth, this gives the number 4 plus 6 plus 4, which equals fourteen. Word play, number play, the Bible finds them difficult to resist.

raise eyebrows of disapproval. In an age when the internet makes tracing family trees a national pastime, many dread what they might uncover in their own past, but I doubt many have found a genealogy more embarrassing than that of Jesus. It illustrates perfectly the old pulpit cliché that God can only work with what we give him and that often what he is given is very poor material indeed. To present day Christians researching their family tree, it says, "Yours could not possibly be more unpromising than the genealogy of Jesus". It's the comedy of surprise and incongruity.

And Judas Begat Phares & Zara of Tamar, and Phares Begat Esrom [Mt 1:3.]

> *Prostitution: selling one's body to keep one's soul: this is the meaning of the sins that were forgiven to the woman because she loved much.*
>
> Sir Compton Mackenzie [1883-1972].

Of the 41 names on Matthew's list, it is Tamar's story [Gen. 38] which is most likely to satisfy lovers of scandal. Tamar was the wife of Er, the first born son of Judah, after whom the Jewish people is named. When Er died, custom decreed that his younger brother Onan should marry her. In this way Tamar would not be left destitute and any children she bore Onan would count as his brother's. This was the custom known as Levirate marriage met with earlier in the story of Ruth and Boaz.

But Onan declined to give his deceased brother children in this way. As the Bible puts it, instead *he spilled his seed on the ground*, a form of birth control known medically as "coitus interuptus;" or, in Liverpool, among Protestants who can never resist rolling two jokes into one, "getting off at Edge Hill," Edge Hill being the station before the Lime Street terminus! Among practising Roman Catholics the preferred euphemism was, "leaving before the gospel." Onan also gave his name to the Victorian euphemism, "Onanism".

After Onan's refusal to beget children for his brother, Judah should have insisted that his third son, Shelah, took on the responsibility, but Judah argued that his son was too young and that Tamar should wait. By now, Tamar was feeling vulnerable and for support returned to her family, where she waited until it became clear that her husband's family had no intention of doing their duty by her. It was then that Tamar planned to entrap the now widowed Judah who was also emotionally vulnerable and missing his wife. Accordingly, Tamar laid aside her widow's weeds, donned a veil and, dressed as a prostitute, sat by the roadside and waited for Judah. Judah took the bait and a price was agreed, *a kid from the flock,* [38:17] but, as Judah hadn't the wherewithal handy to pay, he gave Tamar his signet ring, bracelets and shepherd's staff for security.

Judah later learned that through her prostitution Tamar was pregnant. Full of righteous anger, he used his power as head of the family and sentenced her to death by burning. When she was hauled before him for sentencing, Tamar produced his ring, bracelets and staff so that he was obliged to admit: *She has been more righteous than I.* [38:26]. Eventually, Tamar gave birth to twins, and it was from the first born, Phares, that Jesus traced his decent. The comedy lies in the sport that providence plays with the history of the Messiah. There is no attempt to tidy it up. Like the Hebrew Scriptures the Christian also steered clear of moral revisionism.

Salmon Begat Boaz of Rahab; and Boaz Begat Obed of Ruth; and Obed Begat Jesse

> *I wish either my father or my mother, or indeed both of them, as they were in duty both equally bound to it, had minded what they were about when they got me.*
>
> Lawrence Sterne [1738-1768] *Tristram Shandy.*

Rahab is the other prostitute in Jesus' family tree. According to the Rabbis, she was the fourth most beautiful woman in the world, and from her, it was said, no fewer than eight prophets traced their decent, including Jeremiah.

During the conquest of Canaan, Rahab won everlasting fame by risking her life sheltering the Israelite spies when they came to Jericho on reconnaissance [Josh. 2:1ff]. For this, the writer of Hebrews included her as the only woman among his exemplars of faith [11:31]; while St James [2:25] cites her as someone justified by works. I once heard a lecturer rhapsodising on Rahab's place in the Bible say, with unconscious humour, "Rahab, the harlot, is deeply embedded in scripture." He was surprised at the laughter that followed. It was appropriate!

Yet the significance of Rahab doesn't end there, for Rahab's son was Boaz of Bethlehem, who, when the penniless widow Ruth returned with Naomi her mother-in-law, did his duty by her in Levirate marriage. The result of their union was Obed the father of Jesse, the father of King David. When Ezra was telling the returned exiles to get rid of their foreign wives, they could have challenged him with, "Remember! If Boaz the son of a Canaanite prostitute hadn't married a Moabite there would have been no king David"'; nor, Christians might add, "the Messiah, Jesus of Nazareth."

Jesus' family tree is not at all that we would expect. Morally, things seem the wrong way round. It's a theme we will come across again and again. It's part of the Bible's inescapable comedy and irony.

David the king begat Solomon of her that had been the wife of Uriah

Do not adultery commit; Advantage rarely comes of it.
Arthur Hugh Clough [1819-1861].

Although King David was well provided with wives and concubines, on seeing Bathsheba, the wife of Uriah, one of his Hittite mercenaries, bathing on a rooftop opposite his palace, he cynically engineered Uriah's death in battle. Bathsheba was added to his harem and bore him a son, Solomon, who on David's death became king and an ancestor of Jesus. Matthew carefully avoided using Bathsheba's name. David is named of course, the mention of which Queen Victoria once disapproved! The poet, William Scarwen Blunt, wrote in his diary that he had heard that after dinner, when there was table-talk about meeting the dead in the hereafter the Queen was horrified at the thought of David being introduced to her, on account, she said, of his "inexcusable conduct to Uriah." Like Matthew, she too could not bring herself to mention Bathsheba's name.

And Jehoshaphat begat Jehoram

Do justice to your brother and you will come to love him.
John Ruskin [1819-1900].

King Jehoram[79] did what many monarchs did to stabilise a shaky throne: he murdered, in his case, all six of his brothers, [II Chron. 21:13] while his descendant, Ahaz, who was king[80] when Jerusalem was under siege, offered his son as a burnt sacrifice to one of the gods. [II Kings 16:3]. Again, this not what we would expect in the genealogy of the Messiah. It's the humour of incongruity and of the darkest kind. Jesus is from the right family to qualify as Messiah, but

79 King around 849-842BC.
80 King from 735-715 BC.

his family tree includes a pretty unrighteous mix of characters! It's as well perhaps that it's diluted with a number of unknowns: Abiud, Eliakim, Azor, Zadok, all of whom left no mark on history apart from their names. Even their deeds died with them. Jesus could no more help his family tree than his distant followers can help theirs.

It might be argued that the comic element here is no more than an effect of historical distance, that it would not have been seen in that way by Matthew's first readers. In view, however, of the Bible's strong moral stance on the issues involved that argument fails to convince. Irony was the kind of comic effect biblical writers knew only too well.

The Handicap of Place

The first requisite to happiness is that a man be born in a famous city.

Plutarch [c46-120AD]

If the family we are born into can be a blessing, a curse, a mixture of both or of not much significance at all, then so too can our birth-place. Jesus was born in Nazareth. *Can any good come out of Nazareth*, Nathanial said to Philip [Jn 1:46] when Philip told him that Jesus of Nazareth was the man they were looking for, the man foretold by Moses and the prophets. But no one had any great expectations of Nazareth. Its history had left no prophecies to fulfil, though St Matthew tries hard with a not very successful play on the Hebrew word *Nezer*, a branch, in Isaiah 11:1.

Nazareth was not a place mentioned in the Old Testament, the Talmud or Josephus though it did have a synagogue because, on at least one occasion, to the amazement of the congregation, Jesus went back to preach there. Their surprise was such that Jesus quipped: *a prophet never lacks honour, except in his own town and in his own family.* [St Mt 12:53ff].

Luke's account [4:16ff] is of an unhappy visit. Knowing that not only his family but the whole town were unconvinced of his ministry, he preached to them on some verses from the prophet Isaiah [61:1-2 & 58:6] and referred the promise of good news for the poor, amnesty for prisoners and sight for the blind, to himself. He also took the opportunity to tell them that he was not surprised that they failed to recognise his teaching and healing because it was the same for Elijah 900 years before. The congregation would have known that it took a pagan and foreigner, Naaman the Syrian, to recognise Elijah. The unflattering comparison angered them. At this, *they leapt up, drove him out of the town, and took him to the brow of the hill on which it was built, meaning to hurl him off the edge. But he walked straight through the whole crowd, and went away.*

Today, pilgrims visiting Nazareth are shown the traditional site of Jesus' being run out of town: "The Mount of Precipitation", a phrase as unforgettable as "the Defenestration of Prague".

During his short ministry, Jesus was an "outsider," even to his own family and community. St John, in his prologue, sums it up: "*e came unto his own, and his own received him not.* [1:11]. Later, in the life of the early gentile church, as the Jewish people disagreed over the status of Jesus as Messiah, theologians increasingly understood these words as applying to Judaism as a whole, so beginning a long tragic dispute over the supposed anti-Semitism of the Christian scriptures, a debate which continues to this day The gospels make it clear that Jesus was rejected by his family and home-town long before he moved the centre of his ministry from Capernaum to Jerusalem.

Jesus as a Galilean Jew

I decide who is a Jew.

Dr Karl Lueger [1844-1910], Mayor of Vienna.

One of the consequences of Hitler's assault on Europe's Jews during the Holocaust [1941-45] was that it triggered a great post-war rethink of Christian attitudes towards the Jewish people. Before the Second World War, certainly in Britain, most people would have said that Jesus was the first Christian. Nazi ideology was able to build on centuries of Christian anti-Judaism and transform such contempt into an organised, murderous hatred of Jesus' fellow Jews.

After the war, that ancient prejudice began to change as books were written and sermons preached in which the Church was reminded that Jesus was a Jew. Jewish thinkers, who had been slow to enter into discussions about Jesus, realised that his Jewishness had become a key to combating anti-Semitism. Jesus was a Torah observant Jew from a Torah observant family.

After the Second World War, the transformations in Christian teaching and attitudes towards Jews were greatest in the Roman Catholic Church and were set out by the Second Vatican Council [1962-5] in *Nostre Aetate,* the 1965 *Declaration on the Relation of the Church to Non-Christian Religions,* which banished for ever a hostile anti-Jewish polemic that went back to the Church Fathers. Other churches revised their teaching, and 20 years later, the Church of

England finally replaced its third Good Friday Collect, which had been a cause of much offence. By the 1980s the Jewishness of Jesus was no longer an awareness confined to scholars.

Jesus was a Jew – that was now readily admitted - but what sort of Jew exactly? Many writers on the subject wrote as if, in Jesus' day, there was only one kind, namely today's orthodox Jew projected back into first century Palestine. It was as if, to discover who Jesus was, all that was required was a better understanding of the Old Testament and the Mishnah that lies at the heart of the Talmud, the great Torah commentary which defines today's Judaism. However, the realisation that not everything in the Mishnah goes back to the time of Jesus, together with the publication of the Dead Sea Scrolls, which revealed a non-Mishnaic kind of Judaism, made that over-simplification untenable. The result is our present day interest in Jesus as a first century Galilean Jew.

Galilee lies 80 miles north of Jerusalem. It was a distinctive region, known since Isaiah's time as "Galilee of the Gentiles", that is, Galilee of the Foreigners. To complicate things, it was separated from the Jewish heartland of Judah by the unsympathetic territory of the Samaritans. It was a deeply troubled land with a violent history from which it was finding it difficult to escape. Again, not a place where one might expect the Messiah to be born.

Galilee

Vicisti, Galilaee [Thou hast conquered, O Galilean.]
The last words of the Roman Emperor Julian. [332-62]

Galilee was not an attractive place for empire builders. Would be conquerors usually marched around it to get to more desirable parts of the world. In the end, however, they all had to pacify and occupy it.

In all Galilee covered some 800 square miles, making it slightly smaller than the English Lake District. It was a fertile, hilly region with, in Jesus' day, a population of about 200,000. Its name comes from the Hebrew, *galil,* meaning "ring" or "circle" and refers to the shape of the hills that make up the area.

Until it was conquered in 734 BC by the Assyrian ruler Tiglath-Pileser III, Galilee was part of the northern kingdom of Israel and the tribal home of Issachar, Zebulon and Naphtali. To forestall rebellion, the Assyrians simply took potential trouble-makers into exile. Its leading citizens were never heard of again.

A hundred years later, when Assyria fell, Galilee was ruled first by the Babylonians and then by the Persians with any remaining

Israelites in a minority. After the Persians came other rulers, Greeks, Egyptians, Syrians and finally the Romans. By the time Jesus was born, the Galileans had inherited an altogether unpromising history.

Some idea of the hostility between the northern and southern kingdoms in the days of King Hezekiah [715-687BC] can be found in the account in II Chronicles. 30:10-11. Hezekiah was a pre-exilic reformer who made a determined effort to bring together Jews from both kingdoms in a great Passover held in Jerusalem. *As the couriers passed from town to town throughout the land of Ephraim and Manasseh and as far as Zebulon, they were treated with scorn and ridicule. However, a few people from Asher, Manasseh and Zebulon submitted and came to Jerusalem.*

It was a disappointing response, and for the next 650 years, from 734-80 BC, Galilee was under the control of non-Jews. The Greek Seleucids, ruling one of the sub-divisions of Alexander the Great''s brief empire, were anti-Jewish, and sought to stamp their Hellenistic culture over the whole region. In 169 BC, Jewish resistance to this assault on their religion climaxed in the Maccabean rebellion against the Seleucid king, Antiochus IV. It was a bitter struggle lasting until, in 163 BC, Judas Maccabeus re-dedicated the temple in Jerusalem, an event which is commemorated in the Festival of Hannukah. History had once more become comedy.

After this, Simon invaded Galilee and, after many battles, broke the resistance of the Gentiles. Pursuing them as far as the gates of Ptolemais, he killed nearly three thousand of them, and stripped their corpses. He brought back with him the Jews from Galilee and Arbatta, and amid great jubilation conducted them to Judaea. [I Mac. 5:21ff]

After the Maccabees came the Hasmonean rulers, when Jews again had their own kings. However, the Hasmoneans were not descendants of King David, and when they in turn were followed by the upstart Herodians there could well have been at any one time contenders for the throne of Judah from three royal families. Jesus was born into a very complex political situation!

In order to enlarge their kingdom, the Hasmoneans declared war on the Samaritans who claimed descent from the Israelites of the old Northern kingdom. They even destroyed the rival Samaritan temple on Mount Gerazim. Then, around 80BC, under Alexander Jannaeus, who was both king and high priest, Hasmonean forces invaded Galilee determined to bring it into their new Jewish kingdom, which in scale was soon to rival Solomon's. They forcibly circumcised the men, obliged non-Jews to observe Torah and sent home some of the exiles from the south.

But it was a settlement that didn't last long. In 63 BC, the political situation changed yet again, when the Roman general Pompey annexed the region. When he fell from power, the Romans installed Herod the Great as a client king. As Herod died in 4 BC, Jesus must have been born sometime before that. 7BC is often cited as the most likely date.

After Herod's death, the kingdom was divided between his sons. Herod Antipas became Tetrarch of Galilee and ruled throughout Jesus' lifetime. He made Sepphoris the capital and, to promote the economy, founded Tiberius, naming it after the Emperor. There is no record of Jesus ever visiting Sepphoris even though it was only a few miles from Nazareth.

Because Tiberius was built over a cemetery, few Jews would settle there. Nevertheless, the city flourished until it was destroyed by Vespasian during the war with Rome. When, in 70AD Jerusalem itself fell, Jewish survivors fled to Galilee, and Sepphoris and the rebuilt Tiberius became Jewish towns. For the next four hundred years, Tiberius was the seat of the rabbinical school that produced the Mishnah, the Jerusalem Talmud and the Masoretic text of the Old Testament.

Such an unsettled history raises many questions. Among them, just how Jewish was Galilee in Jesus' lifetime? How orthodox were its Jews? How numerous and influential were Galilee's non-Jews. The large gentile presence was a problem for the righteous, as orthodox Jews normally refrained from business dealing with non-Jews for three days before a gentile religious festival. Again, how did Galilean Jews relate to the Jews of Judah, separated from them as they were by the Samaritans?

Lastly, if temperament can be strengthened by overcoming handicap, then in overcoming the handicaps of family, town and region Jesus' upbringing must have offered rare opportunities for developing his strength of character.

Rebellion at Sepphoris

Rebellion lay in his way, and he found it.
William Shakespeare [1564-1616] *Henry IV pt 1.*

In 4 AD, following the death of Herod the great, the Zealot leader, Judah ben Hezekiah, attacked Sepphoris, a city less than 4 miles from Nazareth, captured the royal palace and armoury and led a revolt against the Herodian family. As Rome needed political stability on its borders with the Parthian Empire, it was unable to tolerate the turmoil and Varus, the Governor of Syria, marched against the rebels. In 6AD he destroyed the city. As Jesus was about 10 years old at the time, and this was a major national event for the Jews, he could hardly have been unaffected by these events. Talk would have been of the Zealots, Josephus' Fourth Philosophy of the Jews, and of their latest attempt to bring in the Kingdom of God by rebellion against Rome. Although the Zealots are not referred to often in the gospels[81], there are echoes throughout the teaching of Jesus which pointedly link violence and Kingdom of God. Galilee was something of a Zealot stronghold with the most extreme among them nationalists who linked strict observance of the Torah with intense hatred of Rome and an overwhelming desire for self-government.

Although over the centuries the causes of political instability were forever changing, the result was always a volatile and troubled Galilee. As Jesus grew up with expectations of a coming Kingdom of God, and in his family this was inevitable, especially if Christian tradition is right and his mother Mary was born there, he would have needed to think very carefully about what sort of kingdom it was. Throughout his ministry, in order to survive the Zealots and their rivals the Pharisees, Jesus would have needed a clear mind and a ready wit.

Galilean Judaism

> *Maximum competition is to be found between species with identical needs.*
>
> Gause's Law, [in Ecology].

Following the realisation that Jesus was not simply a devout first century Jew, but a devout first century Galilean Jew, great efforts have been made to discover how Galilean Judaism compared with that of Judah and Jerusalem. Not that this will necessarily tell us much about Jesus himself, as great men and women always transcend the limitations of their background.

The second century Christian writers Hegesippus and Justin Martyr mention the Galileans as a Jewish party. As this would make them as distinct as the Pharisees and Sadducees, it is unlikely. It's better, perhaps, to recognise Galilean Judaism as modified versions of southern orthodoxies – of which there were several. There is evidence of Galilee and Judah having differing religious customs, for example, widows' rights on the Day of Atonement and of no work being done on the day before Passover. Passover may even have been observed a day earlier, which might explain differing accounts

---

81 Simon, one of Jesus disciples had been a Zealot. [St Luke 6:15.]

of the Last Supper in St John and the Synoptic gospels. In addition, southern rabbis reckoned Galilean olive oil ritually impure and, more seriously, complained that the rabbinic rule separating meat and milk dishes was not observed in Galilee. The Pharisees thought Galileans uncouth, uncultivated and aggressive. Galileans were also noted, it seems, for not going up to Jerusalem at the three major festivals. Jesus' family was clearly an exception here.

In brief, Galileans were looked down on by Judeans. Their accent gave them away. When Peter was sitting in the courtyard at the trial of Jesus [Mt 26:69ff], a servant girl accused him of being with "*the Galilean*". Peter denied it and moved to the gateway where another girl also accused him. Peter again denied it, but a bystander repeated the charge, telling him "*your accent gives you away.*" If accents in England still reveal differences in education and social class, in first century Palestine it's possible that they also reflected differences in adherence to the Jewish Law.

Wherever religious competition is serious, small differences in identity loom large. The adjective, "Judaean", was shortened to Jew, that is someone who came from Judaea. Galileans came from Galilee, a name which was not shortened. Judaeans and Galileans became Jews and Galileans, a geographical distinction which tumbled over into religious difference. This goes some way towards resolving the offence Jews can experience today when coming across the apparently pejorative references to "the Jews" in the Christian Scriptures. The term could mean "non-Galilean.'

The Am Ha-Aretz

> *It's worse than wicked, my dear, it's vulgar.*
>
> Punch magazine, 1872.

As in all traditional societies, among devout Jews social and religious prejudices were seldom far apart and could be mutually reinforcing. The Torah righteous, for example, often referred to less orthodox Jews as *Am Ha'aretz,* "People of the Land." For 600 years, righteousness and its pursuit had been the dominant fact of Jewish life, with the result that most ordinary people were often looked down on by the religious elite. *Am Ha'aretz* was also an expression of superiority used by the descendants of those who had returned from Babylon to refer to the families of those who had been left behind and had assimilated in varying degrees to their pagan neighbours. Much of Galilee was probably seen in this light by devout southerners living in Jerusalem and Judea. In short, the Am Ha'aretz were not considered proper Jews;they had not taught their children Torah, they did not tithe as commanded, observe the rules governing purity or say the Shema twice a day. A devout Jew would not allow his children to marry an Am Ha'aretz.

This hostility between two rankings of Jewishness was a struggle at the heart of Judaism and it could be very bitter. Rabbi Akiva [c40 –c135 CE], who began life as an Am Ha'aretz, confessed that he had once been eager to break the bones of the learned "like those of an ass." As an estrangement between the devout and the unobservant it was part of the background to Jesus' ministry and is reflected in the gospel accounts. It was an alienation that some feel may have contributed to the rise of Christianity with many early converts coming from the Am Ha'aretz. Yet the hostility was never total and later the Talmud advised, *Heed the sons of the Am Ha'aretz for they will be the living source of the Torah.*

Where then did Jesus fit in this religiously vexed scheme of things? The answer would appear to be that the devout found him difficult to place. He wore a prayer shawl, the hem of which was touched by the woman *with an issue of blood*, [Mk 5:25ff] and this and much of his teaching supported the view that he was orthodox. However, he *ate with publicans and sinners*, [Mt 9:11] and this would have led to him being placed with the Am Ha'aretz.

19

JESUS' TROUBLING AND DISTURBING SENSE OF HUMOUR

The widespread failure to recognise and appreciate the humour of Christ is one of the most amazing aspects of the era named for him.
Elton Trueblood [1900-94.].

"John Chrysostom said that Christ never laughed". "Nothing in his human nature forbade it," William remarked.
Umberto Eco [b.1932] *Name of the Rose.*

The sorts of biblical humour we've considered so far, found in the Law, the Prophets and the Writings of the Hebrew Scriptures, were the comic inheritance of Jesus. He would also have been familiar with the banter and humour of Galilean life. Did he simply reflect these traditions or did he add to them something uniquely his own? The answer explored here is that it was very much the latter. His humour was distinctive and an important element in his teaching. It was needed most in the way he managed that other key aspect of his Jewish inheritance: the pursuit of righteousness.

Faithfulness to God was of paramount importance for Jews and it was achieved by leading a life whose righteousness was defined by the Torah. This understanding was as central to Jesus' life as it was for any Jew. As we shall see, his distinctiveness as a teacher lay in the way he interpreted the Torah. It was an understanding of righteousness that in time became through the Church the moral, but misunderstood, heritage of the Western world.

The problem was that while God was One there were many conflicting ways of interpreting his nature and commandments. Jews today joke that wherever there are two Jews you will find three opinions. It was the same in Jesus' day as the Bible testifies.

Can We Ever Know The Man Jesus Behind The Gospels?

Jesus was the greatest of Jewish geniuses.
Harold Bloom [1930-]

One of the great blanks at the heart of Christianity is our ignorance of Jesus as a flesh and blood human being. Interest has focussed chiefly on the theological meaning of his life and work, but of his personal qualities we know very little, certainly not enough to form a clear impression of what he was like as a person. Yet, because it is impossible to talk about Jesus without forming some mental image of him, most Christians have made good the deficiency by picturing him as their ideal man, clothed in what they know or imagine was the ordinary Jewish dress of his time.

After two hundred years of scholarly endeavour the search for the historical Jesus has little to show apart from a few incontrovertible facts: he was a first century Galilean, a controversial teacher and miracle-worker who was crucified. Christians have little more than a name on to which to project their fantasies and prayers. The result is an image filled out by centuries of extraordinarily rich church art and devotional tradition – and, for most of Christian history, this has had to suffice. To that picture we can add from the gospel Jesus' deep concern for the poor and the socially excluded, and his ability to relate sympathetically to women and children. On occasions too he could be as impatient as a prophet as when he drove the money changers out of the temple. Yet, when all is taken into account, we are still left with a figure whose personality and character are largely a product of Christian imagination. Devotion to Christ as Son of God, Redeemer of the World and personal saviour has left us with a name to which we cannot put a face, or anything more than a generalised personality. Unlike Dr Johnson, Jesus did not have his Boswell. Instead, we must manage with gospels containing hundreds of incidents, sayings and parables, each told with great economy making them little more than notes for preachers and catechists. The emphasis is on his teaching and death because it's these that were important to his early followers. Emphasis moved quickly from what Jesus did and said, to who he was in the cosmic scheme of things. He was the risen and ascended Lord, seated at the right hand of God, interceding for his Church as it struggled through the world's last days before his return in glory. Anything else was of less interest.

The first attempts to find "the Jesus of history," the man behind "the Christ of Faith", were made in the 18th century, and the quest continues today though in a more perfunctory sort of way. By seeing Jesus as a figure in a landscape and discovering as much as possible of first century Palestine and the Judaism of the time, it was hoped to bring him into clearer focus as a first century Jew. Much has been achieved and our picture of early Roman Palestine has become a good deal clearer, but though the historical background is now better known, the remoteness of Jesus as a man has not really changed. Was Jesus a kind of shaman, a wandering Galilean charismatic, an apocalypticist, a teacher of wisdom, a moderate zealot, a

Pharisee even, or a philosopher influenced by the Cynics? All, and more, have been seriously proposed.

Summarising earlier efforts to discover the Jesus of History, the liberal German scholar George Tyrrell [1861-1909] compared them to "the reflection of a liberal Protestant face, seen at the bottom of a deep well." Later attempts have only reflected back other faces.

By focussing on Jesus' use of humour it is hoped to avoid some of these limitations, humour being one of the characteristics that define us as individuals. Did Jesus have a sense of humour? Not many have thought so. Did he laugh? Until recently, few seem even to have considered the possibility. Was his style of humour distinctive in a way that made it different from the love of puns and irony that characterise the comic elements of the Old Testament? Those are the questions which underlie the following sections and chapters.

Comedy at the Birth of Jesus

Babies that are not born are rarely missed.
J. K. Galbraith [1908-2006]

One of the constants of biblical comedy is salvation as an escape from tight spots. For example, the Israelites crossing the Red Sea, Daniel surviving the lions' den and, at his birth, Jesus escaping the death-squads of king Herod. Often, the escape is attributed to divine intervention. In this case a timely dream, in which *an angel of the Lord appeared to Joseph and said, "Get up, take the child and his mother and escape with them to Egypt"* [Mt 2:13]. Similarly, the Magi who visited the infant Jesus with gifts of gold, frankincense and myrrh, returned to their country by another route, for they had been warned in a dream not to go back to Herod. [Mt 2:12].

There's comedy too, in the sense of events turning out well, in the angelic vision of the temple shepherds watching over their flocks. There was a widespread belief at the time that after the days of prophecy ended the sky, in the sense of it being heaven, was closed. *O that thou wouldst rend the heavens and come down,* said Isaiah, in a prayer to the God who hid himself. [64:1] For St Luke, the prayer was answered when the shepherds heard the Bat Kol[82], the voice of God, in another message from heaven. [2:8ff]. In short, communication between heaven and earth had been restored. With

82 Bat Kol means literally, "daughter of the voice," in other words, an "echo." For the rabbis it was the voice of God, a message brought by an angel, traditionally that of Gabriel.

the birth of Jesus all had ended well, though there was further comedy in the irony that after his birth the Messiah was *laid in a manger, for there was no room for him at the inn.* [2:7] The translation "manger" conceals the humour of incongruity! The Messiah's crib was an animal eating-trough!

The Naming of Jesus [Mt 1:21]

He is born in a good hour who gets a good name.
15th c. English Proverb.

In naming their children most parents think long and hard. Earlier, we saw how prophets like Hosea and Isaiah gave their children names embodying messages from God. In St Matthew's gospel [1:20], an angel names Joseph's son for him: *you shall give him the name Jesus, for he will save his people from their sins.* As with so many biblical names there's a word-play here which is lost in translation. *You shall call his name Jesus [Yeshua] for he will save [yasha] his people from their sins.* Even though Jesus' name was a common one, it still contained the meaning of his life. The reader, who is in on Jesus' secret, knows that his name means what it says – and more.

St Matthew drives the irony home when he explains to the reader, *All this happened in order to fulfil what the Lord had declared through the prophet: "A virgin will conceive and bear a son, and he shall be called Emmanuel"* [Isaiah 7:14]. Knowing that gentiles may be unable to translate the Hebrew, Matthew adds: *a name which means, "God is with us".* Once again, it is a name which is more than a name. Depending on the level of interpretation, it can be simply a reminder to the devout that God is never far from them, or it could even stretch to St John's pronouncement that, in Jesus, the Word became flesh. In the gospels, humour and ambiguity are often near neighbours.

Growing up in a Family of Devout Galilean Jews

Religion is the best armour in the world, but the worst cloak.
18th c. English Proverb.

Very little is said about Jesus before he began his ministry. Speculation that he studied magic in Egypt, or the secrets of hidden Buddhist masters in Tibet can be confidently dismissed. There is not the slightest trace of these or any other esoteric influences in the gospels. Jesus is a first century Galilean Jew, albeit of debatable orthodoxy as this was set out by his orthodox contemporaries.

Of Jesus' boyhood, only one intriguing story has come down to us, preserved by St Luke [2:41ff], of how, when he was twelve years old, his parents took him to Jerusalem for Passover. Many assume that this was at the time of his Bar Mitzvah but, as Bar Mitzvah as it is observed today was unknown at the times, the idea can be dismissed. Nevertheless, even though there was no ceremony to mark a young man's passage from childhood to his status as a Son of the Commandment, thirteen years plus a day seems to have marked the transition to personal responsibility for Torah observance, while twelve seems to have been the age at which this could be anticipated, [Yoma 82].

When Jesus went up to Jerusalem with his parents he was fulfilling the commandment for adult Jewish men like his father to go up to the temple for the three major festivals of Passover, Pentecost [Shavuot or Weeks] and Tabernacles [Succot].[83]

The Holy Family was a family of observant Galileans and though Mary was not obliged to go with Joseph and Jesus, she went nonetheless, possibly following a ruling of Rabbi Hillel. Jesus' brothers and sisters may have been too young to go with them.

And Jerusalem would have been crowded. Tens, if not hundreds of thousands of pilgrims would have arrived for the festival from all parts of the Jewish diaspora. The list of fifteen places of origin in the Acts of the Apostles [2:9ff] gives some idea of the make-up of the crowds that usually thronged the city. Pilgrims were expected to stay only for the first two days of the feast. The third marked the start of the half holy-days when it was permissible to travel home.

At the end of the first day of their return, Mary and Joseph realised that Jesus was missing, having assumed he was elsewhere in the caravan with relatives or friends. When they discovered that he was not, they returned to Jerusalem. Three days went by before they found him in the temple, *surrounded by the teachers, listening to them and putting questions.* [Lk. 2:46].

The Talmud records that on Sabbaths and feast-days members of the Sanhedrin taught on the Temple terrace, in an open Torah School, for the general public, including boys as young as Jesus. It would be pointless to ask what questions Jesus put to the scholars. All that Luke wants us to know is that Jesus was a good

---

83 Succot, also spelled Sukkot, was the third of the great pilgrim festivals. It celebrated harvest and involved those who celebrated it living in a Tabernacle or Booth.

student, something that still makes Jewish mothers very proud, and one who, even at that young age, was keenly interested in interpreting Torah.

St Luke says his parents were "astonished," but his mother's question, *My son, why have you treated us like this*, suggests too that they were angry. A twelve year old missing for three days calls for explanation. Perhaps his thirteenth birthday had passed and he was claiming his right as a young adult. In addition to having lost track of him, as they had done, the episode would have made most parents feel guilty as well as angry.

Jesus was in a difficult position. As he had just spent three days discussing Torah with the nation's finest minds he must have known that by treating his parents as he had done his behaviour could be thought of as breaking the fifth commandment. And then his wit came to his rescue as he searched for and found a soft answer to deflect their wrath. It was a close call. When his mother, said, *Your father and I have been anxiously searching for you,* Jesus replied, *Why did you search for me?* adding word play which, not surprisingly, St Luke's silence indicates they failed to appreciate. He said, *Did you not know that I was bound to be in my Father's house?* The risky double entendre was on the word, "father." Jesus' answer was sheer chutzpah. He was being a clever adolescent treading a delicate line. As St Luke tells the story, he got away with it. Perhaps his parents pretended not to understand his reference to his "Fathers house". We, of course, do, which adds irony to wit. Most preachers I've heard, keen to emphasise the wisdom of Jesus, as well as his closeness to God as his Father, miss the family dynamics and adolescent cheek here. Whenever a preacher preaches from his own piety, any comedy in the text gets blurred. To discover Jesus the man, we need to explore his sense of humour and the part it played in his ministry.

So we must ask, did his chutzpah, risky though it was, go even further than this? How much of the Christmas story did Jesus know? As much here, perhaps, as St Luke when he was writing the gospel? If Jesus knew of Joseph's dilemma over his birth, and in a small community like Nazareth it's impossible that he didn't, was this a reminder to his parents that God not Joseph was in fact his real father? The chutzpah and irony here went as far as chutzpah and irony could in the circumstances without becoming blatantly offensive. If this was a declaration of independence on Jesus' part, and it certainly looks like it, then he just about got away with it. His answer was soft enough to turn away the wrath it provoked. In which case, what, we may ask, prevented his parents" silence tempting and leading Jesus into becoming egocentric, narcissistic and megalomaniacal, paths followed by other Messianic candidates?

While other Jews acknowledged God as Father, they did so corporately, rather than as individuals like this. Whenever I have taken members of a church congregation to synagogue the conversation afterwards has often focussed on how, in talking to individual Jews, Christians have been surprised to discover that while prayer for them was something of an intimate, ongoing personal conversation with God, for the synagogue members they had been talking to it was less intimate and part of a more formal kind of corporate relationship.

If this is the case and was the case in Jesus' time as well, then behind his chutzpah, his reference to God as his father also represented a break with the tradition he inherited. His relationship with God in his prayers had already become more personal than his fellow Jews might understand or feel comfortable with. It gives us an insight too into his intercession for his disciples in John 17, which forms part of the farewell discourses of John 13-17. Many have wondered how, if the material there is genuine, the author of John's gospel came by such personal material. It is so unusual that some have supposed that it must be a devotional creation on the part of an early follower. My own view is that we need only suppose that among Jesus' disciples "memorisers" were appointed whose role was to remember and perhaps write down the sort of pithy summaries of his teaching that we have in the synoptic gospels. It would have been a role along the lines of Baruch's work as Jeremiah's secretary. We know that one of Jesus' disciples was thought close enough to his master to be known as "the beloved disciple." If anyone would have known Jesus' mind, and had a knowledge of his prayer life, it would have been this man. The authenticity of the material he has left us is supported by what we learn of Jesus as a person from the clues provided elsewhere by his sense of humour.

In Mark 14:36, when Jesus is praying in the garden of Gethsemane within hearing distance of Peter, James and John, he prayed that, if it were possible, the hour might pass from him. *Abba, Father, he said, all things are possible to you; take this cup from me. Yet not my will but yours be done.* The interest lies in Jesus' use of the Aramaic *Abba*, which means Father, as in "my Father" or "our Father." While Jesus' use of the word is found only here it almost certainly lies behind its use in the Lord's Prayer; and St Paul takes it up in Romans 8:15 and Galatians 4:6. And though later rabbis also used the word, the suggestion is that it originated in family life as an informal, intimate form of address. Jesus use of the word in prayer would then have been linked in some way with his growing realisation of his "sonship." For Jews generally, it would have referred to Israel as God's son. When Jesus began to see himself in a "sonship" kind of way, even without the story of his exceptional conception it would have transformed his relationship with God and his whole sense of divine calling. In his prayers, Jesus saw God as his Father in ways that other Jews didn't.

Growing up in the Family of the Messiah: Different but not Dysfunctional

Like father, like son.
14th c. English Proverb.

We are all the products in some way of our families and their stories. If Jesus grew up on the story of Mary''s miraculous conception we might well wonder about its effect on a maturing boy, especially if he accepted it without question, and all that we know leads us to believe that he did: that he accepted that God was Abba, his Father, rather than Joseph.

If this was the case, then such a belief and realisation would have transformed his sense of himself, his place in the world and who he was. If God was his Father, and he prayed to him as such, then in the circumstances of his time and place, he would have been led inevitably to ask himself if he was Israel's expected Messiah.

He would have heard talk of "false Messiahs", and must have wondered in the light of their failures what the true Messiah would be like; what mistakes he himself would need to avoid, what message would identify him as the real Son sent by God, if this indeed was who he was.

Jesus would have pondered texts like psalm 2, one of the royal psalms used in the old days at coronations, but in which the word for king does not appear. Instead, it has the Hebrew word for "anointed", which in English is translated as "Christ" or "Messiah." The key words are those of verse 7, *You are my son, this day I become your father.*

We have so little information to go on in exploring these themes. Did Jesus share his emerging sense of identity with his "cousin" John the Baptist? In view of John''s role in preparing the way for him to eventually step on to the public stage, we may assume, perhaps, that he did.

The Baptism of Jesus: The Messiah as Clown

These men who have turned the world upside down.
[Acts 17:6]

It's a common theme in clowning and certain kinds of humour to turn things the wrong way round or upside down. *I need to be baptised by you, and do you come to me?* John the Baptist asked when Jesus came to him asking to be baptised. As they were close relatives in a small world it's hardly possible that they didn't each know the religious views of the other, especially where the Kingdom of God was concerned. John's was a baptism of repentance to prepare for the arrival of that kingdom and commentators have understandably had difficulty in making sense of the occasion and especially Jesus' answer: *Let it be so now; for thus it is fitting for us to fulfil all righteousness.* [Mt 3:15]. How does repentance fulfil righteousness? Surely, success in righteous living was its own fulfilment. It's what the Torah observant strove for and John was being honest in his own eyes by deferring to Jesus in this way. The more righteous should baptise the less righteous. But Jesus knows that measuring one's own righteousness like this is the way spiritual disaster lies. It was the kind of spiritual pride that he fought against all his ministry.

By being baptised with John's baptism of repentance Jesus was identifying with spiritual struggle, not spiritual success. By turning what was expected of him upside down he was making it a comic sign of God's coming kingdom. "Nothing in the kingdom is as you think it is, but its opposite!" This would be a comic twist in his teaching again and again, a theme that went back to Mary's Magnificat. Fulfilment in the spiritual life is never where we think it is. It's as if Jesus was still testing his growing sense of Messiahship. It was not a role he was rushing into.

The Temptations in the Wilderness

No man that is not tempted shall obtain the Kingdom of Heaven.
An Agraphon[84] of Jesus recorded by Tertullian.

Immediately after his baptism, Jesus went into to the desert to pray and test his vocation as Messiah. Every role or job in life has its temptations. Teachers in my day were tempted by the pleasures of sarcasm, and during my years as a part-time hospital chaplain I met a number of consultants who could not resist the pleasures of a god-like bearing and demeanour. The role of Messiah also had its

[84] "Agraphon" means "not written" and refers to a number of sayings of Jesus not recorded in the gospels but which were accepted as authentic by many writers in the early church.

temptations and it was these that Jesus confronted in the wilderness.

The moral and spiritual courage shown by Jesus in arguing with the Tempter is presented as comedy. Each time Satan comes up with what seems like a winning line, Jesus comes back with a better and escapes the trap. In doing so, it introduces a recurring wisdom theme in his teaching: that the righteous life is one of continually avoiding subtle moral and spiritual snares.

Three times the devil tried to entrap the Messiah in a game as serious as that played with Job, and three times Jesus avoids capture with a well-chosen quotation from the Torah or the Psalms. [Mt 4:1-10]. Each test assails Jesus' vocation where it is most vulnerable.

In a debate reminiscent of those between rabbis, Jesus struggles with the Tempter. His faith and wit see him through. *Resist at the beginning; the remedy may come too late,* Thomas a Kempis advised us. Jesus does exactly that. The integrity of righteousness is where the Devil knows the Messiah will be most vulnerable. Both Matthew and Luke [4:1ff] record that Jesus was guided in his victory by the Spirit of God. "The only temptation for man is to be abandoned to his own resources in the presence of evil," wrote Simone Weil. Without God underpinning the wit of the righteous, comedy would quickly become tragedy. "There is a certain degree of temptation which will overcome any virtue", Dr Johnson declared. The role of grace in bringing events to a good end is always a comic role. Far from remaining a terrifying figure as he beats a retreat, Satan, humbled by prayerful wit, is reduced to a figure of ridicule.

It is important to note that the temptations are not those of an ordinary man. If they had been, they would almost certainly have included sexual temptation and that's missing here. Jesus' temptations are those of the Messiah: they include a test of his ability to provide food for a nation in revolt against an occupying power, his ability to survive physically in prolonged military conflict, and his being able to survive the corruptions of a successful revolt and the gaining of regal power. In the wilderness Jesus tackled successfully the lures of egocentricity, narcissism and megalomania, which awaited all who felt called to be the Messiah.

The Role of Humour in the Ministry of Jesus

> *Humour undiluted is the most depressing of all phenomena. Humour must have its background of seriousness. Without this contrast there comes none of that incongruity which is the mainspring of laughter.*
>
> Sir Max Beerbohm [1872-1953].

The Bible is bursting with incongruity. One of the results of concentrating on Jesus' use of humour will be that we recover something of his personality. His style of humour also demonstrates his humanity and, to some extent, his psychology. This is where the Christ of Faith can conceal the Jesus of History. Jesus was a Jew, Christians are not, though historically in the beginning most Christians were, a fact which focuses a major difference between our two faiths. Jesus worshipped God; Christians come to God through Jesus. Where Jesus related to God through the Torah, or Jewish Law, Christians relate to God through Jesus as God's Christ or Messiah, the Incarnate Word, crucified, risen and ascended. *We know Christ*, as the reformer Melanchthon [1497-1560] said, *through his benefits*. We come to Christ through a number of symbols and titles that describe the work of God through him: Saviour, Lord, Christ, Redeemer, Son of David, Son of Man, Son of God, Word of God, Light of the World, with the result that the man can easily be buried under the theology needed to understand him. All too easily, Jesus the man becomes the casualty of our prayers.

Once Christians came to believe that what God did through Jesus was more important than what Jesus did and taught, it was inevitable that the historic person should be lost to the symbols used to understand him. Recovering his jokes and witticisms could well be a way of finding again the human being hidden by prayer, liturgy and theology.

20

JESUS LEAVES HOME AND MOVES TO CAPERNAUM

Independence, like honour, is a rocky island without a beach.
Napoleon Bonaparte [1769-1821]

In order to make something of themselves, most people have to overcome one or more handicaps in life, most commonly those of family or place, and sometimes both, as was the case with Jesus. If he was to have any ministry at all, he needed to get away from the limitations of his home and from Nazareth, and yet remain in Galilee. His solution was to move to Capernaum and make his headquarters there. It was a good day's walk, 20 miles north-west of Nazareth on the northern shore of the Sea of Galilee. In the synoptic gospels Jesus seems to have gone on his own, but in St John's gospel [2:12] his mother and brothers went with him and stayed for a few days. After Joseph's death, as the first born son, Jesus would have been head of the family and probably the chief breadwinner too. Was there only minimum contact between them, for they seem to have played little further part in his life until its end? Jesus soon settled in, however, and St Mark says he was "at home" in Capernaum [2:1], establishing it as the headquarters for his work in Galilee.

Capernaum was a small, lakeside town, of perhaps 5-15,000 inhabitants. Josephus mentions it only once, yet it boasted a customs house which collected revenue for Herod Antipas. Perhaps Jesus chose it for its Jewishness and its relative freedom from Gentile influence. And because Jesus was a religious Jew, raised in a conservative home, his family probably felt it was safe to leave him there once he had settled in. The more religious the family, the more they would avoid close contact with gentiles. However, the fact that Jesus did not avoid non-Jews but was increasingly open and tolerant towards them is a reminder that short though his ministry was, he was a Jew whose attitudes, outlook and teaching changed and developed becoming ever more liberal with experience.

With Capernaum as his base he began finding and training his disciples, financing the cost from what he could earn through his teaching. It could not have been easy for Jesus to leave home and set up in Capernaum this way. Perhaps it was the difficulty of the move that lay behind his saying, *No one is worthy of me who cares more for father or mother than for me* [Mt 10:37]. Jesus would need his wit and good humour if he was to survive. The fact that it sometimes let him down was evident when a group of Pharisees and scribes, who had probably travelled from Jerusalem, complained about the disciples not washing their hands. [Mt 15:1ff] This was the occasion when Jesus, with a little lavatory humour, said that it's what comes out, not what goes in, that defiles a man. When Peter asked what this parable of bowel movements meant, Jesus lost his sense of humour: *Are you still as dull as the rest?* he asked. It is interesting that as a failure of good humour it was remembered long afterwards.

Rabbi Jesus' First Joke

> *My way of joking is to tell the truth.*
> *It's the funniest joke in the world.*
> George Bernard Shaw [1856-1950].

As John the Baptist was unknowingly coming to the end of his ministry Jesus was beginning his, arriving at Capernaum with a similar message to his cousin saying *repent the kingdom of God is at hand* [Mk 1:16ff], only with this difference that he indulged in a little prophet-like love of word play and cracked a joke. He was walking by the Sea of Galilee when he saw two fishermen casting their nets, Simon and his brother Andrew. Going up to them he said, in a pun as good as any in the Old Testament: *Follow me and I will make you fishers of men.*

Perhaps it was an obvious thing to say. Teachers attempted similar "witty" connection of name and character when I was school. It's humour for breaking ice, or bonding men into a team. But it was a quip the disciples remembered; one that helped establish Jesus as leader and sum-up their ministry. It marked Jesus out as a teacher with a liking for certain kinds of joke.

Jesus Meets Nathaniel

> *Do you think I could buy back my introduction to you?*
> Groucho Marx [1890-1977] [in *Monkey Business*]

In his search for disciples, Jesus recruited Philip, who, like Andrew and Peter came from Bethesda. [Jn 1:44ff] Philip went off to find Nathanael and when Philip told him that Jesus was from Nazareth, Nathaniel quipped, *Can anything good come from Nazareth?*, helping us to understand, perhaps, why Jesus thought it wise to move to Capernaum. Philip replied, *Come and see*. Before Nathaniel even speaks to Jesus, Jesus jokes, *Here is an Israelite worthy of the name. There is nothing false in him.*

To appreciate what lay behind this banter we need to know why anyone might think that an Israelite would not be worthy of the name. Else why say it? We can only assume that social prejudice reckoned Galilee disreputable because it was once part of the old, idolatrous kingdom of Israel, named after the crafty son of Isaac, Israel, or Jacob as he's more often called..

Nathaniel seems taken aback by Jesus' generous reply and play on words but deflects embarrassment with a quip of his own, *How is it that you know me*? Possibly he expects Jesus to say something profound but the banter continues with the let-down reply, *I saw you under the fig tree before Philip spoke to you*. There's nothing deeper than that on one level, but on another, Jesus was hinting that he saw everything and knew all he needed to know from that one sighting.

Nathaniel's reply continues the banter with another, possibly sarcastic, non-sequitur, *Rabbi, you are the Son of God; you are king of Israel*. Was this a joke of the many a truth in a jest kind? It probably was. It took Peter until Caesarea Philippi to recognise Jesus as Messiah, but just as Jesus sees to the heart of Nathaniel, Nathaniel's exaggerated irony affects to see to the very core of Jesus' identity!

This is truth through the comedy of ironic banter. The exchange can be read without humour and is usually read that way in church, though Jesus' reply then makes it even more unlikely that this was an irony and banter free exchange. *Do you believe this*, Jesus asked him, *because I told you I saw you under the fig tree*? Jesus then gives the banter an even more serious twist by saying, *You will see greater things than me seeing you under a fig tree*. He adds, *You will see heaven wide open and God's angels ascending and descending upon the Son of Man*.

The banter is now in danger of becoming too clever by far with more verbal play on the word "Israelite" which could also mean *someone who sees God*, and this was itself something of a joke because of the Jewish belief that no one could see God. The jokey exchange climaxes with Jesus' reference to Jacob's dream at Bethel, [Gen. 28:10-17] where he saw the angels ascending and descending on a ladder that reached into heaven.

It's not easy to keep track of all the humour in this witty exchange. As Israel, also called Jacob, is the most guile-filled character in scripture, what Jesus is saying is, "Nathaniel's a Jacob without deception". Nathaniel the wit, had met his match.

Another Gospel, another Joke

A nickname is the heaviest stone that the devil can throw at a man.

William Hazlitt [1778-1830].

In all four gospels Jesus begins his ministry with a pun. In St John [1:40ff], it centres on a disciple's name. Andrew tells his brother Simon, *We have found the Messiah,* [Hebrew for Christ]. *He brought Simon to Jesus, who looked at him and said, You are Simon, son of John; you shall be called "Cephas," that is Peter the Rock.* All nicknames are attempts at humour and this is no exception.

It's possible that Simon already had Peter as his second name, as two names were not uncommon in Galilee, though if this was the case, the story would lose something of the point it seems to be making, together with its humour, for there is another play on words here. Jesus pointedly renames Simon, *Cephas,* which is Aramaic for "Rock," and translates into Greek as *Petros*, Peter. As Peter was, in character, anything but rock-like, for example, before the crucifixion he denied he knew Jesus, his brother Andrew would have been amused at the irony. In modern slang a more appropriate equivalent of Simon's second name might be "flaky"! "Rocky" in its other sense of "shaky" would also convey the wobbly nature of Simon Peter.

In the 16th century, part of the Reformers' explanation of how God worked the sanctification of Christians was that the change in their status from sinner to child of God would, in time, and by God's grace and the power of the Holy Spirit, lead to a change in nature. This was probably the psychology behind name-change in the Bible. The name changes first, changes in character and personality would then hopefully follow. Simon did eventually become Cephas, the Rock, when he rallied the disciples after the crucifixion. [Lk 22:31]

Tragi-comedy: The Precariousness of Life in Galilee

I am the sovereign of things that cannot last,

Marcel Proust [1871-1922]

Life in Galilee was hard, with many Galileans living in or on the edge of poverty, while for those who failed to pay their way there was always the possibility of selling themselves and their families into slavery.[85] This precariousness of life and the enviable position of the rich were the background constants to the ministry of Jesus.

For the righteous, the way for Galileans to secure the blessing of God, and thereby escape penury, was to keep the commandments as they were kept by the most devout Jews of Judea – an almost impossible task. On one occasion [Mt 24:27ff] , Jesus ended his sermon on his understanding of the Torah with memorable dramatic imagery: *Whoever hears these words of mine and acts on them is like a man who built his house on rock. The rain came down the wind blew and beat upon the house, but it did not fall, because its foundations were on rock.*

In St Mark 6:3, Joseph is described as a τέκτων (tekton). This is usually translated as "carpenter", but it can also mean a builder, in which case Jesus would be experienced in house construction and could therefore say with authority, *whoever hears these words of mine and does not act on them is like the man who was foolish enough to build his house on sand. The rain came down and, the floods rose, the wind blew and battered about that house and it fell with a great crash.* [Mt 7:24ff] We are back again here to the biblical image of the tragic fool as a comic figure.

Having perhaps worked for the rich, Jesus knew their temptation to be greedy, a sin hardly open to the poor. Again, and perhaps from experience, he tells a parable of a greedy farmer: *There was a rich man whose land yielded a good harvest. He debated with himself: "What am I to do? I have not the space to store my produce. This is what I will do', said he, "I will pull down my barns and build them bigger. I will collect in them all my grain and other goods, and I will say to myself, "You have plenty of good things laid by, enough for many years to come: take life easy, eat drink and enjoy yourself" But God said to him, "You fool, this very night you must surrender your life; and the money you have made, who will get it now?"* [Lk 12:16ff]. The farmer provides yet another unforgettable image of the folly of over-confidence in an unpredictable world, and is therefore both a tragic and a comic figure.[86]

---

85 See Catherine Hezser's informative book, *Jewish Slavery in Antiquity,* Oxford University Press, 2005.

86 If, as many believe, the Letter of St James was written by the brother of Jesus, then his warnings to the rich about the spiritual dangers of wealth, could well be echoes of the teaching of Jesus of how wealth can so easily make fools of the rich. *A word with all those who say, "Today or the next day we will go off to such and such a town and spend a year there trading and making money". Yet you*

Comedy and Controversy at Capernaum

Reason itself is a matter of faith.
G.K.Chesterton [1874-1936].

When, as I child, I first heard the story of the paralysed man whose friends took the roof off a house to let down his bed so that Jesus could heal him [Mk 2:1ff], I really did chuckle at the trouble they took. Perhaps it was the way our Sunday School teacher laid on the drama with a ready trowel, though she could not have done that had the humour not been there. It was faith as the humour of incongruity. Because of the happy outcome, all healing counts as comedy.

Because this healing was accompanied by an absolution, *My son, your sins are forgiven,* [2:5] *some of the scribes*[87] *objected within themselves, who can forgive sins but God alone.* Jesus' reply courted controversy: *But that you may know that the Son of Man has authority on earth to forgive sins – he said to the paralytic – "I say to you, rise, take up your pallet and go home."* Comedy, as often happens, has here become contentious. Is the Son of Man Jesus? Or is he everyman? Again, is Jesus here accepting uncritically the prevailing biblical belief that sickness was a punishment for sin, a belief he would later repudiate?[88]

There are other possible comic interpretations surrounding the Son of Man reference. In its Jewish context, Jesus' claim to be able to forgive sins is pure chutzpah! If it is accepted that only God can forgive sins, then is the irony here Matthew's version of John's doctrine of the Incarnation?

The Demoniac and the Gadarene Swine

When the unclean shall be no more, what were modesty
but a fetter and a fouling of the mind.
Kahlil Gibran [1883-1931] *The Prophet.*

(86 continued) have no idea of what tomorrow will bring. What is your life after all? You are no more than a mist, seen for a little while and then disappearing. What you ought to say is: "If it be the Lord's will, we shall live to do so and so."

[87] "Scribes", in Hebrew, sopherim, were interpreters of the Jewish Law [Torah] and in the gospels are usually linked with the Pharisees, though earlier they had been distinct and something of that may survive in the gospels.

[88] See the discussion on The Tower of Siloam [Lk 13:4] and on the healing of the man born blind [Jn 9].

Jesus' healing ministry included his role as an exorcist, casting out demons wherever he found them, and they seemed to be everywhere, signs of a society under spiritual stress. All three synoptic gospels record his encounter with a demon-possessed man somewhere in the predominantly gentile territory on the eastern shore of Galilee. [Mk 5:1ff] Possession by an evil spirit was seen as the triumph of evil over human life, and this was a particularly bad case. The man lived as a feral, self-destructive outcast bound with chains and fetters in a graveyard among unclean tombs. He gave his name as *Legion*[89], because, he said, *there are so many of us.* [5:9]. When the demons were cast out they begged to be sent into a herd of pigs[90], *and the herd of about 2,000 rushed over the edge into the lake and were drowned.* The images are vivid and describe a great victory over evil as the tragedy of the man's life gives place to the comedy of his deliverance.

---

89 A Roman Legion had a core strength of 6,000 augmented by auxiliaries and cavalry.

90 There is a double uncleanness in this story in the mention of first the graves and tombs, and then the herd of swine.

21

THE KINGDOM OF GOD

The state of man, like to a little kingdom, suffers the nature of an insurrection.

William Shakespeare [1564-1616].
Julius Caesar.

The Kingdom of God, or of Heaven, for the devout who avoided uttering the word God,[91] is the dominant theme in Jesus' ministry. It was the apocalypticists who developed the idea that the cruel and ungodly kingdoms of this world would one day be replaced by the righteous kingdom of Heaven. Accordingly, history was divided into the Present Age, an age of injustice and oppression, and the Age to Come, God's age of peace and justice. For the Zealots and perhaps too for the Essenes, God's kingdom would come through armed struggle. Jesus, however, had different ideas.

The Kingdom of God was a metaphor and while metaphors are intended to make some aspect of a matter clear, the effect is often more ambiguous. All truth, religious or scientific, is built on metaphor, the idea that something is like something else. "Boys," our class was told at school one day, "atoms are like little billiard balls." Later, those same atoms were said to be like "like tiny solar systems." Even physics, it seemed, was a system of abstract metaphors where letters and numbers always stood for something. When human beings think, they can only do their thinking through the "as-iffery" of metaphors so that here Jesus was one with all mathematicians, poets and philosophers. "The Kingdom of God is like....." he would say, and a metaphor would follow.

The Feast of Fools: Turning the World Upside Down

The world is a comedy to those who think, a tragedy to those who feel.

Horace Walpole [1717-1797]

Like other Jewish teachers, Jesus would often use the idea of a feast or banquet when he talked about the kingdom of God, and

---

91 To this day, devout Jews often write G-d for God, omitting the vowel as in Hebrew.

being a metaphor for good company and food in abundance, that image was among the most basic of all comic metaphors.

In 1955, during my National Service, I had no idea that Christmas dinner at RAF Yatesbury, in Wiltshire, was but the latest example of one of the oldest comic images in the world, a joke that's spelled out in the Magnificat and is central to the humour of Jesus in the gospels.

Christmas dinner was the one occasion when ranks in the Royal Air Force were turned upside-down. I was, at the time, a humble Aircraftsman Second Class, an "erk," though I'd soon rise to the dizzying heights of Junior Technician, known jocularly in those pre-Harry Potter days as "Junior Magician."

Instead of the "men" taking orders from officers, the officers waited at table and took orders from the men. Later, I realised that for several hours we had been enacting a 20th century version of the ancient *Feast of Fools*, in which all the expectation of daily life were suspended in a kind of comic Song of Mary, prefiguring the Kingdom of God. Years later, this comic yet serious ritual was enacted again throughout Her Majesty's armed forces in Iraq, Afghanistan, Northern Ireland, Bosnia and elsewhere. The custom is all that remains of the feast of Saturnalia in ancient Rome, when masters waited on slaves and the rules governing ordinary behaviour were relaxed. In medieval Christendom, a Lord of Misrule might be appointed, or a King of Fools or even a Boy Bishop. Drinking to excess was common, as was singing vulgar songs and holding mock church services. Not surprisingly, the Feast of Fools was opposed by the Church and, in the 15th and 16th centuries, often suppressed

But interest in the feast has never died out and, in 1969, additional impetus was provided by Harvey Cox's book, *The Feast of Fools, A Theological Fantasy.* Cox was chiefly interested in the feast's witness to our human need for festivity and celebration. Only at the end of the book does he consider "Christianity as Comedy," and ask, as did the 12th c. medieval theologian, Petrus Cantor, whether Christ ever laughed, a question also raised in Umberto Eco's 1980 novel, *The Name of the Rose.* The gospel accounts of Jesus' ministry quickly reveal that the Kingdom of Heaven was both a Feast of Fools and a Divine Comedy, two themes present at the Wedding at Cana.

Preaching a Topsy-Turvy Message

> *You may call it "nonsense" if you like [the Red Queen] said, but I've heard nonsense, compared with which that would be as sensible as a dictionary.*
>
> Lewis Carroll [1832-1898] *Through the Looking Glass.*

Jesus' understanding of righteousness turned conventional morality upside down! It stretched Torah to its moral breaking point. It was ethics for fools. The first would be last and the last first. The Messiah would be baptised by his forerunner in this topsy-turvy, counter-factual kingdom of God, where enemies were to be loved [Mt 5:44], adversaries reconciled before their law suits reached the court [Mt 5:25], assets given away [Mt 12:40], the other cheek turned [Mt 12:39], strangers treated as family and social outcasts as friends [Mt 9:11]. The widow in the temple was to be our example not for the amount she gave as alms but for the amount she kept back, which was nothing! [Mk 12:42]. The kingdom of heaven belonged not to the old and wise but to children [Mk 10:13ff]. Jesus' moral teaching makes no sense at all if it is read as a course in prudential ethics. The kingdom contradicts the world. As a programme for outrageous moral risk-taking it inverts ordinary values as the clown says to his apprentice, "Follow me.'

After 2000 years, not only has the world not taken Jesus' way of looking at moral behaviour seriously but the Church hasn't either. It's a momentous spiritual, theological and ethical mismatch. Jesus' clowning is a far reaching comic reversal of how we normally think morally and for most of us it's too challenging to take seriously.

Jesus' teaching on the Kingdom of Heaven directly confronted the way in which all other Jews thought about righteousness. Everything about the Kingdom was counter-intuitive. It was a world in which, compared with our ordinary, everyday world, everything was upside down. The kingdom was all that contradicted what for devout Jews was unquestionably the moral norm. As it was a kingdom of paradoxes, where sinners were admitted before the righteous, it was inevitable that it would get Jesus into trouble with the religious authorities. Not even Hosea's anticipation of the kingdom in *I desire mercy and not sacrifice* [6:6] was as controversial as the Kingdom of God preached by Jesus. It was what, today, we might call an "alternative reality." It presented in the sharpest possible way his challenge to what was spiritually and morally real. Is the real world the world we are all caught up in and accept as given, or is it the world Jesus called the Kingdom of Heaven, a world which he said was "near?" Which of the two kingdoms was real? For Jesus it was the Kingdom of God. It was also the world as we'd like it to be, unless that was, we were rich and powerful.

If you were not in the top ranks of society, then life was hard, and the lower down the social order you came, the more harsh life could be. Little wonder then that St Mark could say: *the common people heard him gladly.* [12:37]. From their point of view, it was the world as they experienced it that was dystopian, the kingdom of Heaven was the more real because it was how the world should be. But by preaching that that world was near at hand, was Jesus saying that it was historically near and, like the day of the Lord, could arrive in their life-time; or was he saying that it was only just out of reach but could be made real if only we could love our enemies and forgive as God forgave us? He seems to have taught both, the second being a kind of promise of the first. The kingdom of God was the will of God as Father for his children. Of that Jesus had not the slightest doubt. No Jewish teacher had interpreted the Torah like this before.

The Wedding at Cana

O Wedding-Guest! This soul hath been
Alone on a wide, wide sea;
So lonely 'twas that God himself
Scarce seemed there to be.

Samuel Coleridge Taylor [1772-1834]
The Ancient Mariner

Cana, the home town of the disciple Nathanael [Jn 21:2], was a village about 9 miles north of Nazareth. Mary, had been invited to a wedding there and Jesus went along with her, together with his newly recruited disciples.

While I was British Chaplain in Israel, I recall an Arab Christian wedding to which over 1,000 guests had been invited; and another in which the groom's gifts to the bride were shown to all who cared to view them in a room whose walls were hung from floor to ceiling with household goods, shoes, jewellery and outfits for the bride, for all of which the groom had entered into debt for years ahead.

In a culture based on honour and shame, weddings were occasions when a family's reputation was on view before the whole community. If all went well, the family's good name would rise further in public esteem. But, if things went badly ... and unfortunately, at Cana, things did go badly.

What happened next is not easy to interpret. The gospel accounts of any event are little more than summaries and notes, as is the case here. Mary comes to Jesus to tell him that the wine has run out. She didn't need to add, "Cana will never let the family forget this. The memory will haunt them for years." Jesus knew what it meant and how the family would feel. Yet, however cleverly a translator words it, his reply sounds harsh and even rude. *Woman, what have I to do with you? My hour hasn't arrived.* The Revised English Bible even omits the brusque, *gunai,* "woman," in Jesus' answer. What was going on? Clearly, Jesus' ministry is a family problem here and Mary isn't helping. After all, it was the host's problem, not the guests'; besides, Jesus had only just begun his ministry. But Mary rescues the situation she's caused and says, *Do whatever he tells you*. We can hear the maternal irritation in her voice. Family tensions were still there.

Down the centuries Christians have idealised the Holy Family; but the impression given here, as in his staying behind at Jerusalem, is that there are things going on between Jesus and his mother which are troubling family unity – something that happens in the best of families. Why, I ask, have I not only never heard a sermon on Jesus' use of humour, but equally, have never heard one on his awkwardness with his mother? The answer has to do with the way we interpret the doctrine of his sinlessness. Idealising him as the perfect man, people suppose that to imagine there could be any hint of defensiveness in his response to his mother would be sinful on our part, if not his.

The presence of six large water-jars indicates that the wedding was that of a wealthy, Torah observant family, the water being used only for washing the hands before a meal. This was referred to as the "lifting of the hands." Water was drawn with a *Netilah,* poured first on the hands and then on both raised hands so that it ran down to the wrist and, being ritually unclean, did not run back to contaminate the fingers. In contemporary British measurement, each jar held about 25 gallons; and would have been refilled daily by the servants. As all six seem to have been empty, we must conclude that the wedding was a large one and had needed at least 150 gallons if the guests were each to wash their hands.

Jesus instructs the servants to fill the jars with water for the second time that day. Was there a little presumption in this, a guest giving instructions to the family's servants? Already the wedding reception was taking on some of the characteristics of the Feast of Fools. In addition, it was the host's responsibility to provide the wine. He, poor man, was probably occupied in summoning the courage to borrow from a neighbour!

Meanwhile, Jesus gave fresh orders to the servants. They were to draw from the re-filled jars and take it to the "master of the feast", the equivalent of the Best Man at an English wedding. It was an odd thing to ask as he had already washed his hands. Nevertheless, he drinks what he thinks is water, water that wouldn't normally be drunk and discovers that it's vintage wine, Jesus providing the equivalent of about 750 bottles or 4,500 glasses! A guest had come to the rescue on a lavish scale, and in a Feast of Fools, role-inversion kind of way. From that moment on, conversation would not be about the family's shame in letting the wine run out, but its comic provision to excess.

These features of the Magnificat and the Feast of Fools, a reversal of roles and a gracious provision to the point of comic excess, would occur again and again in Jesus' ministry. They were identifying characteristics of the Kingdom of God which lay behind all that Jesus did and said,

The Feeding of the Five Thousand

Miracle is religion's sense of humour.
Ludwig Feuerbach [1804-1872].

There are echoes in the miracle of the loaves and fishes [Lk 9:10ff] otherwise known as The Feeding of the Five Thousand, of both the wedding at Cana and the Feast of Fools. In St Matthew's gospel [14:13ff], when he hears from John's disciples that Herod the Tetrarch had executed the Baptist for no other reason than that his daughter wanted to help her mother, Herodius, settle an old score, Jesus went by boat to a remote spot in order to mourn for his cousin and, probably too, to review his own now more precarious situation.

John's death was a serious business, for not only was he a close relative, but in many ways their mission had been a joint venture: John preached repentance in preparation for the Kingdom as did Jesus, St Mark tells us [1:15] at the beginning of his ministry.

But even while Jesus was in the boat attempting to avoid them, the crowds were following. They were there when he landed, perhaps 10,000 and more of them, men, women and children, waiting with their sick, and growing hungrier. When his perplexed and still novice disciples pointed this out and suggested sending them *off to the villages to buy themselves food,* Jesus' replies with some humour, *give them something to eat yourselves.* As all they had were *five loaves and two fishes,* the joke must have seemed a cruel one. But the crowd was quickly organised into rows, the meagre food supply passed around and, at the end, the joke climaxed with the crowd's hunger satisfied while 12 baskets were inexplicably filled with the left-overs. The disciples had fed the crowd! The joke was on them. The surplus testified to the super-abundance of grace in the kingdom of God. It was prophetic symbolism as comedy; in that what began as a food-shortage ended as a food surplus. In the teaching and works of Jesus, the kingdom of God is always about history as comedy, that is salvation out of disaster.

Always in the Background: the Zealots and Jesus

Satan offered man the power to be like God without loving him.
Thomas Merton. *Disputed Questions.*

After the feeding of the 5,000, the fourth gospel reports that the crowd, thinking that Jesus must be "*the Prophet who was to come into the world*", "*intended to seize him to proclaim him king*". Jesus immediately went into hiding.

The prophet referred to was one *like Moses* [Dt 18:15]; but as Moses was not a king there's a muddle in expectations here. The sort of leader who might hope to be king of the Jews would have been one of Josephus' fourth sect, the Zealots, founded by Judas of Galilee about 6AD. It was the Zealots who, in 66 AD, led the Jews in the bloody and futile revolt against Roman occupation, which ended in the destruction of their homeland. One of their leaders, John of Gischala, a town in Galilee, seems to have tried to make himself king in Jerusalem. He was just one of many "false Messiahs", the role that had tempted Jesus in his 40 days in the wilderness.

The Zealots had a fervent devotion to the Torah, and in addition, Josephus wrote, *they have a passion for liberty which is almost unconquerable, since they are convinced that God alone is their leader and master. They think little of submitting to death*. While Jesus was not a Zealot he was nevertheless executed as one, and given a Zealot's death by crucifixion.

The Zealot presence was strong in Galilee, though scholars differ as to how strong, but at least one of his disciples, Simon the Zealot [Lk 6:15] had, or had had connections with the movement. It's interesting that Mark [3:18] and Matthew [10:4] call him the Cananaean. While this suggests he was from "Cana," or was a "Canaanite," it probably comes from the Aramaic for Zealot. It is possible that when Joseph, Mary and his brothers distanced themselves from Jesus, it was because while they were perhaps moderate Zealots and had brought up Jesus in that philosophy, they were disappointed when he insisted on creating his own understanding of what the true Messiah and his kingdom would be like. The Zealots saw the kingdom arriving through armed resistance to Rome; Jesus saw it arriving non-violently through the grace of God, as much of his preaching and many of his miracles testify.

22

THE SERMON ON THE MOUNT

He that takes pleasure to hear sermons enjoys himself as much as he that hears plays.

John Seldon [1584-1654].

With Capernaum as his base, Jesus travelled about Galilee, teaching in synagogues and *proclaiming the good news of the Kingdom* [Mt 4:23]. Large crowds gathered and, on one occasion, as there were too many to squeeze into a synagogue, he climbed a hillside to address them.

One suggestion is that the crowd was made up of landless peasants, the am ha'aretz, driven off the land by economic and social change, and this is possible. But it's more likely that, Jesus being local and new on the scene, they were the religiously curious drawn from a variety of backgrounds. Life was hard in Galilee and any diversion was an attractive prospect after a day's work. Religious issues dominated Jewish life and a fresh opinion was always welcome. We owe to the Jewish historian, Geza Vermes, the reminder that Galilee was home to at least two other itinerant teachers and miracle workers besides Jesus: Hanina ben Dosa and Honi the Circle-drawer. These were important charismatic figures previously overlooked by Christian scholars. They shed a welcome light on the background to Jesus' ministry.

Hanina ben Dosa was active some thirty years after Jesus. He lived ten miles or so from Nazareth and was a pupil of the great rabbi Yohanan ben Zakkai who, according to tradition, was so disappointed after the failure of his eighteen year ministry to make any impact on the local population he complained, "*Galilee, Galilee, you hate the Torah*". This gives an idea of what Jesus was up against, though Yohanan was a Pharisee from Jerusalem and, as we can see in the gospels, these missionaries from the south did not go down well in the north. Could Jesus do any better?

However, Yohanan's student, Hanina ben Dosa, did fare better. Like Jesus, Hanina also had a reputation for being able to heal at a distance, exorcise evil spirits and influence the weather' and, like Jesus, he too had a sense of humour as well as a close relationship with God. Walking home one day, it rained heavily and as he began to get wet, he prayed, *Lord of the universe, the whole world is in comfort while Hanina is in distress.* The rain stopped. Home and dry, he prayed, *Lord of the universe, the whole world is in distress whereas Hanina is in comfort*, and it began to rain. Humour and religion have always gone together for Jews in a way they don't always for Christians.

Like Jesus, Hanina was a devout teacher of the Torah but did not always follow the strict rules of the Pharisees. One day, while walking on his own it was said that he was met by the queen of demons who said to him that had he not been recommended from heaven she would have harmed him. Hanina, with great good humour and echoes of Jesus replied, *If I'm so highly regarded in heaven, I decree that you shall never again pass through an inhabited place.*

And just as in his encounter with the Pharisees over unwashed hands, Jesus shifted concern from the ritual to the moral, Hanina would do the same. One of his sayings which reflects this is preserved in the *Sayings of the Fathers,* the Pirke Arboth, *Any man whose fear of sin precedes his wisdom* [that is his expertise in the Torah] *his wisdom will endure; but if his wisdom precedes his fear of sin, his wisdom will not endure.* As Hanina probably taught in the generation after Jesus, it could be that he filled a similar role to Jesus and that Jesus is not quite the isolated figure he appears to be in the gospels but is recognisable as a certain kind of Galilean charismatic teacher.

Having attracted a large crowd, Jesus would have had to have held their interest, knowing that what he said would be heard against a background of rival teachers who were equally keen to be heard. To succeed, his message would need to be distinctive as well as clear and helpful to the morally and spiritually perplexed. To do this he leavened his message with humour.

Blessed are the meek

> *The meek do not inherit the earth unless they are prepared to fight for their meekness,*
>
> Harold Laski [1893-1950] [attrib].

Who were the "meek" to whom much was promised? [Mt 5:5] They were not the psychologically faint spirited of contemporary sermons but those at the bottom of the social pecking order, the underprivileged who had no choice but to turn the other cheek. These were the unemployed and the am ha'aretz, all potential recruits for the Zealots. With a few exceptions, like Rabbi Akiva, the Pharisees could only hope to recruit better off Jews, not from those doomed to scratch for a living on the edges of society.

But now, Jesus pronounced them "Blessed," this least blessed and least assertive group of all. Yet what did they understand by his words? Once they realised he was not a recruiting sergeant for the Zealots, they must have smiled, if not laughed. Like the "poor in spirit", "the merciful" and "the peacemakers" these were people whose goodwill and good nature were often exploited. Their blessings were not so much "pie in the sky", as pie at God's own Feast of Fools.

Two thousand years later, the meek have still not inherited the earth and the persecuted are still persecuted. God really would need to turn the world upside down if the promised blessings were to materialise. Communism, the god that failed, promised that it would bring in a just world order, and slew millions in the process. False ideologies are today's false messiahs. Market Capitalism has fared better in its promise of better lives, especially in China and India, yet at the cost of a major banking catastrophe, accelerated global warming, and threatening ecological disasters. All across the world, the meek who are also the poor, are still with us, crowded into slums in the third world and into high-rise, sink-estates in the more prosperous. Unless the irony is grasped, the message is missed. The Kingdom may be desirable, but was it real?

Jesus Lays the Irony on Thick

> *The longing for the truth is the weakest of all the human passions.*
>
> A. E. Housman [1859-1936].

Few expect to find humour in the Sermon on the Mount, but it's there: *Blessed are those,* Jesus said, *who hunger and thirst after righteousness, for they shall be satisfied.* [Mt 5:6]

This must really have made the crowd laugh, because if there was one group which was never satisfied, it was those who pursued righteousness in the single-minded, over-eager way described by Jesus, hungering and thirsting for it and demanding ever more from themselves and from others. Galilee would never be righteous enough for the Torah experts from Jerusalem, just as Jerusalem would never be righteous enough for the Essenes at Qumran; while the most extreme of all the pursuers of righteousness, the Zealots, would never be satisfied not even when their attempt to drive out the unrighteous Romans brought about the destruction of Zion, Herod's Temple and the Jewish communities of Judaea and Galilee.

The poor couldn't afford to observe the Torah in the way

demanded by the ultra-observant, hence Jesus' ironic attack on all who were making the law impossibly difficult to observe.

It may be objected that this is too novel an interpretation of the text. Why cannot the verse be taken at its face value, the way it has always been read? The problem is that this would have Jesus simply repeating what his opponents were saying, reducing righteousness to a cliché when he wasn't that sort of preacher. The text only says something that's worth hearing if it's read ironically. The consequence of taking it non-ironically would mean that Jesus was saying, "Blessed are the Torah extremists."

Righteousness: The Priority for Jews

Be not righteous over much.

Ecclesiastes 7:16.

If the Greeks hungered after knowledge and the Romans after power, then the Jews thirsted for righteousness. This not only meant that the good Jew intended to lead a moral life but that he was bound to observe all of the law's 613 commandments which sanctified every aspect of life through holiness and prayer. At its best, it was a splendid spiritual vision; at its worst, it was a programme of perfection which could corrupt those who lost sight of the ends which the ritual law was there to serve.

Every Jew who took Judaism seriously endeavoured, with God's help, to live according to the Torah. The trouble lay with those for whom Torah observance had become absolute. This was a problem that went back at least as far as the return from exile. The consensus among Judah's leaders was that the nation had been exiled because of its unfaithfulness to God and his Law. The unflinching resolve was that such an apostasy would never happen again. Judaea in Jesus' day was more Torah observant than it had ever been before. Only now there was a new problem: not idolatry as it had been in Jeremiah's day but anxiety as to the degree and extent of Torah righteousness, for not only were there widely divergent degrees of observance but also diverging degrees of expectation of observance. The result was rising anxiety among religious Jews over the details of their observance, an anxiety that radiated outwards from Jerusalem into Galilee and beyond.

Psalm 119 is the passage which best expresses this anxiety. *Happy are they whose way of life is blameless, who conform to the law of the Lord.* [v1] *You, Lord, have laid down your precepts which are to be kept faithfully. If only I might hold a steady course, keeping your statutes. Then if I fixed my eye on all your commandments, I should never be put to shame.* [vv5&6]. The entire psalm is about a young Jew's total devotion to the Torah. It's his life and joy. *How I love your law! It is my study all day long!* [v97].

As in so many psalms, the psalmist's zeal has made enemies and in prayer he vents his anger against them: *The proud have felt your censure; cursed are those who turn from your commandments. Set me free from scorn and insult, for I have obeyed your instruction.* [vv21&22.] The spiritual and social dynamics are revealing. Firstly, the observant appear to antagonise fellow Jews simply by their faithfulness. There is a constant reference to enemies in the psalms and commentators are not agreed on who these enemies are; but it is probable that a good proportion of them are those who are hostile to the more Torah observant.

A second observation is that not only do the observant antagonise the non-observant, but that in the pains they go to to observe even the smallest details, they feel that God owes them blessings in abundance. Psalm 1 expresses this beautifully: *Blessed is the man who has not walked in the counsel of the ungodly, or stood in the way of sinners; and has not sat in the seat of the scornful. But his delight is in the law of the Lord, and in his law he will exercise himself day and night* [vv1&2]. It is because of this that the ultra-righteous so often felt spiritually dissatisfied.

As we have seen, one writer who reacted against this excessive concern with Torah righteousness was Koheleth, the author of Ecclesiastes: *In my futile existence I have seen it all, from the righteous perishing in their righteousness to the wicked growing old in wickedness. Do not be over-righteous and do not be over-wise. Why should you destroy yourself?* [Ecc. 7:15]. A few verses later, he concluded, *There is no one on earth so righteous that he always does right and never does wrong.*

Another sage, Agur son of Jakeh from Massa, wrote, *The leech has two daughters, "Give, give," they cry. Three things are never satisfied, four never say, "Enough": Sheol, the barren womb, the earth ever thirsty for water and the fire which never says, "Enough."* [Prov. 30:15] These are comical enough in a grim sort of way, especially if we read "death" for "Sheol," while a childless woman was likely to exhaust both her husband's physical strength and his patience in her attempt to get pregnant. She would have been the butt of village humour. Now Jesus adds a fifth as the butt of the crowd's humour: the comic figure of the ultra-religious, falling over the smallest details in the pursuit of righteousness, making everyone feel religiously inadequate in the process. Yet, having said this it needs to be remembered that alongside the texts quoted in support of reading the psalms as evidence of Torah anxiety, there are also texts to support a genuine, spiritual joy in the Torah, a joy which as Christian visitors to a synagogue will bear witness often survives in Shabbat morning services to this day.

Throughout Jesus' ministry, the need to live righteously was an inescapable problem, the background to everything he did and taught. His answer seems to have been akin to that of the book of Ecclesiastes, moderation; while his preferred way of dealing publicly with the problem was through humour, especially ridicule.

23

THE BIBLE'S FOURTH DEFINING MOMENT: JESUS REINTERPRETS THE TORAH

It is my judgement that Church interpretation… has tended to trim and domesticate the text…

Walter Breuggemann [b. 1933]

Writing as a gentile convert, a generation after these events, St Luke can see, in a way that the more Jewish gospels of Mark, Matthew and John cannot, how radical Jesus was in his interpretation of Jewish religious law. *I desire mercy and not sacrifice,* Hosea said. In his teaching about the love and forgiveness of the Kingdom, Jesus had shifted the emphasis from sacrifice to mercy even more radically than any prophet before him.

Jesus as an Irresponsible Rabbi

Perhaps it is better to be irresponsible and right than to be responsible and wrong.

Winston Churchill [1874-1965].

Devout Galileans had continually to negotiate the details of their obedience to Jewish law, while those who did not give much attention to their religious practices were reminded constantly that they should try harder, if not by itinerant Pharisees, then by family members and neighbours. Interpretation and obedience to Torah were subjects on which Jesus as a teacher could not avoid making pronouncements.

As with any contentious issue, opinions ranged from the strict to the not so strict with every gradation between. Among the Pharisees, Rabbi Shammai, an older contemporary of Jesus, was reckoned to be strict while Rabbi Hillel was thought more liberal. Their opinions were important and the crowds who turned up to hear Jesus would have been familiar with some of their sayings and legal judgements. Rabbi Shammai's favourite dictum was, *Study Torah regularly, say little, but do much, receive all men in a friendly manner;* while Rabbi Hillel's was, *What is hateful to you, do not do to your neighbour,* which in Jesus' summary of the Torah became The

Golden Rule. Today, Hillel's most quoted saying is: *If I am not for myself, who is for me? And when I am for myself, what am I? And if not now, when?*

In his teaching on Torah observance, Jesus could sound as conservative as Shammai, *Till heaven and earth pass away,* he said, *one jot or tittle shall in no wise pass from the law, till all be fulfilled* [Mt. 5:18]*;* while, in practice, he could seem among the most liberal and irresponsible of interpreters: for example, with the Woman Taken in Adultery, a story, which, because some were afraid of what it might appear to teach, was left out of many gospel manuscripts, and in others can be found in no fewer than five different places. [Jn 7:53; 7:36; 7:52; 7:24 and Lk 21:38].

Most modern translations print it as a codicil to St John's gospel: *At daybreak, Jesus appeared again in the temple, and all the people gathered around him. He had taken his seat and was engaged in teaching them when the scribes and the Pharisees brought in a woman caught committing adultery. Making her stand in the middle, they said to him, "Teacher, this woman was caught in the very act of adultery. In the law Moses has laid down that such women are to be stoned. What do you say about it?"*

His interrogators are eager to know to which school of interpretation he belongs: the literal rigorist or the liberal humanist.[92] In this encounter Jesus is thrown back on his wits; and wit, being clever at finding a way out of a predicament, is often comic, as is the case here, where we have to smile at the ingenuity of his reply. *They put this question as a test, hoping to frame a charge against him. Jesus bent down and wrote with his finger on the ground. When they continued to press their question he sat up straight and said, Let whichever of you is free from sin throw the first stone at her. Then, once again, he bent down and wrote on the ground. When they heard what he said, one by one they went away, the eldest first; and Jesus was left alone, with the woman still standing there. Jesus again sat up and said to the woman, Where are they? Has no one condemned you? She answered, No one, Sir. Neither do I condemn you, Jesus said. Go; do not sin again.*

This is wisdom to rank with Solomon's, and it counts as comedy because we smile at the discomfort of his opponents. But we can also understand why it was omitted in so many manuscripts, becoming a kind of free-floating passage in St John and St Luke. Gentile Christians probably feared it would encourage wives to stray;

---

92 These are modern categories but they do correspond to what we might term the "strict" and "more lenient" schools of interpretation among the scribes and Pharisees.

while Jewish Christians either feared the same result or reckoned it to be so liberal as to encourage adverse comments by the Torah-strict.

A Saying Left Out of the Gospels

Let us never negotiate out of fear. But let us never fear to negotiate

John F. Kennedy [1917-63]

Another instance of Jesus' embarrassing wit in interpreting Jewish law is found in Codex Bezae, an ancient manuscript brought from Lyons in the 16th century and given to the University of Cambridge by the reformer Theodore Beza [1519-1605]. The saying occurs in St Luke 5:6 replacing the well known, *And he said unto them that the Son of Man is Lord also of the Sabbath.* The Bezan text reads: *On the same day, seeing one working on the Sabbath, he said unto him, "Man, if indeed you know what you are doing, you are blessed; but if not, you are cursed and a transgressor of the law."*

To appreciate the radical nature of Jesus' response here, we need to set it against its background story in Numbers 15:32, *While the people of Israel were in the wilderness, they found a man gathering sticks on the Sabbath day. ... They put him into custody, because it had not been made plain what should be done to him. And the Lord said to Moses, "The man shall be put to death; all the congregation shall stone him with stones outside the camp." And all the congregation brought him outside the camp, and stoned him to death..."* Read in this context, the Bezan saying could hardly be more radical, with Jesus going against the plain ruling of scripture, making it among the most radical of his re-interpretations of Torah.

Personally, I have no doubt that the saying is genuine as it embodies in a characteristic, risk-taking way, the wit, ingenuity and humanity of Jesus. It is easy to see how such a story might be omitted from a manuscript but not how it might be invented and written in. There's no purpose its invention might have served, but every reason for church leaders to fear its inclusion.

To see how Jesus applied its principle to himself, we can note his keeping company with tax-collectors and sinners in yet another comic example of the Kingdom of God as a Feast of Fools. [Mk2:16]. In most circumstances it is wise to avoid bad company. But there are exceptions. Like the man in the Bezan text, Jesus is blessed if he knows what he is doing and cursed if he does not. For those who favoured moral strictness in Torah observance Jesus must have seemed the most irresponsible of Rabbis.

When a Good Story is a Comically Dangerous Story

> *Wickedness is always easier than virtue; for it takes the short cut to everything.*
>
> Samuel Johnson [1709-84] Boswell's *Tour of the Hebrides.*

In the Parable of the Unjust Steward [Lk 16:1-9] Jesus tells the story of a servant who fails to do his job and is dismissed for wasting his master's property. His last action before handing back his responsibilities is to "tidy the books." *Summoning his master's debtors one by one, he said to the first, "How much do you owe my master". He said, "A hundred measures of oil." He said to him, "Take your bill and sit down quickly and write fifty. Then he said to another, "And how much do you owe?" He said, "A hundred measures of wheat." He said to him, "Take your bill and write eighty."*

Ingenuity in getting out of a tight spot always raises a smile. Clever escapes are comedy[93] and though what the steward does is theft on a grand scale, he made sure that lots of people owed him favours which he could call in later. If only, Jesus is saying, the *sons of light,* that is the Torah righteous, were as ingenious as *the sons of this age*.

Verse eight has been the source of much discussion among scholars: *The master commended the unjust steward for his prudence.* Is the master here, Jesus or the steward's master? It hardly matters, as either way the steward's wit and ingenuity are the whole point of the parable. Jesus is again treading tricky moral ground and to his critics must have seemed irresponsible as a teacher.

Just as with the woman taken in adultery and the man found working on the Sabbath, Jesus is revealed in this parable as a teacher who departed radically from what was expected of him. The parable makes most sense if Jesus is recommending that his followers be as creative in taking risks with the Torah as the steward was with his book-keeping.

It's not surprising that this parable is found only in St Luke's gospel, and one manuscript at that. Mark and Matthew being nearer to the Jewish-Christian wing of the early Church would have found it

---

[93] We have only to consider the popularity of Baroness Emmuska Orczy's [1865-1947] novels in her Scarlet Pimpernel series, to see the entertainment value of ingenuity.

too liberal in its attitude to the Torah. As an Anglican watching the repeated reluctance of the Church of England's General Synod to depart from "the clear teaching of the Bible", I marvel at how little the conservative mind appreciates the radical stance of Jesus as a teacher.

A Parable of God's Generosity

> *One must be poor to know the generosity of giving.*
> George Eliot [1819-1880] *Middlemarch.*

The best known of Jesus' parables of his Father's remarkable generosity is that of the Prodigal Son, [Lk 15:11ff] in which, rather than wait for his father to die, the younger son asks for his inheritance there and then. The father grants his request, the son turns his good fortune into cash, leaves home, squanders the lot and ends up penniless. To stay alive, he does what no observant Jew would do and looks after pigs, until, brought to his senses, he returns home and throws himself on his father's mercy. His father's welcome knows no restraint: he is given back his old standing and loaded with gifts. Understandably, the elder brother protests at the injustice, only to be told, *"How could you fail to celebrate this happy day? Your brother was dead and has come back to life; he was lost and has been found."* [15:32].

The words which cause the greatest offence to those who hear the parable and take the older brother's side, are these: *But while he was yet at a distance his father saw him and had compassion and ran and embraced him.* That is, long before the returning son had an opportunity to repent and explain himself, or his father reflect on what the Torah expected of him, the father showed his love and forgiveness by running to greet his wastrel of a son. That, in the teaching of Jesus, is how God behaves towards us. Once again, in turning the expected order of things upside down his was not the teaching of a Torah-responsible Rabbi.

When Good is in Conflict with Good: The Priority of Love over Justice

> *I dogmatise and am contradicted, and in this conflict of opinions and sentiments I find delight.*
> Samuel Johnson [1709-84] *Johnsonian Miscellanies.*

The greater tragedy often lies less in the conflict between good and evil than in the conflict between good and good, which was the tragedy that arose in the preaching of Jesus whenever he gave the claims of love priority over those of justice. The parable of the Prodigal son illustrates the conflict perfectly.

'Outrageous" is the word that often summarises Jesus' teaching. In the tension between mercy and justice, Jesus comes down on the side of mercy. For the Torah observant, justice and righteousness were twin virtues. To be righteous was to deal justly and here Jesus was putting the mercy and the generosity of love before righteousness, justice and fair play. To this day, in Jewish/Christian dialogue, Jews will sometimes challenge Christians by declaring that justice is the primary virtue not love.

For 600 years the survival of Israel had been built on Torah righteousness, with the result that most Pharisees saw Jesus' interpretation of the Torah as being too liberal and too radical. He was turning everything they stood for the wrong way round. The Pharisees were not against mercy, indeed the Talmud frequently tempers justice with mercy; but, by prioritising love over justice like this, Jesus could cause great offence. It was taking the comedy of the Kingdom too far.

Jesus: A Different Sort of Rabbi

Love, thou art absolute sole lord of life and death.
Richard Crashaw [c. 1613-1649]

Though there are many instances in the Talmud of Rabbis expanding upon the commandment to love our neighbour as ourselves [Lev. 19:18], it was always seen as part of living righteously, that is justly, as commanded by the Torah. Jesus, on the other hand, would appear to have been unique in his understanding of Jewish Law in the central importance he gave to love. Nowhere is this as clear as on the occasion when Simon, a Pharisee eager to discuss the Torah with him, invited him to a meal. [Lk 7:36-50]

During the meal, *a woman of the city, who was a sinner* arrived. At the very least she failed to keep a kosher kitchen; at worst she was, perhaps, a prostitute. She was not a welcome guest and had brought *an alabaster box of ointment, and standing behind him at his feet, weeping, she began to wet his feet with her tears and wiped them with her hair and anointed them with the ointment.*

The woman's histrionics are a comedy of exaggeration and

they embarrass the host, as does Jesus' response to her behaviour: *If this man were a prophet, he would have known who and what sort of woman this is who is touching him.* In response, Jesus, as a guest teacher, asks his host a question: *A certain creditor had two debtors, one owed five hundred denarii*[94]*, and the other fifty. When they both could not pay, he forgave them both. Now which of them will love him more.* Simon, as a Pharisee dedicated to Torah observance, would have expected this sort of question from another teacher of Torah and said, *The one to whom he forgave more.* It was the right answer, but with the parable, Jesus has turned what was at issue from a question about righteousness to one about love and forgiveness and this is a big leap in the interpretation of Torah.

Although all four gospels include a story of an unnamed woman extravagantly anointing Jesus,[95] Matthew, Mark and John link the incident to Jesus' Passion and the disciple's complaint about it being a waste of money. St Luke, on the other hand, links it to Jesus' understanding of the Kingdom of God as the place of God's love and forgiveness. He compares, unfavourably, Simon's lack of greeting and failure to anoint his feet with oil with the fuss the woman makes and interprets her theatrical behaviour as a response to love: *I tell you, her sins, which are many are forgiven, for she loved much; but he who is forgiven little, loves little. And he said to her, your sins are forgiven.*

To Simon, the Torah observant Pharisee, Jesus' teaching must have seemed as bizarre as the woman's behaviour. If she was a prostitute then of course she had loved much, but only in a perverse ironic sense. Matters were not improved when Jesus further shifted the meaning of her behaviour from moral and social impropriety to the need for forgiveness when, *he said to her, Your sins are forgiven. Your faith has saved you, go in peace.* Not surprisingly, this provoked a general discussion, something all Rabbis aimed to do, *Who is this, who even forgives sins.*

When Jesus says, *she has anointed my body beforehand for its burial* [Mark 14:8], there's irony here, for he knew what we know, that the word Messiah means, "anointed one". Jesus had possibly been anointed as Messiah by a prostitute! Our expectations really are reversed in the Kingdom of God.

Jesus told his followers to take his Torah principle of love as far even as loving one's enemies: *love your enemies, bless them that curse you* [Mt 5:44]. In the comic, turning the expected around,

---

94 The singular, *denarius,* was, at the time, a day's wage for a farm worker.

95 Matthew 26:6-13; Mark 14:3-9; John 12:1-8.

parable of The Good Samaritan, again told only by St Luke [10:29 – 37], Jesus has the mitzvah[96], the good deed, of compassion, rescue and ongoing care, performed by, of all people, a Samaritan, the long-standing enemy of the Jews. This was an another unexpected twist.

In many respects, Jesus can be considered more of a Sage, a Wisdom teacher, than a Rabbi. Rabbis were expected to give precise answers to questions on matters of Jewish Law. For example, how far was it permitted to travel on the Sabbath day? Different Rabbis gave different answers, but 2,000 cubits was the lower figure suggested and 4,000 cubits the upper. Jesus, for his part, appears to have avoided being so definite. Instead, he took both Torah and Wisdom in the opposite direction, to their limits, to the point at which they broke down and lust became equivalent to adultery and anger, murder. *Judge not*, he said, *and you will not be judged.* [Mt 7:1] But a life based on precisely applied rules required the constant making of judgements and the answers he gave were not practical answers to practical questions. To the devout Jew, they were decidedly unhelpful. They opened up a subject to such an extent that righteous living only became possible in an unimaginable Kingdom of God. If the purpose of the Torah was to prescribe the smallest details of righteous living, so that the righteous knew what to do in every situation in life, then the teaching of Jesus undermined that whole approach. He took away the certainties of traditional teaching. Responsibility for living a righteous life was given back to the individual. To the Rabbis and those who lived by their decisions it must have seemed a chaotic, even anarchic way of teaching Torah.

Care must be taken here not to revive the old Christian prejudice that the Rabbis were legalistically minded and organised righteous living around narrow rules and regulations, though some Jews have always been given to casuistic extremes like this. In the early modern period this approach became known as *pilpul* [keen analysis] and was mocked, in typical word-play, by other Jews as *bilbul,* [confusion.] Jesus was not the first, nor the last, to take interpretation in the direction of "wisdom." To Jews who judged others as being insufficiently observant, Rabbi Hillel, the grandfather of Gamaliel, St Paul's teacher, advised, *Do not judge your neighbour*

---

96 *Mitzvah* is Hebrew for "commandment". The rabbis taught that there were 613 commandments in the Torah, of these 365 were negative and 248 positive. In everyday life, Jews speak of any good deed as a mitzvah, indicating that all acts of human goodness have their origin in the promptings of the God of the Covenant with Moses.

until you are in his place. This was an approach Jesus shared, only he took it further in a liberal and non-prescriptive direction than anyone before or since. To his opponents among the Pharisees it must have seemed that he was succeeding where the Seleucid attacks on the religious law had failed. Jesus was unleashing dissonance and the *Nihil* would be not far behind.

Throughout his ministry, Jesus was a Torah observant Jew: he went up to Jerusalem for the festivals and he wore fringes on his garments; yet in many matters he appeared radical or lax. He differed, too, from other interpreters of the Law in that he related its fulfilment to the Kingdom of Heaven rather than to the practicalities of 1st century Judean life. Moreover his message that disasters like the collapse of the Tower of Siloam [Lk 13:4] were not in any way punishment for sins, threatened strict adherence to the Torah as the central, comic guarantee of Jewish survival.

More worryingly, Jesus' non-prescriptive approach to righteous living: *you are blessed if you know what you are doing, cursed if you don't,* placed too great an onus on an individual's capacity to act wisely and rightly,[97] as well as rendering redundant the need for rabbinic and other authoritative interpretations of scripture.

In humanising the Torah Jesus emerges as a Jewish humanist who went far beyond the teaching of the most liberal Pharisees. What makes him so difficult to categorise is that while he exhibits some of the characteristics of the prophet, apocalypticist, rabbi and wisdom teacher, he is far from being comprehended or limited by them.

Whereas the Pharisees, Scribes and Sadducees gave precise rulings to precise questions, Jesus avoided detailed pronouncements and opened the debate for further discussion instead. He was taking the development of Torah studies in a way that must have seemed to other interpreters to run counter to 600 years of history.

Was Jesus too Radical even for the Church?

> *Lest they should see with their eyes and understand with their hearts.* Isaiah 6:10

The advantage of organising morality as a system of rules is that these can be systematised as law and managed by lawyers. Without

---

97 The difficulties of legislating for euthanasia and assisted dying are problems that remain under secular law.

the rule of law societies disintegrate. Little wonder, that the Pharisees were concerned about how Jesus was interpreting the Torah as the rule-free governance of love. Where Jeremiah and Ezekiel saw the Torah as educating the heart by being written upon it, Jesus saw the role of the heart as the interpreter of Torah; so that while the Pharisees, with their desire to humanise the Torah, could go some way with Jesus' view, they soon began to part company with him. To them Jesus seemed not only too radical but also irresponsible. As love and the heart cannot easily be structured, the Torah as a system of wisely devised rules and principles would inevitably be undermined. Its comic purpose of guaranteeing Jewish survival would end. The ministry of Jesus was the fourth defining moment of Judaism.

And not only did the Pharisees find it difficult to follow Jesus in his interpretation of Torah, but clearly the disciples did too. The account of Jesus dining with Simon found a place only in Luke's gospel. There was also a similar lack of enthusiasm for the story of the woman taken in adultery. These were occasions not easily reduced to general principles and they were open to misunderstanding by ordinary people. It was better to play them down. If many thought Rabbi Shammai too strict[98], Jesus could seem too lax. Occasionally he might talk tough, but his actions whether dispensing forgiveness or eating with sinners would take the Torah in ways in which its interpretation could no longer be controlled.

We will see in the next chapter how the gap between Jesus and the Pharisees, the religious group who were nearest to him, widened to the point it could no longer be bridged.

---

98 It may seem paradoxical but strict rules often enhance the survival chances of a religious tradition, and the Pharisees knew this. The phenomenon has been explored by sociologists, psychologists and others. It strengthens group cohesion and seems to limit "free-riding" whereby the poorly committed share the benefits created by the strongly committed. See pp 58ff of Nicholas Wade's, *The Faith Instinct, How Religion Evolved & Why It Endures,* The Penguin Press, 2009.

24

JESUS AND RELIGIOUS RIVALRY IN GALILEE

Thou shalt not covet; but tradition
Approves all forms of competition
Arthur Hugh Clough [1819-1861]

There was no shortage of wandering philosophers and preachers in the ancient world. Established teachers were to be found in cities among the educated, where they could earn a living, while those not so well-established honed their message in marginal regions like Galilee.

For Greek and Roman audiences there would have been teachers in the Stoic, Cynic and other philosophical traditions. These would have kept to the gentile areas of Galilee, but judging from Stoic influences in St Paul's writings, it is clear that even orthodox Jews could be influenced by non-Jewish teaching. Galilee was in many respects a "multi-faith" area, but one in which Jews and gentiles kept largely, though not entirely, to themselves.

Some scholars have explored the influence on Jesus of wandering Cynics, ascetic philosophers who challenged convention and lived close to nature, men like Diogenes, who lived in a barrel and once asked Alexander the Great to step out of his light. It is doubtful if they influenced any but the most Hellenised Jews, and although they taught that by reducing personal needs to a minimum it was possible to control one's soul, there is little evidence of any real influence on Jesus.

While Jesus may have had to deal with Zealots and Essenes, and even Buddhists on their travels to Rome, it is chiefly the Pharisees who challenged him.

The Pharisees

Now is the time of the Pharisees.
Boris Paternak [1890-1960]

Modern Jews are descended spiritually from the Pharisees and few groups in the Bible have been more misunderstood. Millennia of Christian misunderstanding have made an objective view difficult. After the failed rebellions against Rome in 66AD and 135AD, it was the Pharisees who ensured the survival of Judaism. Without them there would be no Jews in the world today. It's because of this that it's important to note that Jews today are not identical in a religious sense with those of Jesus' time. This is because in the intervening years Judaism was redefined by the Talmud, that vast record of debates on the Torah by the Rabbis, the scholarly descendants of the Pharisees. Today, even secular Jews honour the Pharisees as the saviours of Judaism, while, for the religious they are the sages whose lives of prayer and study made the very survival of Israel possible.

This contrasts with the traditional picture Christians have had of the Pharisees in which they seem to be no more than the implacable, fault-finding opponents of Jesus. Only after the Second World War and the evils of the Holocaust have Christians and Jews attempted to come together as men and women of faith seeking to relate to one another with mutual respect. As the Christian poet, W. H. Auden put it, "We must love one another or die."

How then are we to reconcile these views? Although Jesus frequently disputed points of Jewish law with the Pharisees so that on occasions the disagreement between them could hardly have been more marked, it is a travesty to argue that Jesus preached a message of love while the Pharisees preached one of sterile legalism. Nor is it correct to assert that the Pharisees were a party of self-righteous hypocrites whose rejection of his message led to Jesus being crucified. We must be careful not to over-simplify or deal in caricatures. This is important if Christians are to free themselves from a long standing contempt for the Pharisees and their spiritual descendants.

As with any group, there was a range of opinion among New Testament Pharisees from those who managed their religious practice in a relaxed way, to those who were more extreme. The Pharisees were no more monolithic in beliefs and practice than were 17th century English Puritans. The moderates are usually the majority in any group, with the extremists in a minority. This would have been the case with the Pharisees, who in Jesus' day were a minority party. Josephus said they numbered only about 6,000 though a very influential 6,000.

In the gospels, the Pharisees who exhorted Galileans in Torah obedience were probably of the more extreme kind. We know little of their teaching, only that they did not find Jesus to their liking and that in response he made use of comedy, especially satire, to counter their influence. As for Pharisees in general, relations appears to have been friendlier, though far from simple.

St Luke [13:31] recalls that *a number of Pharisees came and warned him, "Leave this place and be on your way; Herod wants to kill you."* As Herod Antipas had already killed Jesus' relative, John the Baptist, it was a plot to be taken seriously and so the warning speaks of a generosity that the Pharisees are not always credited with.[99] Similarly, in the Acts of the Apostles, the influential Pharisee, Gamaliel, speaks before the Sanhedrin on behalf of the Apostles; while in spite of their disagreement with Jesus over dietary laws, St Luke reports a Pharisee inviting Jesus to a meal. We need to note too that a number of Pharisees were sympathetic to Jesus' teaching: the most famous being Nicodemus [Jn 3:1ff].

It is clear from what Jesus said to his disciples and the temple crowds that all that he said against the Pharisees was set within his basic acceptance of them. Even so, his criticism could be comically mocking: *The scribes and the Pharisees occupy Moses seat; so be careful to do whatever they tell you. But do not follow their practice; for they say one thing and do another. They make up heavy loads and pile them on the shoulders of others, but will not themselves lift a finger to ease the burden. Whatever they do is done for show. They go about wearing broad phylacteries and with large tassels on their robes; they love to have the place of honour at feasts and the chief seats in the synagogues, to be greeted respectfully in the street, and to be addressed as "Rabbi".* [Mt 23:1ff]

The issue centred on the way in which some Pharisees promoted their teaching by imposing it on the hearers. As a party, they had developed in the post-exilic period advocating separation from non-Jews as a way of preserving not only their religious identity but also their ritual purity. This approach could, and for many did, lead to excessive pride in their own piety and contempt for gentiles. What Jesus attacked was exaggerated religiosity, and he used humour to do it.

Whited Sepulchres

The only real danger that exists is man himself.
Carl Gustav Jung [1875-1961]

Several times at the funerals of Jewish friends, friendly arms have guided me from unknowingly stepping onto a poorly marked grave. This is a practice Christians observe in graveyards out of respect, but orthodox Jews from the need to avoid ritual impurity. Graves that

[99] We need to recall too that in 62AD it was the Pharisees who protested at the murder of St James, the brother of Jesus, by the Sadducees.

might not otherwise be obvious, especially at dusk, were, in Jesus day, often whitewashed. The practice gave Jesus a comic image for the more extreme behaviour he wanted his followers to avoid. If the pursuit of wisdom could lead to intellectual superiority, then the pursuit of holiness as separation from the ritually impure could lead to attitudes of religious superiority and it was these Jesus would lampoon.

When the Pharisees fell into the temptation of reproving the Judaism they found in Galilee, Jesus countered with: *Alas for you, scribes and Pharisees, hypocrites!*[100] *You are like tombs covered with whitewash; they look fine on the outside, but inside they are full of dead men's bones and of corruption. So it is with you: outwardly you look like honest men, but inside you are full of hypocrisy and lawlessness.* [St Mt. 23:27].

The comedy here is dark as Jesus strikes at the very thing his opponents pride themselves on: their law-abidingness. His image implied that Pharisees were to be avoided in the way tombs were to be avoided. The Greek word hypocrite came from the theatre and referred to "an actor playing a part". As devout Jews did not go to the theatre it was a telling polemic to suggest that the Pharisees were turning their religion into street theatre. To ensure the charge is understood, Jesus goes into details about bones and rotting flesh in a kind of visual slapstick. If the outside of the tomb made someone ritually unclean, then the inside was even more to be avoided. Satire like this would have appealed to Galileans who thought that they were being pressured into being more observant than they were comfortable with. The overly righteous could never be satisfied.[101]

They Disfigure Their Faces

Who are those advertising men kidding?
Mary McCarthy [1912-1989]

Some of those who hungered and thirsted after righteousness went as far as cultivating a pinched and pale look, using wood ash or some other cosmetic device. [Mt 6:16]. Jesus said, *they disfigure* [aphanizousin] *their faces so that they may "figure"* [phanosin] *as*

---

[100] There is an Islamic agraphon or saying of Jesus preserved outside the gospels which reflects the teaching here, *Revere God in the secrecy of your hearts as you revere him in public.*

[101] This problem of "scrupulosity" among the ultra-devout is also one that Christian confessors and counsellors have to deal with.

fasting in public. The wordplay is easily lost in translation.

Disagreements, Arguments and Disputes

Rightly to be great
Is not to stir without great argument,
But rightly to find a quarrel in a straw.
William Shakespeare, [1564-1616], *Hamlet.*

Rabbis in Jesus' day debated points of law. They still do. Arguing is what scholars do the world over. It is the way knowledge grows even in modern science. It's not just that life would be dull without disagreement but that without it there would be no development or progress. What matters is that such disagreements are productive. Disputes become serious when the satire begins, and that happens only when truth is thought to be at issue. Satire marks the shift from the gentlemanly to the gloves-off stage of disagreement.

Like even the best books, the gospels have their limitations, especially in their accounts of Jesus' disputes with the Pharisees where they give mostly his side of the argument. We have no idea if and how they satirized him in turn.

In the Sermon on the Mount, [Mt 5-7], although the subjects of Jesus' warning are not identified, it is clearly the overly religious Pharisees who are the targets. Modern Jews have a word for this kind of excessive zeal: *frum.* I first heard the word when invited to speak at an Orthodox synagogue on Christian-Jewish dialogue. The chairman took me aside to say that I might have some trouble from a convert on the front row who was very "frum". "She's more religious than God!" he said.

In summary, we can note that on the one hand, Jesus had supporters and friends among the Pharisees and reminds his followers that they occupy the teaching chair of Moses, while on the other he warns against the double-standards and hypocrisy to which their zeal tempts them. In this way, we can attempt some sort of balanced judgement about his attack in the Sermon of the Mount on the "ultra-frum". *So, when you give alms, do not announce it with a flourish of trumpets, as the hypocrites do in the synagogues and in the streets to win the praise of others.* [Mt. 6:1-2] In the House of Commons members know that a single luminous phrase will be more effective against an opponent than a string of sound arguments. When in a Commons wrangle over the dismissal of the Director of the Prison Service, the Prisons Minister famously remarked of the then Home Secretary that there was "something of the night about him," that six word, Dracula evoking image ricocheted around the country and is thought to have contributed to his failure at the time to secure the leadership of the Conservative party. "A flourish of trumpets in a synagogue" might have proved an effective equivalent in Galilee.

The Healing of the Man Born Blind

Hatred is blind, as well as love.
18th century English Proverb.

St John's story, [9:1ff] of *The Healing of the Man Born Blind* is difficult. Because the healing took place on the Sabbath [v16] some of the Pharisees took it as evidence that Jesus could not be from God. This was also their reaction to the healings of the man with the withered hand [Mk 3:1 ff], the stooping woman [Lk 13:10ff], and the man with dropsy. [Lk 14:1ff.] To his opponents these were violations of the Sabbath and came automatically under divine condemnation.

Of interest too is the reaction of Jesus' disciples, who find no difficulty in his healing on the Sabbath. Instead they ask, "*Rabbi, why was this man born blind? Who sinned, this man or his parents?"* They accepted as self-evident that his blindness was a punishment for sin; yet, for whose sin was it a punishment? If it was the man who had sinned, then either he had sinned in a previous existence, or his punishment had been backdated to his birth. Both explanations raise as many problems as they solve.

The first might presuppose belief in re-incarnation or the transmigration of souls which, though not orthodox Jewish beliefs, were not unknown in some sects; so, though unlikely, re-incarnation as an explanation cannot be ruled out. Josephus [Jew. War ii, 8.14] seemed to hold that some Pharisees accepted the idea. Moreover, as Buddhist missionaries were not unknown in the Roman Empire, it is possible that the idea was around and had been picked up by the disciples.

Equally, the idea that the man had brought his blindness upon himself could relate to the Pharisaic doctrine of the resurrection. When, at Caesarea Philippi, Jesus asks his disciples "*Who do people say that the Son of Man is? and is told, "Some say John the Baptist, others Elijah, others Jeremiah, or one of the prophets,"* [Mt 16:13ff] they perhaps had in mind some idea of an exceptional resurrection before the End Time.

The second possibility, that the man had been punished by God for his parents' sins, though acceptable in earlier times, for example, the death of David's son following his adultery with

Bathsheba, this had been ruled out by Ezekiel [18:1ff] with his assertion that *the soul that sins, it shall die.*

Within the theology of the time, the disciples' question was one which involved an unresolved contradiction. There are a number of these in the gospels. For example, in Matthew 22:42, Jesus challenges the Pharisees with "*What is your opinion about the Messiah? Whose son is he*?" And when, as expected they reply, "*The Son of David*," then Jesus is ready with a quotation from psalm 110:1 *If then David calls him Lord, how can he be David's son?* It was a trick question designed to score points and there's always a comic element in wrong-footing opponents.

But with the man born blind, the question is a real question involving a contradiction. How then does Jesus respond? His answer, "*he was born blind so that God's power might be displayed in curing him*," [9:3] when taken literally does not so much resolve the disciples' problems as compound them. The thought that God would afflict an unborn child with blindness simply so Jesus could cure him is horrific and one which commentators do their best to circumvent with the suggestion that a practical cure was better than a theological explanation. This is true, of course. In suffering some evil, victims need rescuing, not a crash course in philosophy. But then why would Jesus say something as callous as, "*He was born blind so that God's power might be displayed in curing him?*" This is not the God revealed elsewhere in Jesus' ministry. In fact it is specifically denied in his account of the fatal collapse of the tower at Siloam [Lk 13:4].

However, much is resolved if Jesus' words are read as deflecting a serious question with the humour of absurdity. It is a joke and one of Jesus' best. To see how, consider the comic tale of the Mullah Hodja Nasrudin, a spiritually educative story told among Muslims and Christians in the Middle East.

One evening, the Mullah and his wife retire to bed but are unable to sleep because of a quarrel in the street below. "Nasrudin," his wife says, "See if you can find out what they're fighting about and put an end to it so we can get some sleep." Nasrudin snatches a valuable heirloom, and flings it out of the window. When those quarrelling see what a treasure has landed at their feet, they run off. "What was all that about?" asked his wife. "They were arguing about the antique," says Nasrudin, "because as soon as they had it, they stopped squabbling."

The form of this story, with its misdirecting wit is identical to the tongue-in-cheek response of Jesus to his disciples. He jokes to avoid the theological impasse presented by his disciples; then heals the man.

The Jesus comment only makes sense if it is a "leg-pull" on

his part. Jesus is not doing theology on the hoof and giving a definitive explanation of the problem of evil. There are plenty of indications when the gospels are read in this knowing, word to the wise, comic way, of Jesus using often quite outrageous humour, especially in his teachings about the kingdom. This wry, dry humour of his was there right up to the crucifixion and it survived intact at the resurrection.

Jesus' Response to the Problem of Sin and Punishment

The tears that lie about this plightful scene
Of heavy travail in a suffering soul,
Mocked with the forms and feints of royalty
While scarified by briery Circumstance
Might drive Compassion past her patiency
To hold that some mean, monstrous ironist
Had built this mistimed fabric of the spheres
To watch the throbbing of its captive lives,
(The which may Truth forfend) and not thy said
Unmaliced, unimpassioned, nescient Will.
Thomas Hardy [1840-1928]

If I fixed my eyes on all your commandments I should never be put to shame. [Ps 119:6]. The desire to connect our sense of moral guilt with our desire to punish and be punished runs very deep in human nature. Abraham challenged the assumption and failed to convince, as did Jesus.

It's St Luke who reports the occasion: *some people came and told Jesus about the Galileans whose blood Pilate had mixed with their sacrifices. He answered them: "Do you suppose that, because these Galileans suffered this fate, they must have been greater sinners than anyone else in Galilee? No, I tell you, but unless you repent, you will all of you come to the same end. Or the eighteen people who were killed when the tower fell on them at Siloam – do you imagine they must have been more guilty than all the other people living in Jerusalem. No, I tell you, but unless you repent, you will all come to end like theirs.* [Lk 13:1ff.]

This is a strange, contradictory passage because if such events were not punishments for transgressing the law, as Jesus insists, then why, to evade a similar fate, do his hearers need to repent? Commentators often avoid the problem by losing it in Jesus' advice to prepare for the Kingdom by amendment of life, something they should do anyway, regardless of circumstances. Though that is undoubtedly what he meant, it is not what he said. On the one hand, he denied the connection between moral guilt and accidental misfortune (it was not a direct, punitive action of God); while on the other, he appears to assert that that is exactly what it is because, he says, *unless you repent, you will all come to an end like theirs.* This is confusing, unless, of course, it is a joke, said tongue in cheek to preserve the irony and the paradox, – which it must be if the saying is to work. "No!" he is saying, "these things are not punishments". But, "Yes, we still have to live morally transformed, repentant lives as if the threat of punishment actually hung over us, which we know it doesn't because that is not how God and his universe work". It is a fine example of the humour of ambiguity. Yet, *do not put too fine a point to your wit, for fear it should get blunt,* Miguel de Cervantes reminds us in Don Quixote.

It is a use of humour that closes the door against fear and wrong explanation yet holds it open to truth and integrity. We do not need to be atheists to avoid religious and spiritual nonsense. All that is required is a sense of humour, which is why for Christians and Jews humour is a spiritual necessity, a life-line which runs through the Bible like Ariadne's thread.

In breaking the ancient connection between sin and disaster, a connection also broken in the healing of the man born blind, Jesus is at his most radical. So that his hearers should understand him while at the same time there should be no misunderstanding about the status of the Torah, he places the force of humour on the word "but". Everything turns upon it. He is arguing that there is absolutely no connection between the victims' sins and their being crushed by the tower. God is not like that, "but," having said that, righteous Jews still need to repent. It's just that the fear of retribution is not the right motive for that repentance.

In separating sin and misfortune in this way, Jesus was at his most radical and rational, though it seems to have made little difference to the way Christians see the world. The connection Jesus criticised was still intact at the time of the Lisbon earthquake in 1755, when many concluded that Lisbon must have been the most wicked city on earth to have deserved such a fate. Immanuel Kant [1724-1804] dismissed the idea and wrote a number of tracts offering a natural explanation; yet the connection is still made even now and has plagued discussions about such disasters as the 1980s

AIDS epi-demic and the South Asian Tsunami of 2004.[102]

The Distinctiveness of Jesus' Teaching

I will show you something different…
T. S. Eliot [1888-1965] *The Waste Land.*

Besides the way in which he employed the entire range of the Old Testament comic repertoire, a number of factors distinguished Jesus as a teacher. Firstly, there was the way in which he made the commandments to love God and neighbour central to his understanding of the Torah. This took Hosea's privileging of mercy over sacrifice, which the Pharisees also accepted, much further than anyone had taken it before.

Likewise, before the Sermon on the Mount, no one appears to have taken Ezekiel's reversal of the order of repentance and forgiveness as seriously as Jesus did. In the prayer he taught his disciples he even included one of his, "the sting is in the tail" moments of humour: *forgive us our trespasses,* then comes the comic catch, *as we forgive those who trespass against us.* Commentators assume repentance here though none is mentioned. Something even more important than repentance is involved, the willingness to forgive others. Jesus does, of course, teach repentance but it is made in recognition of God's forgiveness not in order to earn it. When we forgive others as God forgives us, that is before even they repent, then the Kingdom of God just prayed for, *thy Kingdom come,* has already drawn near. It's the gospel summary of Jesus' message, *the Kingdom of Heaven is at hand.* [Mk 1:15].

Lastly, Jesus' insistence that misfortune was not a punishment for sin was yet one more denial of traditional piety. For many Jews, his teachings on God and the Torah were proving too radical.

These aspects of Jesus' teaching are also to be reckoned as comedy because of the way in which they play with expectations and signal the presence of the Kingdom, a kingdom which frequently reverses the order in which the world does things. Oscar Wilde [1854-1900] affords dozens of examples of the way in which wit can use this

---

[102] For Anglicans, there is an interesting parallel in the fire at York Minster on July 9th 1984. It was suggested by some that God was making known his anger at the denial of the Virgin Birth by the outspoken and recently consecrated David Jenkins as Bishop of Durham.

trick: "*Why, she is worse than ugly, she is good.*"[103] "*A little sincerity is a dangerous thing, and a great deal of it, absolutely fatal.*"[104] But whereas Wilde's wit was often world-weary and cynical, that of Jesus aimed at being faith enhancing and life affirming. It was the comedy of surprise.

The Trouble with Righteousness

> *Take care of your own soul and another person's body, not your own body and another person's soul.*
> Jewish saying.

The temptation to resent the repentance of sinners is one to which the righteous are prone. Hence the need for Jesus to say to those who objected to his ministry to tax-collectors and sinners: *I am not come to call the righteous but sinners to repentance.* [Mt. 9:13] And, *I tell you there will be greater joy in heaven over one sinner who repents than over ninety-nine righteous people who do not need to repent.* [Lk 15:7]. These verses make most sense if Jesus is being comically provocative otherwise they merely state the obvious.

During the Exile, the Jews identified the pursuit of righteousness as their nation's most pressing moral concern. It was a quest intimately linked to their relationship with God. These days we prefer to talk of human rights and unmet needs for justice; but though the language is different, morally it amounts to much the same thing. As with the meeting of most human needs, professional elites have sprung up to superintend the organisation of righteousness, with all the temptations to self-righteousness and spiritual pride the role involves. *All professions are conspiracies against the laity,* wrote George Bernard Shaw, and in Jesus' eyes this was what many of those who criticised him were guilty of. The obsession of some Pharisees with an over-detailed application had made the Torah oppressive, and the desire to live righteously a corrupting instead of liberating thing. *Alas for you Pharisees! You pay tithes of mint and rue and every garden herb, but neglect justice and the love of God. It is these you should have practised without over-looking the others.* [Lk 11:42.]

Jesus' use of humour spoke of humanity and a lightness of touch in his approach to righteousness. It contrasted with the crippling seriousness of his opponents. *Come to me, all who are*

---

103 From *The Duchess of Padua.*

104 From *The Critic as Artist.*

weary and whose load is heavy; I will give you rest. Take my yoke upon you, and learn from me, for I am gentle and humble-hearted; and you will find rest for your souls. For my yoke is easy to wear, my load is light. [Mt 11:28.]

On not resolving every contradiction!

Do I contradict myself?
Very well then I contradict myself,
(I am large, I contain multitudes).
Walt Whitman [1819-92] *Song of Myself.*

Non-believers often mock the Bible for its apparent contradictions. For example, while St James believes that good works contribute to our salvation [2:14ff]; St Paul argues that we are justified not by works but by faith [Rom. 4:1ff].

It is here that the poet John Keats'theory of "Negative Capability" can prove helpful. In a letter of 1817 to his brothers George and Thomas he wrote: *it struck me, what quality went to form a Man of Achievement especially in literature & which Shakespeare possessed so enormously - I mean Negative Capability, that is when man is capable of being in uncertainties, Mysteries, doubts without any irritable reaching after fact & reason.*

In this defence of open-mindedness Keats argued that great men like Shakespeare had the ability to live with the fact that not every contradiction in life could be resolved. Life was too rich for that. Many contradictions just had to be lived with; and this is exactly what the Bible does. The extreme righteousness of Ezra co-exists with the tolerance of the book of Ruth. Not everyone can accept this, and many have spent considerable effort reaching after tension-free reasoning in their attempt to turn the comic lack of resolution in the Bible into the tragedy of a closed and harsh text.

The social psychologist, Erich Fromm, believed that the compulsive quest for certainty is not the expression of genuine faith but is rooted in the need to conquer unbearable doubt. The ideas of cognitive dissonance and negative capability are attempts to make sense of the limited capacity of human beings to live with doubt. Religious doubt which centred on the quest for righteousness was a recurring facet of public anxiety at the time of Jesus' ministry. His humour in approaching this vexed pastoral issue shows him to have been a moral teacher of unusual outlook. To many, his interpretation of the Torah was far too relaxed. As the episode of the woman taken in adultery showed, he was a risk-taker in moral choices who encouraged his followers to take responsibility for their decisions, and to take personal risks in making them. In this he was ahead of his time. Even today neither political nor religious leaders feel able to trust us, the general public, with such freedom of personal responsibility.

The Bible as Comedy, the Bible itself that is and not this book, resists every effort to avoid change in religious practice. The Bible is a radical and liberal, not a conservative book. The Old Testament supports the pro-change Pharisees against the no-change Sadducees, just as the New supports the transforming humour of Jesus against the humourless intransigence of many Christian traditionalists.

25

MORE HUMOUR IN THE TEACHING OF JESUS

For every person wishing to teach there are thirty not wanting to be taught.
W.C.Sellar [1898-1951] & R.J.Yeatman [1897-1968].

The Mote and the Beam:
It needs no dictionary of quotations to remind me that the eyes are the windows of the soul.
Max Beerbohm [1872-1956]

Elton Trueblood, whose book, *The Humor of Christ,* alerted the wider public to Jesus' use of comedy, was himself made aware of this forgotten dimension by his eldest son, when the boy was only four years old. In the King James Version, the passage that made his son laugh, read: *Judge not that ye be not judged.... Why beholdest thou the mote that is in thy brother's eye, but considerest not the beam that is in thine own eye. Or how wilt thou say to thy brother, Let me pull the mote out of thine eye; and behold a beam is in thine own eye,* [Mt 7:1ff]. The child knew immediately what a ridiculous image it was: to have a speck of dust in your eye was one thing – but a plank! Was this a childhood image that went back to Jesus helping Joseph in his workshop? Hyperbole, comic exaggeration, outrageous imagery were devices he'd use again and again.

Straining a Gnat and Swallowing a Camel [Mt23:27]

Freeing the gospels from excessive sobriety.
Elton Trueblood [1900-94].

In his argument with the Pharisees, Jesus resorts to hyperbole over their concern for the minutiae of the Torah while ignoring its weightier demands. *Alas for you scribes and Pharisees, hypocrites! You pay tithes of mint and dill and cumin; but you have overlooked the weightier demands of the law – justice, mercy, and good faith. It is these you should have practised without neglecting the others. Blind guides! You strain off a midge, and gulp down a camel.* [Mt 23:23ff]].

Some Jews, wary of drinking anything that might make them

ritually impure, attached fine mesh to the mouths of pouring vessels to filter out the finest of foreign bodies. As the camel was the largest animal normally seen in that part of the world it provided a ready image for the concern of the ultra-frum.

Jesus' Use of Hyperbole

> *He said I was the most sensitive person he had ever seen – that I belonged to the hyper-hyper type…*
>
> Ruth Draper [1884-1956]

Sometimes Jesus uses hyperbole in a perplexing and ambiguous way: *You have heard that they were told, Do not commit adultery. But what I tell you is this: If any man looks at a woman with a lustful eye, he has already committed adultery with her in his heart.* [Mt 5:27]. If this is taken literally, then what healthy, heterosexual man has not committed adultery? As adultery was punishable by death, its seriousness could hardly be exaggerated; but that is exactly what Jesus is doing. Why? And what counts as lust? In their zeal to avoid the lustful gaze, the Pharisees were as severe in their teaching as Jesus seems to be. On the other hand, they also taught that without the evil *yetzer,* or impulse, no man would ever marry or build up a business.

If devout Jewish women were veiled, as some scholars think, then this saying with its outrageous exaggeration is a comment on the sexual and social mores of the time. How is it to be understood? When the verses which follow are taken into account it looks as if Jesus is cautioning his followers against extremes of interpretation and practice, otherwise as moral advice it is oppressive and depressing, not to mention emotionally unhealthy.

If your right eye causes your downfall, tear it out and fling it away; it is better for you to lose one part of your body than for the whole of it to be thrown into hell. If your right hand causes your downfall, cut it off and fling it away; it is better for you to lose one part of your body than for the whole of it to go to hell. [Mt 5:29ff] To counsel against giving free rein to corrupting inclinations is one thing, but if the comic hyperbole is ignored and the passage is taken at face value then its opposition to ordinary sexual desire would be tantamount to spiritual pathology.

Once again, Jesus is using the method of comic exaggeration to find a kingdom perspective on difficult Torah teaching: he takes a matter to its extreme. In Matthew 5:21, he makes anger the Torah equivalent of murder. This is plainly ridiculous. The consequences of looking at things this way, however, are morally worthwhile. At the least, it prevents hypocrisy on our part.

One clue to how we should interpret these hard sayings is to consider the way Jesus himself behaved towards women. Far from being cautious and circumspect, he seems to have been remarkably open. Many judged his behaviour far too risky.

Jesus and Women

I should like to know what is the proper function of women, if it is not to make reasons for husbands to stay at home, and still stronger reasons for bachelors to go out.

George Eliot [1819-1880]

In Jesus' day women could be a problem for Torah righteous men. *A daughter is a secret anxiety to her father, and worry about her keeps him awake at night; when she is young, for fear she may grow too old to marry, and when she is married, for fear her husband may divorce her; when she is a virgin for fear she may be seduced and become pregnant in her father's house; when she has a husband, for fear she may prove unfaithful, and after marriage for fear she may be barren. Keep close watch over a headstrong daughter, or she may give your enemies cause to gloat...give her a bedroom without windows...do not let her display her beauty to any man...Better a man's wickedness than a woman's goodness; it is woman who brings shame and disgrace.* [Ecclesiasticus 42:9ff]

It was against this background that the initial reaction of Joseph towards Mary's pregnancy can perhaps be understood. Joseph was a devout Jew whose righteousness was eventually able to transcend the kind of anxiety about women found in Ecclesiasticus. Thanks to his dream of an angel he was able to marry Mary. As Jesus must have known the family story of his mother's pregnancy and how it divided opinion, we have to ask if it was a key factor in his humanising of the Torah.

For a religious man, women were portrayed as a constant snare so that no man could afford to be careless about their company. This being the case, it is remarkable that several stories of Jesus in the company of women managed to get past the watchful eyes of anxious gospel editors. In the eyes of his critics, Jesus did not always behave like one of the Torah devout.

Jesus and the Syro-Phoenician Woman

Take my word for it, the silliest woman can manage a clever man.

Rudyard Kipling [1865-1936]

From time to time Jesus would seek opportunity for prayer and rest. On one occasion, he left Galilee altogether and travelled 40 miles or so north-west to the non-Jewish district of Tyre. Yet even there he was known *and a Canaanite woman from those parts came to meet him, crying, "Son of David! Have pity on me; my daughter is tormented by a devil. But Jesus said not a word in reply. His disciples came and urged him, "Send her away! See how she comes shouting after us." Jesus replied, I was sent to the lost sheep of the house of Israel, and to them alone."* [Mt 15:21].

This repeats his instruction to the disciples in 10:5, *Do not take the road to gentile lands, and do not enter any Samaritan town; but go rather to the lost sheep of the House of Israel.*

But, *the woman, not to be put off, fell at his feet and cried, "Help me, Sir." Jesus replied, "It is not right to take the children's bread and throw it to the dogs." "True, Sir," she answered, "and yet the dogs eat the scraps that fall from their master's table."*

The woman would have known how devout Jewish men liked to turn the interpretation of the Torah into a kind of holy game in which they tried to outdo one another in producing religious insights. What followed was pure comedy with a woman playing a man's game and beating Jesus at it. Is it reading too much into the account to see a hint of flirting on her part as well?

However we interpret this, Jesus, the out-arguer of the scribes and Pharisees was out-argued by a gentile woman and as a result broke his rule about ministering to non-Jews. As well as a woman getting the better of him, the comedy also lay in its being a story he must have told against himself. All the stories we tell against ourselves are comedies, otherwise why tell them? The story would also have been useful later as a support for the mission of the early church to the gentiles, as well, no doubt, for encouraging the growing place and influence of women in the early church. Turning the world upside down in this kingdom-like way was part of the comic purpose of the gospels.

Jesus and the Woman at the Well

One of the greatest pleasures in life is conversation

Sydney Smith [1771-1845]

While Jesus' disciples *were astonished to find him talking to a woman,* [Jn 4:27] and a Samaritan woman at that, the woman herself appears to have relished the conversation. It took place at Jacob's Well and ranged in subject matter from a Jewish man asking a Samaritan woman to draw water for him to the woman's five husbands and the site of the temple and the coming of the Messiah. The humour lies in the way Jesus uses the woman's love of argument to make a number of claims about himself, including that of giving living water [4:13] and revealing himself as the Messiah. The comedy lies in the reversal of what was expected of a righteous Jew: Jesus has a conversation with a woman as a result of which he accepts Samaritan hospitality for two days! This is a double breach of the accepted code for a religious teacher. Jesus is once more portrayed as a moral risk-taker. It is also another instance of St John and the Synoptic gospels agreeing.

Humanising the Rigours of the Jewish Law

> *I have thought some of nature's journeymen had made men and not made them well, they imitated humanity so abominably.*
>
> William Shakespeare [1564-1616] *Hamlet.*

In the book Exodus, death was the penalty for murder, striking or reviling parents, kidnapping an Israelite, witchcraft, bestiality, idolatry; and the list is extended elsewhere to working on the Sabbath, homosexuality and refusing to obey parents. While some were for imposing these penalties, most Pharisees were for interpreting them as leniently as possible, the principal being, *I desire mercy and not sacrifice,* [Hos. 6:6] quoted twice by Jesus. [Mt 9:13 & 12:7.]

Yet Jesus with his comic use of exaggeration goes far beyond the Pharisees in his humanizing of the Torah. If even to look at a woman with lust is adultery (and this from a man who was unusual in his public liking for their company) then what man should not be put to death? [Mt 5:28] In the same way he equates murder with anger [5:22] making everyone a murderer! He also applies this *reductio ad absurdum* to divorce and oaths, retaliation and hatred of enemies. *There must be no limit to your goodness.* Why? Because *your heavenly Father's goodness [mercy, generosity] knows no bounds.* [5:48]. This is how Jesus interprets his own apparently hard-line stance in 5:17, *Do not suppose that I have come to abolish the law and the prophets; I did not come to abolish, but to complete. Truly I*

tell you: so long as heaven and earth endure, not a letter, not a dot, will disappear from the law until all that must happen has happened. This makes Jesus sound stricter than the strictest of his opponents. He even adds, *I tell you, unless you show yourselves far better than the scribes and Pharisees,* (and this really would have made a Galilean laugh) *you can never enter the kingdom of heaven.* In saying this, in what follows, he sets a supposed ultra-strictness against the comic opposition of divine mercy and generosity! To take this section of the Sermon on the Mount literally, misses not only Jesus' comic exaggeration but also his intention to humanise the law and encourage his followers to behave with the utmost generosity of spirit towards one another.

If we close our eyes to the comic, exaggerating elements in the Sermon on the Mount, then we fall into the trap of making Jesus guilty of the literalism and inhumanity he opposed!

The Outwitting of the Pharisees [Mt 22:15-22]

You have not converted a man because you have silenced him.
Lord Morley [1575-1622]

Beating experts at their own game is not only satisfying it is also comical. The collapse of stout parties always raises smiles among onlookers.

Matthew reports an occasion when the Pharisees and Herodians ganged up against Jesus. The only thing these two parties had in common was their accommodation with the Romans, something which the Zealots and the Qumran sect completely opposed. As it was an issue that divided opinion both in Galilee and Judea they were keen to test Jesus and asked him, "*are we or are we not to pay taxes to the Roman Emperor*?" Not to pay would be seen by the Romans as treason, while many Jews would claim that to pay was idolatry. Jesus said, "*You hypocrites! Why are you trying to catch me out*?" Asking for a coin used to pay the tax, he asked, "*Whose head is this*?" When they told him Caesar's, he said, "*Then pay to Caesar what belongs to Caesar and to God what belongs to God.*" To which they had no answer and "*went away and left him alone.*" [22:22]

The Torah Debate Continues with the Outwitting of the Sadducees [Mt 22:23ff]

Total absence of humour renders life impossible.
Colette [1873-1954]

Of all Jewish sects, the Sadducees were the most conservative; not only did they not believe in the resurrection of the dead, but they did not accept the existence of angels or recognise as scriptures books other than the Torah. As the priestly party of the temple they were politically powerful and eager to limit the growing radicalism of the Pharisees with the oral law and their increasing entry into the daily lives of observant Jews. Being responsible for maintaining order in the temple and safeguarding orthodoxy they were keen to discover what Jesus was up to and so they set him a mischievous question in case law on the subject of levirate marriage: *a man dies childless, his brother shall marry the widow. We know a case involving seven brothers.* The case was hypothetical and although they did not believe in the resurrection they knew Jesus did and so asked him, *whose wife will she be at the resurrection, since they all married her?* It's a contrived question intended to put him on the spot, yet there's no satire or humour in Jesus' reply, that *in the resurrection men and women do not marry; they are like angels in heaven.* Nevertheless the account is a comic one for the way in which the Sadducees receive their come-uppance and the Pharisees hear how their theological rivals have been silenced.

The comedy continues when the Pharisees return [22:34] to ask Jesus, *Teacher, which is the greatest commandment of the Torah,* and Jesus replies by combining two widely separated texts: Deuteronomy 6:5, *you must love the Lord your God with all your heart and with all your soul and with all your strength,* with part of Leviticus 19:18, *you must love your neighbour as yourself.* There's nothing humorous in his reply, except perhaps the comic surprise of finding that their perfectly serious question has been given a creative and worthy answer. Jesus seems to have been the first rabbi to join these texts together like this, though Rabbi Akiva [c50-135], one of the founders of Rabbinic Judaism, called the commandment to love one's neighbour, "the greatest principal of the Torah." He almost certainly knew the saying of Jesus.

And the contest does not end there as it's now his turn to ask the Pharisees a question. *What is your opinion about the Messiah? Whose son is he? [22:42] The son of David, they replied. Then how is it, Jesus asked, that David by inspiration calls him "Lord'? For he says, "The Lord said unto my Lord, "Sit at my right hand until I put your enemies under your feet." If then David calls him "Lord," how can he be David's son?* As the contradiction involved here seems not to have been one explored before, *nobody was able to give him an answer.*

This sort of verbal jousting was common among those who taught Torah. At the more positive end of the spectrum of debate it was used as a method of teaching; but where rivalry between rabbis was involved it could be less friendly. In the Talmud, it is recorded that Rabba bar Chana had a dispute with a group of carriers who had broken a cask of his wine. He responded by confiscating their clothes whereupon they complained to a more respected rabbi, Rab, who said, "*Give them back their clothes*." Rabba asked, "*Is this Torah?*" Rab answered "*Yes*," and referred to Proverbs 2:20, "*See that you follow the footsteps of the good."* Seeing that he had been bettered in Torah interpretation, he returned their clothes. But the carriers were still not satisfied and pleaded, "*We are poor men and have worked all day and we are hungry and have nothing to eat."* Rab said, "*Pay them their wages,"* at which Rabba asked, "*Is this the Torah as well?* He was told it was and was reminded of the rest of the verse, *keep to the path of the righteous.*

When Torah righteousness led to moral goodness and the letter of the law was transcended in holiness, disciples and others would marvel and remember the rabbi's wisdom and spiritual maturity. This is why the Sermon on the Mount and Jesus' encounter with the Pharisees and Sadducees are preserved in the gospel.

It might seem to be stretching things too far to describe such encounters as comic, yet leaving aside their entertainment value, which is considerable, the wit, perception and ingenuity involved either in summarising or applying the law are comedy at its most serious and spiritual.

Outwitting opponents is one of the most pervasive comic themes in the Bible. Jacob outwits Laban; Samson outwits the Philistines; David outwits Goliath; Judith outwits Holophernes. The list is a long one; Jonah attempts to outwit God and in Job, Satan attempts to outwit him too, but fails. In the gospels, the theme reaches its climax in the resurrection as the outwitting of sin and death.

The Occasional Outrageousness of Jesus' Humour

Everything that can be said can be said clearly.

Ludwig Wittgenstein [1889-1951]
Tractatus Logico-Philisophicus

But Wittgenstein was wrong: nothing in this world is as clear as the Vienna School thought it should be. When Jesus told Nicodemus that those who wished to see the kingdom of God must be "*born-again*" [Jn 3:3], he was using metaphor and the humour of incongruity to make his point; but, to Nicodemus the literalist, the truth he was looking for was made more obscure than ever.

After the Feeding of the Five Thousand, [Jn 6] Jesus uses the same comic device when he talks to the Galilean crowd about his being the bread from heaven. Here too he uses metaphor and comic incongruity extending the humour of his being that bread to its breaking point. This proves too much for the strictly orthodox from Jerusalem. "*How can this man give us his flesh to eat*?" [6:52] In extending the metaphor to the point of cannibalism it becomes a joke too far. Only those with a sense of the bizarre will understand the truth Jesus is trying to convey.

St John's gospel is so different from the synoptics that many doubt the historicity of the Jesus they find there – even though the humour across their differing theological standpoints is so often as near identical as matters.

26

COMEDY IN THE PASSION OF JESUS

'Twas the saying of an ancient sage, that humour was the only test of gravity.
Anthony Ashley Cooper [1671-1713]

Why did Jesus go to Jerusalem?

'Tis all a Chequer-board of Nights and Days,
where Destiny with men for pieces plays.
Edward Fitzgerald [1809-83].

It was not the abstract machinations of destiny that took Jesus to Jerusalem but his love for God as his Father and his obedience, as a Passover pilgrim, to the religious Law. Jerusalem as the spiritual centre of the Jewish world was where Torah as the coming of the Kingdom of Heaven would have to be preached. It was an interpretation of Judaism that would clash with the rival interpretations of the Sadducees, Zealots and Pharisees, the first two being the most dangerous for Jesus. As a reforming prophet with a mission and revelation to transform Judaism, Jesus couldn't not go. As early as Peter's confession at Caesarea Philippi [Mk 8:30ff] he had warned his disciples of where his message would ultimately lead him: to suffering, rejection by the elders, chief priests and scribes and finally, to death and resurrection. And, understandably, he was not believed.

Entering Jerusalem. The Two Kingdoms in Conflict

Contrariwise, continued Tweedledee, if it was so, it might be; and if it were so, it would be; but as it isn't it ain't. That's logic!
Lewis Carroll [1832-98] Alice through the Looking Glass.

The logic of the Kingdom determines that in this status-hungry world, the first should be last and the greatest least, including the Messiah who now entered Jerusalem on a borrowed donkey. At the sight of the waving palms, donkey-trodden clothing and shouts of *Hosanna*, the Jerusalemites were *stirred, saying, "Who is this?"* And the crowd, who had perhaps travelled south with Jesus, said: *This is the prophet Jesus from Nazareth of Galilee.* [Mt 21:10] No one in Jerusalem seemed to know who Jesus was: a celebrity no one recognised! This is climax as anti-climax and ironic comedy in the Kingdom's theatre of the absurd.

A Joke about Death. How Humiliation Became its Opposite

> *Do not seek death, death will find you. But seek the road which makes death a fulfilment.*
>
> Dag Hammarskjöld. *Markings.*

When Jesus went up to Jerusalem for the last time [Jn 12:12] and brought his public ministry to an end, it may well have been without the support of his brothers, *for even his brothers did not believe in him,* [Jn 7:5].

Yet the crowds welcomed him like a Messianic king entering his capital in triumph. This alarmed the Pharisees [v19] but only made others want to meet Jesus. [v22]. Understandably, his disciples were basking in the glory of his entry and it was at this point that Jesus [v43] told them just how wrongly they had read the occasion, though he appeared at first to agree with them: *The hour has come,* he said, *for the Son of man to be glorified;* only the "glory" Jesus was predicting was his humiliation, the cross, when he would be exposed publicly, naked and bloody, with his mother and friends seeing his tortured body, defiled by his bowels and bladder.

It was yet more black comedy! In the chiral, mirror image world of the Kingdom of God the humiliation of the Messiah would be his glorification. His jokes and parables were sometimes too subtle. Little wonder they didn't understand and had to wait for the truth to dawn on them.

Woe to the Pharisees

> *The word of him who wishes to speak with men without speaking to God is not fulfilled; but the word of him who wishes to speak with God without speaking with men, goes astray.*
>
> Martin Buber [1878-1965].

Being the cause of trouble, Jesus was expecting trouble. For most Pharisees, much that Jesus had to say about the Kingdom was so far removed from their understanding of Jewish Law as to border on the absurd; while for Jesus, though he told the crowds in the temple and his disciples to *do whatever the* Pharisees *teach you and follow it,* they were not to *do as they do, for they do not practice what they teach.*[Matthew 23:3].

In biology, Gause's Law states that competition is greatest among species that are competing for the same ecological niche. It's a law that offers insight into competition in the religious sphere. Jesus and the Pharisees were in open competition at the very heart of Judaism. His seven woes against the Scribes and Pharisees in Matthew 23:1-36, reflects this.

Jesus is also conscious of the reputation that Jerusalem has for mistreating those who take unwelcome messages there. *Therefore, the Wisdom of God said, "I will send them prophets and apostles, some of whom they will kill and prosecute, so that this generation may be charged with the blood of all the prophets shed since the foundation of the world, from the blood of Abel to the blood of Zechariah, who perished between the altar and the sanctuary."* [*Luke 11:49ff*].

But though the condemnation of Jesus here is against the Pharisees it's important to note that the murder of the prophets referred to was not their doing as the Pharisees didn't exist at that time. When it came to the death penalty the Pharisees were among the most reluctant of groups to resort to it. It was not the Pharisees so much as the Sadducees and Zealots that made Jerusalem such a dangerous place for Jesus.

The woes against the Pharisees were serious in their intent, but, as we have learned to expect, Jesus gets his points across with some humour. He begins with a little verbal clowning and comic exaggeration: *They tie up heavy burdens, hard to bear, but lay them on the shoulders of others.* [Mt 23:4]. Then he mocks their self-importance. *They love...to have people call them rabbi. But you are not to be called rabbi,* [v8] The literal meaning of the Hebrew rabbi is "my great one", which conflicts of course with the upside-down, Feast of Fools values of the Kingdom where *The greatest among you will be your servant.* [v11]

This discrediting of his rivals by highlighting the moral contradictions in their teaching goes on for verse after verse ending with his repeating John the Baptist's name-calling summary of their character, *You brood of vipers!* This is strong language indeed. In other words, your interpretation of Torah is so full of moral contradictions as to be venomous.

The Execution of the Messiah

I hate victims who respect their executioners.

Jean Paul Sartre [1905-1980].

In my teens, I liked to attend the mid-day devotional service on Good Friday. For some reason, three hours of total seriousness in which I pondered life, death and suffering, appealed to me, a child who grew up in all the uncertainties of wartime Britain.

Only later, when I became involved in interfaith dialogue, did it occur to me how strange Christian devotion to the cross of Christ might seem to outsiders. Once, on a family holiday in Spain, we visited the old Ducal palace at Gandia and stepped into the chapel which had been the prayer cell of St Francis Borgia, the only saint that infamous family produced. A teenager present. paused, considered its coffin-shaped walls and as a product of her time said, "This is sick."

I realised that while what I was thinking took me to the dark and truthful depths of the human condition, to a younger person it was all an obsession with death and suffering.

On several occasion Jewish friends have expressed similar bewilderment at Christian devotion to the wounds of Christ; as, for example, in the Passiontide hymn:

Glory be to Jesus,
Who in bitter pains,
Poured for me the life-blood
From his sacred veins.
Grace and life eternal
In that blood I find;
Blest be his compassion
Infinitely kind.

This focus on the blood of Christ seemed to them unhealthy, whereas to me, living in a society in which blood is shed meaninglessly every day, in which it is the political and criminal worlds which have an unhealthy love of death, not the church, these meditations on the paradoxical blood that redeems us from all of that, I find paradoxically healthy.

Abel's blood for vengeance
Pleaded to the skies
But the blood of Jesus
For our pardon cries

And we are back once more to the comic contradictions of the Kingdom.

I grew up too in the last days of the British Empire and military history remains an interest to this day. Perhaps it's inevitable then that to all human wickedness Christ's cross remains for me a spiritual corrective. It might look to some like a pathological obsession related psychologically to the death cult of the Nazis, but its function is the opposite, a God-given antidote to the world as it is. The Passion of Christ was the worst of us, enlisted in the service of the Kingdom. It is not pathological but redemptive.

With such things in mind it seems almost blasphemous to suppose that there might be elements of comedy, however dark and grim, in the Passion of Jesus. Yet, it is there. It is most obvious in the mockery by the nation's leaders and the Roman soldiers as they taunt Jesus, so that comedy itself becomes part of the sufferings of Jesus as Messiah. Torturers the world over use comedy and laughter to humiliate their victims. Evil likes a good laugh.

To complicate matters further, we humans do like to joke in the presence of death. Gallows humour is a comic subject in its own right. Among my favourite last words are those of Archbishop William Laud [1573-1645] at the moment he was about to be beheaded. Laud had been the chief minister of Charles I. When proceedings at the execution-block were going too slowly for his liking, he prayed, "Lord, I am coming as quickly as I can," and went to God with his sense of humour intact. As did Sir Walter Raleigh; as he placed his head on the block he said: "So, the heart be right, it is no matter which way the head lieth." That's cool wit.[105]

In each of the gospels, the passion of Christ forms the climax to the story of his life, and just as comedy and humour were a part of his teaching and the meaning of his miracles, so in the end they were there at their blackest in his crucifixion and all that led to it.

The Woman Who Anointed Jesus with Costly Perfume [Mt 26:6ff]

Wilful waste makes woeful want.

A Scottish proverb from J. Kelly's 1721 collection.

Jesus was at Bethany in the house of Simon the leper. Everyone

---

105 Laud was also the subject of a famous pun by Archie Armstrong, the king's Court Jester. The Archbishop was a short man who felt his lack of height keenly. Armstrong quipped: *Give great praise to the Lord, and little Laud to the devil.*

knew the commandment that lepers were to be avoided. Worse than that, Simon had put on a meal and Jesus was eating with a leper – unless, of course, Jesus had healed him beforehand, though the text does not say that.

During the meal an unnamed woman entered carrying a bottle of perfume of the kind used in wealthy households to anoint the head of honoured guests. It was a luxury of the sort Jesus was not used to and did not expect. To release the perfume, the bottle had to be broken which meant the perfume could only be used once. It was an example of what today's economists call "conspicuous consumption". The woman was not invited and even though she is not identified as a "sinner," the fact that she was a lone woman would have been enough to have offended the strictly observant.

But it was not this that the disciples objected to. It was the waste. The perfume could have been sold and the money given to the poor. Immediately, Jesus goes to her rescue. *Why make trouble for the woman? It is a fine thing she has done for me. You have the poor with you always, but you will not always have me. When she poured this perfume on my body, it was her way of preparing me for burial.* Jesus used the incident to prepare the disciples for his death, but it is his words that are wasted, not the perfume.

Then follows the verse that makes me smile. Jews were and are a people who set great store by memorials. Synagogues are as full of them as churches. Jewish children are brought up to understand that every child is his or her parents' memorial. It's a sobering thought.

Jesus said, *Truly, I tell you: wherever this gospel is proclaimed throughout the world, what she has done will be told as her memorial.* [Mt 26:13], which is fine, except that we are not given her name! What we have then is a memorial with no name attached. "Typical!" my feminist friends say. "You can tell the story was written by a man. That's patriarchy for you!"

"Messiah" means "anointed one" and the Messiah had been anointed by a nameless women. It could only happen in the Kingdom of Heaven!

A Man Carrying a Jar of Water [Mk 14:13]

Modern man has lost the option of silence.
William Burroughs [1914-1997].

As the practice in those days was for men to carry water in skins and for women to carry it in terracotta jars balanced on the head or shoulder, the man chosen to lead the disciples to the upper room would be recognised instantly. And because of the comedy of the role reversal involved, the sign also doubled as a marker for the arrival of the Kingdom in the Passover about to be celebrated, making the Last Supper, the last Feast of Fools in Jesus' ministry. His sense of humour was present even as he was arranging his own farewell.

The man with the water jar balanced on his head would have stood out, otherwise in an overcrowded city he would never have been spotted. Like William Laud and Walter Raleigh, this was Jesus raising a smile as he journeyed to his death.

Peter's Over-confidence

> *If he damned hisself in confidence, o'course that was another thing.*
>
> Charles Dickens [1812-1870] *Old Weller.*

After singing the Passover hymn, they went out to the Mount of Olives. And Jesus said to them, "You will all lose faith; for it is written: I will strike the shepherd and the sheep will be scattered." [Mt 14:26] Peter, in his usual impulsive way, attempts to assure his rabbi that there is one disciple who is not going to run. Everyone else might lose faith, but he will not. Jesus knew better. Peter was always promising more than he could deliver. Jesus knew this and said to him, "*Truly I tell you: today, this very night, before the cock crows twice, you yourself will disown me three times."* Digging deeper, Peter piles on the irony with: "*Even if I have to die with you, I will never disown you." And they all said the same.* The reader knows what will happen! It's why Jesus nicknamed him "the rock!" It's more grim, ironic humour.

Jesus Washes the Disciples' Feet

> *It is difficult to be humble. Even if you aim at humility, there is no guarantee that when you have attained the state you will not be proud of the feat.*
>
> Bonamy Dobrée [1891-1974].

In the topsy-turvy Kingdom of Heaven, God's Comic Feast of Fools, customs and values are turned upside down, and in St John's account of the Last Supper [13:2ff] there are two surprises to remind us of this. The first is that Jesus replaced the customary hand-washing by foot-washing, even though the disciples had been taught that being clean in heart and spirit was the better preparation! The second surprise was that having foregone the washing of hands Jesus washed the disciples' feet instead of having them wash his! This was such a reversal of proper form that the predictable Simon Peter was outraged: *You, Lord, washing my feet?*

Once leadership is established in a group, the status of its members is determined by their closeness to the leader. To maintain their position disciples must also maintain that of their teacher, yet Jesus now appears to be symbolically relinquishing his status. The comic elements lie in the resulting confusion. These are staples of theatrical comedy which here serve as props. This is again the Kingdom of God in a Feast of Fools reversal. Jesus is teaching humility, but there are lessons too about submission to what lies ahead. Peter's initial refusal of Jesus' gesture is overcome less through his understanding of what's happening than by his loyalty as chief disciple.

There is further comedy in Peter's extravagant reply, *Then, Lord, not my feet only; wash my hands and head as well.* The comedy is used by John in the same way that Shakespeare employed comedy in his plays: as steps and highlights to tragedy.

Who Will Betray Jesus? [Mt 26:20ff]

And oftentimes, to win us to our harm,
the instruments of darkness tell us truths,
win us with honest trifles, to betray's
in deepest consequence.

William Shakespeare [1564-1616] *Macbeth.*

The treachery of Judas seems as far removed from comedy as it's possible to get, yet there are tragi-comic elements throughout his story; in the way, for example, in which he is cynically used by the chief priests, in his clumsy exchanges at the last supper and in the way everything finally goes wrong for him. The tragedy of Judas appears the blacker for their presence. Without these elements a straight telling of the story would lack not only narrative power but also theological depth. His motives remain a mystery. It is treachery without explanation and Judas can easily and mistakenly be thought of as no more than a pawn in God's playing out a hidden fulfilment of prophecy.

From our modern viewpoint, the account of Jesus' betrayal by Judas is unsatisfactory. We would much prefer to understand what led to his decision. With so little information it's no surprise that conjectures multiply.

> **Jesus**: *Truly I tell you: one of you will betray me.*
> **Disciples**: *Surely you do not mean me, Lord?*
> **Jesus**: *One who has dipped his hand into the bowl with me will betray me.*

The custom at the time seems to have been for a portion of lamb, together with a piece of unleavened bread and the bitter herbs [maror] to be dipped into the charoset, a sweet mix containing apples, nuts and spices representing the mortar used by the Israelite slaves in building store cities for Pharaoh. As all the disciples would have broken bread and dipped together like this, Jesus' reply is more a riddle than an answer; and this is where the darkly comic begins to heighten the tragic nature of events. In irony, the reader expects to know what remains hidden from the characters within the narrative, but here the reader is no wiser than the disciples. This is irony denied. Wanting to understand what is happening the reader hurls his questions at the text but all that results are more riddles. It preserves intact what St Paul, in the King James Version, calls the *mystery of iniquity* [2 Thess. 2:7], but this inexplicableness of Judas' betrayal can irritate. If irony is a form of comedy, then irony denied where it is most expected simply annoys..

Jesus is no clearer when he expands his answer with a further riddle: *The Son of Man is going the way appointed for him in the scriptures* [Mt 26:24]. This looks as if Jesus is living directly from a selection of biblical texts, as if they were some pre-ordained script for his life. It is possible that he is, though we know that the Bible can't be read like that as the number of possible scripts, even for the Messiah, would be too many for any kind of certainty. A better explanation is that by taking his message to Jerusalem, he set off a train of events that will end in his death and this he accepts as God's will and as his vocation. The scriptures, on this view, would be illustrative rather than predictive.

Jesus then adds: *Alas for that man by whom the Son of Man is betrayed! It would be better for that man if he had never been born.* [26:24] With this, the comedy drops away and Judas is left as the ultimate tragic figure in the gospel story. He betrayed the Saviour of the world to his enemies and ever after became a figure held in contempt by Jesus' followers. The exceptions to this universal hatred were the Gnostic Cainites who perhaps produced the recently discovered Gospel of Judas. Hatred of Judas was a hatred that complicated centuries of Christian contempt for the Jews who were calumnied as the "Christ killers". Judas's name, deriving as it did from the word Jew, did not help matters.[106]

The Words Are Yours

That is a good question for you to ask, not a wise question for me to answer.

Sir Anthony Eden [1897-1977].

After Jesus had said that it would be better for whoever was betraying him never to have been born [Mt 26:24], Judas asked, *Rabbi, surely you don't mean me?* Jesus replied with wit and ambiguity, *You have said it.*

Jesus gives this same riddling reply to the High Priest [26:63] when Caiaphas asks, *By the living God, I charge you to tell us: are you the Messiah, the Son of God.* Jesus replied, *The words are yours,* answering with the same phrase in the Greek, "su eipas." Later, when Pontius Pilate asks him directly, *Are you the king of the Jews?* [27:11] Jesus replies almost identically, *The words are yours.* It is a response which because in answering it withholds the answer can be identified as wit, a comic defence or a polite way for the accused not to incriminate himself.

The Darkest Humour of All

Death thou shalt die.

John Donne [1571?-1631]

The Passover is a meal which over the centuries has added more and more explanatory symbols to itself : for example, a dish of bitter herbs which represented the suffering of the Israelites in Egypt. Later, a bowl of salt water was placed on the table to symbolise the tears shed over the destruction of the temple and, in more recent times, over the Holocaust. For Jesus, on the eve of his crucifixion, to add another layer of meaning to his people's greatest festival was not in

---

[106] As a boy in 1940s Liverpool, on Maundy Thursday each year, I would visit my Roman Catholic cousins whose priest would not allow them to burn Guy Fawkes. "He's one of ours!" he told them. "We're not burning him!" So on Maundy Thursday they burned Judas instead, a custom which I believe ended with the retirement of the priest.

itself surprising. At the breaking of bread there was a set prayer which is there to this day, what Christians would call a grace: *Blessed art Thou O Lord our God, King of the Universe, who has brought forth bread from the earth.* Then, after the blessing, as Jesus took the bread, he broke it, and, as he broke it, he said meaningfully, *Take this and eat; this is my body,* [Mt 26:26] demonstrating dramatically that his body would be broken as surely as he had broken the bread.

To this day, across many communities in the Middle East, the ordinary social act of "breaking bread together" constitutes an act of deeply meaningful fellowship and friendship, so much so that any thought of treachery and betrayal should be unthinkable. It's a bonding action that places guests under the protective roof of the host. And all the time, Judas was sitting there, waiting.

So when Jesus declared that the bread he was tearing in two was his body, the sense of shock must have been palpable. It was the grim humour of surprise at its darkest. He then compounded the gallows-humour over the bread by taking the cup of wine, blessing it and adding bleakly, *this is my blood, the blood of the covenant, shed for many for the forgiveness of sins.* [Mt 26:27].

An ordinary act of blessing, repeated daily in devout families all over Judea had had its meaning transformed for ever. From then on, the followers of Jesus would never be able to separate the tearing apart of the bread at Passover and mealtime from the horrific mutilation of Jesus' body on the cross. It was a chilling action and one that would be repeated to this day at every Eucharist, Mass, Holy Communion and Lord's Supper in the Christian Church.

But comedy? How could something as brutal and inhumane as this be comedy? In the economy of God it became exactly that by becoming a means of grace. This was Divine Comedy. Like the Bible itself, with all its sin and bloodshed, every blessing is a divine comedy. Jesus was counting on the strongest possible emotional reaction in order to open minds to an understanding of his death. Once again, Christian theology has failed to cope with Jesus' Jewish humour.

The Complete Disciple

I know the disciplines of war.

William Shakespeare [1564-1616] *Henry V.*

In St Luke's gospel [22:35], as the Last Supper draws to its close, Jesus says, "*When I sent you out barefoot without purse or pack, were you ever short of anything?" "No," they answered. "It is different now," he said; "whoever has a purse had better take it with him, and his pack too; and if he has no sword, let him sell his cloak to buy one. For scripture says, 'He was reckoned among transgressors,' and this, I tell you, must be fulfilled in me; indeed all that is written of me must reach its fulfilment." "Lord," they said, "we have two swords here."*

In the Revised English Bible, Jesus answers in one word, "*Enough!*" But there are two words in St Luke's Greek, so that the Authorised Version's, "*It is enough,*" is better.

This is a disturbingly comic little scene which most commentators interpret symbolically. Yet, in order to be identified as law-breakers and fulfil scripture, Jesus and his disciples must at least look as if they are dangerous and for that it would help if they were armed. They might even be mistaken for Zealots! It is clear from this charade that carrying swords was optional among them, some of the disciples did and some did not. In the event, we learn that only two did, one of the swords being used later to cut off the right ear of the High Priest's servant [Lk 22:50]. In effect, Jesus is saying, "two swords will be quite enough for what I have in mind."

Jesus knows the authorities plan to remove him from the national stage. All they need is a reason, and in that case he will provide one. Like other candidate Messiahs before and after him, he and his followers will be armed; then, when the Romans ask just how dangerous a threat he posed, a couple of swords will be all his accusers can produce. The Romans will smile, the Sadducees will be discredited and Jesus will have the last laugh, his sense of humour intact to the end.

The Mystery of Judas

> *Suicide is the only logical reaction to the death of God.*
>
> Kirilov, a character in Dostoievsky's *The Devils*.

Why did Judas betray Jesus for the price of a slave or the equivalent of a few months' wages for a labourer? Matthew [26:13] thought greed was his motive while St Luke [22:3ff] and St John [13:2, 27] believed the cause was Satanic possession. These days we seek deeper explanations.

When confronted with suspicion at the Last Supper, Judas says to Jesus, *Rabbi, surely you don't mean me?* He says this even though, not long before, Jesus had forbidden his followers to call anyone Rabbi. And again, in the Garden of Gethsemene, in the very act of betraying Jesus with a kiss, Judas used the same title, saying *Hail Rabbi*. [Mt 26:49]. The other disciple recorded as calling Jesus

"Rabbi" was Nathaniel and that was in the banter before his recruitment [Jn 1:49.], all of which would indicate mockery in Judas' greeting. Was he being sarcastic, or ironical in his insolence, using a formula of respect to show contempt? In his reply, Jesus will not play Judas's game: *Friend* ,he says obliquely, *do what you are here to do.*

The most convincing explanation for Judas' rejection of Jesus is some sort of disillusionment with his teaching and ministry, and as this had always centred on the nature and coming of the Kingdom, we may reasonably suppose that it's Jesus' version of the Kingdom of Heaven that Judas has lost confidence in.

Little is known of Judas Iscariot. Iscariot may mean "man from Kerioth" or "man from Sychar", or "man from Issacah", none of which are very helpful. If Iscariot, on the other hand, derives from *sicarios*,it could even mean "assassin." All that we know for certain is that until the Last Supper his commitment to Jesus was not in question. And then, for reasons unknown, his belief in Jesus as the Messiah failed and was replaced by hostility and rejection. What could possibly have caused that? It was as if a spell had been broken; that one moment the promise of the Kingdom preached by Jesus had seemed the best and most real way of obedience to the Torah being fulfilled, while next it seemed no more than an illusion, a dream that could never be realised within the reality of the world. If this was the case, then Jesus, the prophet of the Kingdom, was no harmless dreamer but dangerous and liable to lead the nation astray. He would have to be stopped.

It's important to note that Judas did not betray Jesus to the Pharisees. Had he done so, Jesus might only have been led off for a another discussion on the interpretation of Torah. Instead, he handed Jesus over to the Sadducees, the religiously conservative group who ruled Judea under Roman authority and for whom anything but the safest talk of the Kingdom of God was judged a threat to the Roman occupation and therefore a political risk. Judas could not have handed Jesus over to a more dangerous enemy. He knew what he was doing. He was sentencing Jesus to death. That was the measure of his disillusionment. His sarcasm was the comedy that showed the depth of his disappointment.

Then, when Jesus was condemned, as suddenly as he had turned against him, Judas had doubts about what he'd done and repented. He tried to return the thirty pieces of silver only to have the offer refused. In this sudden descent from contempt to despair, from the blackest comedy to the darkest tragedy, Judas committed suicide.

Twice in the Lord's prayer, Jesus' disciples prayed for the Kingdom: *Thy Kingdom Come, Thy will be done,* near its beginning and at the end, *for Thine is the Kingdom, the power and the glory.*

The problem was that unless God himself blessed that topsy-turvy Kingdom in which the last were first, the meek inherited the earth, forgiveness came before repentance and justice was about love, the Kingdom was no more than a political fantasy. Yet, except for the rich and powerful, it was the dream of people everywhere, especially slaves, the poor and downtrodden. It was the achievement of Jesus to have brought these hopes to the very centre of the Jewish faith and made them the heart of his message. Through his parables and miracles they seemed not only believable but, under God, realistic. It was, after all, not a human but God's Kingdom he was talking about.

Had Judas only lost his faith in the Kingdom of God he would have needed to do no more than hand back the money bag and cease being a disciple. But he did far more than that. He handed Jesus over to the Sadducees who would label him as yet another false prophet and deal with him accordingly. Judas' betrayal of Jesus to the Sadducees decided everything.

Poor Judas! His dilemma is still with us. Human beings still dream of secular utopias and of political ways to achieve them. The trouble is that even the most sophisticated have so far proved not only unattainable but also so destructive of human life. Only one kind of humanism preserves our humanity: Jesus vision of the Kingdom of God and that's a religious not a secular vision. Its agents are God and those who love him. By keeping it out of the hands of clergy and politicians Jesus safeguarded its humanity! With the Kingdom of God as the only possible loving, just and righteous society, Judas was wrestling with things too deep and complex for him. It's the situation the Church has inherited today.

An Ineradicable Love of Irony

> *The archetype of the incongruously ironic is Christ, the perfectly innocent victim excluded from human society.*
>
> Northrop Frye [1912-1991]

Because they took such pains to record it, for reasons we can only guess at, the comedy that surrounded Jesus seems to have been as important to the gospel writers as to Jesus himself.

In the episode of Simon of Cyrene [Lk 23:26], the irony lies in the phrase that Simon was *on his way in from the country.* He was an unsuspecting visitor who was about to become involved in an event of major historical importance. Jerusalem was so crowded for the festival that Simon had been obliged to lodge outside its walls, perhaps in one of the thousands of tents pitched on the surrounding hillsides. The poor man, who St Mark tells us was the father of the now forgotten Alexander and Rufus, was only coming into the city for the feast yet ended up carrying a cross! The episode was doubtless remembered because of the personal connections cited, but the irony is there underlying the cruel sense of privilege: a devout Torah-righteous Jew walking into the city suddenly finding himself a part of a condemned man's walk to his execution which later turns out to be part of the drama of the world's redemption. If irony was found only here, it would be of minor interest only, but it crops up throughout the entire crucifixion story. When Jesus was nailed to the cross, *There was an inscription above his head which ran: "This is the king of the Jews."* [Lk 23:38]. The soldiers who put it there knew that, as a Galilean, Jesus' own king was Herod Antipas, while the reader knows that, as Messiah, Jesus was exactly who the inscription said he was.

Even though St Luke was a gentile, he lived among Jewish Christians who, like Jesus, were at home with irony. He even has two ironies in one verse! During Jesus' last moments: the *sun's light failed* and *the curtain of the temple was torn in two.* [23:45]. Jesus is the light of the world, but with the sun clouded over, both of the world's lights are going out. Meanwhile, the curtain separating the Holy of Holies, the shrine of God's presence, from the rest of the temple and so symbolising the separation of humankind from God, this great emblem of the God and human divide was torn in two. No wonder Honoré de Balzac could write in *Eugénie Grandet* that *Irony is the essence of the character of Providence.* It points to the presence of God. It is why there is so much of it in scripture.

Avoiding The Question

No question is ever settled until it is settled right.
Ella Wheeler Wilcox [1855-1919].

Throughout his ministry Jesus was asked questions. It's what rabbis were for: people asked them for decisions on matters of law, while the rabbis in turn asked questions of those who came to them in order to open their minds to wisdom and understanding. Those who disagreed with Jesus would often ask questions calculated to catch him out and discredit him. In meeting this threat, Jesus developed a number of techniques designed to thwart them, one of which is used in some forms of modern counselling. This is to reflect what someone says back to them. *As soon as it was day, ... he was brought before their Council. "Tell us," they said, "are you the Messiah?" "If I tell you," he replied, "you will not believe me; and if I ask questions you will not answer. But from now on, the Son of Man will be seated at the right hand of Almighty God." "You are the Son of God, then?" they all said, and he replied, "It is you who say that I am."*

In their efforts to get Jesus to incriminate himself, a game is being played between them. It may not be high comedy, but it is comedy all the same. The process is repeated when Jesus is brought before Pilate [23:2]. *They opened the case against him by saying, "We found this man subverting our nation, opposing the payment of taxes to Caesar and claiming to be a Messiah, a king." Pilate asked him, "Are you the king of the Jews?" He replied, "The words are yours."*

There are echoes here of Jesus being quizzed by his parents after he had gone missing in the temple. Again, he is just sufficiently respectful to avoid offending those in authority. Nor is he overawed by the trouble he's in. His chutzpah is mischievous enough to show that he is still in charge of himself and his predicament, without making matters worse. In the circumstances, Pilate's reply is inevitable; *I find no case for this man to answer.* In the end, Jesus is executed by an authority that finds he has no charge to answer. It's history as a kind of gallows humour.

Irony in a Variant Reading

> *I have called this principle, by which each slight variation, if useful, is preserved, by the term of Natural Selection.*
>
> Charles Robert Darwin [1809-1882].

Those Christians who believe that they base their faith wholly upon the Bible must reckon with the awkward fact that there is no definitive Greek or Hebrew text upon which they can base their claims of absolute certainty. The text, on which all our translations are based, has been reconstructed by scholars from the many hundreds of ancient manuscripts and fragments that have come down to us; and, though we can for the most part be reasonably certain that what we have before us in our Bibles is what was originally written, there is no final certainty. For example, in St Matthew's account of Pilate asking the crowd to choose between Jesus and Barabbas [Mt 27:15ff] in the Revised Standard Version a footnote tells us: "other ancient authorities read *Jesus Barabbas*". While my Revised English Version now cites that variant reading as accepted Bible text: *There was then in custody a man of some notoriety, called Jesus Barabbas.*

The scholars who changed their minds on this were doubtless swayed not only by the antiquity of the manuscripts that called the other prisoner Jesus Barabbas, but also because it made more sense to conclude that copyists were more likely to omit the word "Jesus," than include it. It would not have seemed appropriate to an older generation of scholars that a common criminal should share the sacred name, Jesus; even thought it was not uncommon.

But, there is not just one irony here but two. The first is that both prisoners are called Jesus which for Christian readers is irony enough, but, in addition, the name *Bar Abbas* meant in Aramaic, *son of the father.* The man freed by Pilate was called "Jesus Son of the father." We can see why so many manuscripts dropped Barabbas' first name. It was a jest too far.

Texts with Blood on Them

Here's the smell of the blood still.

William Shakespeare [1564-1616] *Macbeth*

All irony is comical, but occasionally the comic element is overwhelmed by the tragic. For example, in St Luke's parable of the Great Supper [14:15ff] Jesus tells of a man who gave a banquet which no one could be bothered to attend. The guests sent their excuses: one had bought a field and wished to inspect it, someone else had purchased five yoke of oxen and, best of all, another had married and explained, *therefore I cannot come.* Jesus said, *The master of the house was furious and said to the servant, "Go out quickly into the streets and alleys of the town, and bring in the poor, the crippled, the blind and the lame".* Already, a little humour has crept into the parable because normally these were people who might have been allowed to crowd at the edge of the feast waiting for the leftovers, and here they are arriving as principal guests. It is the Kingdom as the Feast of Fools all over again, but with a twist. Yet, even after they sit down, there's still room. In desperation, the master tells his servant. *Go out on the highways and along the hedgerows and compel them to come in; I want my house full.* In short, there's room in the Kingdom for everyone, even the most unlikely! Besides, any one throwing a party who has to "compel" guests to attend is a comic figure.

The story also appears to be a parable of the Messianic Banquet in which Jewish leaders who refuse Jesus' ministry are accused of refusing God's invitation to his feast. The invitation is then extended to Jews who'd normally be excluded by the righteous and, after they have been invited, it is the turn of the gentiles. Tragically, the great Church Father, St Augustine of Hippo [354-430], misinterpreted the parable in that when reading it with the Donatists in mind, heretics who had separated themselves from the church, he believed that the words *compel them to come in,* were words from God to help him resolve his difficulties with them. As a result, he called in the civil authority and the Roman Army in an attempt to force people back to church. There was bloodshed. Unfortunately, his misreading of this text was taken as gospel justification by a number of Popes and Christian rulers anxious to force heretics back into the churches. It was the justification for those burnings at the stake for which the Church is now rightly ashamed. The Church is not the Kingdom of God, though on rare occasions, and briefly, it might just reflect something of its character.

Even more tragic is the passage in St Matthew's gospel where, after Pilate offers to release either Jesus, or Jesus Barabbas, the chief priests and elders persuade the crowd to demand that Barabbas be released and Jesus crucified. *When Pilate saw that he was getting nowhere, and that there was danger of a riot, he took water and washed his hands in full view of the crowd. "My hands are clean of this man's blood," he declared. "See to that yourselves." With one voice the people cried, "His blood be on us and our children,"* words that are as blood-soaked and tragic as Augustine's *compel them to come in.*

Today, a Jew who finds a Gideon's Bible in his hotel bedroom may ask for it to be removed, complaining, "Someone's left anti-Semitic literature in my room," and, if asked to explain, will point to the text: "*His blood be on us and our children*. [Mt 27:25]. On one level, the words can be rightly read as an example of middle-eastern hyperbole, as for example, in Genesis [2:23] when Adam first sees his wife, taken from his rib, he says: *this is now bone of my bones and flesh of my flesh.* The irony is that though the crowd probably intended their words to mean, "we accept responsibility for his death", modern readers know that their words led in time to the Jews becoming victims of the Christian church. Gentile Christians read the words as meaning that the Jewish people as a whole were guilty of Christ's death having confessed to it in that verse[107]. Down the years,

---

[107] The crowd that yelled for Jesus' death were supporters of the Sadducees, who wanted Jesus dead because he might destabilise the political status quo. Modern Jews are descended from the Pharisees who, though they often quarrelled with Jesus' teaching, were not responsible for his trial and crucifixion. The Sadducean High Priest, Caiaphas, who said, *It is expedient that one man should die for the people,* is making a political point. St John, of course, uses it ironically to make a theological one.

in tragic irony, it was used to justify the most appalling pogroms.

What Is Truth?

> *Truth is God's daughter.*
>
> Proverb quoted by T. Fuller in 1732.

> **Pilate**: *So you are the king of the Jews.*
> **Jesus**: *Is that your own question, or have others suggested it to you?*
> **Pilate**: *Am I a Jew?*[108] *Your own nation and its chief priests have brought you before me. What have you done?*
> **Jesus**: *My kingdom does not belong to this world.*

As Pilate knew the king of the Jews personally, he was being sarcastic. There could be no clearer statement for a politician of the non-threatening nature of the Kingdom of God than Jesus' reply. Only when politics became ideologically based was there a possibility of the Kingdom, as Jesus preached it, clashing with secular politics.

> **Pilate**: *You are a king then?*
> **Jesus**: *"King" is your word. My task is to bear witness to the truth. For this I was born; for this I came into the world, and all who are not deaf to truth listen to my voice.*
> **Pilate**: *What is truth?*

If Jesus can play word games so can Pilate. His question, *What is truth?* [Jn 18:38] can be read as Roman cynicism, or as the question of a trial judge perplexed by this sudden shift into philosophy. Its function is to heighten the drama. The reader knows that as Pilate asks the question, Jesus, who is the truth, is standing before him.

For John, truth is a key word and occurs 22 times in his gospel. Here Pilate is paradoxically brought into its service by focussing our attention on its importance: *I am the way and the truth and the life,* said Jesus [14:6] *He [that is the Holy Spirit] will guide you into all truth.* [16:12]

The Comic Nature of Ambiguity

> *Seven Types of Ambiguity*
>
> William Empson [1906-84]. Book Title.

---

[108] Pilate is being sarcastic. He knows that Jews love debating points of law.

The evangelist who relies most heavily on ambiguity, that close relative of irony, is St John. Wherever he can, he uses it to say one thing and hint at another. He is even ambiguous in its use, as when it is sometimes his own, as the gospel's editor, and sometimes as it belongs to Jesus who also revelled in its use.

Ambiguity is John's device for opening up the depths in narrative. For him, the whole of life is ambiguous, especially the life of Jesus, the incarnate Logos of God. God and his kingdom are active everywhere: they are there in the inescapable ambiguities of his trial. When the crowd yells, *If you let this man go you are no friend of Caesar,* at one level they are only telling him what is politically obvious, at least to their Sadducee masters: Jesus will be political trouble which is what Caesar put Pilate there to prevent. The other side of the ambiguity lies in the reader knowing that the teaching of Jesus subverts all power, including its worship by the Romans. The message of Jesus is the best hope the Romans have.

In modern communication theory, ambiguity is seen as something to be avoided as communicators constantly seek the "disambiguation of miscommunication!" Applying this principle to the gospels would only make them something they are not. Jesus' own love of irony and ambiguity were two things that were passed on to those who left us their extended notes upon his life.

The Power of those in Power

> *The wrong sort of people are always in power because they would not be in power if they were not the wrong sort of people.*
> Jon Wynne-Tyson [1924-]

Pilate: *Where have you come from?*
Jesus: [remains silent.]
Pilate: *Do you refuse to speak to me? Surely you know that I have authority to release you, and authority to crucify you?*
Jesus: *You would have no authority at all over me, if it had not been granted from above; and therefore the deeper guilt lies with the one who handed me over to you.* [Jn 19:9]

In St John's gospel what is said here is said at several levels. The answer to *Where have you come from?* Could well be "Galilee" and in St Luke's gospel when Pilate learns that that is where Jesus is from, he sends him to see Herod Antipas, its ruler. Or it could be an answer at the spiritual level, and the reader is meant to understand, "I have come from the Father to be the light of the world".

There is ambiguity too, in Jesus saying *You would have no authority at all over me, if it had not been granted from above.* Pilate probably took this to refer to Tiberius Caesar who appointed him. The reader, on the other hand, knows that Jesus is referring to his Father in heaven. He knows that his death is inevitable. Pilate will give way to the demands of the Sadducees and the mob and be guilty of condemning an innocent man, but the real guilt will belong to Judas, *the deeper guilt lies with the one who handed me over to you.*

Suffering and Comedy Go Together

Can I learn to suffer
Without saying something ironic or funny
On suffering.

W.H.Auden [1907-73]

In the Bible, suffering and comedy are seldom far apart, as in the setting of Job's misfortunes within a wager between God and Satan. The thought offends us and yet it is such dislocations in experience that intrude in life again and again, as something out of place is juxtaposed with the deepest pain and sorrow.

Jesus is passed from the Sanhedrin to Pilate and from Pilate to Herod Antipas, in whose territory Galilee lay. Pilate asked Jesus if he was the king of the Jews then sends him to the man who was king of the Jews. Jesus had avoided Herod throughout his ministry. When he was on his way to Jerusalem, some Pharisees had warned him, "*Leave this place and be on your way; Herod wants to kill you."* [St Luke 13:23]. In his reply, Jesus characterises Herod as a fox, *Go and tell that fox.* Today, the fox represents cunning; in Jesus' day foxes were vermin and symbolised destruction. Herod had, after all, killed John the Baptist. Was Jesus next on his list? The reason was that as well as threatening the political stability of Galilee, Jesus was a member of the old royal house of David and a possible rival to the throne.

Yet, even with his life in danger, Jesus could not resist a little humour on this occasion. Herod is a fox and that suggests to Jesus that he must be the hen! So, far from being the fox's victim, Jesus sees himself as a mother hen that wants only to gather her chickens under her wing, *O Jerusalem, Jerusalem,* Jesus says to the friendly Pharisees, *city that murders the prophets and stones the messengers sent to her, How often have I longed to gather your children, as a hen gathers her chickens under her wing; but you would not let me.* [Luke 13:34] Yet again, this is humour as the turning of tables.

When therefore Jesus appeared before Herod as his prisoner, St Luke, aware of the irony, said, *When Herod saw Jesus he was greatly pleased; he had heard about him and had long been wanting to see some miracle performed by him.* But, the reader knows that there was more than this involved in this encounter.

Herod questioned Jesus *at some length* but *without getting any reply.* As the Sabbath was only hours away, the chief priests and scribes, concerned that progress was slow, arrived on the scene to press the case more vigorously. But Jesus still would not give them what they needed for a successful prosecution. It's then that Herod's patience runs out and he hands Jesus over to his soldiers for what today might be called "a bit of fun." Luke says, *Herod and his troops treated him with contempt and ridicule.* One suspects that by this time Jesus' reputation for satire had reached Jerusalem. He had even ridden into Jerusalem on a donkey which fulfilled the prophecy of Zechariah [9:9] but it was hardly what was expected of a king.

In 2003, events at Abu Ghraib[109] showed how easily prison life can plummet out of control whenever unsupervised guards lose respect for a prisoner. Jesus was abused and his suffering provided the comedy. In words familiar in courts all over Britain, his guards were doing it "for a laugh." But St Luke had not finished with the irony. Herod sends Jesus back to Pilate *dressed in a gorgeous robe,* then adds, *that same day Herod and Pilate became friends; till then there had been a feud between them.* In other words, the comic cruelty of the soldiers turned out to be redemptive for their superiors. Herod and Pilate were reconciled and as Christian readers know reconciliation was the hidden purpose of God throughout Jesus' passion.

The Soldiers Make Jesus a Parody of Himself as King

It is a modest creed, and yet
Pleasant if one considers it,
To own that death itself must be,
Like all the rest, a mockery.

Percy Bysshe Shelley [1792-1822].

---

[109] Abu Ghraib was the Iraqi prison taken over by the USA where, in 2003, there as a scandal over the way in which Iraqi prisoners had been tortured and appallingly mistreated by members of the US military.

As teachers everywhere know, unless it is held in check, comedy can easily get out of hand. It was now the turn of Pilate's guards to amuse themselves by torturing Jesus. They heard perhaps that he belonged to Judah's oldest royal family, but raised by a carpenter and was of dubious parentage. Because Jesus was a condemned man about to die a slave's death, they felt they had licence to do as they pleased, and so they played with him the game of *King Fool.* In Jerusalem, the Sisters of Zion show visitors the pavement of the Antonia Fortress preserved in the basement of their convent. On it is preserved the crudely carved setting of the game of dice played by Pilate's soldiers.

The condemned man was dressed as a king and then abused in a parody of judicial ritual. It was a perverted version of the Feast of Fools that Jesus had used throughout his ministry as an emblem of the Kingdom of Heaven. *Then the soldiers of the governor took Jesus into his residence, the Praetorium, where they collected the whole company around him. They stripped him and dressed him in a scarlet cloak; and plaiting a crown of thorns they placed it on his head, and a stick in his right hand. Falling on their knees before him they jeered at him: "Hail, king of the Jews."* [Mt 27:27ff].

All mockery is enjoyable for those doing the mocking. The passage is so full of ironies and reversals which parody the Kingdom of God as to constitute the ultimate comic contempt for Jesus as a man and a teacher. He was of the House of David and a candidate for the throne of Judah. His trial was an opportunity for the weak to mock the strong. Seeing how comedy can serve evil as well as it can serve righteousness we understand that it too needs to be redeemed.

Ezekiel and Jeremiah at the Cross: Banter Crucified

Wit shall not go unrewarded while I am king of this country.
William Shakespeare, *The Tempest.*

Crucifixion first humiliated its victims, then tortured them to death. Mockery was part of the humiliation. The charge against the condemned man was written on a board nailed above his head. Lest anyone fail to see the joke, the charge against Jesus was written in three languages: Hebrew, Latin and Greek: *Jesus of Nazareth, King of the Jews.* [Jn 19:19]. The crowd, taking their cue from the sign, added their own comic touch: *He saved others: now let him save himself.* [Lk 23:35] The soldiers also joined in: *If you are the king of the Jews, save yourself.*

Men crucified together would often try to talk to one another and one of the two criminals crucified with Jesus, they were probably Zealots, couldn't resist a little gallows humour: *Are you not the Messiah? Save yourself and us.* Everyone was having a joke at Jesus' expense.

At first, it looked as if the second man dying with Jesus, the so-called Penitent Thief, would have none of this and began by telling his friend off: *Have you no fear of God? You are under the same sentence as he is. In our case it is plain justice; we are paying the price for our misdeeds. But this man has done nothing wrong.* But then he spoils his case, by adding ironically, if not sarcastically: *Jesus, Remember me when you come into your kingdom.* [Lk 23:42.] Though perhaps, like a skilled counsellor entering into a client's fantasies, he was attempting to comfort this poor, deluded, false Messiah? But Jesus, never one to resist irony if it pointed to a deeper truth, entered into the spirit of the banter with: *Truly I tell you: today you will be with me in Paradise.*[110] The "thief" did not actually repent and his request had something of a dying man's chutzpah about it, chutzpah being something Jesus understood well. Had they been able to hear it, those who hungered and thirsted after righteousness would have been angry at this opening of the kingdom beyond even tax collectors and sinners. An executed man was a curse upon the land; this time, Jesus' humanising of the Torah had stretched mercy's priority over justice too far.

Like the Jews in Ezekiel's prophecy for the returning exiles [Ezek. 36:24], all was put right for the dying Zealot even before he repented. Christians often assume that his repentance followed on from the words of Jesus, but Jesus' theology of forgiveness was built on the comic reversals of Ezekiel and Jeremiah. In the Kingdom of God you were forgiven first and then you repented.

In St John's account, with the Sabbath almost upon them, the soldiers speeded death up by breaking the legs of the crucified. When they came to Jesus, however, they discovered that he was already dead and so the cruelty was unnecessary, Jesus having had, as it were, the last laugh. *As no bone* of the Passover Lamb *shall be broken* [Ex. 12:46] it was a faintly comic way of making the theological point that Jesus was the lamb of God sacrificed for the sins of the world. However, to make sure, one of the soldiers *thrust a*

---

110 It's possible, but very unlikely that the dying thief was not being ironical and that he meant what he said in the way that most preachers understand him. The more likely explanation, however, is that he was humouring Jesus in a good-natured way and that St Luke used his words to point to the deeper truth they contained.

lance into his side illustrating a prophecy of Zechariah, *They shall look on him whom they pierced.* [12:10].

Entering the Nihil

> *I believe in God, the Holy Nothingness, known to mystics of all ages, out of which we have come and to which we shall ultimately return,*
>
> Richard Rubinstein [b. 1924][111]

Why did Jesus quote Psalm 22:1, *My God, my God, why hast thou forsaken me,* and why did Matthew and Luke preserve the quotation in Aramaic if it did not express a real experience on Jesus' part? The *Shekhinah*, the indwelling presence of God, which was signalled at Jesus' baptism by the appearance of the dove of the Holy Spirit, had abandoned him. This was the cross experienced as the death of prayer. For devout Jews, to be deserted by God was the ultimate spiritual catastrophe.[112] It was the one tragedy that made life as comedy impossible. In the absence of God there could be no salvation. In the Bible, to be without God when life amounts to nothing, nihil, is as dark as it gets. It is the awful possibility underlying all human existence, even the lives of those closest to God. For a time Jesus entered the negative reality behind our every day human existence. The nihil is an even darker night than the dark night of the soul in the prayer life of mystics.

The Bible as Comedy founders on this bleakest of verses and experience. In Matthew and Luke, Jesus cries with a loud voice and dies. In St Luke's gospel as the sun's light is eclipsed and the veil of the temple torn in two that cry becomes a final act of faith as Jesus cries from the nothingness, *Father, into thy hands I commend my spirit.* [23:46]. Thus, the last word from the cross becomes a comic word of salvation. Jesus died as he lived, a Jew about his Father's business.

---

[111] Writing in "The State of Jewish Belief" in the journal *Commentary*, August 1966, the quotation continued, "I concur with atheistic existentialists such as Sartre and Camus, in much of their analysis of the broken condition of human finitude. We must endure that condition without illusion or hope."

[112] The departure of the Shekhinah from the temple in the visions of Ezekiel [11:1-25], would become a focus for much rabbinic debate.

27

THE RESURRECTION THE DISAPPEARING WITNESS AND BEYOND

The unexpected always happens.

Latin Proverb.

In the Bible, the Resurrection of Jesus is the greatest comic moment in the history of the world. It was the day when the tables were turned on death. All was well that ended well and St Matthew especially cannot resist a little comedy: *Suddenly there was a violent earthquake; an angel of the Lord descended from heaven and came and rolled away the stone, and sat on it.* [Mt 28:2]. Worn out by his exertions but, with the job done, the angel sits on the stone and rests, like God on the first Sabbath! It's a splendid touch and we have to smile.

And John too, in his gospel, cannot resist a little joke. Being fleeter than Peter, John gets to the tomb first but does not enter. Peter, however, goes in and *saw the linen wrappings lying there, and the napkin which had been around his head, not with the wrappings but rolled up in a place by itself.* [20:6] In other words, Jesus, after getting up from his burial slab and flinging aside the grave clothes couldn't resist taking the cloth that was over his face and carefully folding it up. In short, he left the tomb tidy! Partly, anyway. Jesus had risen with his sense of humour intact. Had he grown up in a home without servants? Was he used to making his own bed like this? However we view it, it's a nice aside by a man again in charge of his life and with his faith in God as his father vindicated.

All four gospels agree that Mary Magdalene was among the first witnesses to the empty tomb. As Jewish law reckoned that women make less credible witnesses than men, there was something almost tongue-in-cheek here about the way in which God, the hidden agent in the account, is acting. Just when you need the most reliable of witnesses, God gives you the least! Who says that God doesn't have a sense of humour? In this most improbable of events, it's the comedy in the detail that makes the account ring true.

And it gets worse, or better, depending on your point of view, when St Paul gave the church at Corinth his summary of what had happened at the empty tomb. He wrote: Jesus *appeared to Cephas, and afterwards to the Twelve. Then he appeared to over five hundred of our brothers at once, most of whom are still alive, though some have died. Then he appeared to James, and afterwards to all the apostles.* [I Cor. 15:5ff]. But what's happened to Mary Magdalene, the first witnesses to the resurrection? Not sharing Jesus' attitude to women, St Paul has air-brushed her out of the picture!

On that first Easter Day, St John [20:19ff] reports one other reversal of the ordinary way of things and that was how while the disciples were all together behind locked doors Jesus appeared, showed them his wounds, said *As the Father sent me, so I send you,* and as he breathed on them, said, *Receive the Holy Spirit. If you forgive anyone's sins, they are forgiven; if you pronounce them unforgiven, unforgiven they remain.* This was an extraordinary assertion, not only because it gave them the controversial power to pronounce forgiveness which he had exercised during his healing ministry, but because it turned upside down one of the central beliefs of the classical world which was summed up in the ancient formula, *as above so below.* It was part of the magical view of reality and can be found even in Plato where the world of ideal and mathematical forms is prior to and makes possible the realities of our everyday world.

At Jesus' birth, when the heavens were telling in stars and angels, it was an *as above, so below* series of events. And now, where sins are concerned, there's a comic reversal of that world view. Here, in the Kingdom, it's reversed and what happens on earth determines what happens in heaven! If the disciples needed proof that Jesus had risen from the dead, this survival of his unique brand of spiritual truth as comic truth should have been more convincing than the sight of his hands, feet and side!

Jesus' Last Jokes [Lk 24:13]

> *Humour remains a phenomenon that stands alone with no obvious place in the scientific understanding of our species.*
>
> Dr John Hewitt, in a scientific paper on humour.

Jesus: [Feigning ignorance.] *What is this conversation you are holding with each other as you walk?*
Cleopas: [Puzzled] *Are you the only visitor to Jerusalem who does not know the things that have happened there in these days?*
Jesus: *What things?* [Lk 24:19].

It was during Easter 1963 that I first came to appreciate Jesus' sense of humour. My Vicar, a prince among preachers, while expounding Luke's account of Jesus appearing to his disciples on the road to Emmaus, said, "It's the best joke in the Bible!" The Passover Moon was beginning to wane, though casting enough light to travel by. Jesus joined the disciples as they walked but as they couldn't believe he'd risen from the dead they failed to recognise him. Being a rabbi who liked to tease his students, Jesus, fresh from the grave, could not resist a little mischief and asks what they are talking about. They are talking about him. What other topic of conversation could there be? *Are you the only visitor to Jerusalem who does not know the things that have happened there in these days?* They asked. *What things?* he replied. It's a one word question in Greek, ποîα, poia, a piece of comic understatement to rival anything an Englishman could come up with. On the Road to Emmaus, the Bible as comedy climaxes in the resurrection because resurrection by its very nature must generate comedy.

In St Luke's gospel it is the verbal humour that survives the crucifixion, in St John it is Gematria, the Jewish love of playing with numbers. St John tells how seven of Jesus' disciples go night-fishing on the sea of Tiberius and catch nothing. But when Jesus tells them to cast their nets on the starboard side, *they did so and found they could not haul the net on board, there were so many fish in it.* [21:6]. When they count the fish, there are 153.

Knowing the Bible's love of number-play, commentators have long thought that 153 must represent something theologically and spiritually significant; it was, after all, the seventeenth triangular number and as such figured in the number mysticism of the Pythagoreans and others.

If numbers are represented by dots, e.g. 1 = . 2 = .. 3= ... and so on, then the dots when placed one above the other, form a triangle like this:

.
. .
. . .

A triangular number is defined as the sum of all the dots in the triangle that ends with that number. As the triangular number three contains six dots, six is the third triangular number; ten will be the fourth, fifteen the sixth and so on, until we reach the number 17. As the sum of all the numbers from one to seventeen add up to 153 it is defined as the 17th triangular number. Christian and Jewish scholars knew this. They also knew that if each of the three digits 1, 5 and 3 are cubed, they also add up to 153; for 1x1x1 = 1; 5x5x5 = 125; 3x3x3 = 27, and 1+125 + 27 = 153.

To the ancient mind, the mystery didn't end there, for any third number treated in this way will always result in the number 153. There was something fishy about the number 153! Even the number of the Beast, in the Book of Revelation, 666, the 36th triangular number, being divisible by 3, will also reduce to 153, and in a manner of speaking end up in God's net! On this interpretation, in the comedy of redemption even the Beast it seems will be redeemed.

For the mathematically minded, playing with numbers is always fun. For Jews and early Christians the fun was also Divine Comedy. However, the problem for commentators, number fun aside, has been to discover what it all meant. St Jerome's explanation, quoting the *Helieutica of Oppian*[113], was that as there were 153 different kinds of fish in the world, all the nations of the world would one day belong to the Church. Jesus' first joke was, after all, that he would make his disciples "fishers of men." Other commentators have fixed on 153 as the triangular number 17[114] and concluded that as 17 is the sum of 7 plus 10; and as 7 in biblical number symbolism is the number of completeness and 10 that of perfection, 153 is the number of the universal and apostolic Church. It's a similar conclusion arrived at in a different way. Things become even more interesting because the cubes of any number that is divisible by 3, will also converge on the mysterious, irreducible 153.

The trouble is, of course, that in this kind of Christian gematria while the number is interesting mathematically it carries no clear meaning. It is another of Jesus' jokes, only this time the punch line is lost! Leaving the tomb tidy after the resurrection; an angel sitting nonchalantly on a tomb-stone, his quip on the road to Emmaus and now the strange count of fish; the humour and the word play just goes on and on. If satanic evil had its cruel fun and games in the crucifixion of Jesus, then the gospels reveal the gentler playfulness of the divine comedy in his resurrection.

Jesus the Man

Behold the man.

Pontius Pilate [Jn 19:5]

---

113 The quotation has not been found.

114 153 is the sum of all the whole numbers from 1 to 17.

What sort of man, then, was Jesus? He was a first century Galilean, a religious Jew, born of a good, Torah observant family and into the traditions of those whose loyalty to the Torah had preserved Judaism through six hundred difficult and testing years. Yet he was a devout Jew with a difference. Jesus adapted the wordplay and humour of the Hebrew Scriptures and took them to new heights of invention and ingenuity making them more central to his ministry than any prophet or teacher before him.

History as comedy in the coming Kingdom of God was the heart of his theology. What made Jesus so radical and iconoclastic was that his use of humour was no mere adjunct to his teaching. Its function was spiritual and defining. Just as humour takes conventional expectations and treats them to sudden and unanticipated transformations in order to reveal some surprise latent within them, so Jesus did something similar with his theology. All humour involves some kind of double take. First the penny fails to drop; then it falls and we get the joke. It's the same with Jesus' theology. We need a double-take before we understand it.

Everyone thought they knew what righteousness was until, in making jokes out of it, Jesus revealed where authentic righteousness and its Kingdom lay.

Mere religious convention, however devoutly and intelligently held, is vulnerable to this sort of humour because being at root conventional its psychological structures are often devised to avoid difficult spiritual truths. This is why Jesus' theology shares the same debunking, teasing structures as his jokes. Making his humour central like this also reveals more of Jesus the man than do any of the more conventional approaches. It also makes him less tameable by theologians. Those who like to intellectualise know what a menace the intellect can be.

Jesus was concerned that believers should not be imprisoned by the well-intentioned prescriptions of those who believed they had the right to determine how others should live. Religious practice and religious belief should make us more human and not less. Increase of humanity was the acid test. We should always ask of some belief, can you build a civilisation on it, and what sort of civilisation would result? Jesus can be described therefore as a Jewish humanist, a humaniser of Judaism who used humour to expose the spiritually oppressive nature of Torah extremism. And because, from the human side, few things conceal the reality of God quite so much as religious convention and the narrow controlling of other people's lives, Jesus' sense of humour opens the way to a deeper experience of the God hidden not only behind the text of the Bible, but by the structures that make up our social and religious world.

What Exactly was Jesus trying to do during his Ministry?

> *The Kingdom is always that which is worth more to me than anything I have; that which I want more, need more than anything I possess.*
>
> Werner Peltz. *The Listener* 12.7.62.

So, what was Jesus attempting to do when he went about Galilee teaching and healing and what was his purpose in making that final journey to Jerusalem? The usual answers to these important questions are often wrong.

Did he, for example, attempt and then succeed in founding the religion we know as Christianity? There's not the slightest hint of this in the gospels and besides, such a thing was unthinkable even for the most radical Jew, yet this was often the assumption in church circles when I was growing up in the 1940s.

Was he trying, then, to reform Judaism? This is much nearer the mark. In sayings like, *The Sabbath was made for man, not man for the Sabbath*, Jesus was clearly trying to turn the usual way of understanding the Torah on its head. It was a text that set out a great humanising and legally transforming principle in the relationship of Jews to their religious law. To that extent, Jesus was following in the steps of prophets and teachers like Hosea and Jeremiah. He was a reformer with a radical understanding of the Kingdom of God as the key to the Torah. His own deep relationship with God as Father was what lay behind his decision to take his message from Capernaum to the spiritual heart of Judea and Judaism in Jerusalem. In doing this he believed that he would be fulfilling the true role of Messiah, the anointed one.

Tragically, as he knew they would be, his views on Messiahship were misunderstood, and in the religious confusions and corruptions of the capital he was crucified with Zealots. The irony being that the Zealot ideas of the Kingdom, based as they were on hatred and violence, were exactly opposed to his own. It's an opposition which is as central to terrorist dominated world politics today as it was then. Jesus is no less relevant for us as he was for Caiaphas and Pilate. The humanism of the Kingdom of God is for ever at odds with the kingdoms, systems and anti-human ideologies and beliefs of our world. History as tragi-comedy is our story. The Kingdom of the Father is Christ's upside-down Kingdom of love.

Those who think they know a better have so far only added to the horrors of human existence.

The Ascension of Christ as a Comic Exit

Thou hast ascended on high, thou hast led captivity captive.
Psalm 68:18.

In the Acts of the Apostles, the earthly ministry of Jesus, validated in his resurrection, reaches its climax with his ascension into heaven. [1:9ff] There's no humour here, unless it is in the attempts of some artists to represent it visually, but it is in its theological meaning a true comic ending; for all's well that ends well, and much more: the Son returns to the Father and sits at God's right hand. He intercedes for the world and sends to his Church the Holy Spirit, and through the Holy Spirit the many gifts of God's Kingdom of grace. All that is needed now is the final triumph of righteousness and the restoration of nature on the eighth and last day of the world.

Humour in the Rest of the New Testament

They are ill discoverers who think that there is no land, when they can see nothing but sea.
Francis Bacon [1561-1626].

In the Acts of the Apostles [2:14], St Luke reports St Peter attempting a little humour in his day of Pentecost speech when he and the other disciples are filled with the Holy Spirit and speaking in tongues. He says to the crowd, *These people are not drunk. It is only nine o'clock in the morning.*

Much of the Bible's humour of incongruity has to do with extremes of inappropriateness; for example, in St Peter's defence before the Sanhedrin in which he employs the paradoxical image of God choosing Jesus like an architect selecting for the corner stone of a building a stone rejected by the builders. [Acts 4:11] This was a reference to Psalm 118:22, a verse used previously by Jesus himself [Lk 20:17], though in a comic, slapstick sort of link with Isaiah 8:14, making it also a stone to trip over. This doubly comic image of tripping over a stone that nobody wanted clearly amused early Christian theologians because it's repeated in the First Letter of St Peter to represent the fate of those who refuse to believe the gospel. [2:7].

Because the New Testament is written in Greek and not

Hebrew, puns don't features in it as they do in the Old; but irony is occasionally there. For example, at the martyrdom of St Stephen the witnesses lay *their coats at the feet of a young man named Saul* who *was among those who approved of his execution.* [Acts 7:57ff] The reader knows that this Saul will shortly be converted and become St Paul the most effective of all the champions of the Christian Church. And when it comes to comedy of the darkest sort, the New Testament can be as black as the Old; this is especially so where the wicked get what is deemed to be their well deserved deserts. *A man called Ananias sold a property, and with the connivance of his wife Sapphira kept back some of the proceeds and brought part only to lay at the apostle's feet. Peter said, "Ananias, how was it that Satan so possessed your mind that you kept back part of the price of the land. While it remained unsold, did it not remain yours? Even after it was turned into money, was it not still at your disposal? What made you think of doing this? You have lied not to me but to God." When Ananias heard these words he dropped dead; and all who heard it were awestruck.* [Acts 5:1ff]

I've been a member of several church groups when they discussed this passage and each one found it both disturbing and difficult, only to discover, when they read further, how their first shock was only the beginnings of the passage's moral challenge. *About three hours passed, and his wife came in unaware of what happened. Peter asked her, "Tell me, were you paid such and such a price for the land?" "Yes," she replied, "that was the price." Peter said, "Why did the two of you conspire to put the Spirit of the Lord to the test? Those who buried your husband are there at the door, and they will carry you away. At once she dropped dead at his feet."* [5:7ff]

Did Peter deliberately frighten Sapphira to death, or was he merely predicting what her reaction would be? In either case, the implied comedy of just deserts is frightening to the modern mind. The whole episode can, of course, be explained away rationally though the reason St Luke included it in his history of the early church was to produce what he considered an appropriate response of fear to the working of the Holy Spirit.

St Luke also thought that the sudden death of Herod Agrippa I also qualified as a well-deserved, and therefore comic, punishment. In Caesarea, Herod, *attired in his royal robes and seated on the rostrum,* received the ambassadors of Tyre and Sidon who were suing for peace. A crowd of sycophants shouted, "*It is a god speaking, not a man!" Instantly an angel of the Lord struck him down, because he had usurped the honour due to God; he was eaten up with worms and so died.* [12:22ff]

Together with the story of Ananias and Sapphira, we may

assume that the early Christians found this an edifying tale. More to modern tastes in comedy is the story of Eutychus, a member of the church at Troas, who is so eager to hear Paul preach that he sat in the only place available, a window ledge. Paul *went on speaking until midnight.* The room was lit by a large number of oil lamps. The young man *grew more and more drowsy,* Paul *went on talking, until, completely overcome by sleep,* Eutychus *fell from the third story to the ground.* [20:7ff]

At first, it was thought that he was dead, but the boy survived and was taken home. There's no serious point to this story, no miracle, no work of the Holy Spirit, and yet St Luke obviously relished telling it. We can only conclude that we were intended to smile at the effect and length of Paul's sermons and enjoy with the writer this evidence of the great man's weakness for lengthy and soporific preaching.

St Paul has come down to us not as a storyteller like Jesus, but as a writer of serious letters. What humour there is, is found in their pastoral advice rather than in their theology. He advises the Christians at Corinth, for example, that it is *better to marry than to burn.* [I Cor. 7:9] Many a groom has smiled at that thought! Later, the apostle ridicules some in the congregation, who at the Lord's Supper take and eat their own food, with the result that *one goes hungry and another has too much to drink. Have you no homes of your own to eat and drink in?* If the humour here is barely noticeable, things are very different when the apostle has cause to rebuke the Galatian church for its drift towards a Christian version of Torah righteousness. A group of visiting Jewish Christians have attempted to persuade Gentile Christians that they need to become Jews by being circumcised before they can become Christians. Paul's argument against the "Judaisers" gathers force until finally his patience snaps and in the crudest of vulgar jokes he wishes that those who would have the Galatians circumcised would *cut themselves off* or *mutilate themselves* or *make eunuchs of themselves* [5:12], depending on the coyness of the translation.

On occasions, Paul can turn on the sarcasm like a prophet, as in his Letter to the Romans where, tongue in cheek, he praises the Jews of the Empire's capital for their faithfulness to the Torah: *you rely on the law;* he says, *you take pride in your God; you know his will; taught by the law, you know what really matters; you are confident that you are a guide to the blind, a light to those in darkness, an instructor to the foolish, and a teacher of the immature.* [2:17ff]. This doubles as the humour of sarcasm and comic exaggeration.

Like all Jewish scholars, Paul loved to argue points of Torah.

It was how the Rabbis did their theology. This can be seen very clearly again in his letter to the Roman Church whose congregation he planned to visit. Much of the letter is written as a series of discussions on a number of subjects raised by reports he's heard. The problem, of course, is that having never met the Roman Christians he can only fill out what little he knows about their problems with assumptions, and this he does with tremendous insight and depth. Sometimes, though, he appears to be arguing with himself, at others with an imaginary opponent. We have to smile at his earnestness here, for it is after all only a rhetorical device: *You will say, "Then why does God find fault, if no one can resist his will?" Who do you think you are to answer God back?* [9:19]

But when it comes to predestination, Paul is as much out of his depth as any man. His greatness as a theologian has run up against the limitations of all thinking on the matter, and as St Luke did over the effect of his preaching on Eutychus, we have to smile as he gets trapped in the subject's complications.

Although Paul does not directly quote the teaching of Jesus, in his First Letter to the Corinthians he does reflect Jesus' comic theme of things being the other way round in the Kingdom of Heaven where *God chose what was foolish in the world to shame the wise, God chose what is weak in the world to shame the strong, God chose what is low and despised in the world, even things that are not, to bring to nothing things that are, so that no human being might boast in the presence of God.* [1:17ff]

However, writing to Philemon, Paul does have a pun equal to the best elsewhere in the Bible. A runaway slave, the convert, Onesimus, is returning to his Christian master, Philemon, and because they are brothers in Christ, Paul provides a covering letter. The pun is on the slave's name which means, "the useful one." *I, Paul, appeal to you about my child, whose father I have become in this prison. I mean Onesimus, once so useless to you, but useful indeed, both to you and to me.* [v 10].

Whether or not in writing to Titus, Paul realised there was paradox in his quoting [1:12] the 6th c. BC poet and philosopher, Epimenides [1:12]. Titus was bishop in Crete and there were problems in the church there. Epimenides was a Cretan and Paul thought it appropriate to quote his saying, *Cretans are always liars.* If the statement is true, then Epimenides being a Cretan, must have been lying, and therefore the statement is a lie. But, if he's telling the truth, then the statement must again be false because being truthful he can't be a lying Cretan! The assertion is a paradox of the kind much discussed by modern philosophers. Today, philosophy and mathematics thrive on them. Paradoxes are philosophically a serious business, yet comical at the same time; as in the theologian's paradoxical question: "Can God make a stone that he can't lift?"

Comedy and the Cosmos

If I had been present at the creation, I would have given some useful hints for the better arrangement of the universe.
King Alfonso the Wise of Castile [1221-1284]

The early Church's comic vision of salvation permeates the New Testament. Here, for example, is St Paul writing to the Ephesians: *God has made known to us his secret purpose, in accordance with the plan which he determined beforehand in Christ, to be put into effect when the time was ripe: namely that the universe, everything in heaven and on earth, might be brought into a unity in Christ* [1:9-10]. As we shall see, this theology is echoed in the Book of Revelation in more traditional apocalyptic language.

If Only the Letters of the New Testament Sparkled More With Humour

Religion is a way of walking, not a way of talking.
Dean W. R. Inge [1860-1954]

There is an attempt at humour in the Letter to the Hebrews where its unknown author, having written more of a theological tract than a letter, hopes to humour his readers with: *I beg you, friends, bear with my appeal; for this is after all a short letter.* Only it's not. Its thirteen chapters make it the fourth longest of the New Testament's twenty one epistles!

An argument in favour of Jesus' brother James being the writer of the letter that bears his name is that for all that he seemed absent in the latter part of Jesus' ministry, after the resurrection he does appear to have come round to Jesus' comic vision of the Kingdom. The following quotation from his letter reads very like Jesus in its message: *If a person with gold rings and in fine clothes comes into your assembly, and if a poor person in dirty clothes also comes in, and if you take notice of the one wearing the fine clothes and say, "Have a seat here, please", while to the one who is poor you say, "Stand there", or, "Sit at my feet", have you not made distinctions among yourselves, and become judges with evil thoughts? Listen, my beloved brothers and sisters. Has not God chosen the poor in the world to be rich in faith and to be heirs of the kingdom that he has promised to those who love him?* [James 2:2ff]

28

MORE ON PAUL THE APOSTLE: THE BIBLE'S FIFTH DEFINING MOMENT

Tell me now, you that are so anxious to be under the Torah...
St Paul's letter to the Galatians [4:21]

It is often said that the real founder of Christianity was St Paul, and that though he had no personal knowledge of Jesus he nevertheless turned Jesus' own religion into a faith about Jesus; that through his travels and writings, the Jesus of history became the Christ of faith. This is far too simplistic a view, as the Christ of faith can also be found in the epistles of John and Peter, the letter to the Hebrews and the Apocalypse.

As we have seen, at the time of Jesus there were two quite distinctive types of Judaism: the Palestinian[115] and the Hellenistic. Jesus was a Palestinian Jew and Paul, Hellenistic. Palestinian Jews numbered about one million,[116] spoke Aramaic and Hebrew, their Bible was the Hebrew Bible, they lived in and around Judah and Galilee and had largely resisted the influence of Greek and Roman culture. Their religion was conservative and traditionalist. They were not very missionary minded.

Hellenistic Jews numbered about four million, spoke Greek and had largely assimilated to Greek culture. Their Bible was the Septuagint. They lived mostly outside the historic Jewish heartland, being scattered in communities all around the Mediterranean. Through intermarriage and missionary activity, they attracted large numbers of interested gentiles known as "God-fearers"[117].

It was, it seems, these more sophisticated and culturally open

---

115 The use of the word here parallels its use in the phrase, "The Palestinian Talmud", which served to differentiate it from "The Babylonian Talmud", produced by the Jewish Community in Babylon.

116 These figures are rough estimates only. Historians reckon the population of the Roman Empire to have been between 55-70 million, putting the proportion who were Jews at about 8%.

117 Godfearers [see Acts 13:16 etc and Josephus *Antiquities* 14:110] were non-Jews who attended a synagogue, yet were spared circumcision and full Torah observance which were required for conversion.

Hellenistic Jews who responded to the preaching of St Paul and other Christian evangelists. The tensions which arose between the two groups are evident in Acts chapter six.

Because of its high birth rate and social cohesion, its missionary outreach and moral attractiveness, Hellenistic Christianity began to displace Hellenistic Judaism throughout the Empire. As Jewish Christianity was marginalised after the fall of Jerusalem in 70AD, and Rabbinic Judaism grew in vitality as Jews rallied around the Torah, the separation of Church and Synagogue became inevitable. The Christian Church was now the Christian Hellenised Judaism of St Paul built upon the Palestinian Judaism of Jesus. This is why, in the New Testament, the revisionist Judaism of Jesus is succeeded by its Hellenised interpretation as St Paul redirected Hellenistic Judaism along the Christian track. Only in this sense can Paul be described as being the founder of Christianity. It explains why the comic Palestinian folk elements in the parables and teaching of Jesus were replaced by the abstract teaching of Paul in which comedy as humour is much, much rarer.

We have seen how by emphasising the love and graciousness of God and urging his fellow-Jews to treat Jew and non-Jew, righteous and unrighteous in the same way, Jesus liberalised and transformed the central meaning of the Torah. Paul's problem was how to achieve the same transformation for Gentile Christians who had no background in the Torah. The key to understanding Paul's success lies in the fact that the love, graciousness and forgiveness of God as understood by Jesus are, at root, comic concepts. They remain comic concepts with or without their Palestinian Jewish wrappings of parable, irony, hyperbole and chutzpah.

Events qualify as comedy in our study's first sense of the word whenever they result in happiness, fulfilment and well-being. The Bible's central themes of deliverance and salvation are by this definition comic themes. In the Old Testament, they were linked to Israel's faithful observance of the Torah. In his letters to the churches[118], St Paul strove to show how, for the Gentiles, the redemptive comic role of the Torah had been replaced by faith in Christ. This left, however, an important gap in the pastoral care of Gentile converts. Without the Torah, how would these Hellenist Christians receive the moral training necessary for their Christian

---

[118] In the New Testament, there were seven of these: Romans, Corinthians, Galatians, Ephesians, Philippians, Colossians and Thessalonians; plus letters to three individuals: Timothy, Titus and Philemon.

formation? This omission Paul made good in the extended last, pastoral, sections of his letters. After a personal introduction, the major section was always concerned with explaining some aspect of the comedy of God's love in the Christian's salvation in Christ; this was then followed by a long section on living out that love morally in daily life, whether in the Church or in the world. Paul's letters end with the ethical aspects of the Torah, interpreted as Jesus interpreted it, by divine love.

St Paul's Theology of the Love of God

> *Love is the only enduring power, since it is the only power which is not ultimately self-defeating.*
>
> Philip Toynbee [1916-1981] *Part of a Journey.*

St Paul's theology of love is centred on the key word, "Grace"; in Greek *charis*. The roots of the idea lie deep in the Hebrew Scriptures in its concept of divine favour. For St Paul, grace was the transforming power of God's love towards us. It was shown in such things as his forbearance and forgiveness. Its effect was to create in a Christian the sort of love he described in his famous chapter on Charity in 1 Corinthians 13: *Love is patient and kind. Love envies no one, is never boastful, never conceited, never rude; love is never selfish, never quick to take offence. Love keeps no score of wrongs, takes no pleasure in the sins of others, but delights in the truth. There is nothing love cannot face; there is no limit to its faith, its hope, its endurance.* [vv4-7]

It is because God is gracious that the world can live in hope, history come to a glorious conclusion in Christ, and Christians are able to love one another as God in Christ loved them. Grace is the Bible's ultimate comic expression and unites the theologies of Paul and Jesus; though Jesus' theology is largely comedy with humour and Paul's comedy without it.

Paul and the Problem of Righteousness

> *But now, quite independently of the law*[119]*, though with the law and the prophets bearing witness to it, the righteousness of God has been made known.*
>
> St Paul, Romans 3:21.

---

119 Torah is translated as "Law" wherever the Jewish law is referred to.

How should Christians observe the Torah? This was the question that troubled the first generation of Church members. Was the answer the same for both Jewish and Gentile Christians? The matter was dealt with at the first council of the Christian Church held in Jerusalem and chaired by St James, the brother of Jesus. Though the biblical text [Acts 15:15] and its interpretation are far from agreed, what is clear is that while Jewish Christians were to continue to observe the Jewish Law, gentile Christians had only to *abstain from the pollution of idols, and from unchastity*[120] *and from what is strangled*[121] *and from blood;* in other words, to observe the Noachic Commandments[122] as Godfearers had always done.

Unfortunately, this did not answer the problem that some Torah devout Christian Jews, St Paul called them Judaisers, had with Christian Gentiles. They insisted that gentile Christians should be circumcised. St Paul dealt with the problems this raises at length in his letters to the Galatians and to Rome. What is significant for this study is that his resolution kept close to the Old Testament's comic view of salvation.

Firstly, as Jeremiah and Ezekiel had taught, God offered salvation *for the sake of his Name;* that is, it was an offer of grace which preceded all human effort at keeping the commandments. God underwrote human existence and our response was to be one of trust or faith. Paul's doctrine of Justification by Faith is a comic doctrine. God's redemption of his own creation, its eventual happy and therefore comic outcome, was God's own work, to which Jewish and Gentile believers respond with worthy lives. This is why he ends all his letters with a section on what it means for Gentiles to keep the moral, though not the ritual, Torah of God. There was, alas, no Christian midrashim or humour in this.

And then came tragedy when the great reformer, Martin Luther [1483-1546], angry that the Jews did not convert at his preaching of justification by faith, argued erroneously that Jews

---

[120] Some texts omit *and from unchastity.*

[121] Many important ancient texts omitted *and from what is strangled.*

[122] This was roughly in keeping with the Talmud which listed, as derived from Genesis, seven prohibitions against Blasphemy, Idolatry, Sexual immorality, Murder, Theft, Eating part of a living animal, acting justly. A gentile who kept these laws as God-given was reckoned worthy of the Kingdom of Heaven. [Sanh. 105a]

believed in salvation by works[123] whenever they were obedient to the Torah. He contrasted it to Christian salvation by faith in God's grace in Christ. Modern Protestant scholarship has challenged this interpretation as unfair to 1st century Judaism[124]. The arguments are complex[125]. The good thing is that Christian scholars are now reading Paul more carefully and viewing Judaism more charitably. Christian/Jewish dialogue has been essential in improving understanding and relations between the two faiths. It has been a happy and therefore comic turn in relationships after 2,000 years of tragic Christian hostility and contempt.

---

[123] This was Luther's argument against the Vatican's sale of indulgences projected on to the synagogues and Jews of 16th century Germany.

[124] The debate really got underway with E.P.Sanders 1977 book, *Paul and Palestinian Judaism.* In 1982, James D.G.Dunne labelled this important revisionist movement, "The New Perspective on St Paul."

[125] The arguments centre on the charge that, beginning with St James, St Paul has too often been read out of context.

29

THE BOOK OF REVELATION: THE BIBLE'S COMIC FINALE

Apocalypse Now
The 1979 Francis Ford Coppola film.

The Christian Bible begins with creation and the woes of Eden and ends with the violent, two part comedy of the book of Revelation, the earliest Christian Apocalypse. The book's first section uses the comedy of come-uppance to tell of the overthrow of Satan and the forces of evil. In the second part, the whole created order is renewed in *a new heaven and a new earth.* [21:1] and the history of the world ends with a classic comic conclusion in *the Marriage Feast of the Lamb* [19:6-10 & 21:9].

The Apocalypse is a record of the visions of a Christian prophet, John, who may or may not have been the apostle of that name. The visions were for the encouragement of churches persecuted for their refusal to worship the Emperor as a god. These were congregations who longed to see Jesus the Messiah vindicated and the powers of evil overthrown. The Apocalypse was written to encourage them to remain faithful to Christ, for Satan would not triumph for ever and God's glorious kingdom would eventually arrive.

As was usual in apocalyptic, the message was delivered through dramatic and often impenetrable symbolism. Many of the images it employs, such as the Four Horsemen of the Apocalypse [6:1ff], the number of the beast, 666[126], [13:18] and the final battle of Armageddon [16:16] have, through books and film, become part of popular western culture and its love of violence. It is, however, a violence taken out of context, as popular culture has no interest in the triumph of God, only in the world-wide cataclysm and destruction that precedes it, a time known in Jewish apocalyptic as "the birth pangs of the Messiah". The Book of Revelation goes into vivid detail with these as seven seals are broken, seven trumpets blown, seven visions seen and seven bowls full of the wrath of God poured on the earth. In this comedy of deserved retribution, Rome, the great whore of

---

126 This is a rare example in the New Testament of numerology or gematria. In Hebrew, the numerical value of the letters of "Nero Caesar" come to 666.

Babylon, is destroyed while an angel seized *the dragon, that ancient serpent, who is the Devil, or Satan, and chained him up for a thousand years. He threw him into the abyss, shutting and sealing it over him, so that he might not seduce the nations again till the thousand years were ended.* [20:2-3]

Finally, the Devil will be *flung into the lake of fire and sulphur, where the beast and the false prophet had been flung to be tormented day and night for ever,* [20:10]; which is a comic but hardly a happy ending for those concerned. That comes in the last two chapters: *I saw a new heaven and a new earth, for the first heaven and the first earth had vanished and there was no longer any sea. I saw the Holy City, New Jerusalem, coming down from God out of heaven, made ready like a bride adorned for her husband* [21:1-2]. "All comedies are ended by a marriage," said Lord Byron.

It's a splendid vision and one that presumably comforted its first readers however much it might trouble us today with its body-count and descriptions of terrible destruction; even though that dreadful cost in human misery is no more than what we humans make of history with our human capacity to inflict death and appalling suffering upon one another.

However, as a vehicle for conveying Jesus' teaching on the grace, love and forgiveness of God, the apocalyptic tradition found here does not sit easily with the gospels. Jesus was an apocalypticist, as Schweitzer and others made clear, but he humanised that tradition in his teaching about the kingdom just as he humanised the teaching of Torah. The Apocalypse as comedy needs to be read in the gospel light of the Kingdom as comedy.

Though the Good News of God's grace is central to its message, we search the New Testament beyond the gospels in vain for illustrations which reflect the storytelling genius of Jesus. In the Revelation of St John, the vengeful figure of the divine Jesus hardly seems the same person as the Christ of the gospels, as if not only had the Church been infiltrated by those who had opposed Jesus' understanding of the Torah but whose apocalyptic ideas were more in keeping with those of the Zealots and Essenes.

30

BIBLICAL CRITICISM: THE BIBLE'S SIXTH DEFINING MOMENT

Life is doubt, and faith without doubt is nothing but death.
Miguel de Unamuno [1864-1936]

During the first hundred years of the Protestant Reformation, the Bible was unchallenged as a source of revealed truth, not only in Christian doctrine, but in science and history too. Its authority and comic vision extended into all aspects of European life. Its transforming power was such that in Britain it led to the triumph of Parliament, the beheading of the King and to the Church of England even becoming briefly Presbyterian.

However, early in the 17th century the rise of experimental science in England, Italy, Germany and France meant that a second source of truth developed alongside the Bible's.[127] It was in the spirit of scientific enquiry to question everything, even the thinking and opinions of once revered authorities like Plato and Aristotle. It was therefore inevitable that systematic doubt would eventually spread to the way in which the scholars of Christian Europe read their Bible.

At first, the new approach concerned itself with sorting through the hundreds of ancient manuscripts whose texts were becoming more readily available through printing. The aim was to establish the original Hebrew and Greek wording of the biblical text. It was not long, however, before the methods of rational enquiry applied to the study of Greek and Roman history were applied to the Bible and the Christian doctrines derived from it. This happened most radically and quickly in German universities though the approach and its conclusions spread slowly elsewhere.

This "scientific" approach to establishing the original biblical text was seldom controversial and was known as *Textual* or *Lower Criticism* in order to distinguish it from criticism of the history and meanings of that text, which, accordingly, became known as *Higher Criticism.*

---

127 This was the idea, found in Galileo, Newton and others, that there were two books of divine revelation: the Bible, and the Book of Nature which it was the task of experimental and mathematical science to read.

In their radical use of the critical method, biblical scholars questioned every received belief and opinion. Not only did they assert that St Paul was not the writer of the Letter to the Hebrews, but some questioned that Jesus ever existed as an historical person. Others concluded that John's Gospel, almost in its entirety, was without historical value and that the synoptic gospels contained little of what Jesus had actually said and done. What had once been understood as history was declared to be little more than "myth."[128] Old moral certainties such as the existence of hell as a place of everlasting punishment were abandoned. For many, the doctrines of the Trinity and the Incarnation were redundant. History and belief, it was believed, were catching up with science.

One effect of this flood of new ideas from Germany was that many in educated Victorian society lost their faith. It was cognitive dissonance on a grand scale. It was the biblical dread of entering the Nihil of meaninglessness. A typical case was that of Mary Anne Evans, later to become famous under her pen name, George Eliot[129]. Eliot had been brought up as a conventional, low church, evangelical Anglican, a tradition that read the Bible in its literal sense. In the 1830s, she was introduced to an educated circle whose reading included the liberal German theologians David Strauss [1808 – 1874], who denied Christ's divinity, and Ludwig Feuerbach [1804-1872], who believed that religion resulted from the projection of human needs and desires on to nature and the idea of God. By 1849, when Eliot

---

[128] Few words have proved as confusing as the word "myth." It is, for example, often overlooked that a historical fact can also operate as a myth; for instance, the events known as the French Revolution actually occurred and yet they also function today as the French Republic's founding myth. The same is true of the American Revolution. Historic facts double up as myths whenever they shape some aspect of culture. Albert Einstein, for example, acts as a powerful mythological figure in inspiring in many the study of science. Facts only operate spiritually and psychologically when they take on a mythological role. Jesus is no exception. To use "myth" as a synonym for "fairytale" could not be more mistaken. Fairy tales shape no one's inner life, myths do.

[129] Eliot's loss of faith is movingly described in her 1867 poem, *O May I Join the Choir Invisible,* especially the lines: *To higher worship mixed with love/ that better self shall live till Human Time shall fold its eyelids, and the human sky/ be gathered like a scroll within the tomb/ unread for ever.* The poem's Latin epigraph from Cicero, translates as "That long span of years when I shall be no longer, moves me more that this brief life-span".

translated Strauss's *Life of Jesus* into English, Christianity as historical fact had vanished for her and Jesus been reduced to a symbol of moral virtue.

Another famous Victorian who lost his faith in this way was Matthew Arnold [1822-1888] whose love poem *Dover Beach* of 1867, reflected the impact of German biblical criticism[130] on a previously uncritical faith. For Arnold, the best we could hope for in the meaninglessness of life[131] was human love. [132]

While some resolved the dissonance by abandoning their faith, others like Samuel Taylor Coleridge [1772-1834], one of the few to have studied in Germany and mastered the language, sought to place the reading of the Bible on a more philosophical basis.[133] "The Bible and Christianity," he wrote, "are their own sufficient evidence."[134]

It was the growing and largely negative impact of Higher Criticism upon traditional Christian belief which became the Bible's Sixth Defining Moment. Well-read Christians felt that they were standing at the edge of an abyss looking out over nothingness. For

---

130 By this date the impact of Darwin's *Origin of Species* [1859] was also taking its intellectual toll. Leslie Stephen, an Anglican priest, had renounced his orders after reading Darwin. In his essay, *Religion as a Fine Art,* he rejected the attempts of "liberal" clergy to reconcile science and theology.

131

Ah, love, let us be true
To one another! For the world, which seems
To lie before us like a land of dreams.
So various, so beautiful so new,
Have really neither joy, nor love, nor light,
Nor certitude, nor peace, nor help for pain;

132 In 1848, the poet Arthur Hugh Clough [1819-1861] also resigned his Fellowship at Oriel College, Oxford, having read Strauss.

133 Not all educated Christians by any means lost their faith, but they all had to reformulate it to take account of the challenge posed by biblical criticism. John Henry Newman [1801-1890] dealt with the challenge by exploring the idea of doctrinal development.

134 Other poets who retained their faith in this difficult intellectual climate were Alfred, Lord Tennyson [1809-1892], Robert Browning [1812-1889], Emily Bronte [1818-1848], Christina Rossetti [1830-1894] and Gerard Manley Hopkins [1844-1889].

2,000 years, Christians and Jews had read their Bible devotionally. Bible reading was linked directly to individual and corporate spiritual formation. Its primary function was to educate the soul in the things of God. The inner, spiritual life of Jews and Christians can only be built upon a comic, all's well that ends well, theistic framework. As the Psalms in their reflections on the Torah make clear, without the under-girding of biblical comedy, prayer and all sense of a relationship with God are impossible. And the new, critical ways of reading the Bible were not devotional. They did not pre-suppose a happy final outcome to the world. They were academic and so unsuited to meeting the traditional pastoral need of the care of souls. Instead of being helpful to the struggling believer, they dissolved prayer and inhibited the exercise of faith. So, how did the churches respond to this unparalleled assault on traditional ways of using the Bible?

We have seen earlier that in coping with cognitive dissonance and the threat of the nihil of meaninglessness on this scale three strategies are available: [1] Loss of Faith, [2] Accommodating the challenge by re-interpreting faith, [3] avoiding all challenges to that faith and insisting aggressively that nothing has changed.[135]

An Anglican Response

To the Church nothing is secular but what is sinful.
Archbishop E. W. Benson [1829-1896]

While many Victorians felt obliged to abandon their faith in the Bible, others strove to reconcile their beliefs to the new critical standpoint and radical views crossing the North Sea from Germany. In 1860, seven Anglican clergy, all academics and writing independently of each other, published their responses to the new challenges in *Essays and Reviews.* Frederick Temple's[136] article, *The Education of the World,* was the first in the volume, and made use of the idea that the history of revelation paralleled the growth of human understanding from childhood through to maturity. Benjamin Jowett's[137], *On the Interpretation of Scripture,* argued for

[135] I recall an anthropologist saying to me once that, "When the tribe is dying, the dance gets faster!"

[136] Temple later [1896] became Archbishop of Canterbury, showing how quickly the Church of England had accommodated itself to views which had at first seemed disturbing to so many.

[137] Jowett was a Fellow of Balliol College, Oxford, and later became Regius Professor of Greek.

understanding the Bible as progressive revelation. Its constant reinterpretation was a continual necessity.

The book went largely unnoticed until Samuel Wilberforce, the Bishop of Oxford, denounced it in an anonymous review for its liberalism. In February 1861, it was condemned by a meeting of bishops in Fulham. A petition signed by 11,000 Church of England clergy[138] declared their belief in the inspiration of Scripture and the eternity of Hell.[139] In 1863, Jowett was brought before the Vice-Chancellor's Court charged with teaching doctrines contrary to the Church of England. The case was later dropped.[140] It was a sign that not all Anglicans were against the views of the essayists.[141] Once the fear of having their faith cut from under them had passed, the majority of clergy learned to accept the new critical methods which were then taught in theological colleges; though the doctrinal divide created between "liberals" and "conservatives" remains to this day. On the whole, evangelical Anglicans rejected what became known as "liberalism," but not all. Indeed, St Aidan's, Birkenhead, where I trained was known as a "liberal evangelical" college.

The Roman Catholic Response

The march of the human mind is slow.
Edmund Burke [1729-1797]

The attempts to reconcile the Bible and Church teaching with developments in philosophy and the new academic understanding of history eventually made their way into the educational systems of the

---

[138] There were at the time almost 25,000 Anglican clergy in the country.

[139] In 1853, the theologian F.D.Maurice [1805-72] had been dismissed from his Chair at King's College, London, for teaching that "eternity" in the New Testament had nothing to do with time.

[140] Legal action was also taken against Henry Bristow Wilson, Fellow of St John's, and Rowland Williams, later the Professor and Vice-Principal of St David's University College, Lampeter. They were found guilty, but the verdict was later reversed by the Judicial Committee of the Privy Council.

[141] Those view were far from static, and the seven authors took opposing standpoints on some matters. Their unity was in their intellectual freedom of approach.

Roman Catholic Church. This was especially the case in France[142]. The official reaction was slow but in the end decisive as Roman Catholic Church leaders were just as fearful as Anglicans had been that basic Christian truths were being undermined. In addition, it was believed that the Magisterium, the "teaching authority of the Church" was being by-passed in universities, colleges and seminaries. The work of interpreting the Word of God was emphasised as the proper responsibility of the Pope and the bishops in communion with him.

Under Pope Leo XIII[143], no action was taken, but to his successor, Pius IX[144], Modernism, as the movement had become known, was "the synthesis of all heresies". Its official condemnation came in 1907 with the decree *Lamentibili*[145] and the encyclical *Pascendi.* In 1910, the motu proprio[146], *Sacrorum Antistitum,* obliged all clergy at their ordination and on taking up a teaching post to swear an anti-modernist oath. Modernism in the Roman Catholic Church had been successfully repressed but the cost was its intellectual isolation.

In 1902, however, the Pope kept the door ajar by setting up a Biblical Commission whose task was to promote biblical studies within the Roman Catholic Church; which, while they conformed to modern scholarship also safeguarded the Bible from the sort of criticism thought to undermine its authority. Its conclusions were always cautious and though authoritative were never "infallible."[147] The Vatican's chief concern throughout was to protect its clergy and laity from the sort of doubts that had afflicted Anglicans half a century before.

In 1943, with the publication of Pius XII's encyclical *Divino Afflante Spiritu,* the atmosphere of reactionary conservatism that dominated Roman Catholic life began to give way to a more liberal outlook which was further developed at the Second Vatican Council

---

142 In France, among those pressing for the modernisation of church teaching were the historian, Alfred Loisy [1857-1940] and the philosopher, Maurice Blondel [1861-1949].

143 Pope from 1878-1903.

144 Pope from 1903-1914.

145 The decree listed 65 propositions which the Vatican believed summarised accurately the teachings of the Modernists.

146 "Motu proprio" is Latin for "On his own impulse" and is a personal letter from the Pope.

147 The doctrine of the Pope's Infallibility when speaking *ex cathedra*, was defined at the Vatican Council in 1870. Unfortunately it was open to the sort of continual interpretation it was intended to guard against.

[1962-65]. After this, Roman Catholic scholars, though in general cautious and always having to write and teach with a regard to official Vatican pronouncements, were in essence as free as academics in other churches. In the Editors' Preface to *The Jerome Bible Commentary*, the editors were able to write: *The principles of literary and historical criticism, so long regarded with suspicion, are now at last accepted and applied by Catholic exegetes.*

The Rise of Protestant Fundamentalism

Progress would be wonderful – if only it would stop.
Robert Musil [1880-1942]

In the late 19th century, a number of Bible Conferences were convened by Protestants in the USA concerned about the doubts raised in traditional believers by the teaching of evolution, liberal theology and biblical criticism. In 1895, a conference at Niagara drew up a list of non-negotiable fundamentals of evangelical truth: these were the plenary, verbal inspiration and inerrancy of Scripture; the divinity, virgin birth and physical resurrection of Christ; salvation through his work of substitutionary atonement and his physical and literal second coming. A series of tracts, *The Fundamentals,* published between 1910 and 1915 spelled out the conservative position clearly and were the origin of the word "fundamentalist". The "sticking-points" listed at Niagara defined the battle-lines drawn up against liberalism and modernism. For conservative evangelicals they remain to this day, with the addition of the rejection of legalised abortion, homosexual practices and in the USA, the theory of evolution. In Britain, "conservative evangelical" is the term preferred.

Fundamentalism as a Defence of Scripture as Comedy

If a man will begin with certainties, he shall end in doubts; but if he will be content to begin with doubts, he shall end in certainties.
Francis Bacon [1561-1626]

In churches that had once preached their message clearly and authoritatively, the fear of the Nihil released by the tentativeness of biblical scholarship[148] proved too much for many believers. For peace of mind they needed the certainty of beliefs that were beyond challenge. For Roman Catholics infallibility rested in the Pope; for conservative Protestants in the Bible. If the sophistication of the modern world challenged those beliefs then the modern world was wrong it was argued. The force of feeling produced in this clash of belief with belief is evident in the violent invective that theological disputes can still unleash.

Those not raised on the old certainties of the Bible can have little idea of the cultural trauma that resulted from attempts to re-define those certainties. Biblical criticism had produced in the western world the nihilism that biblical comedy had held in check since the exile of the Jews to Babylon. The Nihil, the ultimate dread of nothingness, had been unleashed as a fifth horseman of apocalyptic truth riding across the modern world. Cultural historians can trace his death-ride across the west in movements like Anarchism, Dada, Death of God theologies, Deconstructionism, Existentialism, Futurism, Moral relativism, Postmodernism, the Theatre of the Absurd and so on. These, however, were all minor encounters with the Nihil compared with what was unleashed in the Holocaust[149], or Shoah[150], the Bible's most recent defining moment and the truest measure yet of the loss of the Bible's comic vision in the western world.

---

[148] It is the job of scholars in all subjects to be forever coming up with new ideas while challenging old one. Their task is to suggest better answers to old problems. Their inner lives are given meaning by the ever-changing directions of the search for truth. Most people seem not to be made that way, however, and want only clear and authoritative answers to basic questions. This is the appeal of Fundamentalism in all religions.

[149] The Holocaust was the Greek word for the Whole Burnt Offering in the sacrifices at the Temple in Jerusalem. While as a metaphor it usually refers to the mass-murder of Jews under Hitler it is sometimes used to describe the genocide of other peoples, for example that of the suffering of the Armenians under the late Ottoman Empire.

[150] Shoah is a Hebrew word meaning calamity or disaster and is the term preferred by many Jews.

31

THE HOLOCAUST: THE BIBLE'S SEVENTH DEFINING MOMENT

Life is a long lesson in humility.
J. M. Barrie [1860-1937] *Little Minister*

The Holocaust [1941-45] was the state-managed genocide of six million out of Europe's nine million Jews. It can be understood as an inevitable result of the Nazis' ecstatic embrace of spiritual, moral, philosophical, political and other nihilisms. Many regard it as the defining event of the 20th century, one that cannot be contemplated without being over-whelmed by the dread of the meaninglessness of the Nihil. It was an event that called and still calls all values and beliefs about humankind and God into doubt.

After 1933, Nazism quickly emerged as a total way of life based on unquestioning obedience to Hitler as the Fuhrer. Its values were derived from the racial worship of the German people and a loathing for all non-Aryans, with the Jews as the most hated race in the Nazi hierarchy of contempt. For Hitler, Jews were a disease of civilisation. All the world's woes were attributable to them and the "rational" solution[151], the *Endlösung,* or "Final Solution", was their complete elimination. Nazi self-deception was such that in a perverse inversion of Judeo-Christian ethics they convinced themselves that what they were doing was right and good.[152]

From 1933-1939, this was done legally through oppressive

---

151 Reason also dictated A *Law for the Prevention of Hereditary Diseased Offspring* by which 360,000 social misfits and mentally-ill Germans were compulsorily sterilised. This particular eugenics measure was halted at the sterilisation of the physically disabled because Joseph Goebbels the Minister of Propaganda suffered from a congenital club foot. The heartless applications of rational argument prepared the way for the war without limits against the Jews.

152 Recalling Satan's "*Evil, be thou my good*" in John Milton's *Paradise Lost.*

laws which "encouraged" Jews like Albert Einstein and Sigmund Freud to emigrate[153]. But in 1941, beginning in the conquered territories of Poland and Russia, Jews were shot and gassed by the ten thousand[154]. Vast, industrial-scale death camps like Auschwitz were set up, backed by an efficient bureaucracy and transport system. The SS was the organ of state, entrusted with ridding Europe of its Jewish contagion with state of the art crematoria to obliterate the evidence.

The world had known many genocides but none on the scale of the Holocaust. It was modernity in the service of evil: the best employed by the worst. The armed forces, the civil service, the churches, education, law, medicine, the press, radio, films, science, technology; all were made use of by the party machine. To the Nazis it was part of their grand comic vision of history; an unconscious perversion of the biblical.

It has not been easy for European Christians[155] to come to terms with the Holocaust and the way in which a democratically elected leader was able to hijack a political party and through it a whole nation, persuading it to adopt a programme which, until then, the majority would have found unthinkably wicked.

Hitler was arguably the most spiritual man of the 20th century[156], and the German churches and universities in not resisting him effectively, were Europe's most flawed institutions.

In Hitler and the Nazi party, biblical comedy and the civilisation based upon it had encountered its most powerful rival and briefly lost the struggle. Only the Apocalypse had imagery dark enough to do justice to that irony and briefly and locally lost the struggle.

---

153 In 1933 laws were passed which marginalised and isolated German Jews. They could not belong to a profession and were excluded from schools and universities. In 1938, with the *Nuremberg Laws* they lost their citizenship and civil rights.

154 The work was entrusted to a special SS task force, whose four Death Squads, the *Einsatzgruppen,* murdered by the ten thousand.

155 During my time as British Chaplain in Israel [1966-69] it was noticeable how differently many Israeli Jews behaved towards African Christians whose identities had not been tarnished by the Holocaust and centuries of anti-Jewish prejudice.

156 How else can we account for his hold and power? Certainly Europe produced no spiritual power for good to equal him.

Making Sense of the Holocaust

What I mean by moral progress is an increasing and active recognition of the fact that other human beings are fully as human as oneself.

Philip Toynbee [1916-1981]

Although the state of Israel held its first *Yom HaShoah*, Holocaust Memorial Day, on 27th Nisan[157] 1951, the United Nations did not declare 27th January[158] as an International Day of Commemoration to Honour the Victims of the Holocaust until 2001. Likewise, though *Yad VaShem*, the Israel Holocaust Museum in Jerusalem was opened in 1953, the exhibition at the Imperial War Museum in London was not set up until 2000.

Generally speaking, even in Israel, it was only after the War of June 1967 that the enormity of the Holocaust was recognised in public debate. Until then, survivors were reluctant to speak and historians slow to write. Even the execution of Adolf Eichmann [1906-1962], dubbed "the Architect of the Holocaust", did not arouse anything on the scale of later interest. The subject seemed just too painful, the public insufficiently interested. Since then, the dam of reluctance has been breached. In Britain, Holocaust Memorial Day is a day in the civic calendar, and commemorative events are attended by civic and religious leaders, In addition, the Holocaust has become part of the National Curriculum in Schools.

Yet for all the recognition of what for many is the worst crime in history, two related problems remain: that of safeguarding the Holocaust against subtle forms of trivialisation and the ability of Christians to face up to the questions it raises. How could such a thing have happened in the most cultured and scientifically[159] advanced country in Europe? How did Hitler conceive such a hatred of the Jews? How did he persuade so many Germans to participate? Why did God not intervene? Why did the churches not resist more

---

157 In the Jewish calendar, which is a lunar calendar, Nisan falls April/May.

158 This was the day in 1945 when the Russian army liberated the infamous death camp at Auschwitz.

159 The following quotation throws some light on this question: "Modern Physics is an instrument of Jewry for the destruction of Nordic science… True physics is the creation of the German spirit." Rudolphe Tomaschek, a leading Nazi physicist quoted in William Shirer's, *The Rise and Fall of the Third Reich.*

effectively or its members refuse more often to participate? Did Christian anti-Judaism and its ancient theology of contempt for the Jewish people help build the road to the gas chambers? Why was Pope Pius XII so silent? Couldn't the allies have bombed the railway to Auschwitz?

The Threat of the Nihil: Can the Bible as Comedy Survive the Holocaust?

> *The expression often used by Mr Herbert Spencer of the Survival of the Fittest is more accurate, and is sometimes equally convenient.*
>
> Charles Darwin [1809-1882]

Some Jewish Responses: In 1949, after reading *Todesfuge,* Death Fugue, a poem by the holocaust survivor, Paul Celan, the literary critic, Theodore Adorno [1903-69], made his famous comment that "*To write poetry after Auschwitz would be barbaric.*" Though he later withdrew the remark, the Holocaust as the sum of the 20th century's darkest nihilism has the power to call all that human beings value into doubt: including reason, humanity, the existence of God and the biblical message that history is a Divine Comedy. The Holocaust is humankind's greatest experience of dissonance and many attempts have been made to resolve it. For believers, the key question is: how could an all-knowing, all-loving, all-powerful[160] Lord of History stand aside and do nothing while his Chosen People suffered for the very name Jew, the name he gave them? How could they continue to approach him through the Torah, the book that recorded his saving acts in Egypt and Babylon?

Some Haredi[161] Jews accept even the Holocaust as divine punishment for sin; believing that it changed nothing and that the Torah's view of history remains. Others, like the Lubavitcher Rebbe, Menachem Mendel Schneerson, argued that such a view was blasphemous. A rational explanation is impossible. The Holocaust cannot be explained and God cannot be justified by human reason.

---

160 Rabbis like Harold Kushner and William E. Kaufman have argued that for the Holocaust to have happened God cannot be all-powerful.

161 These are the most conservative Jews. The word Haredi means "one who, in awe of God, trembles."

The only answer we will accept[162] *is the immediate and complete Redemption that will forever banish evil from the face of the earth and bring to the intrinsic goodness and perfection of God's creation*. In other words, the Bible as Comedy remains the ultimate statement of faith.

More than any other historical event, the Holocaust has compelled thinkers from all traditions to re-examine their explanations in order to maintain the biblical insistence that history will finally have a redemptive outcome[163]. Others hold that God's apparent absence is explained by Deuteronomy 31:18, *I will surely hide my face on that day.*[164]

The fear that the Holocaust might be the Nihil that threatens all religious faith has led both Christian and Jewish thinkers to explore the idea that even God is limited; or that perhaps after all that the Deists are right and the Bible wrong and that God does not intervene in history.

Among the mystical traditions of Judaism based on the Kabbalah there is the idea that sin is a descent of the soul in which the greater the sin, the deeper the accompanying descent, but that through *Teshuvah*, repentance and return, the soul has the possibility of an even greater spiritual ascent. To the ordinary believer, any idea that the Holocaust was a blessing in disguise like this can seem perverse.

Some Christian Responses: As a much needed and practical theological reform, the important Vatican document *Nostra Aetate*[165] redefined radically the relationship of the Roman Catholic Church to the Jewish people, setting all discussion of the Holocaust within a positive and constructive framework of respect, dialogue and acceptance. It stated that even though some Jewish authorities called

---

[162] This is identical in form to the traditional explanations of Jesus healing the man born blind in St John's gospel; that what's needed is a cure, not an explanation.

[163] In a radical and much criticised break with Jewish tradition, Rabbi Irving Greenberg has argued that by allowing the Holocaust God has unilaterally broken the covenant with his people and no longer hears their prayers. After the Holocaust the Torah can only be observed by Jews on a voluntary basis because God has lost the authority to enforce obedience. The Holocaust was the worst that God could do.

[164] This is the idea of *Hester Panim,* in which inexplicably God hides the Divine Face.

[165] Promulgated by Pope Paul VI on 28th October 1965.

for Jesus' crucifixion, all Jews could not be blamed for his death, either then or now. This repudiated the ancient charge of deicide[166]. Nor could Jews be thought of as people rejected or accursed by God. *Nostra Aetate* also condemned all forms of anti-Semitism and spoke positively of other faiths.

On 28th May 2006, Pope Benedict XVI visited the site of the death-camp at Auschwitz-Birkenau. The Holocaust, he suggested, was motivated by a hatred of the God of Abraham. God had to die and with him the people who witnessed to him.[167]

In his book, *The Gay Science* [1882], Friedrich Nietzsche had a madman proclaim, *Gott ist tot,* God is dead. By this he meant that in late 19th c. Europe, God no longer functioned as a cultural reality. It was an idea that lay dormant outside philosophical circles until a group of theologians which included Thomas J. Altizer, Paul Van Buren, William Hamilton, Bishop John Robinson, Rabbi Richard Rubenstein and Gabriel Vahanian took up the idea and on 8th April 1966, the front cover of *Time* magazine made the public aware of the Death of God Movement in theology. This was a heroic response to a growing awareness that contemporary culture no longer supposed the existence of a transcendent being who intervened in history. Humanity was on its own. Man had come of age. A new morality was required. There was at this time a buoyant confidence in the human ability to manage the world now that it was no longer tied in a childish dependence to God's apron strings. And though it did not say so in as many words, it meant that the comic vision of the Bible was neither sustainable nor required.

The Death of God movement[168] was not a direct response to the Holocaust, which was still to become the defining problem of the 20th c; rather, it set it aside for a while as it enjoyed a short interval of over-confidence in human nature and its abilities.

Can Secular Humanism Survive the Holocaust?

> *We do not need to prove religion to men but to prove to them that they are religious.*
> George Tyrrell [1861-1909]

---

166 This was the charge that in crucifying Jesus the Jews were God-killers. The charge lay behind many a massacre and pogrom.

167 St Augustine had suggested that the reason God had allowed the Jews to survive was as a perpetual witness to Christ.

168 The over-confidence of the Death of God theologians was short-lived and came at the end of a century of a humanism which with its secular beliefs in progress, social utopianism and human perfectibility had been every bit as triumphalist as the Church.

In January 2009, a group of British secular humanists launched an advertising campaign in which buses in a number of cities carried the slogan: *There's probably no God. Now stop worrying and enjoy your life.*[169] In the view of the advertisers the contemporary experience of the meaninglessness of life could be replaced by the ability to enjoy it, once people ceased believing in God. History as comedy was not the outcome of belief in the God of the Bible but on reason and basic human decency. Secular humanism was believed to be spiritually self-sufficient and well able to provide history with a comic outcome.

This challenge to the Bible as Comedy is a strong one providing that only the evils of a pathological religion are the issue. But most of the world's troubles are not caused by bad religion. That's far too simplistic a view. The evidence is that in the absence of religion what results is not a secular heaven on earth but a variety of nihilisms, all of which clamour for dominance and can only be silenced by some sort of human sacrifice.

Secular humanism fails to take seriously the egotism of the atheist ego, the innate evil in pathological personalities and unjust social systems. Reason and benevolence need motivating and organising and only facts as myths can do that. As secularist thinking rejects all myths except the uncritical and romantic myths of its own inherent power and decency, it is under-equipped to take on reality and its current nihilisms. Its message seems to be that the Holocaust was only possible in a world built on religion. In a world built on enlightened secularism it could not have happened. The irony was that the Holocaust was devised largely by those who had cast off religion. No one suggests that contemporary secularists are from that mould, only that they should be aware that just as God is hidden, so is the Nihil that his departure in secularism leaves. Nothing ever seems enough for its hunger. The Nihil needs constant feeding and always seeks to satisfy its appetite on some aspect of the very humanity that humanists wish to promote. The irony is that here believers and humanists are on the same side.

The bus campaign began a much needed dialogue. Many secular criticisms of religion are correct. Religion can be oppressive. It can encourage spiritual and emotional infantilism, closed minds, extremisms and prejudiced societies. But it's a mistake to think that getting rid of all religion is the answer. In practice, Christianity is not yet "true" in the full, mature sense of "true to God" that its members

[169] The bus campaign was in response to extremist Christian advertising which said that those who rejected God would spend eternity in the torments of Hell.

would wish. One essential way to that much prayed for, spiritual, human maturity is through dialogue with its critics, including secular humanists.

At the moment, the Bible as Comedy remains an unrealised vision and an unfulfilled hope. The Bible as Comedy underwrites history as comedy and so far all attempts to secularise that have failed. To be successful it would need a powerful, spiritual and factually based myth to rival that of the Bible, and so far, none is even on the horizon.

32

FURTHER THOUGHTS ON THE NATURE OF THE BIBLE

There is scarcely a text in the Holy Scriptures to which there is not an opposite text written in characters equally large and legible.
Walter Savage Landor [1775-1864]

Landor's imaginary conversation with the reformer Melanchthon sums up most people's experience when they begin to get to grips with their Bible.

When Billy Graham first visited Britain, he would clinch his arguments with the phrase, "the Bible says," giving a wrong impression of what sort of book most Christians, at most times and in most places, have believed the Bible to be. It was as if he believed it had been infallibly dictated, word for word, by the Holy Spirit, even though the Bible does not read like that kind of work. It contains so many opposing ideas that this fact alone should dispel such a simplification. Then there's the humour. The Bible is so full of humour that it could only be inspired in the fundamentalist sense if God had deliberately set out either to override human creativity or to counterfeit it. If, in response to this, it is recognised that God revealed himself through our human sense of comedy, then our artistic and intellectual endeavours being such fuzzy and fallible things, any claim to infallibility would itself be a poor joke.

Twice in The Book of Revelation, John the Christian prophet prostrates himself in self-abnegation before an angel [19:10ff & 22:8ff] and twice he is told: *You must not do that! I am a fellow-servant with you and your brothers who bear their witness to Jesus. It is God you must worship.* John is commanded to stand in the presence of the angels of revelation and not set his humanity aside.

The Clue to How We Should View the Bible is How the Bible Views Itself

> *The modern world seems to have no notion of preserving different things side by side, of allowing its proper and proportionate place to each, of saving the whole varied heritage of culture. It has no notion except that of simplifying something by destroying nearly everything else.*
>
> Gilbert Keith Chesterton [1874-1936].

Jesus the rabbi was an interpreter of scripture in the humanist tradition of the Old Testament storytellers. He was not a moral rigorist, that is a fundamentalist in today's language. As a teacher of Torah, Jesus was too liberal for his family and too liberal also for the Jerusalem Pharisees monitoring his preaching; while often his disciples failed to understand his comic and radical approach to the pursuit of righteousness.

Righteousness was a problem for devout Jews. Jesus clearly thought his opponents were expecting more from men and women than God expected, and said so, but with a mocking humour that tested the limits of the Jewish comic tradition.

In 70AD, the failure of the Zealots to defeat the Romans brought to an end a 600 year belief that history could be managed through the formula of Torah faithfulness guaranteeing Jewish survival. Those six centuries gave the Bible its comic structure and content. When, after the fall of Jerusalem, the rabbis defined the Hebrew canon of scripture, followed in the 4th century by the Church closing that of the New Testament, the Bible's overall shape had been established as a comic vision of world history. For more than 1500 years that comic vision shaped the moral and intellectual development of the western world. Although the canon of scripture was closed, the debate over the righteousness that shaped it went on and continues to this day. Jesus' teaching and St Paul's victory at the Council of Jerusalem on the priority of grace over law defined the debate on the Christian side; while the Talmud, with its leniency and prophetic privileging of mercy over sacrifice partly paralleled that development for Jews.

After the Religious Wars of 17th century Europe[170] the Bible's comic vision survived in various secularised forms, to become a blueprint for liberal optimism: Enlightenment belief in progress, the Marxist view of history and to some extent, as a template, even the evil, perverse ideology of the Nazis.

The illusion that by understanding history we can control it was re-asserted after the collapse of communism by the American intellectual Francis Fukuyama with his claim that, with the triumph of liberal democracy and market capitalism, history had reached its final form[171]. His claim, however, was challenged by the 2008 crisis in the global finance markets, an upheaval which appeared to threaten a

---

170 Which were often fought over failures to agree on the interpretation of the Bible.

171 See his 1992 book, *The End of History and the Last Man*.

total systems failure like that of the 5th c. Roman Empire in the west.

Yet, as we have seen, even before confidence in consumer capitalism was shaken, the moral and political disasters of the Holocaust had led both Jews and Christians to question their comic vision of history. How can a moral and spiritual optimism based on the Bible's comic overview of history survive the death camps?

For want of better labels we could characterise this two and a half thousand year debate over history as comedy as one between ideologues and humanists. Is the purpose of religious practice to make us perfect after some given idea of what it is to be human; or is the purpose of religious practice to promote a richer and more mature humanity through a relationship with God and righteous dealings with other human beings? Ezra was an ideologue on this way of describing the different approaches; Koheleth and Jesus were humanists.

Christian Homosexuals: a Test Case

> *We have just enough religion to make us hate, but not enough to make us love one another.*
>
> Jonathan Swift [1667-1745]

For Anglicans, the 2008 Lambeth Conference intensified the debate between those who stood by a conservative understanding of scripture and those who wished to interpret it as it interprets itself, dynamically, developmentally and creatively.

The comic opposition of Ruth and Jonah to Ezra's extremism is reflected in contemporary Anglicanism's confusion over the moral and spiritual status of Christian homosexuals[172]. Rigorists assert that what is needed is a strict moral purity based on a plain reading of the text; but just as the Pharisees' accommodation with the Romans was destroyed by extremists so the Anglican accommodation with contemporary culture seems likely to be brought to a tragic end by its inflexible traditionalists.

How easily today's conservative Christians have given up following Jesus in his radical, risk taking ways of interpreting scripture! In the expanding economies of the 17th century, Protestant Reformers were able to circumvent the commandments forbidding usury in economically static societies and by doing so helped

---

[172] The ordination of women to the priesthood and their consecration as bishops is also an issue that threatens to divide the church.

transform the European economy from one of static to dynamic markets. Could today's conservatives be as radical? Likewise, in the 19th century, by bold re-interpretation, evangelicals especially were able to read texts which had once supported the institution of slavery as no longer doing so. Both these reforms were energetically resisted by biblical conservatives who clung to the "plain reading" of scripture.

Because the text of the Bible is more or less fixed, only flexible, adaptive interpretations can see it safely through new challenges. We have followed this process through seven defining moments in biblical history when to have read it literally would have brought its comic story to a tragic end. And now, with the controversy over Christian homosexuals, we have reached another seeming impasse. *Yet we possess the mind of Christ,* St Paul wrote to the Corinthians [I:2v16]; though clearly in our reluctance to take risks and interpret scripture ever more compassionately and humanely, many Anglicans could not be further from that mind. It is an irony that though the interpretation of the Biblical text became ever more compassionate and humanitarian, beginning with the Pharisees and reaching its zenith in the teaching of Jesus, those who today appeal to it as their authority in righteous living should in their hard-line attitudes to homosexuality move counter to the direction of its teaching. *Man, if indeed you know what you are doing, you are blessed; but if not, you are cursed and a transgressor of the law.*

Judaism is a religion based on law, Torah, and interpreted by religious lawyers, rabbis, who, when they felt it right, interpreted it in the direction of a generous humanity. Christianity is not a religion of law, but of grace and it should be interpreted as Jesus interpreted Judaism, radically and generously and in the direction of an ever greater humanity. Morally and spiritually this can be a high risk strategy, but the main thrust of the Bible, especially the New Testament is subverted if Christian theologians become religious lawyers.

The fact is that no one understands either the origins or the nature or biological purpose, if any, of homosexuality. There are only theories and attitudes and a marked lack of humility or compassion in the whole debate. It's not a time to be saying, "The Bible says." But it is a time to ask where the Bible was going with moral questions like this when the canon was closed. What is certain is that for Christians the gates of interpretation are always open and that the Biblical direction in these things was always one of ever greater humility, understanding, compassion, inclusiveness and humanity.

A rigorist, ideological reading of the Bible tends inevitably to violence, self-righteousness and self-destruction. It is a belief in biblical comedy without the Bible's humour. Once we take the promise of history ending well out of the hands of God and into our own, fantasising that we can read the Bible infallibly, then idolatry becomes the spectre at our literalist feast.

When the Bible is read ideologically, texts which were once attacks on idolatry can become its defence. The reality of idolatry, religious and secular, is still with us. It is perhaps the one subject on which Christians and Jews could profitably engage in dialogue, as the ancient quarrel between religion as ideology and religion as the true humanism continues to tear all three faiths apart. Once we let go of the Bible's comic vision of life with all its humour, then for the church and for humankind the hope of history as comedy has ended.

Yet that need not happen. The canon of scripture might be closed but the dialogues that shaped it continue within and between the Abrahamic faiths. Recently there are signs that that dialogue is beginning to extend to a wider and much needed dialogue with atheists and secular humanists. Because the Bible was written by writers who did not always agree, it is important that its readers reflect that diversity in dealing with one another. Without communities discussing it openly in shared difference, the Bible must remain a closed book. It is continuous discussion that keeps the Bible open to its readers. That's the lesson of the Talmud for Christians.

There are risks for all who are involved in dialogue. It is therefore important that we avoid extremes and remember the words of Ecclesiastes, *be not righteous over much* as well as those of Hosea, *I desire mercy and not sacrifice.* [6:6]

33

HUMAN BEINGS AS THEIR OWN CREATORS: THE BIBLE'S EIGHTH DEFINING MOMENT

Nature admits no lie.

Thomas Carlyle [1795-1881]

When faced with Darwin's *Origin of Species,* Victorian theologians like Charles Kingsley [1819-75] responded to its challenge by arguing that God had created a universe that creates itself. Within that universe, human beings have reached the point at which they can create automatic systems whose algorithms can make moral decisions[173] and others with software programmes which by trial and error can modify and direct their improvements to themselves. It's a defining and critical moment in human affairs and in the Church's relationship to the Bible.

If the present rate of technological advance continues it will soon be possible for human beings to transform, in whatever way they think desirable, their own genetic make-up, while, at the same time, chemically and electronically enhancing many of the capabilities of the mind. This vision of a human/ technological chimera, has already been given a name, *transhumanism,* by its supporters. Like the Kingdom, as a reality it's drawing near. How are they related?

Behold, the man has become like one of us, knowing good and evil; and now, lest he put forth his hand and take also of the tree of life, and eat, and live for ever – therefore the Lord God sent him forth from the garden of Eden. [Gen:3:22] The truth of this verse still haunts us as do the words: *From now on nothing they have a mind to do will be beyond their reach* [Gen. 11:6]. Human beings will shape the future of the world and determine what kind of creatures they will be.

The automated electronic creatures we call robots and those other extensions of ourselves known as cyborgs have arrived. On past performance, the outlook for such developments does not look good. In the last half of the 20th century, management theory fell well

---

173 Robot sentries with artificial intelligence are currently being developed by the military. They can not only challenge intruders but by using advanced algorithms can decide without human intervention whether or not to shoot!

short of what was required to control such complex systems as wars, economies and global weather. Because our ability to manage a system depends on being able to predict its behaviour, it follows that the more complex it is the less well we are able to control it. That's why, like the Garden of Eden, so many systems expel their managers! And there's no going back to any time of technological innocence. The gate to that garden is closed behind us.

For the Bible, every historical crisis so far has been underwritten by God as Creator; but, when human beings become their own creators and create other creators, what then?

That important and tragedy-laden text from the story of the Tower of Babel, *From now on nothing they have a mind to do will be beyond their reach,* [Gen 11:6] is about the seemingly limitless power of the human imagination. Whatever human beings have created existed first in the imagination, including all those aspects of the strange, new run-away world taking shape around us. It's our world, we have made it, yet already, as it leaves our control it seems to have to have a mind and imagination of its own. What use now is the Bible?

It's here that Jesus' teaching about the Kingdom of Heaven is important; for, like the world we live in, the Kingdom too is a powerful product of the imagination. It is what many modern writers know as a "paracosm", that is a detailed imaginary world that exists solely in the mind. Literary examples abound, Narnia, for example, and alternative realities in science fiction. Such fictions are easy to mock, yet without them human beings would not be human. We have only to think of the Standard Model of the Atom, which, for the moment, is the best description of physical reality that we have, to know that without such experimentally based and mathematically grounded imaginary realms, science would not progress or be science. The deciding factor in evaluating all paracosms is whether as metaphors they are a good or bad fit to reality. The Standard Model is a good fit, and so too is the Kingdom of God, which Jesus said was always near, always arriving.

The Kingdom is a state of affairs unlike any known in society or in politics. It's the most desirable of worlds in which the poor and weak take precedence over the rich and strong, in which repentance is prompted by the realisation that we are already forgiven; in which enemies and the undeserving are loved and our every attempt to earn acceptance by God subverted by grace. It's the political world turned upside down. It's the Father's Kingdom that Jesus offers his followers.

I first experienced how near it was when I was ten years old. After much discussion my parents told me that they could not afford to send me to the local grammar school. Then, within months, with the new government came the welfare state with free education and, weeks later, I began grammar school. The meek had inherited the earth and the Kingdom of Heaven seemed at hand. The welfare state wasn't the Kingdom, but in it the Kingdom had drawn nearer, just as it has in the spread of human rights. This has been a predominantly secular process often shaming the Church, the Kingdom being the test for all social, religious and political change. The vision of Jesus may have begun as a spiritual paracosm, but it embodied truths that could be realised politically at least partially. The Bible is relevant and its divine comedy still a player on the world stage.

The Bibles continuing importance comes from its warnings and lessons about idolatry, that what we create we all too easily end up worshipping. Idols and graven images were the original temptation, contemporary ideas and ideologies are less easy to spot, and, when we sacrifice ourselves to them, just as destructive. The test is always, do we serve them or do they serve us? Or as Jesus put it in his humanist manifesto, *The Sabbath was made for man, not man for the Sabbath.* Atheists who turn science into an ideology are as much idolaters as Christians who make the same mistake with their theology. The consequence is always bloodshed. Science is made for humankind, not humankind for science.

The Bible is a library that argues with itself and provokes discussion among its readers. It has the unique ability of keeping life open to the Comedy of God as it holds the tragedy of idolatry at bay.

A SHORT BIBLIOGRAPHY

The Oxford Study Bible, Revised English Bible with the Apocrypha, edited by M. Jack Suggs, Katharine Doob Sakenfeld, James R. Mueller, Oxford University Press, New York, 1992.

The Oxford Bible Commentary, Edited by John Barton and John Muddiman, OUP, 2000.

The Jewish Annotated New Testament, Amy-Jill Levine and Marc Zvi Brettler, OUP , 2011.

Aspects of Rabbinic Theology, Major Concepts of the Talmud, Solomon Schechter, Schocken Books, New York, 1961.

Everyman's Talmud, The Rev. Dr. A. Cohen, Dent Dutton, 1932.

The Human Christ, The Search for the Historical Jesus, Allen, Charlotte, 1998, Lion Books.

Paronomasia in the Old Testament, Immanuel L. Casanowicz, Journal of Biblical Literature, Volume 12, No. 2, 1893. Usefully lists some 500 examples of witty wordplay from the Old Testament.

Paronomasia and Kindred Phenomena in the New Testament, Elbert Russell, University of Chicago [Ph D. Dissertation], 1920. Gives some 200 examples of punning wordplay from the New Testament.

Salvation by Laughter, D. Zuver, 1933.

The Humour of Christ, Elton Trueblood, Harper and Row, New York, 1964.

The Feast of Fools: A Theological Essay on Festivity and Fantasy, New York and London, Harper and Row, 1969.

Holy Laughter: Essays on Religion in the Comic Perspective, Conrad Hyers, New York, The Seabury Press. 1969.

Kerygma and Comedy in the New Testament, A Structuralist Approach to Hermeneutic, Dan O. Via, Jr., Fortress Press, Philadelphia, 1975.

The Name of the Rose: Umberto Eco, [1980] Vintage 2004. A novel which contains some fascinating discussion on humour centring on the supposed lost second book of Aristotle's Poetics.

And God Created Laughter, The Bible as Divine Comedy, Conrad Hyers, Atlanta, John Knox Press, 1984.

On Humour and the Comic in the Hebrew Bible, Yehudah Raddeh and Athalya Brenner, Sheffield Academic Press, 1990.

The Prostitute in the Family Tree, Discovering Humor and Irony in the Bible, Douglas Adams, Westminster John Knox Press, 1997.

Jesus the Holy Fool, Elizabeth-Anne Stewart, Franklin, Wisconsin: Sheed & Ward, 1998.

Jesus Laughed. The Redemptive Power of Humor, Abingdon Press. 2008.

The Bible and the Comic Vision, J. William Whedbee, Fortress Press, 2002.

Wrestling Jacob, Deception, Identity, and Freudian Slips in Genesis, Klitsner, Shmuel, Urim Publications, Jerusalem, 2006.

Black Mass, Apocalyptic Religion and the Death of Utopia, John Gray, Penguin Books, 2008.

25153998R00193

Printed in Great Britain
by Amazon